INTERNET
IN A NUTSHELL

A Desktop Quick Reference

Valerie Quercia

O'REILLY™

Cambridge · *Köln* · *Paris* · *Sebastopol* · *Tokyo*

Internet in a Nutshell
by Valerie Quercia

Copyright © 1997 O'Reilly & Associates, Inc. All rights reserved.
Printed in the United States of America.

Published by O'Reilly & Associates, Inc., 101 Morris Street, Sebastopol, CA 95472.

Editor: Linda Mui

Production Editor: Clairemarie Fisher O'Leary

Printing History:

      October 1997:   First Edition

This book is printed on acid-free paper with 10% recycled content, 15% post-consumer waste. O'Reilly & Associates is committed to using paper with the highest recycled content available consistent with high quality.

ISBN: 1-56592-323-5

Table of Contents

v

Part III: Finding Stuff

Part IV: Email and News

Part V: File Handling

Part VI: Helpers and Plug-ins

Part VII: Web Authoring

Part VIII: Internet Relay Chat

Foreword

In 1991 when I was writing *The Whole Internet Users Guide and Catalog*, George Bush was president of the U.S., the Gulf War was being fought, real networking was done by IBM computers using something called SNA, and the Internet was viewed as an unreliable academic plaything. The Internet had perhaps 10,000 users, who used programs like *telnet*, *ftp*, and *mail* to do work. Most of them were computer geeks or scientists who were dragged onto the Net kicking and screaming to get their research done.

There was virtually no documentation about how to use the Internet at the time Tracy LaQuey-Parker (author of *The Internet Companion*) and I each started writing a book to help people understand and use the Internet. Each of these books spent as much time trying to convince the reader that the Internet was good, useful and the thing of the future as it did trying to tell you how to use it. Most people still did not believe.

Now everyone believes. The Internet has permeated out culture. Some still don't think it's good but all you need to do is turn on the TV to hear, "To find out how to be a contestant, see **http://www.sony.com**." It has become the basis of so much corporate networking that it took me about ten minutes to remember the acronym SNA. Gone are the arcane command lines, although they are still documented in the hundreds of books still available about the Internet.

Yet with commercial success comes new complexity. The Web is so easy to use and so extensible that everyone is hoping to make a buck (actually millions of them) by producing new things for it. When I did my first resource catalog we had to look hard and wide to find 500 good sites. Now you can find hundreds of thousands with the help of search sites. When you arrive, the site will tell you need a new a new plug-in, the next version of a browser, or Java. "Push" technology is now the rage. Suddenly the Internet isn't so simple any more.

Most people can get by as long as they limit themselves to familiar sites, but the fun of the Internet is the lack of limits. People no longer need Internet promotion, they get that everywhere: TV, posters, work, and especially their kids. What they do need is a book which tells them just the facts, a ready reference to sit by the side of their computer in case they wander into unfamiliar territory. *Internet in a Nutshell* is that book.

Ed Krol

Preface

With everything being written and said about the Internet, it's still difficult to get a clear picture of what the thing's about and what you can get out of it. If you've explored the Net for a while, you've very likely encountered some of the various services it makes available, such as the World Wide Web, electronic mail, Usenet news, and chat. You might think of the Internet as a glue that binds these interrelated, yet independent, modes of communication—much in the same way that telephone lines are used for conversation, faxing, modem connections, credit card verification, etc.

At this point, (just about) everyone and her mother knows about email, a quick, cheap method of sending messages across the globe. The World Wide Web represents some of the fancier technology available on the Net. The Web is sort of a hybrid between a research library and an entertainment channel—letting you access (and publish) multimedia documents (i.e., documents that contain text, sound, images, video, etc.). Usenet news is a forum for people all over the world to discuss their common interests. Chat is a facility that lets people have interactive discussions with friends and online acquaintances. Although each of these services is distinct, they all involve communication, and they're all made possible by the Internet.

It isn't possible to catalog everything that's out there on the Internet. Given the vast amount of information and its rapidly changing nature, this kind of catalog wouldn't even be particularly helpful. You're a lot better off knowing *how* to find out what's out there and how to access it effectively.

That's where the current book comes in. We've tried to rope together some general information about the various services you can access on the Net, as well as to provide a reference to the tools and tricks that will help you get the most out of them. The book moves quickly because there's a lot of ground to cover. If you already have a basic understanding of the Net and what's out there, this book should have you accessing those resources quickly and effectively.

Contents

This book is for the new and eager Internet user, for the seasoned surfer who occasionally needs to remember shortcuts or syntax, and for everyone in between. The book is separated into eight parts, as follows:

Part One, *Getting Oriented*

If you're just getting started on the Internet, or if you learned it in an ad-hoc manner (as most of us did), Part One gives a fast-moving overview of the Net and helps clarify how everything fits together.

Part Two, *Your Browser Inside-Out*

For most people, their primary Internet tool is their Web browser. In Part Two, we cover Netscape Navigator (version 4.01) and Microsoft Internet Explorer (version 3.02), the two most widely used browsers.

Part Three, *Finding Stuff*

Now the fun part. In Part Three we point you to sites of general interest, and explain how to use the search engines that help you find sites related to your own personal interests.

Part Four, *Electronic Mail and Usenet News*

Email is arguably the most essential Internet service. News is less prominent in the public eye, yet is also one of the backbone services of the Internet. Part Four has tips on how to get along in email and news, including coverage of "netiquette," and how to use the email and news programs distributed with your browser.

Part Five, *File Handling*

When you strip away all the bells and whistles, you'll find that the Internet is just about sharing files from one system to another. While many of the tools covered in this book manage most file types automatically, it frequently happens that you have to figure out file management yourself. Part Five covers the various file types, how to transfer them with FTP, and how to work with compressed and archived files.

Part Six, *Helpers and Plug-ins*

Your Web browser has been designed to deal automatically with many types of files, but occasionally you need to dig up another application to read incoming data. Part Six covers helper applications, which are external applications your browser can call upon to handle particluar files, and plug-ins, which are helper apps that are incorporated directly into the browser.

Part Seven, *Web Authoring*

On the Web, you aren't confined to being a user; you can also publish your own Web documents. In Part Seven we discuss how to create HTML files, and also give a brief introduction to incorporating static images, animation, and even Java applets into your page.

Part Eight, *Internet Relay Chat*

Chat allows users to communicate with each other with an immediacy not available with other Internet services. In Part Eight, we give an overview and reference to Internet Relay Chat (IRC).

Conventions Used in This Book

The following typographical conventions are used in this book:

Bold
> is used for URLs and Menu names.

Letter Gothic
> is used to indicate computer examples.

Italic
> is used to indicate filenames and command names and emphasis.

Request for Comments

We invite you to help us improve this book. If you have an idea that could make this a more useful quick reference, or if you find a bug in an example or an error in the text, let us know by writing:

```
O'Reilly & Associates, Inc.
101 Morris Street
Sebastopol, CA  95472
1-800-998-9938 (in the U.S. or Canada)
1-707-829-0515 (international/local)
1-707-829-0104 (FAX)
```

You can also send us messages electronically. To be put on the mailing list or request a catalog, send email to *nuts@oreilly.com*. To ask technical questions or comment on a book, send email to *bookquestions@oreilly.com*.

Acknowledgments

Many people were instrumental in making this book happen. Thanks to Linda Mui, my pal and the developmental editor of this book. Thanks also to Tim O'Reilly for his general wisdom and editorial guidance.

Clairemarie Fisher O'Leary managed the arduous production process and put up with my schedule-slipping and other antics to boot, for which no amount of thanks are sufficient.

Frank Willison managed many of us with an even hand and a sense of humor, long after mine was exhausted.

Steve Kleinedler did a fine copyedit, while taking delays and obstacles in stride. Seth Maislin did a bang-up job on the index. Elissa Haney and Gabe Weiss provided production assistance.

Thanks to Edie Freedman for designing the cover, as well as hammering out some problems with the internal presentation. The tireless Lenny Muellner made these refinements possible with his terrific formatting work. Thanks also to Robert Romano for creating the illustrations under a good deal of pressure.

Thanks to John Files, Nicole Gipson Arigo, and Nancy Wolfe Kotary for handling the quality assurance checks before this thing went to print.

Thanks to Sheryl Avruch for managing the numerous production staff members involved in this project, which entailed a number of difficult constraints.

Kiersten Conner wrote the bulk of Chapter 26, *GIFs, Applets, and Other Enhancements*, which appears in Part Seven, *Web Authoring*. Much of the HTML reference material in this same part was adapted from work done by Chuck Musciano and Bill Kennedy for *The HTML Handbook* and Stephen Spainhour for *WebMaster in a Nutshell* (both published by O'Reilly & Associates).

Thanks to Tim O'Reilly, Frank Willison, Mike Loukides, Kiersten Conner, and Jessica Perry Hekman for providing essential review comments.

I'd also like to thank my family and friends for putting up with me for the past few months, and in general.

PART I

Getting Oriented

CHAPTER 1

A Living Glossary of the Internet

For the most part, this book is intended to serve as a reference for anyone who's exploring the Internet. Thus, much of this information is only useful if you've already dived in—or at least gotten your feet wet—and have some understanding of what's out there and how to get around.

However, we think even a novice (or "newbie," as the Net crowd says) can quickly take advantage of this reference book, once they get oriented. The tools that let you explore the Internet and the information available on it, are not designed to be confusing or unintuitive—on the contrary. Even if you're a new kid on the Net, it shouldn't take long for you to get comfortable. Keep in mind that there's not really anything you can do out there (barring writing something you may regret) that can cause much trouble to you or anyone else.

This chapter introduces some of the sights and concepts you're likely to encounter when exploring the Internet. The format of the chapter is a series of illustrations showing typical Internet offerings, with an accompanying narrative. Let's call this approach a "living glossary"—the idea being that it's easier to understand any defined terms when you see them in a context that is true to life. And what better way to explain how the parts of a *network* relate to one another?

Of course, there are also limitations in defining terms using this method. The Internet is a large topic, and this brief chapter could never illustrate all of the related concepts. But for anyone who's a beginner, it should cover most of the basics.

For those who already know their way around the Net, you can take advantage of the reference chapters right away. And you may be able to fill in some gaps of understanding using the conventional glossary, which appears (by convention) at the end of the book.

The Internet, the Web, and Everything

These days, there are few topics hotter than the Internet. Television programs cover it, newspapers and magazines write about it (and publish over it as well), even the President and Vice President of the United States have cut a presence on the Net. They and other self-appointed visionaries call it the "information super-highway," which sounds pretty good, but doesn't tell anybody very much.

If you really have no idea what the Internet is, and if the World Wide Web sounds like a hostile takeover attempt by a group of spiders, this is the section for you. If you already have a (hairy?) leg up on the Web but don't always understand every-thing you encounter, the illustrated part of this chapter may still be helpful.

The simplest definition of the Internet is that it's the largest computer network in the world. A January 1997 estimate set the Internet at 16.1 million "hosts" (or com-puters). Two years earlier, the estimate was only 4.8 million hosts.[*]

Technically speaking, the Internet is actually a network of many smaller networks that exist all over the world, but this organization is as invisible to the user as the telephone companies who cooperate to help us place international calls.

Keep in mind that in order to be considered an Internet host, a computer must be connected to the network at all times, and thus be accessible to other computers. Most universities have at least one computer that is a legitimate Internet host, whereas a personal computer (PC) you use to connect to the Net from time to time doesn't qualify.

A networked computer is also commonly called a *server* because it provides some kind of service or information. Internet servers are classified by the type(s) of information they offer. A mail server provides electronic mail. A World Wide Web server provides so-called *hypertext* documents (more about the Web in a minute). A Web server works by way of the Hypertext Transfer Protocol, or HTTP, and is thus more specifically called an HTTP server. An FTP server makes files accessible to users via the File Transfer Protocol. Technically, a single computer can act as a number of different servers. For example, a host might be both a mail and an HTTP server.

There are many different ways to get access to the Internet. Many businesses, uni-versities, schools, libraries, and other organizations are connected to the Net. If you're connected to the Internet courtesy of an organization, they've probably also provided you with software to explore and use the Net's resources.

If you want to obtain Internet access for yourself or your organization, you have more connection options than you'll want to think about. With this industry boom-ing, there are a growing number of Internet Service Providers (ISPs) for both orga-nizations and individuals. You've probably seen the television ads offering 10 free hours of Internet access if you'll try a particular service.

---

[*] These estimates were made by Mark Lottor of Network Wizards, Menlo Park, California. The results of the surveys are available on the World Wide Web at the URL **http://www.nw.com**, or in the *zone* directory at the FTP site **ftp.nw.com**. (If this all sounds like gibberish, check out Chapter 4, *Internet Addressing*.)

America Online (AOL), Compuserve, and Prodigy are among the premier services that are intended primarily for individuals who want to connect to the Internet using a personal computer and a modem. These services are very appealing because they offer a "plug-'n'-play" solution: you simply pop in the disk or CD-ROM they give you, follow some simple installation instructions, and you're on the Net before you know it. They even provide an integrated software package that lets you take advantage of the Net's resources, as well as certain resources they provide specifically for their own subscribers. Voila!

Keep in mind, however, that the resources provided by services like these are more heavily weighted towards their own offerings—both in software and informational content. You *can* use a more mainstream browsing program, such as Netscape Navigator, with a service like AOL, but it requires you to mess around a bit with configuration files, specifically something called a Winsock file.

As an alternative, there are many ISPs that offer connection time at a bargain rate, and let you sort out your own software needs. A Web site known as "The List" lets you search through a list of thousands of ISPs in the U.S. and elsewhere. The address of this site is:

```
http://www.thelist.com/
```

We'll see how addresses play a role in the course of the chapter.

What Can the Internet Do for Me?

So, there's this worldwide computer network. Great. But what do people really do on the Internet? Well, they exchange email, participate in discussion groups (known as newsgroups), socialize (one forum for such activities being called "chat"), retrieve data files, and access all sorts of information in a wide variety of formats.

The types of information available on the Internet are as diverse as the people interested in it. You can log on to many libraries, take a tour of the White House, read literature, magazines, and newspapers, look at maps, get a weather forecast, review Supreme Court decisions, get travel advice, exchange recipes, view paintings, find out the latest baseball trades, learn about the environment, shop, listen to music, see the Net version of movies, you name it.

Where does all this information come from? Everywhere. Because not only can just about anyone access info on the Net, they can also publish it. The Internet has no central authority.* There is no organization. In one sense, you can think of the Internet as a vast and growing online library in which anyone can publish anything they want. Unfortunately, there are plenty of people who publish material others might consider offensive. Fortunately, as in other media, those people are in the minority. However, as with any other information, you should definitely consider the source before accepting something you read on the Internet as the truth.

---

* The First Amendment protects our freedom of electronic expression, but there have been challenges. To learn more about this issue, use your browser to go to **http://www.yahoo.com/** and select the following links in this order: 1. **Society and Culture**, 2. **Civil Rights**, 3. **Censorship**, and 4. **Censorship and the Net**.

Most of the (more useful) information available on the Internet exists in a variety of forms to allow people with different computer hardware and software to access it. At the low end of the spectrum are simple text files accessible by a variety of tried-and-true methods, such as FTP, Gopher, and WAIS. These programs are the old war horses of Internet information distribution and access.

The high end of the spectrum, the kind of information that is drawing people onto the Net, is hypertext (and hypermedia)—files that can incorporate text, graphic images, audio and video tracks, and most importantly, dynamic connections, or links, to related files all over the Net. The sum of all the hypertext and hypermedia connected via the Internet form what is known as the World Wide Web (sometimes abbreviated WWW, or "the Web"). The Web lets you move among linked documents stored on host computers that may be very distant from one another. It is currently the most powerful and flexible Internet navigation system around.

What does all this mean in practice? Well, you can read a hypertext file, look at its illustrations, and even listen to it, if that's how it's set up. You can follow its links where your curiosity takes you. Unlike traditional file organization in which there is a set hierarchy, hypertext files are linked logically. How you navigate the file system largely depends on how you personally perceive the information. No matter where these links may take you, you can always retrace your steps. You can also save any of the information you want on your local system.

Here's a more concrete example. Let's say we've accessed a hypertext file containing an article about dolphins, maybe distributed in one of the growing number of online magazines. The hypertext file would undoubtedly include text about dolphins, and pictures of them, of course. It might also provide a link you can select to hear some of the sounds a dolphin makes. During the course of the article, it might also provide hypertext links to other information about dolphins. Perhaps you can click on the word "anatomy" and retrieve a document containing anatomical diagrams. Following links, you might be able to read about related species, navigation using sonar, or the study of dolphin intelligence. Maybe you can link to a society that protects dolphins, or even book an Earthwatch voyage to study them yourself.

Those Funny Looking Names

Just as you need an email address so people can communicate with you, files on the Internet need an address so people can access them. A file's address is more formally known as its *Uniform Resource Locator*, or *URL*. Admittedly this is not the friendliest handle, but the Internet addressing system is simpler than the term URL suggests.

Even if you're a complete novice, you've undoubtedly seen some Internet addresses on billboards, in print ads, and on television. Many organizations, especially in the media, have begun to make themselves accessible via email and the World Wide Web. As a matter of fact, if you've seen a television magazine program recently, they've probably closed with an arcane list of symbols beginning with the letters "http://www." This is the address of their Web site; "http" stands for "hypertext transfer protocol," the technology behind the Web. The "www" is obvious. A

TV show's Web address would probably then give the name of their program, followed by the suffix ".com"—which indicates they are a commercial enterprise.

This sort of naming scheme may sound complicated, but there is actually a fairly limited set of components and a simple logic to using them. For a more systematic look, see Chapter 4, *Internet Addressing*.

By now you're probably getting the idea that the Internet is making its way into many areas of our daily lives. If you've never had access to Internet before, it may seem like yet another layer of complication in our already complex modern world. Don't fall into that trap. The Internet is a tool and it can work for you in ways you haven't yet imagined. First, however, you have to get onto it.

The World's Fastest Internet Tour

This book can't take you on a comprehensive tour of the Internet any more than a doctor can examine every cell in your body. There's too much territory, and nobody cares about all of it. But the current section should give you an idea of the general kinds of information that exist out there, as well as some of the tools and skills you'll need to access it.

The most important piece of software you'll need is called a *browser*, a program that lets you visit different sites on the Net and display their offerings on your own computer. You visit a site by supplying the browser with an address, or URL. At the address is a file, or *document*, you can view in the browser window. In order for you to see the document, the browser makes a copy of it on your local computer (i.e., it *downloads* the file).

Specifically, browsers are intended to let you access resources on the World Wide Web—the hypertext files discussed earlier in this chapter. However, you *can* use a browser to access other types of file systems as well. More about this later.

Browsers are a little bit like colas: there are worlds of them, but only two of them appear just about everywhere. Think of Netscape Navigator and Microsoft Internet Explore (MSIE) as the Coke and Pepsi of browsers. (Or Pepsi and Coke. We don't want anyone to sue us.) Chapters 2 and 3 deal with Netscape Navigator and MSIE, respectively.

A browser displays a document from the Internet on your computer screen. Like any window-based program, a browser has a number of features—buttons, menus, scrollbars, etc.—that let you control its operation. Depending on the browser you choose, there may be superficial differences in the way displayed documents look. Having a more recent version of a browser is much more significant than the particular browser you choose. Since the technologies involved in publishing information over the Net are constantly changing, your browser has to keep pace.

What's Out There

The first document you access at any site is called the *home page*. The term "home page" is also used more loosely to refer to the primary document about any subject or person. Many individuals on the Internet have their own home page—a document about them and their interests—that anyone on the Net can access. This can be a useful way to represent your company or organization. However, the current trend to include all kinds of personal minutiae on one's home page is sometimes carried to a bizarre extreme.

From a particular Web page, you can access other related sites and information by clicking on *links*. These generally take the form of pictures, or of text that somehow stands out from the rest (by being underlined, a different color, etc.). Another clue: when you place the pointer on a link, the symbol changes to a small hand—in a way, to suggest that you can "grab on" to this spot. As described earlier in this chapter, the links among files are the basis for hypertext.

When you access a document that interests you, you can use the browser to print the file or to save a copy of it on your hard disk. (The copy made by the browser for viewing purposes will be erased when you exit the program.) Browsers also let you keep a list of the sites you want to visit over and over again. Instead of typing in the site's address every time, you simply open the list and select the site you want. In the Netscape environment, this list is called "Bookmarks." Microsoft Internet Explorer uses the terminology "Favorites." "Hotlist" is a comparable term used by some other browsing programs.

Now let's do a little browsing. The first time you start up your browser, it automatically takes you to the home page of the company that makes it. Thus, Figure 1–1 shows us the Netscape Navigator window open to the Netscape home page: Many hypertext documents are large, and they can take a long time to load into your browser window. While the data is being downloaded, system messages will report the progress in a small box near the bottom of the window.

Also, notice the Netscape logo in the upper-right corner of the window: a graphic of a capital letter "N" riding atop the planet. While a document is being loaded, the planet revolves and stars and other planets rush past. When a file is finished loading, the Netscape logo returns to its original state. The MSIE browser's logo looks like a round letter "e" with a ring diagonally around it, suggesting some kind of orbit. While a download happens, the "e" begins to rotate and look like the earth; it then reverts to an "e" when the process is done.

Notice that the address, or URL, for the page appears in the box labeled "Netsite" near the top of the window. (Actually, with Navigator, this label varies depending on the content you're viewing. The current document is a Web page, with the address **http://home.netscape.com/**; Web addresses get the label Netsite.) If you're using MSIE, the URL appears in a box labeled "Address."

The Netscape home page is chock full of links to information about Netscape products. Some of these links are labeled in the preceding figure. Naturally our black-and-white illustrations can't show you, but when you access a link, it changes color. Thus, you can generally glance at a page and know which links you've followed.

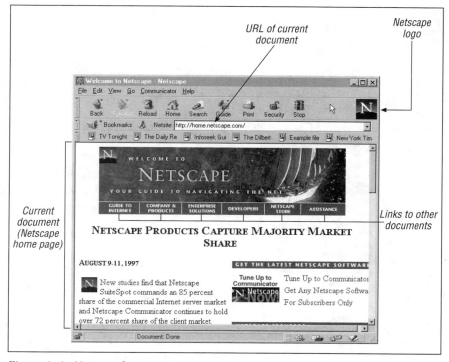

URL of current
document

Netscape
logo

Current
document
(Netscape
home page)

Links to other
documents

Figure 1–1: Netscape home page

Finding Your Way Around

When you're viewing a page, you can access a related document by clicking on a link. Or, you can go to an entirely unrelated document by providing its address, or URL. There are a number of ways to do this. Chapters 2 and 3 summarize these and other operations for Netscape and MSIE, respectively. For now, know that you can edit the current address field in the browser window, and then press the Return key to download the new file. Use the same techniques to edit the text in this box as you would in any field in a Windows-based program.

My employer and the publisher of this book, O'Reilly & Associates, has a fairly snazzy Web site, with the address **http://www.oreilly.com/**. (The older URL, **http://www.ora.com/**, still works too.) Figure 1–2 shows the O'Reilly & Associates home page. The O'Reilly home page features a primitive kind of animation using files called *animated GIFs*. GIF is a particular graphic file format popular on Web pages. Web artists can easily turn a series of related GIFs into a little cartoon-in-place. And your browser doesn't have to be very new or fancy to display animated GIFs. So many pages have dancin' GIFs galore. The GIF animation on the O'Reilly home page is much more subtle. If you watch the animal (a tarsier) in the banner across the top of the page, you'll notice that every so often he *blinks* his eyes.

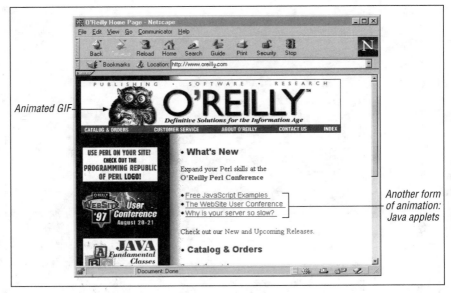

Animated GIF—

Another form of animation: Java applets

Figure 1–2: Watch a while and you'll see the banner guy blink

In the current incarnation of this page, there is some even fancier animation. The text items that keep moving on and off the page like a news ticker are *Java applets.* These "images in motion" are in reality small applications created by routines using a programming language called Java. You need a fairly recent version of a browser to display Java applets. A browser with this capability is called *Java-enabled.* The latest versions of Netscape Navigator and MSIE are Java-enabled. Many Web sites now sport Java applets, so a Java-enabled browser is worth having.

Well, enough of this shameless self-promotion. Let's look at somebody else's site for a while. Here's the address of a site called Yahoo!: **http://www.yahoo.com/.** The Yahoo! home page appears in Figure 1–3. Yahoo! is one of the most famous sites on the Net, and also one of the most useful. With the huge number of resources out there and the sheer chaos of it all, you need guidance in figuring out what's available, what matches your interests, etc. Yahoo! provides two related tools to help you:

- A *directory* of resources. This takes the form of a skeletal outline of links organized by subject, not unlike a very simple card catalog for a library. Each of the subjects/links in the directory connects to related documents or categories of documents. This nesting can be fairly deep: a single category may have many thousands of links branching out under it.

- A *search engine.* You can use the search engine to look for certain terms in the documents referenced by Yahoo!'s directory.

Yahoo! is more of a directory than a search engine in the strictest sense, but these distinctions are sorted out in Chapter 6, *Internet Directories and Search Engines.*

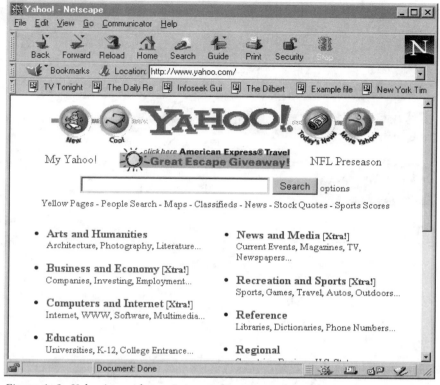
Figure 1–3: Yahoo! provides an Internet directory and search engine

Suffice it to say that you can use a service like Yahoo! to help you navigate the frequently overwhelming resources of the Internet. Let's try it out.

The directory takes up most of the Yahoo! home page. However, notice the text box above the directory. You can use this to enter words you want to search for in the Yahoo! database of resources (which is derived from all the links in the directory tree). You can opt to search the entire Yahoo! database, or limit your search to a particular category or subcategory within the directory. Chances are you'll want to do a combination of clicking on the category links and searching.

For starters, I'm going to choose the link **Travel** (under the top-level link **Recreation and Sports**), on the right side of the directory list. Now I get a page of travel-related categories and links from the Yahoo! directory (see Figure 1–4). I'm interested in finding information about traveling in England, so I'll search for some terms that are likely to be relevant. First I'll click the box to limit my search to the Travel section, then enter the search phrase:

```
UK OR England OR Britain.
```

(How you phrase a query depends on the search engine; see Chapter 6 for details.) After I've entered the query, I hit Return to initiate the search.

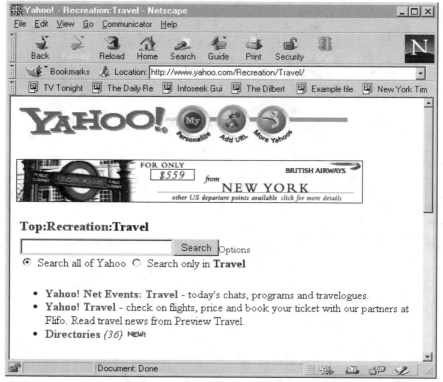

Figure 1–4: The Yahoo! Travel link reveals a number of related categories and links

When you search, the top portion of the results page will show categories from the Yahoo! directory that matched your search, while the lower portion (below the line) will show matching sites. Figure 1–5 shows the substantial results this particular search turned up. Notice that there are more than 6000 site matches. Of course, this isn't particularly practical. (That's why you should take the trouble to learn how to narrow a search.) But I can follow any number of links at this point, and then follow the links they reveal, and so on.

As you look at page after page, the browser records where you've been and in what order. This record forms something commonly known as your browser *history* or *history list*. Most browsers provide a way for you to open the history list at any time, and select one of the links from it. Both Chapter 2 and Chapter 3 explain how to use a history list to help you get where you want to go.

However, the history also helps you perform a much simpler and more common operation. It lets you move backward and forward through the pages you've accessed, in the order you've seen them. Thus, now that I've looked at a couple of related pages, I can retrace my steps. The most obvious way to do this is to click on the Back button, labeled with a left-arrow, near the upper-left corner of the browser window. That takes me back to the previous URL I accessed (the one in

Figure 1-3). I can go to the next URL in the list by clicking the Forward button, which is next to Back, and labeled with a right-arrow.

If you find a page that really interests you, you can print it and/or save it onto your local computer's disk. All browsers provide menu commands and other short-cuts that let you perform operations like these. See Chapters 2 and 3 for some of the ways to perform these functions using Netscape Navigator or Microsoft Internet Explorer.

Authentication, Cookies, and Privacy

All of the Web sites we've looked at in this chapter have extremely easy access—namely, you just enter their URL or follow a link, and you're in. But some sites will actually require you to register with them before you can use their resources. In many cases, this registration is free. The people running the site just want to have an idea who you are. They may want to tailor information to you. Or they may want to know what kinds of people are interested in their various offerings.

Registering often means coming up with a username and password that you will then supply whenever you connect. This lets the server perform *user authentication*—to make sure you're really you. (However, as we'll see, the login process is often simplified for you, using a mechanism called *cookies*—which have a whole slew of other implications as well.)

Some sites will require not only registration, but payment—at least for certain content. ESPNet SportsZone (**http://espnet.sportszone.com/**) is a freebie, unless you want to read their "premium" content. Then you need to be a subscriber (though you can do so for the day). The quote.com financial site (**http://www.quote.com/**) has a lot of free information; but you'll have to pay for their more elaborate reporting and tracking services. Still other services, like *Wall Street Journal* online, may offer a free trial, but for the most part are a paying proposition.

Whether you register to have access to a particular Web site or not, keep in mind that remote servers can gather a certain amount of information about your online activities using *cookies*. A "cookie" is a small piece of information shared between your browser and certain servers—basically to let the server know you're visiting.

The first time you connect to a site that uses cookies, the server sends a bit of information to your browser; each time you return to the same server, your browser sends the cookie back. In this way, the server can keep track of who's coming and going. (This is an oversimplification; in reality, a single server may exchange many cookies with your browser containing a variety of data—but you get the idea.)

You don't have to register with a site for cookies to be exchanged; it's happening all the time. Both Netscape Navigator and MSIE can be configured to tell you when a server tries to send a cookie to your browser, and to let you accept or refuse. I've configured my browser to inform me about cookies, and I'm amazed at how often even a single server may want to send them.

For the most part, the contents of a cookie are pretty harmless—and anonymous, since much of the information they contain is encoded. Cookies are also generally used for innocuous, if not downright helpful, reasons. In many cases, cookies are also unavoidable; if you don't accept one, you don't get onto a server.

The use of cookies worries some people because, hypothetically, one server can pose as another, retrieve your cookie information, and then pretend to be you. Personally, I don't care *all that much* if someone else wants to do my online crossword puzzles. Or go around visiting my favorite baseball sites in my stead—unless they try to pass me off as a Yankee fan. (Hey, I'm from Boston.)

But retrieving your cookies *can* tell someone about you and your interests— maybe some interests you'd prefer remain private. That's not to say that there's a ton of snooping going on out there. Sure, there are marketing efforts that involve figuring out what people are looking at on the Web, but no one is really sure how widely and deeply these efforts extend. There are reports of one company passing cookies to people's browsers to track the ads they look at online. This doesn't bother me terribly either.

The truth is, you can't do much of anything on the Internet and expect to leave no trace. Electronic mail can be forwarded to people you didn't intend to see it. It can be read by employers who expect to be privy to what happens on their system. It can even be cracked or intercepted by someone outside. (But they'd have to be pretty bored to be interested in mine—and I don't think I'm alone.)

Usenet news is intended to be broadcast to a limited audience of people interested in the same subject. But anyone can search through old news messages if they want to find out something about you and your opinions.

With all sorts of servers exchanging information about us via cookies and getting our email addresses when we register, and with the number of online directories of people and organizations, it's no wonder there's a growing onslaught of junk email. One strategy to get you to read this mail is to put a friendly greeting in the Subject line of the message. Sort of a "Hi, I am the stranger who wants to sell you stuff."

Am I worried about my privacy online? Not particularly. I'm one of those people who thinks that anyone who's terribly interested in my activities must have something better to do. I'm just not that fascinating.

Does the open-ended nature of Net communications give me a "Big Brother" paranoia? Nah. But many people have this kind of concern. What if your health insurance company could find out that you've been visting Web sites that provide information about AIDS? In theory, couldn't an insurance company try to exclude people who seem to be very interested in such a subject? What about an employer who finds out you're reading about drug rehabilitation? I'm not saying this kind of electronic investigation is going on now. Frankly, I don't believe it is. But it's feasible, and there are no widespread security measures to prevent it.

Now you're going to have a ton of fun on the Internet, aren't you? Well, I'm still not worried. I don't do anything on the Net that I would have to worry about becoming public. And I actually don't believe that the Big Brother level of scrutiny we've considered will ever happen.

Just keep in mind that someone somewhere might possibly find out what you do and say on the Internet. If you really want your activities to remain private, you're going to have to stay off the Net entirely. But that's kind of like staying in the house because sometimes it rains.

Hypertext Is Not Alone

While the primary function of both Netscape Navigator and Microsoft Internet Explorer is to let you browse through hypertext documents on the World Wide Web, keep in mind that there are other types of sites on the Net as well. Before hypertext technology existed, a lot of data was transferred by way of the File Transfer Protocol, or FTP. And FTP is still a popular way to make files available to the public. The average FTP site stores a number of large data files, such as documents, software, and graphic images. Public FTP servers allow people to connect via a facility called *anonymous FTP* (described in Chapter 17, *FTP and File Transfer*), which allows anyone to download files from the server. You can also connect to an FTP site using your browser by giving it an FTP-specific address. The following URL connects you to the FTP site of O'Reilly & Associates:

```
ftp://ftp.oreilly.com/
```

When your browser connects to an FTP site, it displays a graphical representation of the FTP file system, which looks something like a table of contents (see Figure 1-5). You navigate through an FTP file system much as you would the file system on your PC—by clicking on symbols that correspond to directories (folders) and files. When you open a text file, it will be displayed in your browser window. You can then read it, save it, etc. If you try to open a file that contains compiled data, in many cases the browser won't be able to display it; instead you'll be prompted to save the file to your hard disk. In these ways, you can use your browser to access the resources at FTP sites. However, if you're going to make a habit of frequenting such sites, it's a good idea to use a special FTP program. See Chapter 17 for more information.

You may also run across *telnet sites*, which are common at libraries around the world, but also have other uses. Telnet sites have a very simple interface, and they're definitely not on the cutting edge. But in some cases, connecting to a telnet site is the only way to access certain information online. For more info, see Chapter 8, *Accessing Libraries and Other Resources with Telnet*.

Is That All There Is?

The Internet is not only for browsing. Here are just a few of the other things you can do:

- Send and receive electronic mail

- Participate in Usenet news (a forum for discussion on a variety of topics)

- Transfer and download files of all types (including images, video, sound, etc.)

- Connect to thousands of libraries worldwide, using Telnet

- Enhance your browser (with *plug-ins*) to be able to display additional data types, and even to perform fancier tasks

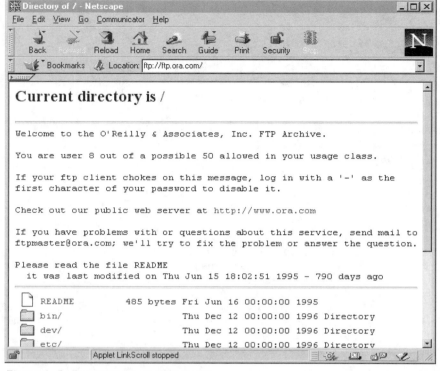

Figure 1–5: Browsing on an FTP server

- Participate in "chat" sessions

- Create your own hypertext documents and "publish" them over the Net

This book should help you take advantage of these and other Internet resources. It's primarily a reference, and it's designed to let you skip around. But some sections also include a fair amount of explanation, and even some brief tutorials.

No book can hope to acquaint you with all you can find and do on the Internet. Beyond the quickie tour you've had so far, here's what the current book gives you:

- Part Two, *Your Browser Inside Out*, gives you more than you ever wanted to know about your browser if you're using Netscape Navigator or Microsoft Internet Explorer. Chapter 2, *Netscape Navigator*, and Chapter 3, *Microsoft Internet Explorer*, deal with these programs. These chapters won't teach you the fundamentals of browsing—which take seconds to master—but give you some pointers on getting more out of your browser. These chapters also include extensive reference pages for the various browser functions.

- Part Three, *Finding Stuff*, provides extensive information on how and where to find what you want on the Net, including chapters that should help you:

  - Understand URLs (Chapter 4, *Internet Addressing*)

  - Find some of the more prominent and useful sites (Chapter 5, *Landmark Sites and Other Resources*)

  - Track down whatever interests you (Chapter 6, *Internet Directories and Search Engines*)

  - Locate names, email addresses, and businesses, get directions, phone numbers, etc. (Chapter 7, *Finding People and Places*)

  - Scan card catalogs from libraries all over the world (Chapter 8, *Accessing Libraries and Other Resources with Telnet*)

- Part Four, *Electronic Mail and Usenet News*, covers both of the these distinct services, with an emphasis on the programs that let you access them:

  - Chapter 9, *Why Email and News*, explains why we've bundled these two largely different subjects together in a single section, and reviews what is covered in this part.

  - Chapter 10, *Email Strategies and Survival Tips*, introduces some of the concepts related to email management and culture.

  - *Mailing Lists* (Chapter 11) are a form of discussion carried on over email, with lists devoted to thousands of different interests.

  - Usenet newsgroups are also conversation groups, but are run somewhat like bulletin boards, with messages "posted" via a news server. Chapter 12, *Getting Along in Usenet*, explains the types of groups you can subscribe to, what goes on in Usenet, the netiquette you should follow, how to search for certain information in news, etc.

  - Netscape Communicator provides an email program called Messenger and a news program called Collabra Discussions. However, in practical terms, these are really no more than two sides of the same application. Chapter 13, *Netscape Messenger and Collabra Discussions*, includes tips on using these modules more effectively, and extensive reference pages for the various program functions.

  - MSIE's Internet Mail and Internet News modules are more clearly separate applications, though there are still many similarities. Chapter 14, *MSIE Internet Mail*, and Chapter 15, *MSIE Internet News*, introduce these modules. Again, there are lots of tips to help you use the programs, as well as a reference to their functions.

- Part Five, *File Handling*, deals with topics that should help you send and receive files of various kinds:

  - Filename extensions give a clue to a file's type and help you decide what special handling it might need. Chapter 16, *File Types and Extensions*, covers common file types, their extensions, and corresponding MIME types.

- FTP is good for transferring large files, or multiple files at once. Many FTP sites provide free software and other files to the public. Chapter 17, *FTP and File Transfer*, explains how to use some of the available FTP programs; Chapter 18, *FTP Command Reference*, is the place to go to look up FTP commands and syntax.

- When you're sending files via email or downloading them from an FTP site, you'll need to know a bit about compressing and archiving files. Chapter 19, *File Compression and Archiving*, covers various formats and tools for sending files that can't be easily transferred in their native format.

- Part Six, *Helpers and Plug-Ins*, covers some of the programs you can use to extend your browser's capabilities, either separately (Chapter 20, *Helper Applications*), or as a part of the browser itself (Chapter 21, *Plug-ins and ActiveX Controls*).

- Part Seven, *Web Authoring*, deals with some of the topics you may need to understand in order to create your own home page or other Web documents:

  - Chapter 22, *Authoring for the Web*, gives a speedy introduction to HTML, the markup language for the Web.

  - Chapter 23, *HTML Tags and Attributes*, serves as a quick reference to HTML.

  - Chapter 24, *Color Names and Values*, and Chapter 25, *Character Entities*, provide additional reference material for effective HTML authoring.

  - Chapter 26, *GIFs, Applets, and Other Enhancements*, is a quickie introduction to Web page "enhancements" such as animated GIFs and Java for those who want to use new technology without knowing too much about it.

- Part Eight, *Internet Relay Chat*, covers chat, an enormously popular service that's the closest thing to having a real conversation on the Internet. Chapter 27, *It's About Chat*, provides an overview, while Chapter 28, *IRC Command Reference*, lets you look up some of the confusing syntax.

PART II

Your Browser Inside Out

CHAPTER 2

Netscape Navigator

The latest incarnation of Netscape's Internet software is a suite called Netscape Communicator, which is composed of a number of modules, including:

- Navigator—the browser program, new and improved

- Messenger—electronic mail

- Collabra Discussions—Usenet newsgroups

- Composer—HTML authoring software

- Conference—Internet conferencing program

The current chapter provides an overview of and a quick reference to Netscape Navigator for the Windows platform, along with some suggestions on using the program more effectively. This information is based on the most recent version of Communicator for Windows available as of this writing (Version 4.01). Note that if you're running Communicator on a UNIX or Macintosh platform, some of the functions, shortcuts, menu items, etc., may be different. If you are using Navigator 3.*x*, some of the functions will not be available. (To move up to Communicator, visit the Netscape home page.)

For more about *Netscape Messenger and Collabra Discussions*, see Chapter 13.

Navigator Illustrated

In order for you to know what menus, buttons, etc., we're talking about, Figure 2-1 shows the various parts of the Navigator window, complete with labels.

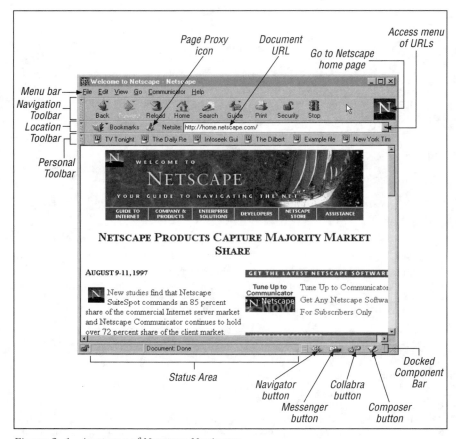

Figure 2-1: Anatomy of Netscape Navigator

Tips, Tricks, and Hidden Stuff

Browsers are supposed to work intuitively, and Netscape Navigator is no exception. However, Navigator also has a lot of depth. Certainly you can open it up and browse around without knowing much about the program. And many people undoubtedly restrict their browser use to a few functions—typing in URLs, visiting sites via link, saving files, etc.

Frankly, that may be all that you want to do as well. The purpose of this section is not to tell you that you should become some sort of browser jock. But certainly there's a lot more to Netscape Navigator than simply following links, if you want to become familiar with its various dimensions.

What the current section does do is highlight some of the functions you may not immediately notice, but that you might enjoy or benefit from using.

Keyboard Shortcuts for Common Functions

If you check out the reference pages for Navigator functions (later in this chapter), you'll see that there's a keyboard shortcut, or accelerator, for just about every one. However, many of these shortcuts are no more than the keys that let you access the various menus items. For instance, you can open a new browser window using the menu sequence **File** → **New** → **Navigator Window**. The key sequence "Alt+F, N, N" does the same thing because Alt+F brings up the **File** menu, N reveals the **New** submenu, and then N invokes the **Navigator Window** item.

However, for the most commonly used functions, there are true—and simpler—keyboard shortcuts, many of which require the use of the Ctrl key. Since opening a new browser window is something you might want to do fairly often, there's a better shortcut: Ctrl+N.

Table 2-1 summarizes this and other common functions and the keyboard shortcuts for them. Remember that these are Windows-specific shortcuts. However, some of them may still apply if you're working in a UNIX or Macintosh environment.

Table 2-1: Keyboard Shortcuts for Common Navigator Functions

Function	Shortcut
Address book	Ctrl+Shift+2
Back one document in history list	Alt+←
Bookmarks, add	Ctrl+D
Bookmarks, edit	Ctrl+B
Close window	Ctrl+W
Collabra Discussions	Ctrl+3
Composer	Ctrl+4
Conference	Ctrl+5
Copy (selected text)	Ctrl+C
Cut (selected text)	Ctrl+X
Decrease font	Ctrl+[
Exit program	Ctrl+Q
Find text on current page	Ctrl+F
Find text again	Ctrl+G
Forward one document in history list	Alt+→
Frames, move between	Ctrl+Shift+Tab
Help	F1
History	Ctrl+H
Increase font	Ctrl+]
Message Center	Ctrl+Shift+1
Messenger mailbox	Ctrl+2
Netcaster	Ctrl+8
New browser window	Ctrl+N
New Composer document	Ctrl+Shift+N

Table 2–1: Keyboard Shortcuts for Common Navigator Functions (continued)

Function	Shortcut
New mail message	Ctrl+M
News, read	Ctrl+3
Open Document	Ctrl+O
Open/raise browser	Ctrl+1
Page info	Ctrl+I
Paste (last cut/copied text)	Ctrl+V
Pop up menu for document (To use menu on a link or image, click right pointer button in that context)	Shift+F10
Print page	Ctrl+P
Reload document	Ctrl+R
Save in file	Ctrl+S
Security info	Ctrl+Shift+I
Select all	Ctrl+A
Source code, view	Ctrl+U
Stop download	Esc

Speedy URLs

This is one of my favorite Navigator features. If you supply Navigator with a URL, you can omit one or more elements, and it will still do its best to find the right address. What exactly does this mean? Well, you can actually omit any or all of the following parts of a URL:

- The **http://** prefix

- The **http://www.** part of a URL

- A **.com** suffix

What this boils down to is that if you want to get to the home page of a commercial enterprise, there's a good chance all you need to supply is a tiny bit of the domain name. As a matter of fact, if I want to get to **http://www.redsox.com/**, the Web site of my favorite team, the Boston Red Sox, all I have to enter is:

```
redsox
```

Navigator figures out the rest. It takes a little longer than if I give the whole URL upfront, but it's still pretty cool.

Of course, if you want to go to a non-commercial site, such as that of a university, you'd have to supply the appropriate suffix. The following info would suffice:

```
ucla.edu
```

This feature certainly can't get you to a lower level in the site's directory structure.

You'd have to supply additional pathname information or follow links once you get there. However, Navigator does remember URL information from your previous Net travels, as explained in the next section.

Navigator Will Complete URLs You Begin, if You've Visited Them Before

This is a Windows-only feature. The first time I saw it in action, it freaked me out a little bit. But it is actually fairly neat and also very useful. As you probably know, Navigator keeps a detailed history of all the URLs you visit. (You can edit your History file, if you really want; more about that later.)

When you begin to type a URL in the box in the location toolbar, Navigator will compare what you type to the URLs in your History file. If you type what looks like the beginning of an entry in the file, Navigator will supply the end for you— as you type—before your very eyes. You hit Return to open the document named.

What if there are a bunch of URLs that start the same way? Navigator starts its matching process pretty quickly. In fact, if you have 25 URLs in your history that begin with **http://www.g** (e.g., **http://www.gray.com**, **http://www.gibbs.org**, etc.), the matching will start as soon as you get to the "g," and it will match all 25 entries. The one that's displayed first is the most recent one from the history.

If Navigator finds multiple URLs that begin the same way, you can cycle through them using the down-arrow key on your keypad. Each time you hit the down arrow, a new (matching) URL from the History is displayed in the location box. You can select whatever one you want by hitting Return.

Of course, practically speaking, you don't want to have to cycle through 25 matches. A couple is OK. But what you actually want to do when you get the wrong match is to keep typing. When you type, you overwrite what Navigator has typed, and Navigator continues to try to match you. Generally it just takes a few letters of the domain name to get the right match.

Note that this only works in the URL box in the location toolbar. If you use the **Open Page . . .** dialog (accessible from the **File** menu or Ctrl+O), URL completion isn't done for you. (But the omission rules from the previous section still apply.)

Getting to the Netscape Home Page

This is a boring one. And it may be a very obvious one, but . . . sooner or later— sooner, now—you'll figure out that the Netscape logo in the upper-right part of your Navigator window is actually a link to **http://home.netscape.com**. From the Netscape home page, you can inquire about their other products, download demos and other software, get upgrades, etc.

This brings us to a potentially confusing point about home pages. The expression "home page" is actually used in a number of different senses. When you connect to the Web site of an organization (like Netscape) or an individual, you're looking at their home page. However, the first URL your browser loads is referred to as its home page (or start page).

By default, the home page of the Navigator browsing program—the first one it displays—happens to be the home page of Netscape (the company). However, you can change the URL your browser first loads, using the procedure outlined in the next section.

Keep in mind that whatever URL you specify as your browser's home page will also be the one you go to if you click on the Home button. However, clicking on the N will always take you to Netscape.

Specifying a Different Home Page

You can specify a different page to be the first one that's loaded when you start the browser—and the one you go to when you click on the Home button. Use the Preferences dialog, which you open up by selecting **Preferences** from the **Edit** menu. Under Category, select Navigator. Then enter the URL you want in the Location box under Home Page. Click OK to get out of the dialog. The next time you start up the browser, it will open to the page you've specified.

Making the Component Bar Easier to Take

Netscape Communicator is set up to let you switch between modules fairly easily. You can do this with the **Communicator** menu that all of the components share. Another way to do it is with the *Component Bar*, a tool that has icons representing the some of the more popular modules, specifically, Navigator, Messenger (email), Collabra Discussions (news), and Composer (HTML editor).

By default, the Component Bar is a small, separate window with a vertical orientation (see Figure 2–2).

Figure 2–2: The Component Bar is useful but easy to lose track of

Although it's a good tool to have, the Component Bar in this form is also awkward. You can lose it under other windows. It takes up space—and unnecessarily, as it turns out, because you can choose to *dock* the Component Bar.

This means that the separate window will be converted to a tiny horizontal bar that becomes part of the Navigator window. As wise planning would have it, closing the Component Bar actually docks it onto the Navigator window—just click on the X button on the Component Bar's frame.

You can also switch to this more practical configuration by selecting **Dock Component Bar** from the **Communicator** menu. The docked Component Bar appears in the lower-right corner of the application, shown in Figure 2–3.

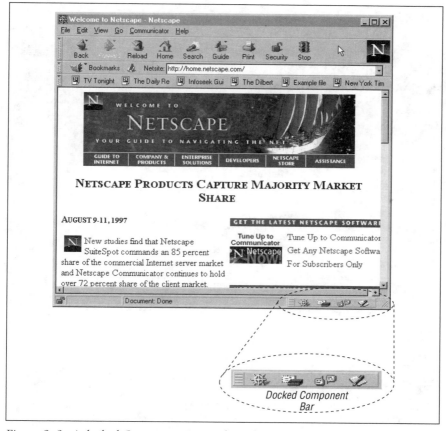

Figure 2–3: A docked Component Bar makes a lot more sense

You can switch the Component Bar back to a separate window by clicking on the small tab symbol at the left end of the bar. Or you can select **Show Component Bar** from the **Communicator** menu.

Since the Component Bar is designed to work with a number of the other Communicator modules as well, you can dock or show it from any of those modules. However you configure the Component Bar in one module is how it will appear in all modules.

Note that when you have new mail, the component bar icon that represents the mailer will have a small green dot next to it.

URLs Entered in the Location Toolbar Are Saved

The location toolbar displays the URL of the page currently displayed in your browser window. What might not be immediately obvious is that this text box provides access to a pulldown menu of URLs. Click on the down arrow to the right of the URL box to display the menu, shown in Figure 2–4.

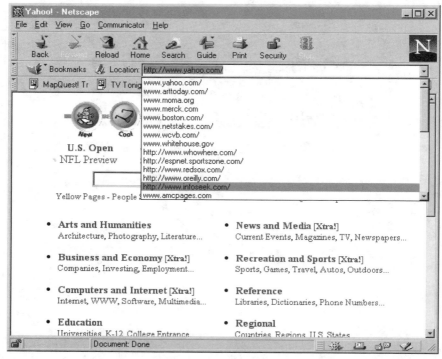

Figure 2–4: Drop-down menu reveals recently entered URLs

You'll probably find a seemingly random assortment of URLs from relatively recent memory. And you'll ask yourself, "Where the heck did these come from? And what do they have in common?"

As it turns out, all that the URLs on this menu have in common is that someone has *entered them in the URL box.* In other words, the URLs on the menu are those that have been typed or cut-and-pasted in, rather than links you've simply followed. The menu shows the last 14 URLs entered in this way.

Saving an Image, Wallpapering Your Screen

A lot of the fun of the Web comes from the multimedia touches you find on many documents. I personally come across tons of images I'd like to save for my own use. I should point out that, techically speaking, this is not entirely, um, legal. But if you photocopy an image from the newspaper to put up on your wall, nobody's going to care. And no one's going to care if you take an image from the Net and use it as wallpaper on your own computer screen.

You don't have to save an entire document to save an image, and you don't have to look at the document source code and find the location of the image file on the remote server. This is the hard way (although it works).

Here's the easy way. One of those subtler Navigator features is a *popup menu*, the items on which vary depending on the *pointer context*. If you didn't realize Navigator had any popup menus, you're probably not alone. It certainly has plenty of conventional pulldown menus (on the menu bar) to keep you busy.

However, if you place the pointer on various parts of a displayed document, and then click the second pointer button (the one you *don't use* to follow links), a small menu will pop up.

The items available on this menu depend on where the pointer is when you click it. If you have the pointer over a graphic image, among the popup menu options will be one that lets you save the image in a file on your own system (**Save Image As . . .**), shown in Figure 2–5. When you select this item, you'll get a dialog in which to specify a filename and directory for the image file.

If you're working in a Windows environment, you don't even have to save an image in order to decorate your screen background with it. The popup menu also offers an item called **Set as Wallpaper** that will cover your screen with a *tiled* pattern of the image in question—that is, a grid of the same image over and over. Note, however, that if you change your background decoration, Windows will wipe this image out of memory—not a very friendly or even logical arrangement. So it's a good idea to save the image anyway. Then you can open up the image file in your browser any time you want, and use the popup menu to use the image as your wallpaper pattern.

What Plug-ins Do I Have?

If you're not sure what plug-ins you have installed for Navigator, you can get a summary by selecting **About Plugins** from the **Help** menu.

For more about the commonly useful plug-ins and their installation, see Chapter 21, *Plug-ins and ActiveX Controls* .

Yellow and White Page Searches

One of the less obvious and potentially very useful features of Navigator is that it lets you search for people and organizations using a variety of white and yellow page services (described in Chapter 7, *Finding People and Places*).

one way is to use the **Search Directory** item on the **Edit** menu, which opens up a dialog in which you can enter the words to search for. The "Search for items" box in the dialog is actually a menu from which you can choose a particular directory, including Four11, InfoSpace, WhoWhere, and Bigfoot. (You can customize what directories are available on this list; see the Directory section, under Mail &

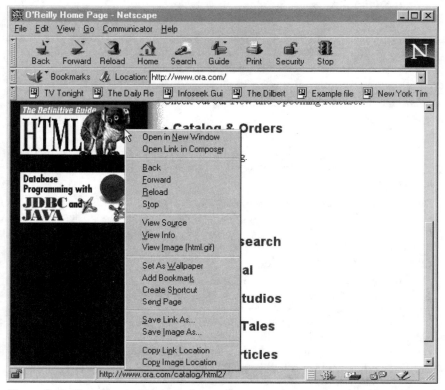

Figure 2-5: You can use Navigator's popup menu to save and use an image

Groups, in the Preferences dialog. The final section of this chapter deals with customization.) The Guide button on the Navigation toolbar also reveals a menu with the relevant choices **People** and **Yellow Pages**.

Suppressing Graphics, Java, and JavaScript for Faster Operation

OK, so the Web is a lot more fun with pictures and animation—but they can also slow your browser down to a crawl. If you really need to move around fast and the text is the thing you care about, the Advanced section of the Preferences dialog box (described later in this chapter) lets you enable or disable a number of features, including:

- Automatic loading of images

- Java

- JavaScript

If you disable all three, you'll definitely speed up your navigation—but you won't get the full effect of most sites. Select **Preferences** from the **Edit** menu in order to play around with settings. Note that the preferences you set will apply to all of the Communicator modules.

The Page Proxy Icon: Links, Bookmarks, and Shortcuts

Every top-level Communicator module window has what's called a Page Proxy icon, which lives on the Location toolbar to the left of the box that tells you the location. The Page Proxy icon represents the URL of whatever is displayed in the window: for Navigator, the URL of the current document; for Messenger (the mail module), it can represent a particular mail folder (e.g., Inbox); etc. (Unfortunately, the Macintosh implementation doesn't provide Page Proxy icons.)

You can drag and drop the Page Proxy icon to do the following:

- Create a desktop shortcut.

- Create a Bookmark entry. Drop the icon into the Bookmarks editing window, described later in this chapter.

- Create a Personal Toolbar link to the window. If you drag the Page Proxy icon from the current Navigator window onto the window's Personal Toolbar, you'll add a link to the currently displayed page. (More about this in the next section.)

- Open the current document/folder in another window. For instance, if you drop the Page Proxy icon from a Navigator window into another Navigator window, the URL will be opened in the second window.

Creating a Personal Toolbar

OK. So the default Navigator window has a navigation toolbar (with command buttons) and a location toolbar (with a Bookmarks button and URL box). You can also configure Navigator to have a Personal Toolbar, which contains links to sites you visit often. You can even create links to your various Netscape Messenger email folders and Netscape Collabra newsgroups.

Think of the Personal Toolbar as kind of a (short) Bookmark list in graphic form. (Currently the Personal Toolbar feature is not available in the Macintosh implementation.)

Setting up a Personal Toolbar is easy.

1. First you need to create a folder, under your Bookmarks, in which the URL info for the links will be stored. In order to edit your Bookmarks, you begin by using any one of the following methods:

   - Use the keyboard shortcut Ctrl+B

   - Select **Edit Bookmarks** from the **Bookmarks** menu on the location toolbar

- Open the **Communicator** menu, select **Bookmarks**, and then select **Edit Bookmarks**

Any of these sequences opens up a Bookmarks window, displayed in Figure 2–6.

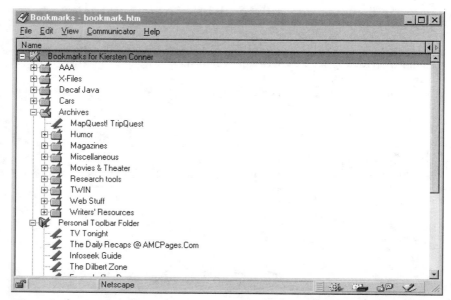

Figure 2–6: View, edit, and organize your Bookmarks in a special subwindow

Within the Bookmarks window, select **New Folder...** from the **File** menu. (Typing Alt+F, then F works too.) This opens up a dialog in which you can name the folder.

Replace the template name "New Folder" with "Personal Toolbar Folder." Then hit Return or click OK. Your Bookmarks file now includes a Personal Toolbar Folder.

2. Select **Show Personal Toolbar** from the **View** menu. (This item is a toggle; when the toolbar is displayed, the item is **Hide Personal Toolbar**.)

3. The next thing to do is to add items to your Personal Toolbar. There are a number of ways to do this:

- To create a Personal Toolbar link to any of the module windows, drag the window's Page Proxy icon onto the bar. (Dragging the Page Proxy icon into the Personal Toolbar Folder in the Bookmarks editing window works, too.) If you drag the Page Proxy icon from the same Navigator window, you add a link to the currently displayed page.

- You can also add a link to the current page using the following menu sequence: **Communicator** → **Bookmarks** → **File Bookmark** → **Personal Toolbar Folder**.

- If you already have a Bookmark to a URL you want to put on the Personal Toolbar, open the Bookmarks window (Ctrl+B); select the Bookmark you want; then choose **Add Selection to Toolbar** from the Bookmark window's **File** menu.

To remove entries from your Personal Toolbar, open up the Bookmarks window and delete the relevant URLs.

More About Bookmark Management

In order to use the Personal Toolbar, you absolutely need to have a Personal Toolbar Folder in your Bookmarks. But, if you have a lot of Bookmarks, you probably also want to have additional folders in which to organize them—otherwise the top-level **Bookmarks** menu becomes too long for practical use.

Suppose, for instance, you have a number of URLs for sites related to cars. Why not create a folder with that name, in which to store the whole bunch? To create a folder, first open up the Bookmarks edit window (as explained in the preceding section). Then select **New Folder** from the **File** menu (Alt+F, F works too). You'll get a Bookmark Properties dialog box in which to enter the name of the folder; then click OK. The folder appears in the Bookmarks editing window.

You can move URLs from elsewhere on the Bookmarks list into the new folder by clicking on the folder to open it, and then cutting (or copying) and pasting the entries into it. The **Edit** menu offers the necessary commands; there are also keyboard shortcuts for the **Cut** (Ctrl+X), **Copy** (Ctrl+C), and **Paste** (Ctrl+V) menu items.

If there's a page currently in the Navigator window that you want to add to a particular Bookmarks folder, use one of the following sequences:

- The menu choices **Communicator** → **Bookmarks** → **File Bookmark** → Choose the folder name

- The Bookmarks button → **File Bookmark** → Choose the folder name

- The key shortcut Alt+C, B, F; then use the arrow keys on your keyboard to highlight the correct folder name, and press Return

If a URL changes, you can update the Bookmark for it. Open the Bookmarks editing window (Ctrl+B). Select the Bookmark you want to edit. Then use the menu sequence, **Edit** → **Bookmark Properties** to open a Bookmark Properties dialog for the entry. Change the URL in this dialog box.

Navigator's interface is not your only option for managing Bookmark info, but it is the safest and most friendly. Bookmark info is stored in an HTML file on your system. In Windows environments, the Bookmarks file lives in *C:\program files\netscape\users\your_name\bookmark.htm*.

Hypothetically, you can open up this file with a text or HTML editor and add and remove entries. However, the file format is not very friendly, and it includes values for the time the entry was added and the last time accessed. If you really want to muck around with the file, you should be very comfortable with HTML and confident you know what you're doing. I'm happy to edit files on a UNIX system (where text is still king), but Windows is not designed to be managed like this on the user level. In truth, I always use the interface.

Playing Tricks with History

The URLs you've visited during the current session are listed on the **Go** menu, in the last section. You can go back to any one by selecting it from the menu.

These same entries are also available on two popup menus you might not have noticed. You can click the left mouse button on the Back button (on the Navigation toolbar) to go back a single URL, or on the Forward button to go forward one URL. But if you click the right mouse button on the Back or Forward button, you'll display a menu of URLs that come before and after the current URL in the session history. You can skip back or forward multiple pages at a time by choosing a URL from one of these menus (just as you can with the **Go** menu entries). The URLs you've visited in the current session are wiped off the **Go** menu and the popup menus when you exit Navigator.

Now suppose you want to go back to a site you haven't visited in the current session. You can't remember the URL, and you don't feel like searching for it. Well, if it's been within the last 21 days (this number is customizable), the link should still be saved in your History list.

You can view and access the History list's entries by selecting **History** from the **Communicator** menu (the keyboard shortcut Ctrl+H works too). You'll get a History editing window, as shown in Figure 2–7.

Within the History window is a list of the URLs you've visited, with the most recent ones at the top. The "Location" column gives the URL. "First Visited" and "Last Visited" give the timestamps from the first and last times you viewed this page. "Expiration" gives the date/time at which the entry will be automatically deleted from the file.

Each of the entries is actually a link to the page in question. Double-click on any line to open that URL in the Navigator window. You can also edit the file's contents. For example, you might highlight and delete entries yourself, or move them around using the **Edit** menu at the top of the History window.

By default, the browser keeps pages in your History list for 21 days. You can change this number in the Preferences dialog. Select **Preferences** from the **Edit** menu. Then expand the Navigation category, and change the number following "Pages in history expire after" in the History section.

Cookies, Security, and You

As explained in Chapter 1, *A Living Glossary of the Internet*, a "cookie" is a small piece of information shared between your browser and certain servers—basically to let the server know you're visiting. The first time you connect, the server sends a bit of information to your browser; then each time you return to the same server, your browser sends the cookie back. In this way, the server can keep track of who's coming and going.

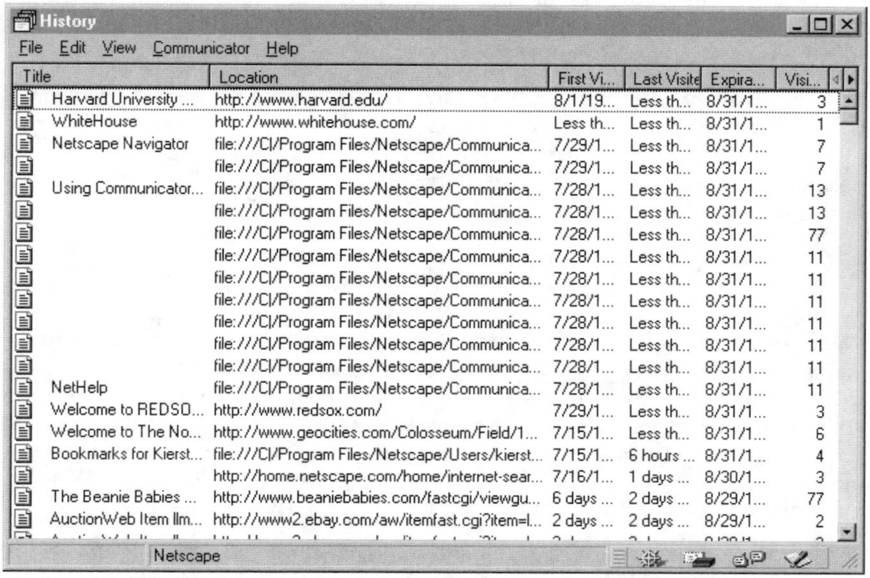

Figure 2–7: Use this window to view, edit, and access URLs from your history

For the most part, the use of cookies is relatively harmless. They're often employed for user authentication, for instance. (A cookie can store your encoded username and password where these are required and security isn't a big issue.) Some servers won't even let you on unless your browser accepts a cookie.

However, if you are concerned about someone keeping tabs on you via cookies, you can open your browser's cookies file and delete anything in it you like. The worst thing that can happen is that another cookie will have to be set, or you'll have to reregister for a free service, or something along that order.

On Windows systems, Navigator cookies live in the file *C:\program files\netscape\users\your_name\cookies.txt* Each line in the file is a cookie. Here's the beginning of a typical cookies file:

```
# Netscape HTTP Cookie File
# http://www.netscape.com/newsref/std/cookie_spec.html
# This is a generated file!  Do not edit.

web.ukonline.co.uk   FALSE   /Squatt   FALSE   883562401   SQUCookie  3

www.webthumper.com   FALSE   /cgi-bin  FALSE   946598401   status on

.netscape.com        TRUE    /custom   FALSE   946635179   version 01.50E00

.internet.net        TRUE    /         FALSE   946684799   ISNER 5650457

www.toyota.com       FALSE   /         FALSE   946684799   REPEAT OnlkhKH1qLe

.boston.com          TRUE    /         FALSE   946684799   INTERSE pc40.ora.com9269

.realaudio.com       TRUE    /         FALSE   946684740   uid 19811714835364495610
```

Obviously this file is much more friendly to servers than to people. Generally the first column will clue you in as to the server that set the cookie originally. Our sample cookie file contains entries from Netscape, Toyota, RealAudio, etc.

The entries themselves contain things like encoded user ID numbers and passwords. If you visit a Web site that requires some kind of user registration, commonly this information will be stored for you in a cookie. Then, when you go back to the site, the server gets that info from your browser—saving you the trouble of having to type it in again. Not a bad idea.

The top of the cookies file offers this ominous warning:

```
# This is a generated file!  Do not edit.
```

There's some wisdom in this. You can't muck around with an individual cookie entry and expect it to do you any good in the future. However, you can't actually cause much trouble by editing the cookie file either. While there's no point in changing anything within a particular cookie, you might want to delete an entry if you consider it to be questionable—in other words, if you think a server is tracking information about you for no good reason. So, if you see something that looks questionable, don't worry about deleting it.

Some people actually suggest you periodically delete all of your cookies. However, I know that my friend whose file we're examining is registered with the *New York Times* online. I assume that particular cookie gets her logged on automatically to the server. Why get rid of that?

In the default Netscape environment, cookies are exchanged without causing a ripple you'd notice. If you'd like Netscape to inform you each time a cookie is supposed to be set—and to ask your permission for it to happen—open up the Preferences dialog (**Edit → Preferences**). Then expand the category titled "Advanced." In the Cookies section, toggle on the setting "Warn me before accepting a cookie." Then each time a server tries to create a cookie on your system, you'll be informed by dialog and given the choice of accepting or not. Figure 2–8 shows the dialog I got when I tried to go to the Toyota Web site. Keep in mind that refusing generally means you won't get access to the server. However, it can still be interesting to see which servers are doing this, and how often. (It can also be a pain to have to respond to so many dialog boxes.)

The same section of the Preferences dialog also lets you set up some minimal cookie security. While the default is to "accept all cookies," you can instead toggle on the Preference:

```
Accept only cookies that get sent back to the originating server.
```

This setting makes it more difficult for someone to retrieve a particular cookie under false pretenses.

Quick Reference to Navigator for Windows

The following pages provide a reference to the functions you can perform with Netscape Navigator. Note that this reference covers the version of Navigator shipped as part of Netscape Communicator 4.01 and installed on a Windows

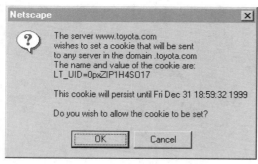

Figure 2-8: You can customize so that Navigator tells you when cookies are set

system. If you're running Communicator on a UNIX or Macintosh platform, some of the functions, shortcuts, menu items, etc., may be different. If you are using Navigator 3.*x*, many of the functions will not be available.

In using the following reference pages, keep in mind that they are organized according to the action you want to perform using your browser. For each action, the pages show the various ways you can perform it:

- Menu items

- Keyboard shortcuts

- Buttons, scrollbars, and other features of the browser window itself (where applicable)

Following the reference to functions is a shorter reference to the possible customization options, also called Preferences. Note that this reference includes Preferences for some of the other Communicator modules as well—since they are all set using the same dialog box.

Address book, open
    Communicator → Address Book
    Ctrl+Shift+2
    Alt+C, A

Animations, stop
    View → Stop Animations
    Alt+V, A

Back one document in history list
    Go → Back
    Alt+←
    Alt+G, B
    Back button

Bookmarks
    access
        Communicator → Bookmarks

        Alt+C, B
        Bookmarks button on Location
           toolbar reveals menu
    add current page to
        Communicator → Bookmarks →
           Add Bookmark
        Ctrl+D
        Alt+C, B, K
        Bookmarks button on Location
           toolbar reveals menu; select
           Add Bookmark menu item
    edit
        Communicator → Bookmarks →
           Edit Bookmarks . . .
        Ctrl+B
        Alt+C, B, B
        Bookmarks button on Location
           toolbar reveals menu; select

Edit Bookmarks . . . menu item
file current under existing folder
    Communicator → Bookmarks →
    File Bookmark → Select from
    menu of folders
    Alt+C, B, F, up/down arrow keys
    to highlight folder, Return
    Bookmarks button on Location
    toolbar reveals menu; select
    File Bookmark menu item,
    folder

Character set (Western, Japanese, etc.)
    View → Encoding → Select Language
    Alt+V, E, down arrow to desired
    language, press Return

Close current Navigator window
    File → Close
    Ctrl+W
    Alt+F, C

Collabra, open news/discussion window
    Communicator → Collabra Discussions
    Ctrl+3
    Alt+C, D

Communicator modules, open active module and move to front of display
    Communicator → Select component from third part of menu
    Alt+C, number corresponding to desired component/window
    Click on component bar icon
    Deiconify appropriate window

Component Bar, show/dock
    Communicator → Show/Dock Component Bar
    Alt+C, T
    Click on grid to left of docked bar to show it; close separate component bar window to dock

Composer, open new edit window
    Communicator → Page Composer
    File → New → Blank Page
    Ctrl+4
    Ctrl+Shift+N
    Alt+C, P
    Alt+F, N, P
    Composer button on Component Bar

Conference, open window
    Communicator → Conference
    Ctrl+5
    Alt+C, C

Copy selected text
    Edit → Copy
    Ctrl+C
    Alt+E, C

Cut selected text
    Edit → Cut
    Ctrl+X
    Alt+E, T

Disconnect from the Net (dialog lets you download mail/news first; first specify newsgroups under Preferences)
    File → Go Offline
    Alt+F, L

Document info, display
    View → Page Info
    Ctrl+I
    Alt+V, I

Edit
    copy of current document in Composer
    File → Edit Page
    Alt+F, E
    copy of current frame in Composer
    File → Edit Frame
    Alt+F, F

Exit program
    File → Exit
    Ctrl+Q
    Alt+F, X

Find

text in current document
Edit → Find in Page . . .
Ctrl+F
Alt+E, F
text, repeat
Edit → Find Again
Ctrl+G
Alt+E, G

Font

displayers, info about installed
Help → About Font Displayers
Alt+H, D
make larger
View → Increase Font
Ctrl+]
Alt-V, C
make smaller
View → Decrease Font
Ctrl+[
Alt-V, D

Forward one document in history list

Go → Forward
Alt+→
Alt+G, F
Forward button

Frame, send URL in mail

File → Send Frame . . . → Navigator
Alt+F, D

Go

to document/file
File → Open Page . . . , enter URL
or file path
Ctrl+O, enter URL/file, Open button
Alt+F, O, enter URL/file, Open button
Edit URL in location toolbar, hit Return
to document in history list
Go → Choose menu item corresponding to page
Alt+G, type number corresponding to page
Hold down mouse on Back or

Forward toolbar button to reveal menu of pages prior to or after the current page in history; select page

Help

display
Help → Display Contents
F1
Alt+H, H
for international users
Help → International Users
Alt+H, I

History, open window to view, edit, etc.

Communicator → History
Ctrl+H
Alt+C, H

Home page

change
Edit → Preferences . . .
Alt+E, E
open
Go → Home
Alt+G, H
Home button

Java console, open compiler

Communicator → Java Console
Alt+C, J

Mail

get new
Mail button on Component toolbar
open composition window
File → New Message
Ctrl+M
Alt+F, N, M

Member services, access

Help → Member Services
Alt+H, M

Message Center (for mail and news), open

Communicator → Message Center

Ctrl+Shift+1
Alt+C, G

Messenger mailbox, open (default folder: Inbox)
Communicator → Messenger Mailbox
Ctrl+2
Alt+C, M
Mail button on Component toolbar (button also retrieves mail)

Netiquette info
Help → Net Etiquette
Alt+H, U

Netscape's
Guide to the Net (provided by Yahoo!)
Guide button → The Internet
home page, go to
Click on the Netscape logo in the upper-right corner of the browser window

New browser window
Communicator → Navigator
File → New → Navigator Window
Ctrl+1
Ctrl+N
Alt+C, N
Alt+F, N, N

News, open Collabra Discussions for
Communicator → Collabra Discussions
Ctrl+3
Alt+C, D

Open
document in Composer window
File → Open Page . . . , toggle Composer setting, enter URL or file path, Open button
Ctrl+O, enter URL/file, Open button
Alt+F, O, enter URL/file, Open button
document in Navigator window

File → Open Page . . . , toggle Navigator setting, enter URL or file path, Open button
Ctrl+O, enter URL/file, Open button
Alt+F, O, enter URL/file, Open button

Open/raise module window
Communicator → select window from last section of menu
Alt+C, number corresponding to menu selection

Page Services (only available when an Enterprise Server has provided the current page)
View → Page Services
Alt+V, V

Paste selected text
Edit → Paste
Ctrl+V
Alt+E, P

Personal Toolbar
add icon for current page to
Communicator → Bookmarks → File Bookmark → select Personal Toolbar Folder
Alt+C, B, F, down arrow to Personal Toolbar folder, press Return
Drag Page Proxy icon (left of Location field) onto Personal Toolbar
create folder for contents
Communicator → Bookmarks → Edit Bookmarks, then in Bookmarks window: File → New ("Personal Toolbar Folder")
Alt+C, B, B; then in Bookmarks window: Alt+F, N, name folder Personal Toolbar Folder
edit contents
Communicator → Bookmarks → Edit Bookmarks → Then edit Personal Toolbar Folder
Ctrl+B, edit P.T. Folder

Alt+C, B, B, edit P.T. Folder
Bookmarks button → Edit Book-
marks → Then edit Personal
Toolbar Folder
specify Bookmarks folder to fill
Communicator → Bookmarks →
Edit Bookmarks; then within
Bookmarks window, click on
folder name, and choose Set as
Toolbar Folder from the View
menu
Ctrl+B, select folder, Alt+V, F
Alt+C, B, B, select folder, Alt+V, F

Bookmarks button → Edit Bookmarks, select folder, View
menu → Set as Toolbar Folder

Plug-ins, info about installed
Help → About Plug-ins
Alt+H, T

**Preferences, view/edit (see also
Browser Preferences)**
Edit → Preferences . . .
Alt+E, E

Print
document
File → Print . . .
Ctrl+P
Alt+F, P
Print button
format page to
File → Page Setup
Alt+F, G
preview
File → Print Preview
Alt+F, V
properties, display/edit
File → Print . . . select Properties
button
Ctrl+P, Alt+P
Alt+F, P, P
Print button (then select Proper-
ties button)

Refresh window contents
View → Refresh
Ctrl+V, F

Register your copy of Netscape
Help → Register Now
Alt+H, W

Release Notes
Help → Release Notes
Alt+H, R

Reload current document
View → Reload
Ctrl+R
Alt+V, R
Reload button

Save
document in file
File → Save As . . .
Ctrl+S
Alt+F, S
frame in file
File → Save Frame As . . .
Alt+F, F

Search
for text in current document
Edit → Find in Page . . .
Ctrl+F
Alt+E, F
for text, repeat
Edit → Find Again
Ctrl+G
Alt+E, G
the Net (go to Netscape search page)
Edit → Search Internet
Alt+E, I
Search button

Security
help info
Help → Security
Alt+H, E
info, show for current page
Communicator → Security Info
Ctrl+Shift+I
Alt+C, S

Select entire text of document
Edit → Select All

Ctrl+A
Alt+E, A

Show images
View → Show Images
Alt+V, W

Software updates
Help → Software Updates
Alt+H, S

Source code, view document
View → Page Source
Ctrl+U
Alt+V, U

Stop page loading
View → Stop Page Loading
Esc
Alt+V, S
Stop button

Support, product info and
Help → Product Information and
Support
Alt+H, P

Toolbar
hide/show location
View → Hide/Show Location
Toolbar
Alt+V, L
Arrow button on left margin of
toolbar
hide/show navigation
View → Hide/Show Navigation
Toolbar
Alt+V, N
Arrow button on left margin of
toolbar
hide/show personal
View → Hide/Show Personal
Toolbar

Alt+V, P
Arrow button on left margin of
toolbar

Upload file
File → Upload File . . .
Alt+F, U

What's Cool?, go to Netscape's
Guide button → What's Cool?

What's New?, go to Netscape's
Guide button → What's New?

White pages
search selected directories
Edit → Search Directory
Alt+E, Y
go to page with relevant links
Guide button → People

Window, open additional browser
Communicator → Navigator
File → New → Navigator Win-
dow
Ctrl+1
Ctrl+N
Alt+C, N
Alt+F, N, N

Yellow pages
go to page with relevant links
Guide button → Yellow Pages
search selected directories
Edit → Search Directory
Alt+E, Y

Netscape Communicator Preferences

You can set a number of preferences that determine how the various components of Netscape Communicator look and operate. All of these preferences are set using the Preferences dialog box, which is displayed from any module using this menu sequence:

    Edit → Preferences

Or the keyboard shortcut:

    Alt+E, and then E

Within the Preferences dialog, the various preferences are organized in six categories, each of which has a number of subcategories, much like a file directory structure. In order to see the subcategories under a particular category, click on the plus sign preceding the category name. Here are the six top categories, listed with their subcategories:

- Appearance
    - Fonts
    - Colors
- Navigator
    - Languages
    - Applications
- Mail and Groups (i.e., newsgroups)
    - Identity
    - Messages
    - Mail Server
    - Groups Server
    - Directory
- Composer
    - Publisher
- Offline
    - Download
- Advanced
    - Cache
    - Proxies
    - Disk Space

How do you know what options are available in each category? You don't. And that's where the following reference pages come in. They list each of the preferences in alphabetical order, along with the appropriate category in which to find it, as well as the default and other possible settings.

Note that these preferences apply to Communicator 4.01 for Windows. If you're running Communicator on another platform, options and defaults may vary.

AutoInstall
> On by default
> Advanced tab

Character (encoding) set
> Western, Central European,
>> Japanese, Cyrillic, Traditional
>> Chinese, Simplified Chinese,
>> Korean, Greek
> Western by default

Color
> *Background*
> If Use Windows Colors is on,
>> default is white
> To specify another color, turn Use
>> Windows Colors off; then click
>> on Background color box to
>> open color editor
> Appearance → Colors
> *Text*
> If Use Windows Colors is on,
>> default is black
> To specify another color, turn Use
>> Windows Colors off; the click
>> on Text color box to open
>> color editor
> Appearance → Colors
> *Unvisited links*
> Array of choices in color dialog
> Blue by default
> Appearance → Colors
> *Visited links*
> Array of choices in color dialog
> Purple by default
> Appearance → Colors

Cookies
> *Accept all; accept only those sent*
>> *back to originating server; or dis-*
>> *able.*

> Default is to accept all
> Advanced tab
> *Warn user before accepting*
> Off by default
> Advanced tab

Directory searches
> *Directories to be searched*
> Default list: Personal address
>> book, Bigfoot, Four11, InfoS-
>> pace, Switchboard, WhoWhere
> Mail & Groups → Directory
> *Format of returned names*
> First name, last name; or last
>> name, first name
> Default is first name, last name
> Mail & Groups → Directory

Disk space, mail and news
> *Don't load messages larger than x*
>> *KB*
> Off by default; 50KB when on
> Advanced → Disk Space
> *Auto compact folders larger than x*
>> *KB*
> Off by default; 100KB when on
> Advanced → Disk Space

Disk space, news only
> *Keep all messages; newest x mes-*
>> *sages; or messages from past x*
>> *days*
> Default is to keep all messages
> Advanced → Disk Space
> *Keep only unread messages*
> Off by default
> Advanced → Disk Space

External viewers/players
> *Add new type*
> Navigator → Applications
> *Edit existing type*

Navigator → Applications
Remove entry
Navigator → Applications

First page opened by Navigator
Blank Page; Home Page; or Last
Page Visited
Home Page by default
Navigator, tab

Font
Character (encoding) set
Western, Central European,
Japanese, Cyrillic, Traditional
Chinese, Simplified Chinese,
Korean, Greek
Western by default
Appearance → Fonts
Fixed-width font
Courier New, Courier New CE,
Lucida Console, OCR A
Extended
Courier New by default
Appearance → Fonts
Fixed-width font size
Assorted sizes, 8-72 points
10 points by default
Appearance → Fonts
Font set to use
User's default; document-specific
(except dynamic fonts); docu-
ment-specific (including
dynamic fonts)
Default is document-specific
(including dynamic fonts)
Appearance → Fonts
For mail and news messages
Fixed-width or variable-width
Fixed-width by default
Mail & Groups tab
For quoted text (in mail/news)
Specify type (bold, italic, bold
italic), size (regular, bigger,
smaller), and color
Defaults are bold, regular, and
red
Mail & Groups tab
Variable-width font
Times New Roman, Times Gothic
MT, Playbill, Wide Latin, Times

New Roman CE, etc.
Times New Roman by default
Appearance → Fonts
Variable-width font size
Assorted sizes, 8-72 points
12 points by default
Appearance → Fonts

FTP password, anonymous
Send email address by default
Advanced tab

Helper applications
Add new entry
Navigator → Applications
Edit existing entry
Navigator → Applications
Remove entry
Navigator → Applications

History entries, number of days saved
Default is 21 days
Navigator tab

Home page
Default is Netscape home page
Navigator tab

Images, autoload
On by default
Advanced tab

Java, enable/disable
Enabled by default
Advanced tab

JavaScript, enable/disable
Enabled by default
Advanced tab

Language
Range of choices from Afrikaans
(af) to Ukranian (uk), or
another you add
English (en) by default
Navigator → Languages

Links
Color of unvisited
Array of choices in color dialog

Blue by default
Appearance → Colors
Color of visited
Array of choices in color dialog
Purple by default
Appearance → Colors
Underline or not
Not underlined by default
Appearance → Colors

Mail (See also Messages)
Message List window, use only one
On by default
Mail & Groups tab
Notify with sound when arrives
On by default
Mail & Groups tab
Read window, use only one
On by default
Mail & Groups tab
Send replies in HTML
Off by default
Mail & Groups → Messages
Servers to use
Server names given at installation
are defaults
Mail & Groups → Mail Server
Server type
POP3 (local storage) or IMAP
(remote storage)
POP3 by default
Mail & Groups → Mail Server
Wrap lines at x characters
Default is 72 characters
Mail & Groups → Messages

Messages
*Auto-mail copy of outgoing mail to
self*
Off by default
Mail & Groups → Messages
*Auto-mail copy of outgoing mail to
other address*
Off by default
Mail & Groups → Messages
*Auto-mail copy of outgoing news to
self*
Off by default
Mail & Groups → Messages
Auto-mail copy of outgoing news to

other address
Off by default
Mail & Groups → Messages
Copy outgoing mail to folder
On by default
Mail & Groups → Messages
Copy outgoing news to folder
On by default
Mail & Groups → Messages
Quote original message in reply
Off by default
Mail & Groups → Messages
Send replies in HTML
Off by default
Mail & Groups → Messages
Wrap lines at x characters
Default is 72 characters
Mail & Groups → Messages

News (See also Messages)
Download unread only
On by default
Offline → Download
Download by date
Previous month, week, two
weeks, six months, year, x days
Default is one month
Offline → Download
Folder in which stored
Defaults: (Windows) *C:\Program
Files\Netscape\Users\login_name
news*; (UNIX)
/usr/spool/news/login_name;
(MAC) N/A
Mail & Groups → Group Server
*Groups to download before going
offline*
Default is none
Offline → Download
*Number of articles downloaded at
once*
Default is 400
Mail & Groups → Group Server
Server name and port
Name given during installation;
port 119 (with exceptions)
Mail & Groups → Group Server

Online/offline, start Communicator
Online work mode (on Net all the

time); offline work mode
(modem); ask me (prompt)
Default is online work mode
Offline tab

Proxy servers
Direct connection; manual proxy
configuration; or auto-proxy
configuration (URL)
Default is direct connection
Advanced → Proxies

Signature file
Default is
C:\Eudora\signature.pce (Win-
dows)
Mail & Groups → Identity

Style sheets, enable/disable
Enabled by default
Advanced tab

Toolbar appearance
Text only; pictures only; or both
Default is both
Appearance tab

User information
Needed in order to receive mail
Default is email address given at
installation
Mail & Groups → Mail Server
Needed in order to send email and
news
Name; email address; reply-to
address; organization; signature
file
Defaults taken from installation
info
Mail & Groups → Identity

CHAPTER 3

Microsoft Internet Explorer

Just about anyone who's ever sat in front of a computer should be able to figure out the basic functions performed by Microsoft Internet Explorer. The current chapter explains some of the less obvious browser features you may find useful.

This chapter also provides a quick reference to the menu items, keyboard short-cuts, and toolbar and other browser window features you can use to perform the various MSIE functions. In order for you to understand the reference better, we've included a figure in which the various parts of the application are labeled.

Note that this chapter is based on Microsoft internet Explorer 3.02. If you're run-ning a different version of Internet Explorer, some of the functions, shortcuts, menu items, etc. may be different.

Following the reference to browser functions is a reference to browser customiza-tion options.

For a similar reference to MSIE's mail and news applications, Internet Mail and Internet News, see Chapters 14 and 15, respectively.

Tips, Tricks, and Hidden Stuff

If all you want to accomplish with your browser is to hop from site to site, it prob-ably doesn't matter which program you use. If you want to fiddle around with your browser and make it do strange and amazing things, Navigator has more bells and whistles than MSIE. But MSIE is also less confusing and more to the point. It also has some interesting features (see Figure 3–1).

The following sections highlight some of the MSIE browser functions you might not notice immediately. This information should help you get more out of your browser, if that appeals to you.

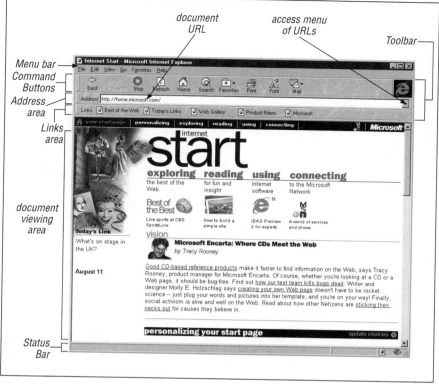

document URL · access menu of URLs · Toolbar

Menu bar · Command Buttons · Address area · Links area · document viewing area · Status Bar

Figure 3–1: Anatomy of Microsoft Internet Explorer

You Will Go to Microsoft Now

The logo for Internet Explorer in the upper-right part of the window is actually a link to **http://www.microsoft.com/**. (This may not be a big surprise to you.) At the Microsoft Web site, you can learn about Microsoft products and services galore.

The Links area of the Toolbar has a number of other related links that take you to various parts of Microsoft's site.

Changing Your Start Page

If you don't want the URL **http://home.microsoft.com/** to load first every time you open MSIE, you can specify an alternative in your browser options. Use the menu sequence **View → Options . . .** to open the Options dialog. Then click on the Navigation tab at the top of the box. Under the Customize section, change the Address of the Start Page to any URL you like. That's the document that will load when you start MSIE. Be sure to click the Apply button, and then OK in the dialog box to save the settings.

Hiding/Showing the Toolbar and Status Bar

If you'd like a larger pane in which to view documents, you can enlarge the window. You can also opt to hide one or more parts of the Toolbar and the Status Bar.

MSIE identifies all of the various tools at the top of the window (except the menus) as a single toolbar, with a number of different parts:

- Command buttons

- Address area (where the URL box is)

- Links area (containing links to some Microsoft info)

If you toggle off the **Toolbar** item on the **View** menu, you'll lose the whole she-bang. You can instead opt to drag closed one or more parts. The double-ridge symbol that appears on the left side of each area is actually a tool you can use to drag that part of the bar up and down, right and left. The thick border below the toolbar also can be dragged up and down to close and open the various parts.

When you drag up to close one part, a small tab corresponding to that part is added to the next part up. For instance, if you drag the Links area closed, a small "Links" tab will be added at the end of the Address area, as shown in Figure 3–2.

Figure 3–2: The minimized Links area appears at the end of the Address area

The tab works something like an icon for the corresponding part of the toolbar. If you click on the Links tab, for example, the Links area will be opened up again. However, it will be expanded on the current horizontal partition—that is, *over* the Address area.

You can also use this tab to drag the corresponding part of the toolbar open and closed horizontally (on the same row). For instance, if you drag the double-ridge symbol to the left, you can create a small Links area *next to* the Address area, as displayed in Figure 3–3.

Figure 3–3: Drag the toolbar tabs to open and close parts on the same line

As you can see, there are many configurations possible here. What you can't tell without playing around is that you can't close the entire toolbar using this method.

(Use the **View** menu for that.) You'll always have at least a single partition, with each of the three parts of the original toolbar represented (by tabs or abbreviated versions).

If you want to combine the three parts into one tier, it's easy to use the double-ridge symbols to open and close parts within the tier.

If you want to specify an abbreviated Toolbar layout as the default, there are MSIE Options to do that. The **Options** . . . item on the **View** menu opens the dialog box in which you can make your specifications. Check out the Toolbar section of the General tab. (You'll need to click Apply in the dialog box, and then OK, in order for your settings to take effect during the current session.)

One more tiny space-saving tip: You can close the Status Bar at the bottom of the browser window using the corresponding toggle on the **View** menu. (Dragging the bottom border won't do it—it will just resize the window.) But think twice about obscuring the Status Bar indefinitely. The information it provides about what's going on in your window is pretty handy.

Surprise! The Address Area Has a URL Menu

Clicking on the down-arrow button at the right end of the URL box in the Address area reveals a drop-down menu of URLs. These are all addresses you have entered during the current session, either by having typed or pasted them into the URL box. You can return to any of these URLs by selecting them from the menu.

This feature makes typing in URLs a lot less painful. Don't forget to add pages to your Favorites list (described later in this chapter) before you quit the browser— the menu will be cleared when you exit.

Customizing the Links Area

The default links that MSIE provides in the Links area of the Toolbar are—let's face it—boring. You're limited to five links here, but you can specify your own URLs in the MSIE Options dialog (**View → Options**). Within the dialog, go to the Navigation tab. Notice that "Page" is listed as "Start Page"—but clicking on the arrow at the end of the text box reveals a menu with a number of other choices. "Quick Link #1" through "Quick Link #5" correspond to the five links in the Links area. If you select one of these, you can specify whatever URL you like in the Address box below it. You can also supply a text name, in the Name field.

When you're done editing, click Apply and then OK in the dialog box. The pages you've specified will have shortcuts in the Links area of the toolbar.

Suppress Pictures, Sounds, Video, and Java for Faster Operation

OK, so this is the Web, and the pictures are a lot of what it's about. But download-ing them can also really slow things down. If you want to move around quickly, and you don't need to see the pretty pictures, MSIE lets you specify an Option that turns them off. There are similar options for sounds and video.

Select **Options**... from the **View** menu to open up the Options dialog box. The first group of options, titled "General," begins with a Multimedia section, with checkboxes for pictures, sounds, and videos. These boxes are toggles—if a checkmark appears, the option is on. Click off one or more of "Show pictures," "Play sounds," and "Play videos," to speed up your browser.

For the sake of speed, you might also opt to disable Java. The Security tab in the Options dialog has an Active Content section with the appropriate toggle. You can also disable ActiveX and other plug-ins here, if you so desire.

You'll need to click Apply in the Options dialog, and then OK, in order for your settings to take effect during the current session.

Managing Your List of Favorites

Every browser lets you keep a list of Internet addresses you like to visit. MSIE makes no bones about what these are, calling them your Favorites. The browser has both a menu and a command button that let you access functions related to managing your Favorites list. Here are the main things you'll probably want to do:

- Add addresses to your Favorites list

- Open addresses from your Favorites in the MSIE window

- Organize your Favorites (e.g., into folders)

- Remove entries from your Favorites list

Menus, buttons, and dialog boxes are the interface MSIE provides to let you work with Favorites. A UNIX-y type like me would just as soon open a text file up in my editor of choice and muck around with the Favorites list that way. However, that's not how things are set up.

There is actually no Favorites file. Rather, there is a folder (usually *c:\windows\profiles\your_name\favorites*) in which are stored your Favorites in the form of Internet shortcuts. So, you do have the option of opening the folder in your Windows Explorer and dragging shortcuts in or deleting them. When you drag a shortcut in, it appears immediately on your **Favorites** menu; likewise, those you delete are removed from **Favorites**.

However, MSIE intends for you to manage your Favorites using its interface, and this is actually pretty easy. You can add the currently displayed page to Favorites by following one of these steps:

- Selecting **Add to Favorites** from either **Favorites** menu (the one on the menu bar or the one revealed by the Favorites toolbar button)

- Using the keyboard accelerator: Alt+A, then A

- Clicking the right pointer button on the page to reveal a (context-sensitive) popup menu; then selecting **Add to Favorites**... (Shift+F10 also pops up menu)

Once a shortcut is added, it will appear on both **Favorites** menus (on the menu bar and the Toolbar). You can go to an address by selecting it from either **Favorites** menu.

Note that when you add an entry using these methods, it appears at the top level of your Favorites. You can also create folders in which to organize your Favorites. Select **Organize Favorites . . .** from either **Favorites** menu to open a dialog box for this purpose, as shown in Figure 3–4.

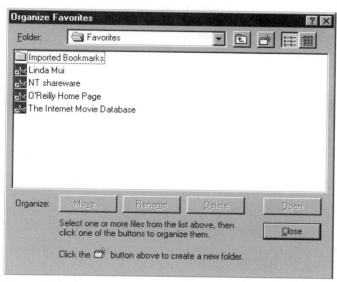

Figure 3–4: Organize Favorites dialog box

The top part of the dialog shows us that we're seeing the contents of the Favorites folder. It happens to have one subfolder called *Imported Bookmarks* and four Internet shortcuts. If I opened the subfolder, I'd reveal a number of additional shortcuts nested down one level. Create a new folder by using the rightmost folder button at the top of the dialog.

You need to have a folder or shortcut selected in order to use the command buttons at the bottom of the dialog. These buttons let you Move, Rename, Delete, or Open the folder/shortcut; the final button simply Closes the dialog when you're done organizing. If you select Move (or type Alt+V), you'll get a second dialog in which to identify the folder into which to move the selected shortcut(s) or folder(s). (If you're moving something from a higher level into a lower one, you can simply drag the symbol for it into the lower folder.)

Deleting is also easy. You can delete a single shortcut, multiple shortcuts, or one or more entire folders. Just select them, and then use the Delete button (or Alt+D or the Delete key on your keyboard).

Adding Netscape Navigator Bookmarks to Your MSIE Favorites

Every browser has a way for you to save your favorite URLs. Netscape Navigator calls this list Bookmarks. If you've been running both Netscape Navigator and Microsoft Internet Explorer, you can take Navigator Bookmarks and add them to your MSIE Favorites list. Here's one way to do it:

1. In the Netscape Navigator window, open the Bookmarks window. Ctrl+B is the fastest way; you can also use the Bookmarks button on the Location Toolbar to open a menu and select **Edit Bookmarks** from it.

2. In MSIE, choose **Organize Favorites** from the **Favorites** menu. This opens the Organize Favorites dialog box (pictured in the previous section).

3. Drag whatever item you want from the Bookmarks window and drop it in the Organize Favorites dialog box. It will appear at the bottom of the Favorites tree.

4. When you close the Organize Favorites dialog, you'll find that the bookmark you grabbed is now available on the **Favorites** menu. Ta-da.

In our sample Favorites window (in the previous section), you may have noticed a folder titled Imported Bookmarks. This folder actually contains the Navigator Bookmarks that were on the system when MSIE was configured. Internet Explorer "imports" them all at once during the initial setup of the program, if you want it to. But this process is not repeated, so if you want to add more Navigator Bookmarks, you'll have to do it yourself. The procedure outlined above should work fine.

Accessing Pages from Previous Sessions: The History List

The URLs you've visited during the current session are listed on the **Go** menu, in the next-to-last section. You can go back to any URL by selecting it from the menu. These entries are wiped out when you quit MSIE.

What if you want to go back to a site you haven't visited for a while? You can't remember the URL, and you don't feel like searching for it. Well, if it's been within the last 20 days (this number is customizable), the link should still be saved in your History Folder.

You can view and access the History Folder's entries by selecting **Open History Folder** from the **Go** menu. You'll get a History editing window, as displayed in Figure 3-5.

As is the case with Favorites, your browsing History takes the form of a folder (generally *c:\windows\history*) in which are stored a number of Internet shortcuts. Within the History folder, the shortcuts for the addresses you've visited most recently are at the bottom. The "Internet Address" column gives the URL; "Last Visited" is a timestamp from the last time you went there. The "Expires" column gives the date/time at which the entry will be automatically deleted from the file.

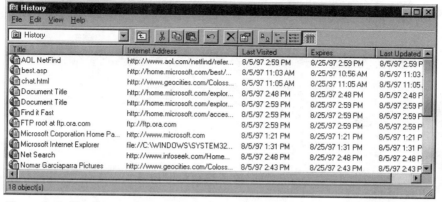

Figure 3-5: Use this window to view, edit, and access URLs from your history

By default, the browser keeps pages in your History list for 20 days. You can change this number in the Options dialog. Select **Options**... from the **View** menu. Then go to the Navigation tab, and change the "number of days" specification under History.

You can open one of these URLs in MSIE by double-clicking on its entry in the History list. You can also edit the file's contents. For example, you might highlight and delete entries yourself, or you can move them around using the Edit menu at the top of the History window.

There is an optional toolbar that can help you with editing. Toggle it on using the window's own **View** menu.

Cookies, Security, and You

As explained in Chapter 1, *A Living Glossary of the Internet*, a "cookie" is a small piece of information shared between your browser and certain servers—basically to let the server know you're visiting. The first time you connect, the server sends a bit of information to your browser; then each time you return to the same server, your browser sends the cookie back. In this way, the server can keep track of who's coming and going.

For the most part, the use of cookies is relatively harmless. They're often employed for user authentication, for instance. They can even be helpful: many sites have you register for free accounts, and cookies can save you from having to supply the same information each time you connect. Many sites will also deny you access if your browser does not accept a cookie. (See Chapter 1 for a more extensive explanation.)

However, if you are concerned about someone keeping tabs on you via cookies, you can open the cookies folder and delete anything in it you like. The worst thing that can happen is that another cookie will have to be set, you'll have to reregister for a free service, or something along that order.

On Windows systems, MSIE cookies live in the folder *c:\windows\cookies*. Each one is stored as an individual text file. Figure 3–6 shows the contents of a typical cookies folder.

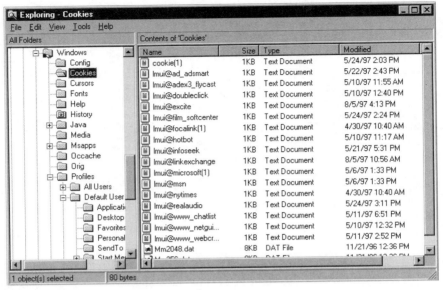

Figure 3–6: Each file contains a cookie

Generally the name of the file will clue you in as to the server that set it originally. Our sample cookie folder contains entries from Microsoft, Infoseek, HotBot, the *New York Times*, etc.

If you see something that looks questionable, go ahead and delete it. Some people actually suggest you periodically delete all of your cookies. However, I know that my friend whose file we're examining is registered with the *New York Times* online. I assume that particular cookie gets her logged on automatically to the server. Why get rid of that?

In the default MSIE environment, cookies are exchanged without causing a ripple you'd notice. If you'd like MSIE to inform you each time a cookie is supposed to be set—and to ask your permission for it to happen—open up the Options dialog (**View → Options**). Then open up the tab titled "Advanced." In the Warnings section is an option to "Warn before accepting cookies." Toggling this on causes MSIE to send you a dialog box each time a server tries to send a cookie to your browser. The dialog box gives you the option of accepting or refusing the cookie. Keep in mind that refusing generally means you won't get access to the server. However, it can still be interesting to see what servers are doing this, and how often. (It can also be a pain to be interrupted.)

Keyboard Shortcuts for Common Functions

If you check out the reference pages for MSIE browser functions later in this chapter, you'll see that there's a keyboard shortcut, or accelerator, for just about every one. However, many of these shortcuts are no more than the keys that let you access the various menu items. For instance, you can open a new browser window using the menu sequence **File → New Window**. The key sequence "Alt+F, N" does the same thing because Alt+F brings up the **File** menu, and then N invokes the **New Window** item.

For the most commonly used functions, there are true keyboard shortcuts, many of which require the use of the Ctrl key. Since opening a new window is something you might want to do fairly often, there's a better shortcut: Ctrl+N.

Table 3–1 summarizes this and other common functions and the keyboard shortcuts for them.

Table 3–1: Keyboard Shortcuts for Common MSIE Browser Functions

Function	Shortcut
Back one document in history list	Alt+←
Copy (selected text)	Ctrl+C
Cut (selected text)	Ctrl+X
Find text on current page	Ctrl+F
Forward one document in history list	Alt+→
Frames, move between	Ctrl+Shift+Tab
New browser window	Ctrl+N
Open Document	Ctrl+O
Paste (last cut/copied text)	Ctrl+V
Pop up menu for document (To use menu on a link or image, click right pointer button in that context)	Shift+F10
Print page	Ctrl+P
Reload document	F5
Stop download	Esc

Quick Reference to MSIE Browser Functions

The following pages provide an index to the various actions you can perform using MSIE. Beneath each possible function are the various ways you can perform it: menu options, keyboard shortcuts, and pointer actions on parts of the browser window (e.g., command buttons).

Note that this reference covers MSIE 3.02. If you're running a different version of the browser, the functions, shortcuts, menu items, etc. may be different. However, most versions after 3.*x* are very similar.

Back one document in history list
    Go → Back
    Alt+←
    Alt+G, B
    Left Arrow Button (toolbar)
    Backspace

Best of the Web
    Go → Best of the Web
    Help → Microsoft on the Web →
        Best of the Web
    Alt+G, E
    Alt+H, W, B

Close browser window
    File → Close
    Alt+F, C

Copy selected text
    Edit → Copy
    Ctrl+C
    Alt+E, C

Cut selected text
    Edit → Cut
    Ctrl+X
    Alt+E, T

Document, open
    File → Open . . .
    Ctrl+O
    Alt+F, O
    Enter URL in Address box, and hit
        Return

Edit current page (in Microsoft Front Page)
    Edit → Current page
    Alt+E, R
    Edit button (toolbar)

Exit browser window
    File → Close
    Alt+F, C

Favorites
    add to list of
        Favorites → Add To Favorites . . .
        Alt+A, A
        Favorites button on toolbar, then
            select Add To Favorites . . .
    open page from list
        Favorites → Choose from list
        Alt+A, choose from list
        Favorites button on toolbar, then
            select page
    organize list of
        Favorites → Organize
            Favorites . . .
        Alt+A, O
        Favorites button on toolbar, then
            select Organize Favorites . . .

Find text on current page
    Edit → Find (on this page) . . .
    Ctrl+F
    Alt+E, F

Font, change size
    (see also Fonts under Browser
        Options, later in this chapter)
    View → Fonts → item for desired
        size (five choices between
        Smallest and Largest)
    Alt+V, then N, then one of: R (for
        Largest), L (for Large), M (for
        Medium), S (for Small), A (for
        Smallest)
    Font button (toolbar); click the up
        arrow to make the font larger,
        down arrow to make font
        smaller

Forward one document in history list
    Go → Forward
    Alt+→
    Alt+G, F
    Right Arrow button (toolbar)
    Shift+Backspace

Frames, move between
 Shift+Ctrl+Tab

Frequently Asked Questions
 Help → Microsoft on the Web →
  Frequently Asked Questions
 Alt+H, W, Q

Go
 to document
  File → Open . . .
  Ctrl+O
  Alt+F, O
  Enter URL in Address box, hit
   Return
 to page in history list
  Go → Choose menu item corre-
   sponding to page
  Alt+G, type number correspond-
   ing to page
 to page in links toolbar
  Click on link

Help
 access topics
  Help → Help Topics
  Alt+H, H
 online support
  Help → Online Support
  Alt+H, S
 Web tutorial
  Help → Web Tutorial
  Alt+H, T

History folder, open
 Go → Open History Folder
 Alt+G, H

Home page (initial page)
 Go → Start Page
 Alt+G, S
 Home button on toolbar

**Links toolbar, specify links for (see
Browser Options)**
 View → Options → Navigation
  tab, Customization section
 Alt+V, O

Mail
 open Internet Mail
  Go → Read Mail
  Alt+G, M
  Mail/News button on toolbar,
   select Read Mail
 open window to compose message
  File → New Message . . .
  Alt+F, M
  Mail button on toolbar; select
   New Message . . .
 send link to current page in
  Mail button on toolbar; select
   Send a Link . . .

Menu, toggle pop-up
 Click right mouse button to dis-
  play pop-up menu
 Click elsewhere to pop it down
 Esc also pops menu down
 Shift+F10 toggles menu on and
  off for a link

Microsoft
 feedback
  Help → Microsoft on the Web →
   Send Feedback . . .
  Alt+H, W, K
 home page
  Help → Microsoft on the Web →
   Microsoft Home Page
  Alt+H, W, H
  Click on the Internet Explorer
   logo
 product news
  Help → Microsoft on the Web →
   Product News
  Alt+H, W, P

Move
 to beginning of page
  Home
 to end of page
  End

New browser window, open
 File → New Window
 Ctrl+N
 Alt+F, N

News
> Go → Read News
> Alt+G, N
> Mail/News button on toolbar,
> select Read News

Open document
> File → Open . . .
> Ctrl+O
> Alt+F, O
> Enter URL in Address box and hit
> Return

Options, edit browser (see also Browser Options section)
> View → Options . . .
> Alt+V, O

Paste last selected text
> Edit → Paste
> Ctrl+V
> Alt+E, P

Preferences, change browser (see also Browser Options)
> View → Options . . .
> Alt+V, O

Printing
> *layout, check/modify*
> File → Page Setup
> Alt+F, U
> Print button on toolbar, click
>   Properties button
> Type Alt+P, edit Paper Properties
> *print page*
> File → Print
> Ctrl+P
> Alt+F, P
> Print button on toolbar
> *properties, check/modify*
> File → Print, select Properties
> Ctrl+P, Alt+P
> Alt+F, P, Alt+P
> Print button on toolbar; click
>   Properties button or type Alt+P

Properties, display page
> File → Properties
> Alt+F, R

Quit browser
> File → Close
> Alt+F, C

Reload document
> View → Refresh
> F5
> Alt+F, C
> Refresh button on toolbar

Save
> *document*
> File → Save
> Ctrl+S
> Alt+F, A
> *document in file*
> File → Save As File . . .
> Alt+F, A

Scroll towards
> *beginning of page (see also Move)*
> Scrollbar on right side of frame
> *end of page*
> Scrollbar to the right of frame

Search the Web
> Go → Search the Web
> Help → Microsoft on the Web →
>   Search the Web
> Alt+G, W
> Alt+H, W, W

Select all
> Edit → Select All
> Alt+E, A

Shortcut, create for current page
> File → Create Shortcut
> Alt+F, R
> Drag and drop link onto desktop

Software, access Microsoft
> Help → Microsoft on the Web →
>   Free Stuff
> Alt+H, W, F

Source, view document
> View → Source
> Alt+V, C

Start page (initial page), go to
    Go → Start Page
    Alt+G, S
    Home button on toolbar

Status bar, show/hide
    View → Status Bar
    Alt+V, B

Stop download
    View → Stop
    Esc
    Alt+V, P
    Stop button on toolbar

Toolbar, show/hide
    View → Toolbar
    Alt+V, T

Version of browser
    Help → About Internet Explorer
    Alt+H, A

Web tutorial, access
    Help → Web Tutorial
    Alt+H, T

Window, open additional browser
    File → New Window
    Ctrl+N
    Alt+F, N

Browser Options

You can set a number of preferences that determine how MSIE looks and operates. All of these preferences are set using the Options dialog box, which is displayed using this menu sequence:

```
View → Options
```

Or the keyboard shortcut:

```
Alt+V, and then O
```

Within the Options dialog, the various preferences are organized on six overlapping tabbed windows, which look something like file folders. The tabs reveal the following categories:

- General

- Connection

- Navigation

- Programs

- Security

- Advanced

How do you know what options are available on what tab? You don't. That's where the following reference section comes in. It lists the possible options in alphabetical order, along with the appropriate tab on which to find them, as well as the default and other possible settings.

Once you specify a setting you want, you can invoke it for the current session by clicking on the Apply button. Then click OK to close the Options dialog.

The current chapter covers MSIE 3.02. If you're using an earlier version, the settable options may vary. In a couple of cases there have been noteworthy changes since version 3.0—so we've noted them!

Active content, enable/disable downloading of
    Enabled by default
    Security tab → Active content section

ActiveX
    Enable/disable controls, plug-ins
    Enabled by default
    Security tab → Active content section
    Enable/disable running of ActiveX scripts
    Enabled by default

    Security tab → Active content section

Authentication, use certificate system for automatic
    Specify certificates for personal, site, and publisher identification
    Defaults are no personal certificates, a number of sites (see dialog), and no publisher certificates
    Security tab → Certificates section

Color

Background
Click on color box to access palette of choices and custom color editor
Default is white
General tab → Colors section

Text
Click on color box to access palette of choices and custom color editor
Default is black
General tab → Colors section

Unvisited links
Click on color box to access palette of choices and custom color editor
Default is blue
General tab → Links section

Visited links
Click on color box to access palette of choices and custom color editor
Default is green
General tab → Links section

Use Microsoft palette
Off by default
General tab → Colors section

Connection (version 3.0 only)

Connect to the Internet as needed (i.e., enable/disable modem function)
Disabled by default
Connection tab → Dialing section

Disconnect if idle for x minutes
Off by default; no number specified
Connection tab → Dialing section

Number(s) to dial
No default
Connection tab → Dialing section

Cryptography settings

Allow/disallow PCT connections
Allowed by default
Advanced tab → Cryptography button

Allow/disallow SSL2 connections
Allowed by default

Advanced tab → Cryptography button

Allow/disallow SSL3 connections
Allowed by default
Advanced tab → Cryptography button

External viewers/players, specify for MIME types

Defaults provided in File Types dialog
Programs tab → Viewers section → File Types button

Font

Character set
Central European, Cyrillic, Greek, Western
Default is Western
General tab → Select Font Settings . . . → Character sets section

Fixed-width text
Courier New, Lucida Console
Default is Courier New
General tab → Select Font Settings . . . → Character sets section

Language
Central European, Cyrillic, Greek, Western
Default is Western
General tab → Select Font Settings . . . → Languages section

Proportional-width text
Matura MT Script Capitals, Monotype Corsiva, Playbill, Times New Roman, Wide Latin
Default is Times New Roman
General tab → Select Font Settings . . . → Character sets section

---

History list, number of days to save entries

Default is 20 days
Navigation tab → History section

Java
Enable/disable
Enabled by default
Security tab → Active content
section
Enable/disable JIT compiler
Enabled by default
Advanced tab
Enable/disable logging
Disabled by default
Advanced tab

Links
Color of unvisited
Click on color box to access
palette of choices and custom
color editor
Default is blue
General tab → Links section
Color of visited
Click on color box to access
palette of choices and custom
color editor
Default is green
General tab → Links section
Highlight when selected
On by default
Advanced tab
Underlining, enable/disable
Enabled by default
General tab → Links section

Links toolbar, specify up to five links for
Defaults are: Quick Link #1: Best
of the Web,
http://home.microsoft.com/
best/best.asp
Quick Link #2: Today's Links,
http://home.microsoft.com/
links/links.asp
Quick Link #3: Web Gallery,
http://home.microsoft.com/
isapi/ . . .
Quick Link #4: Product News,
http://home.microsoft.com/ie
Quick Link #5: Microsoft,
http://www.microsoft.com
Navigation tab → Customize section → Select a Quick Link

from the Page drop-down
menu

Mail and news programs to use
Defaults are Internet Mail and
Internet News
Programs tab → Mail and news
section

MIME encoding version (not settable)
Default is Windows-1252
General tab → Font Settings . . .
→ Character sets section

Pictures, show or not
Default is to show pictures
General tab → Multimedia section

Proxy server(s)
*Address and port for any of these
proxy servers (HTTP, Secure, FTP,
Gopher, Socks)*
Default is none
Connection tab → Servers section
Connect through
Off by default
Connection tab → Servers section
*Do not use for addresses beginning
with (list protocols)*
Default is none
Connection tab → Servers section
*Do not use proxy server for local
(intranet) addresses*
Disabled by default
Connection tab → Servers section
*Use the same proxy server for all pro-
tocols*
Off by default
Connection tab → Servers section

Ratings (to restrict access to content)
*Enable/disable to filter out objection-
able content*
Disabled by default
Security tab → Content advisor
section → Enable Ratings but-
ton
*Create login and password for
access to restricted content*
Default is no login or password

Security tab → Content advisor
section → Settings button

Scrolling, use smooth
On by default
Advanced tab

Search page, specify URL and text name for
Defaults are
http://home.microsoft.com/
access/allinone.asp; Search
Page
Navigation tab → Customize section → Select Search Page from the Page drop-down menu

Sounds, play or not
Default is to play sounds
General tab → Multimedia section

Start page (browser's home page)
Specify a URL (address) and text name
Defaults are
http://home.microsoft.com/;
Start Page.
Navigation tab → Customize section

Toolbar layout (standard buttons, address bar, links, text labels, background bitmap)
Check each feature on or off
All of these features are on by default
General tab → Toolbar section

URLs, show friendly
On by default
Advanced tab

Videos, play or not
Default is to play videos
General tab → Multimedia section

Warnings, enable/disable display of warnings when
Accepting cookies
Disabled by default
Advanced tab → Warnings section
Transmissions happen over an open connection
Enabled by default
Advanced tab → Warnings section
Changing between secure and insecure mode
Enabled by default
Advanced tab → Warnings section
Site certificate is invalid
Enabled by default
Advanced tab → Warnings section

PART III

Finding Stuff

CHAPTER 4

Internet Addressing

By now, you've probably seen quite a few Internet addresses, also known as URLs—even if you don't know that you have. TV programs, newspapers, magazines, billboards—they're all tattooed with the addresses of Web sites. Watch NBC's news program *Dateline*, and they ask you to visit their Web site at http://www.dateline.com/. The *New York Times* is at http://www.nytimes.com/. Harvard University is at http://www.harvard.edu/. The White House is at http://www.whitehouse.gov/.

If you take the time to look more carefully at some of these hieroglyphics, you'll notice a lot of similarities, as well as some superficial differences. For instance, all of these particular addresses begin in the exact same way:

```
http://www.
```

But some of them end differently:

```
.com        Commercial enterprises
.edu        Educational institutions
.gov        Government agencies
```

This chapter explains the addressing conventions that apply to files on the Internet. Understanding these conventions should help you understand the addresses you encounter, as well as to put addresses together on the fly.

Servers, Protocols, and Pathnames

As explained in Chapter 1, *A Living Glossary of the Internet*, a networked computer is commonly called a *server* because it provides some kind of service or information. Internet servers are classified by the type(s) of information they offer. A mail server provides electronic mail. A World Wide Web server provides hypertext documents. A single computer can act as a number of different servers (e.g., a host might be both a mail and an HTTP server).

The reason servers of the same type can communicate with each other is because, in effect, they speak the same language, known in computerese as a *protocol*. A protocol is simply a standard way to send and receive information. Each type of server communicates using a different protocol.

Each file on the Internet has a unique address, also called a Uniform Resource Locator, or URL. This is one of the least friendly terms you'll encounter on the Net; it's also one of the most important. If someone tells you about an interesting Net offering, maybe a Web site, you may need to ask "What's the URL?" In other words, "What's the address? Where can I find it?" You'll certainly see "URL" in print quite often—followed by an address of some kind. Many advertisements now assume people understand URL syntax and simply include addresses without explanation.

A file's Internet address, or URL, is determined by the following:

- The type of server or protocol

- The name/address of the server on the Internet

- The location of the file on the server (this location may be related as a "path" through the file hierarchy)

An intelligent browsing program, like Netscape Navigator or Microsoft Internet Explorer, can display files in just about any format available on any of the common types of servers. Table 4–1 lists the types of servers you may encounter, along with the protocol they use, and the type(s) of information they provide.

Table 4–1: Internet Servers and What They Provide

So, enough of these details. What does an actual address look like? Here is a typical one, the home page of the Yahoo! Web site. (Yahoo! is one of the more popular online Internet guides):

```
http://www.yahoo.com/
```

The "http" identifies both the protocol and server. According to standard URL syntax, a colon (:) and two forward slashes (//) follow the protocol/server.

The next component of the address is the name of the server, in this case, **www.yahoo.com**. Server names have multiple components. Commonly a Web server's name will begin "www" for World Wide Web. The ".com" suffix indicates that Yahoo! is a commercial entity, as opposed to a nonprofit organization (".org"), a school (".edu"), a branch of the government (".gov"), etc. The naming scheme by which servers are identified is also known as the *domain name system*. Each component of a name is a *domain*. Suffixes like ".com," ".org," ".edu," etc., correspond to what are known as *top-level* domains.

As explained earlier in this section, most URLs have three components: the protocol/server type, the name of the server, and the location of the file on the server (also known as the file's path or pathname). Virtually every server provides an introductory document, which you access when you link to the server. When you're dealing with hypertext documents on the World Wide Web, this introductory file is known as a *home page*. But "home page" is also used more generically to mean the basic document about a particular subject (or person!), regardless of whether it's the first page you encounter on a server.

Our sample address accesses the Yahoo! home page, which offers a directory of Web pages organized by subject, as well as a search engine that lets you search for particular words among these pages. (For more information, see Chapter 6, *Internet Directories and Search Engines*). The Yahoo! home page is pictured in Figure 4–1.

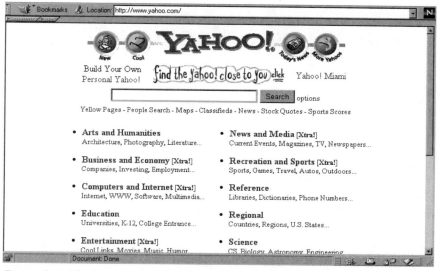

Figure 4–1: The home page of the Yahoo! directory

More often you'll encounter addresses with at least one additional component, which corresponds to the filename. Keep in mind that an address has to pinpoint a file on a server. Since files are arranged in some sort of hierarchy, you often need to supply a path through the file structure to get to the file you want. Thus, often an address will include a long pathname following the name of the server. For example, the following address corresponds to a file on the Yahoo! server:

```
http://www.yahoo.com/reference/dictionaries/english.htm
```

The file's name is *english.htm*; the exact place it occurs on the Yahoo! server (*www.yahoo.com*) is identified by the pathname */reference/dictionaries/ english.htm*. Don't worry about having to come up with addresses like this off the top of your head. In some cases, you'll read an exact address somewhere and simply type it into your browser in order to access the file. But in most cases, you'll come upon files simply by following links, and you won't have to think about the exact address. Whether you supply an address or come upon one, the exact syntax appears in the address box in your browser window, above where the file is displayed.

CHAPTER 5

Landmark Sites and Other Resources

The Internet has no central organization. Millions of people—more every day—contribute to its content. The people and organizations behind the Internet are constantly changing. And, let's face it, there's little information of any kind that remains stable for all time.

As a matter of fact, the Internet may be the largest moving target in history—and it's getting bigger by the moment. New sites are added all the time. Resources are constantly updated. Sometimes they move to new addresses, or they may go away entirely. The innovative young company with the flashy Web site goes out of business. You like to visit the Web site of the Cleveland Browns—and then they go off and become the Baltimore Ravens. Don't get attached to the Official Groundhog Day Site—the Webmaster is liable to see his shadow and take the URL into permanent hibernation.

Still, there are a reasonable number of Internet sites whose appeal is so widespread, maintained by organizations that are so stable that you can pretty much count on them being right where you remember. This chapter takes a look at some of these "landmark" sites, as well as a few other that may have less history, but manage to suggest that same staying power. You may want to add a number of these addresses to your browser's list of your favorite sites.

All of the sites mentioned in this chapter offer substantial resources for free. Keep in mind, however, that some organizations may offer a basic level of information for free, but expect you to pay for extras. *Sports Illustrated* comes to mind. You can certainly read some articles and find out scores, but if you want to download video files of bikini-clad models, you'll have to show them the money.

In addition, there are some very established sites—ones that might legitimately be classified as landmarks—which unfortunately offer information only at a subscription rate. For instance, The *Wall Street Journal* online (**http://www.wsj.com/**) is free for two weeks; after that you're expected to pay a subscription fee, with the rate depending upon whether you also get the print edition. This chapter will not cover sites of this type. It doesn't mean they might not be very valuable to particular individuals.

So, let's take a look at some of the sites that give you substantial resources for free. Of course, your Internet exploration will lead you beyond these well-traveled paths. Although the vast and changing nature of the Net makes it impossible to catalog everything that's out there at any given time, there are a number of tools to help you find what you're looking for. (See Chapter 6, *Internet Directories and Search Engines*, for more information.)

A Directory for Every Topic: Yahoo!

http://www.yahoo.com/

When Yahoo! first appeared online, they had clearly broken a special piece of Internet turf. Yahoo! is an online directory of Web sites, organized by subject area. Among the topic headings are Arts and Humanities, Health, Government, Entertainment, Science, Education, and Recreation and Sports.

The resources Yahoo! lists are growing all the time. As a matter of fact, unless you want to do a very comprehensive search of Internet resources, or the information you're looking for is fairly esoteric, Yahoo! may be the best place to start. Certainly it's a great launching point for general exploration.

The Yahoo! home page offers links to a number of other special features that make it virtually invaluable, including:

- The latest news stories, stock market quotations, and sports scores (This information may not be literally up-to-the-minute, but it's pretty close.)

  Yahoo! gathers its news from a number of sources, including Reuters, the Associated Press, ESPNET SportsZone, and the *New York Times*. Read national and international news in a wide range of categories, including top stories, politics, world, technology, business, sports, entertainment, and weather.

  There are a number of sources of stock market updates online, but Yahoo!'s service is one of the simpler ones to use. For instance, you don't have to specify the particular stock exchange on which a security is listed in order to get a quotation. Yahoo!'s stock quote system also takes in more territory, extending to the rarer listings for "penny stocks," cheap securities that are like lottery tickets to the small-time investor and that appear on the lesser "bulletin boards."

  The news section also covers sports, including stories, results, and scores for college and professional teams.

- Business "yellow pages"—an online directory of businesses (including directions)

- A people search facility

You can also set up a personalized directory called MyYahoo!, which, if you're inclined to tread over the same familiar set of Internet paths, will help you quickly cut to the chase.

Yahoo! is also expanding its resources to provide special directory for particular geographic regions. Yahoo! directories currently exist for certain countries (including Canada, France, Germany, Japan, and the U.K. and Ireland), as well as a number of U.S. cities (Austin, Boston, Chicago, Los Angeles, New York, Seattle, Washington D.C., etc.). All of these sites are accessible from the Yahoo! home page.

About the Internet

Every medium loves self-reference, and the Internet community wallows in it. Here are some of the sites that can tell you about the turf.

Internet World

http://www.iworld.com/

An online magazine about Internet news and resources, *iWORLD* also offers a searchable list of Internet Service Providers (**http://www.thelist.com**). Select the **Search** link to search the magazine's issues (past and present), a number of news sources, as well as the Internet at large—using the search engines Excite and Infoseek. (See Chapter 6 for more information about finding stuff on the Net.)

HotWired

http://www.hotwired.com/

The online version of Wired, the ultra-trendy magazine about the Internet and all things Cyber. (I am not cool enough to read it.) If you like the magazine, you'll like the site—and vice versa.

Web Review

http://www.webreview.com/

If you create Web pages professionally, or you just want to make Web pages that look professional, *Web Review* is a site you'll want to put on your hotlist. *Web Review* features articles, tutorials, and demos that showcase and teach you the latest Web authoring techniques and tools: graphic design, animation, information architecture, audio/video, scripting languages, databases, etc. *Web Review* is produced by Songline Studios, an affiliate of O'Reilly & Associates, and published in partnership with Miller Freeman, Inc. (Miller Freeman publishes the print magazine *Web Techniques*.)

CNET: The Computer Network

http://www.cnet.com/

CNET.COM is an excellent source of information about the Internet and its various technologies. Their Web site offers reviews of and tips for using some of the hottest new software products. You can also download a number of products from here. CNET's efforts also extend to television programming, both in syndication and on networks including USA Network and the Sci-Fi Channel. Check out the TV.com link for details.

CNET offers a free membership that will get you access to their online discussions, as well as their electronic publication, *CNET Digital Dispatch*, which tells you what's happening at CNET.COM and on CNET TV.

Government

Whether they're putting resources online, or being concerned about what you and I do electronically, the federal government is a considerable presence on the Internet. There's certainly a lot of useful information put out there by the government at all levels. Check it out.

Everything Starts at The White House

http://www.whitehouse.gov/

The White House Web site has been designed in such a way that it is a reasonable gateway to all of the online resources of the federal government. At the top level, the site offers links to the following:

- Information about the President and Vice President (and their families), including how to send them email

- Information specifically for kids—don't miss the White House Pets

- A history of the Presidency and the White House (including online tours)

- Various White House documents, speeches, and photographs

- What's happening at the White House—and at the Web site

- The Interactive Citizens' Handbook

- Commonly requested federal services

The final two links merit a bit more discussion. The Interactive Citizens' Handbook is not an actual book, but a collection of software tools and links that help you navigate the government's electronic offerings. For instance, you can search through the offerings of the White House Web site—or extend your search through all federal government Web sites!

The Interactive Citizens' Handbook also offers a link to the germinal Government Information Locator Service (GILS), which will eventually contain records of all public government information, not only the subset that's available online.

Finally, the Interactive Citizens' Handbook offers links to the various branches of the government, federal agencies and commissions, as well as government-supplied information about education, employment, health, safety, travel, arts, housing, and state and local governments. Keep in mind that each of these links provides a number of very useful ones. For instance, if you follow the link to

Travel and Tourism, you'll then be able to access weather maps, national park information, passport and customs information, etc.

Another far-reaching link at the White House Web site is "Commonly Requested Federal Services," which provides a directory of government-offered services, organized by type:

- Benefits & Assistance (Social Security, veterans, pensions, etc.)
- Consumer Protection (automobile recall, product safety, fraud investigation, etc.)
- Education (student aid, grants, loans, etc.)
- Employment & Taxes (IRS, Department of Labor, government and military job opportunities, Peace Corps, etc.)
- Government Property (what's for sale and how to buy it)
- Health (Medicare, Medicaid, aging, AIDS, National Cancer Institute, the FDA and food safety, nutrition, etc.)
- Housing (home-buying and rental assistance, HUD, fire and flood protection, urban planning, etc.)
- Publications & Mail (U.S. Postal Service, government publications, electronic "blue pages"—phone listings for the federal government, etc.)
- Science & Technology (patent information and patent searching; NASA and EPA online offerings; etc.)
- Travel & Tourism (passport and visa information, travel warnings, health, import/export guidelines, etc.)
- U.S. Business Advisor (doing business with the government, finance, international trade, labor and employment, laws and regulations, etc.)

The Library of Congress

http://www.loc.gov/

Read any of the bills currently before the House and Senate; search through the online catalog as well as through the catalogs of more than 200 affiliated libraries.

The Internal Revenue Service

http://www.irs.gov/

You can run, but you can't hide. So why not save some paper and file your return electronically? The IRS Web site says that most people who use electronic filing will get their refunds within three weeks—that's nice. Our men in the Treasury Department have tried to soften the annual blow even further by giving electronic filing a cute acronym, namely, ELF. (Hey, it doesn't work for me either.) Oh, and you can get tax forms and publications here, too.

The United States Postal Service

http://www.usps.gov/

Find out postage rates, track express mail deliveries, view the the latest stamps, etc. You can also look up Zip Codes; to get there directly, use the URL http://www.usps.gov/ncsc/.

Newspapers, Magazines, and Other Periodicals

Whether or not you like to read publications on paper, the online versions of many newspapers and magazines can give you additional info, as well as deliver it in a fun way. You'll also be able to read news that happened too late to make the morning edition. The offerings should become more and more interesting as publications learn to maximize Internet resources.

Newspapers Online

http://www.newspapers.com/

One of the newer sites in this chapter, Newspapers Online is worth a special mention for its breadth of coverage. You can use it to locate the Web sites of hundreds of newspapers both in the U.S. and abroad. (Where else are you going to find links to the *Jerusalem Post* and the *Manila Bulletin?*) The site's listings also include trade journals, university and college papers, and specialty publications.

Finding Stuff

The New York Times

http://www.nytimes.com/

When the *New York Times* first cut an online presence, they decided their Web paper needed a more appropriate slogan than "All the news that's fit to print," which has served the newspaper so well. But then they changed their minds. And what you get online is very much true to the spirit of one of the most established and respected publications of its kind. They'll make you register and get a login name and password, but the most of the information is free. (If you want the crossword, however, it will cost you—unless you're a print subscriber.)

USA Today Online

http://www.usatoday.com/

You've seen the paper; the online offering has the same no-frills, plenty-of-facts feeling. Get news, weather, sports, financial updates and stock reports, columns, etc. *USA Today Online* is especially strong on financial matters. See the *Money* section later in this chapter.

Reuters News Service

http://www.reuters.com/

One of the oldest and most esteemed news wire services, Reuters is going the way of the future. Their primary online service provides the top national and international news stories, as well as extensive financial news. Reuters also offers news in multimedia form: charts and graphs, photos, and audio and video clips. For casual news updates, keep in mind that you may be better off checking other services (e.g., Pathfinder). Reuters is intended more as a feed for other services that synthesize news rather than as an information solution for individuals.

Netgazettes

http://www.netgazettes.com/

A directory to some artsy Web magazines, or Webzines, as they're called. Access electronic publications like *Poetry Magazine*, *Greenwich Village*, and *Chelsea Art*.

Pathfinder

http://www.pathfinder.com/

Is it a search engine? Is it a publication? It's actually both a search engine and a collection of Web sites, all affiliated in some way with Time-Warner. Among the searchable resources are the Web sites for magazines like *Time*, *Life*, *Fortune*, *Sports Illustrated*, and *People*, as well as television networks like the Weather Channel and CNN.

But that's really only the tip of the iceberg. You can also reach dozens of other related publishing, news, and entertainment sites. Select the **Help** link, and then **Site Directory** for a complete list of cooperating sites. Among the more useful sites are the following:

- MusicSeek—a searchable database of more than 200,000 albums and 16,000 artists; read reviews, and discographies; browse through hundreds of musical categories.
- MovieSeek—a database of thousands of films; search by title, actors, genre, year, etc.
- ArtsLink—a site from which you can reach museums, galleries, and art organizations online as well as read about and view art.
- Kidstuff—a site that links to *Sports Illustrated for Kids*, *TIME for Kids*, Warner Brothers Animation, and others geared toward younger people.

Pathfinder's SiteSeeker Search facility lets you search the various Pathfinder resources or opt to search beyond—to the Internet. There should be a search button on the home page and every other document at the Pathfinder site. Use it to access Pathfinder resources (e.g., MovieSearch) that don't have an obvious link.

Reference

Availability, ease of use, and economy, are all great features. But, let's face it, the most important characteristic of a source of reference is that it be right. There's plenty of reference material on the Net, but how much is truly authoritative is a tougher question than I'm willing to answer. You expect an encyclopedia to be as accurate and up-to-date as possible. But phone listings change every day. You'd think it would be easier for an online reference to keep pace with change, and in many cases it works that way, but you're still better off calling 4-1-1 for a friend's brand new phone number than using one of the Internet "white pages" facilities. And, on many topics, I still trust a dusty old tome before a dusty new terminal.

All of this faint praise aside, there is still plenty of useful reference information on the Net. Among the advantages of looking up information on the Net are that it's (generally) fast, readily available (unlike books that you don't already have), and (often) free. I don't really want to call information for Hawaii if I can get it online. The Net also lets you search through multiple reference sources at once. As a matter of fact, a well-maintained reference site can save people a lot of time and bother.

While the Internet is crawling with sites that let you search telephone and email listings, there aren't many free authoritative resources of a higher caliber. For instance, Encyclopaedia Britannica Online (**http://www.eb.com/**) is a landmark site, but it's only free for the first seven days.

Still, most of us need to know phone numbers and the like more often than the annual rainfall in Uganda. (For more about *Finding People and Places*, including email and telephone listings, see Chapter 7.) The Net also has libraries, dictionaries, almanacs, quotations, acronyms, abbreviations, maps, charts, tables, etc. Here are some useful resources:

Finding Stuff

The Merck Manual

http://www.merck.com/

There's plenty of superficial medical information available on the Net. Anyone who's familiar with the printed version of *The Merck Manual* knows that it goes several steps better in describing health problems and treatments. The online version is just as useful.

WWWebster Dictionary

http://www.m-w.com/netdict.htm/

Merriam-Webster (an old name that happens to include a trendy syllable) is proud to offer their online WWWebster Dictionary (of the English language). Look up words using their simple search engine. When search results are returned, you also have the option of checking Thesaurus entries for the word.

OneLook Dictionaries

http://www.onelook.com/

For fast, reliable definitions of English words in common usage, rely on the aforementioned WWWebster Dictionary. To go beyond the everyday, use the OneLook Dictionaries, which indexes more than 100 dictionaries covering a variety of disciplines. In one fell swoop, you can search dictionaries of science, business, religion, sports, technology, medicine, even acronyms—as well as a number of general dictionaries. OneLook Dictionaries is not as established as some of the other recommended sites, but it has the potential to be a uniquely valuable resource. (However, why the site lists the *Italian Cooking Glossary* under *Technologies Dictionaries* remains a mystery.)

The Old Farmer's Almanac

http://www.almanac.com/

Who would have thought that such a traditional book would work so well online? Not only is it cheery and engaging, it can tell you the current weather conditions in more than 800 U.S. cities, as well as give five-day forecasts, complete with maps and illustrations. If you want to know when to do your spring or fall planting, this is the place to come.

The Weather Channel

http://www.weather.com/

The Web site of the Weather Channel provides forecast information for locales at home and abroad. Here you can find bulletins, maps, travel advisories, allergy info, beach and boating reports, etc. If there's something in the air, here's where to read about it. It's also easy to customize your **weather.com** home page to provide the forecasts, maps, and other information most meaningful to you.

Usenet News

Most Web browsers come with a Usenet news module that lets you read and post news. (See Chapter 12, *Getting Along in Usenet*, for more information about Usenet.) The amount of information exchanged via Usenet is vast. The following sites should help you navigate it more effectively.

DejaNews

http://www.dejanews.com/

A search engine that lets you search for words in Usenet news postings, both past and present. It's a great way to extract what interests you or pick up a message thread. You can also use DejaNews to post messages. (This is not an anonymous posting service; you have to register first, so they know to whom the message should be attributed.)

Archive of FAQs (in Text Form)

ftp://ftp.uu.net/usenet/news.answers/

A collection of Frequently Asked Questions (FAQs) for almost any Usenet newsgroup. The files are in text form only. For HTML versions, the following site is helpful.

Search FAQs

http://www.lib.ox.ac.uk/search/search_faqs.html

A service of Oxford University, Search FAQs lets you search through FAQs and retrieve them in HTML form.

Sports

Although surfing the Net could hardly be viewed as a physical activity, the subject of sports is actually a great fit for the Internet. Everything about sports is dynamic, and the Net allows fans to get the latest information in a flash. No more waiting for the evening news; you can read about the controversial trade a few minutes after it's a done deal. You want to make a point about a particular player, and you'd love to call on that one very meaningful statistic you just can't remember? Look it up on the Net.

It's not surprising then there are thousands of sites related to sports and games, both amateur and professional, played by just about anyone you can think of. Just about every pro team has its own Web site, where you can get news, player profiles, team history, tickets, you name it. Many amateur teams are jumping on the Web bandwagon too. There are also Usenet newsgroups and chat rooms you can use to discuss your favorite sports with other fans.

The following selection are among the more stable and reliable sports sites:

Major League Baseball@BAT

http://www.majorleaguebaseball.com/

The official Web site of Major League Baseball, MLB@BAT, brings you news, features, scores, stats, MLB merchandise, links to the Web sites for the various teams, etc. Many of the stories run by MLB@BAT deal with baseball history as well as the trends of the current day. The site also hosts online chat sessions about various aspects of the game. In a typical session, fans are invited to celebrate Jackie Robinson's life, 50 years after he became the first African-American to play Major League Baseball.

NBA.com

http://www.nba.com/

The official Web site of the National Basketball Association, NBA.com, brings you scores, stats, news, features, audio and video takes of big game moments, links to the Web sites for all the pro teams, and (of course) access to the online NBA store.

NFL.com

http://www.nfl.com/

The official Web site of the National Football League, NFL.com has news, stats, features, NFL merchandise, and links to the team Web sites.

NHL.com

http://www.nhl.com/

The current Web site of the National Hockey League describes hockey as the "coolest game on earth." The site isn't bad either. Visit it to get scores, stats, game schedules, and news; to spout off about hockey; or to visit the Web sites of the various teams. You can also buy NHL clothing and products.

The Sports Network

http://www.sportsnetwork.com/

The Sports Network may be the best source of sports news online. As a matter of fact, the only decade-old Sports Network has become a wire service for many more established media entities, including ABC, *Sports Illustrated*, *The Sporting News*, The Sports Channel, and *TV Guide*. This is a great place to come for the latest scores, trades and other news, postgame summaries, statistics, as well as intelligent articles and discussion.

ESPNet SportsZone

http://espnet.sportszone.com/

This site is heavy on news, columns, and features. Read all about the latest trades, games, trends, and events. Download audio and video files. While most of these offerings are free, certain articles are considered to be "premium content," and can only be read if you pay a subscription fee. These articles are identified by a small symbol in front of the title. You can pay for one day of access, though it's much cheaper to subscribe for the year if you intend to read premium articles on a regular basis. ESPNet SportsZone also offers fantasy league play at a price.

CBS SportsLine

http://www.sportsline.com/

One of the fastest growing sports sites on the Web, CBS SportsLine is just the kind of multimedia extravaganza you'd expect. In addition to articles, news, interviews, scores, and the like, there are live audio broadcasts and simulated games. Customize the SportsLine home page to suit your interests.

Nando.net SportServer

http://www.nando.net/SportServer/

Here you can find scores, stats, trades, playoffs, sports chat, photos, history, etc., of the major professional and college sports, as well as Olympic competition, racing, etc. The PressBox features articles written by well-known newspaper columnists.

Money

If you have it, want it, or just want some more, there are a number of online resources that can help you.

Quote.com

http://www.quote.com/

Quote.com provides a lot more than stock market quotations, including information on options, commodities futures, mutual funds, financial indices for markets worldwide, business news, earnings forecasts, market analysis, company profiles, and a whole lot more. You can access quite a bit of this information for free. If you're willing to pay for an additional subscription, you can get extensive information designed specifically for you (e.g., customized charts, reports about the competition, etc.).

USA Today on Money

http://www.usatoday.com/

USA Today Online has dozens of links to useful financial information. Choose Money from the top-level domain to access the latest financial news. Then explore links like Moneyline, Stock quotes, Market indexes, Futures, Mutual funds, Currencies, Global markets, etc. The USA Today stock quote facility can return the values of ten securities at once.

Museums

A "virtual" visit to a museum isn't as good as the real thing, but it's still a lot of fun. More and more museums are going online, and the audio-visual capabilities of the Web make it a good fit.

National Gallery of Art, Washington, D.C.

http://www.nga.gov/

A vast collection of American and European paintings, sculptures, and decorative arts from the 13th through the 20th centuries.

The Smithsonian Institution

http://www.si.edu/

The following is a list of the Smithsonian member museums, most of which are located around The Mall in Washington, D.C. (exceptions are noted). Each of these museums is accessible from the Smithsonian home page.

- National Air and Space Museum
- National Museum of American History
- National Museum of Natural History
- Arthur M. Sackler Gallery (Asian art)
- Freer Gallery of Art (Asian and 19th- and 20th-century American art)
- National Museum of African Art
- Hirshhorn Museum and Sculpture Garden (19th-century through contemporary art)
- National Museum of American Art
- National Portrait Gallery
- National Postal Museum
- Anacostia Museum (Contributions of African-Americans to American society; located in the Fort Stanton area of Washington D.C.)
- National Zoo (Located along Washington's Rock Creek)
- National Museum of the American Indian (New York City)
- The Cooper-Hewitt National Design Museum (Historical and contemporary design; located in New York City)

The United States Holocaust Memorial Museum, Washington, D.C.

http://www.ushmm.org/

You don't find much on the Web that is truly important. This Web site provides online exhibits drawn from the United States Holocaust Memorial Museum's collections. It also makes available some of the most significant historical and artistic works to have arisen from the Holocaust.

The WebMuseum Network

http://sunsite.unc.edu/wm/

What better way to take advantage of computer graphics and color capabilities than to view some of the greatest paintings and sculptures in the world? Not as historic as it sounds, the WebMuseum Network is a relatively young cooperative venture of a number of organizations (primarily universities, but some galleries and other networks) around the world. One of the more amazing things about WebMuseum is that it was started by one person, a computer consultant by the name of Nicholas Pioch. He was assisted by a grant from the BMW Foundation, and has found partners in Encyclopaedia Britannica and Netscape Communications Corporation. With enthusiastic help from universities worldwide, the network continues to grow.

The URL listed above is the recommended point of first entry, but you're then asked to choose a mirror site as close to home as possible. There are no shortage of mirror sites all over the world. New artworks are added all the time.

For Kids, Parents, Teachers (and the Rest of Us)

While many people are worried about kids' access to the less savory content available on the Net, there's also a lot of fun and informative stuff to be explored.

Teachers, you can't go wrong by starting with one of the Internet directories (mentioned in Chapter 6) on Education. If you're ready to involve your students, you might try the book *Net Lessons: Web-Based Projects For Your Classroom*, published by O'Reilly & Associates.

Yahooligans!™: The Web Guide for Kids

http://www.yahooligans.com/

From the people who brought you Yahoo-know-what, here's a Web directory geared towards younger browsers. Yahooligans! features links to subjects like news, entertainment, school, games, sports, science, and comics—just like Yahoo!, only they're not embarrassed to put the fun stuff up front. You can also access this site from the Yahoo! home page.

Crayola Art Site

http://www.crayola.com/art_education/

Classroom activities, contests, etc., from your favorite crayon makers.

KidsWeb

http://www.npac.syr.edu/textbook/kidsweb/

An online library for kids, with links to art, drama, science, social studies, games, and other online libraries.

Education World

http://www.educationworld.com/

A gateway to the top 10,000 education Web sites; search by keyword or topic, or check out award-winning sites.

Web66: A K-12 World Wide Web Project

http://web66.coled.umn.edu/new/new.html

The name for Web66 comes from Route 66—a cultural icon that suggests inspiration, ingenuity, and going places. The Web66 site is geared toward helping students and teachers use the Web. Many terrific projects are shared here.

Colleges and Universities

Just about every legitimate institution of higher learning should have a fairly established presence on the Internet. Certainly this book can't catalog the thousands of addresses for you. However, many of them will be obvious. You certainly don't need to be a Phi Beta Kappa to figure out where these URLs will take you:

```
http://www.harvard.edu/
http://www.purdue.edu/
http://www.ucla.edu/
```

If you can't figure out the address of a college's Web site, you can check in Yahoo! (choose the link **Universities** under the heading **Education**, in the Yahoo! directory), search for the name of the college using an Internet search engine (as described in Chapter 6); or use the old standby method—call the school and ask.

Animals, Nature, and the Environment

The Web certainly isn't a natural phenomenon, but its multimedia capabilities make it a terrific venue for information about the natural world.

NetVet and the Electronic Zoo

http://netvet.wustl.edu/

NetVet and the Electronic Zoo are complimentary sets of Web resources about animals and veterinary medicine, accessible from the same URL. Both concepts were originated by Dr. Ken Boschert, Doctor of Veterinary Medicine at Washington University in St. Louis, Missouri. NetVet provides a wide array of information about pets and their medical care—while reminding visitors that none of this is a substitute for actually taking your pet to the doctor. The Electronic Zoo is an extension of NetVet, with additional resources about veterinary medicine and animals, including image and sound files.

American Zoo and Aquarium Association (AZA)

http://www.aza.org/

The AZA's Web site provides links to the sites of dozens of zoos and aquaria around the U.S. and Canada, as well as to various conservation programs it also provides information about related career opportunities.

ZooNet

http://www.mindspring.com/~zoonet/

ZooNet is a comprehensive online source of information about zoos in the U.S. and around the world, with lots of animal pictures, animal-related links, and endangered species information. ZooNet is currently sponsored by MindSpring Enterprises, Inc., which is also ZooNet's Internet Service Provider, and Personal Computer Services, which is also contributing its image processing capabilities to assist in the site's extensive photo archive. If the link moves, you should be able to turn up the new one using a search engine (see Chapter 6).

Sea World (and the Animal Information Database)

http://www.seaworld.com/

In addition to some fun online adventures for the whole family, Sea World and Busch Gardens have created an animal information database, which is great for school projects. The database has been recognized for its significant achievement in education by the American Zoo and Aquarium Association (AZA).

WhaleNet

http://whale.wheelock.edu/

Hey, we knew they were *smart*, but their own network? Seriously, WhaleNet provides a veritable sea of information about whales and marine research, including interdisciplinary curricula. An impressive collaborative project developed by Wheelock and Simmons Colleges in Massachusetts, with support from the National Science Foundation and technical assistance from MUSE (the Multi-User Science Education Network), WhaleNet has won a number of education awards. Check out the **WhaleNet Affiliates** for links to dozens of cooperating zoos, aquaria, schools, agencies, societies, and other organizations in the United States and Canada.

Travel

Internet exploration may be a form of travel—but I prefer the kind where you get out of town. Travel is expected to be one of the top industries in the 21st century. It's already big on the Web, where virtual visits are the norm. Many destinations have put information for tourists on the Net. You can also find hotels, airline reservations, advisories, weather, language help, etc. For more information on how to use Net resources to plan a trip, see the book *NetTravel: How Travelers Use the Internet*, published by O'Reilly & Associates.

The Bureau of Consular Affairs (Customs, Passports, and Visas)

http://travel.state.gov/

The Web site of the U.S. State Department's Bureau of Consular Affairs is a good place to check on customs regulations, travel warnings and advisories, visa requirements for various countries, the Web sites and contact information for U.S. Embassies and Consulates, and even regulations governing international adoptions. International travelers can benefit greatly from the online passport services, which allow you to download applications and provide detailed instructions, including nationwide lists of agencies that can help you get a passport. There's also a list of frequently asked questions about passports.

travlang

http://www.travlang.com/

A meaty travel Web site, travlang offers links to transportation (airlines, trains, rental cars, etc.), accommodations, travel guides, newsletters, currency rates, ATM locations, etc., for travelers headed for places all over the world. And if that isn't enough, there are also dictionaries and tutorials for more than 35 languages, from Afrikaans to Zulu.

MapQuest

http://www.mapquest.com/

MapQuest provides regional and local maps for locations around the world. This site is especially helpful if you want to go by car from one spot to another in the U.S., since it also provides driving directions. If you want to sign up for a free MapQuest membership, you can customize maps (e.g., add a labeled icon to mark where an event is going to be held), post maps to a public bulletin board (called the DashBoard), and save them for future use. You'll also receive email notifying you of changes to the service.

(Note that many of the yellow and white page services described in Chapter 7 also provide maps and directions.)

Yahoo! on Travel

http://www.yahoo.com/travel/

Yahoo! Travel lets you check on flight availability, schedules, and travel news. But if you follow the links **Recreation** → **Travel** from the Yahoo! home page, you'll find links to dozens of other travel-related resources, including additional directories of similar info.

Lycos City Guides

http://cityguide.lycos.com/

A branch of the Lycos search engine site (see Chapter 6), Lycos City Guides lets you specify a destination—if you want, you can click on a series of maps to narrow your choice. Then learn all about the the area: history, entertainment and culture, how to get there, accomodations, weather, and assorted information for visitors.

Arts and Entertainment

The multimedia capabilities of the Web are a great fit for sites that specialize in arts and entertainment. The Web can present images of artistic masterpieces stored in museums worldwide. It can also keep pace with the more mundane and fleeting visions produced in Hollywood and other tinsel towns. (In fact, just about every mainstream movie released these days has a Web site created specifically to publicize it.) The Web enables you to read literature online, to read about it, and to buy it. You can read interviews with artists, writers, and celebrities, and sometimes even chat with them. There are also plenty of Usenet newsgroups devoted to arts and entertainment, from the serious to the silly, where you can share your enthusiasms or just be fans together.

BookWire

http://www.bookwire.com/

BookWire is a repository of information about books on the Web. You can find reviews, bestseller lists, author events, and even download some books in their entirety. There's also a searchable index of online book information as well as links to a number of relevant sites, including:

- Publishers Weekly
- The Quarterly Black Review of Books
- The Boston Book Review
- Poetry Society of America
- Mystery Writers of America
- National Book Critics Circle

Amazon.com

http://www.amazon.com/

Reading stuff on the Net has its place, but give me a real book any day. The people at Amazon.com bill it as "Earth's Biggest Bookstore." Given the 2.5 million titles you can buy at this site, it's hard to argue with them. Their prices are also substantially discounted from those of retail chains, even the so-called "superstores." Check out Amazon.com's links to book reviews, author interviews, literary history, etc. Amazon.com also holds writing contests, publishes excerpts from new books by well-known authors, and offers a number of other interesting promotions.

CultureFinder

http://www.culturefinder.com/

An online calendar of performances in theater, classical music, opera, and dance, CultureFinder lets you search events by city, type, arts organization, etc. Currently more than 800 arts organizations in the U.S. and Canada contribute to these listings. Three online "Answer Men" field questions about classical music, musical theater, and opera. You can also learn more about classical music, dance, and theater using the online library, and you can track down classical music broadcasts using RadioFinder.

The Academy of Motion Picture Arts and Sciences

http://www.ampas.org/

Get the inside story on the annual Academy Awards, including lists of all the movies and people eligible for nomination, voting procedures, etc. Learn about the other activities of the Academy, such as student awards and fellowships, publications, and events.

The Internet Movie Database

http://www.imdb.com/

Perhaps the ultimate online movie (and television) reference, the Internet Movie Database contains millions of bits of information about movies and TV shows past and present. Look up a movie by title; search for a performer, writer, or director; check out cast lists, awards; film-related biographies; and link to virtually countless related sites.

The Internet Movie Database is an ongoing project to which you can actually contribute. If you know something that should appear in the database, the site allows you to submit a form with this information.

The database is vast. It's also free. The only downside is that with so much information and so many people attempting to contribute, the database is not as authoritative as it might be. In other words, on occasion the information it provides is incomplete—or simply wrong. Still, the important facts all seem to be straight, and you have to be a complete, grew-up-in-the-dark film nut (who me?) to notice any problems. If you do, the database's forms also allow you to submit corrections.

TV Guide Online

http://www.tvguide.com/

Not only can you provide your Zip Code and get a program listing for your area for the next two weeks (including cable and pay channels), TV Guide Online can send you daily viewing suggestions tailor-made for you. All you have to do is register for this free service, and then supply your own television preferences. Accomplish both tasks using forms provided at the site. You can request that specific programs be included in your personal viewing guide as well as express general preferences. Naturally, you can update this information at any time. And you'll need to stay "tuned in" to the site in order to request specific programs for the coming weeks. Still, it's kinda fun, and if you spend more time in front of a computer than in front of the TV, it's also very useful to figure out what's going to be on a week from Thursday.

The Movie Critic

http://www.moviecritic.com/

The Movie Critic is a fun service that suggests movies you might like, based on how you rate a number of films from its database. For an easy-going movie lover, this service is fast and effective. Keep in mind that if you're a very particular viewer (ahem), you may need to rate a lot of movies to educate the program that's making these recommendations for you. I actually rated about 300 before the program seemed to catch on about what I might like. But it was a whole lot of fun.

Note that the Movie Critic's recommendations extend to classics, foreign films, etc.

What's New on the Net?

You could easily take Mark Twain's (much better) joke about the weather in New England and apply it to the Net:

```
Don't like what you find on the Internet?  Just wait a minute.
```

During the time it took me to type that line, the Internet changed more than I'll ever know.

Given the size, complexity, and changeability of the Net, the concept of keeping track of what's new on it is a little specious. You'll never know everything that's out there. What's more, you'll never care—any more than you'll want to read every book in every library in the world or every news story for every country on every single day of your life. And many offerings on the Internet are a whole lot less authoritative.

But you might care about new offerings in some areas in which you're interested. And it doesn't hurt to know how to spot new stuff when you see it. Thus, here are some guidelines for recognizing some of the new material on the Net:

- Here's a tough one: Most sites label new offerings. Be on the lookout for a little "New!" symbol—or something else that's eye-catching. Some sites even have a link to new resources.

- The link to **What's New** at WebCrawler Select (**http://webcrawler.com/select/**) gives reviews of and links to some of the best new sites of the week.

- Yahoo!'s What's New (**http://www.yahoo.com/new/**) tells about some of the new offerings at Yahoo! and around the Web, including "daily picks."

- LinkMonster What's New Catalog, **http://www.linkmonster.com/ whatsnew.hmtl**, is a searchable database of new stuff.

- The Librarians' Index to the Internet, **http://sunsite.berkeley.edu/ InternetIndex/**, is a cool (and searchable) resource, put together by the Berkeley Public Library, with "New This Week" and "Last Week" sections. But it goes much further—check it out.

For a look back at *what used to be new* ;-), check out the What's New Archive, which was last published in June of 1996:

```
http://www.ncsa.uiuc.edu/SDG/Docs/archive-whats-new.html
```

This archive was a joint venture of NCSA (the National Center for Supercomputing Applications) and the former GNN (the Global Network Navigator, originally a product of O'Reilly & Associates, later bought by America Online). The archive includes summaries of interesting new sites, compiled on a monthly basis going back to 1993.

CHAPTER 6

Internet Directories and Search Engines

While there are some fairly stable sites on the World Wide Web (see Chapter 5, *Landmark Sites and Other Resources*), the changing nature of the Net and of information has necessitated the development of tools that allow people to search for what they want. Each of these so-called *search engines* collects a database of information about documents on the Web. The search engine then allows you to look for particular words in the database, and it returns links to the documents that contain your search terms. A search engine generally ranks the documents that match your search, listing what it thinks are the closest matches first. If you select your search terms effectively, you should be able to find Web pages relevant to your topic of interest.

What kind of information is a search engine supposed to help you find? Well, all of the tools covered in this chapter are intended, basically, to locate general information across the Web. However, the label of "search engine" is not limited to these powerful tools with a wide scope. A single Web site might provide its own search tool to help you find what's there. There are specialized databases of telephone numbers, street addresses, email addresses, etc., and the tools provided for you to search through this information are also search engines. Many of these services are covered in Chapter 7, *Finding People and Places*.

Now, since this is the Internet, and it's overrun with enthusiastic developers, there is an abundance of search engines. If you go to the Yahoo! site (**http://www.yahoo.com/**) and follow the links **Computers and Internet → Internet → World Wide Web → Searching the Web → Search Engines**, you'll see a list of dozens of mainstream and alternative search tools. While Yahoo!, Lycos, AltaVista, Infoseek, and other big search tools will do for the most of us, there also seems to be a market for, shall we say, niche products—like the James Kirk Search Engine (**http://www.webwombat.com.au/trek/**), which searches only sites related to Star Trek.

The current chapter is only concerned with the premier tools that let you search a wide array of documents. Although all of the search engines described in this chapter are good, they are not interchangeable. Different search engines index data differently. One search engine may gather only document titles for its database, while another may also include links, headings, and content keywords; some even index every word in every document. Search engines also vary in the method they use to rank the documents that match your search. Some search engines even let you specify parameters that determine how documents are selected, how many are returned on each screen of results, etc. What this boils down to is that results vary even among the more reliable search engines. However, if you phrase your search well, there should be significant overlap, and you should find what you want (presuming it's out there).

There isn't necessarily a *best* search engine, or even a best one for certain types of searches. Each of the various tools has a different look and feel, and your comfort in using one may be the most important factor in choosing. However, since no two search engines are likely to return identical results, and since tracking down information in this vast sea can be difficult, you'll naturally be using multiple search engines all the time.

While a basic search engine provides a simple box in which you enter a word or words to search for, some tools have a more elaborate user interface. The following section describes two broad classes of search engines. Keep in mind, however, that as developers try to extend the powers and parameters of their searching tools, fewer and fewer tools are fitting neatly into one category or another. There are increasing numbers of search engines that offer a variety of searching methods and that allow you to search not only the Web, but also Usenet news, phone and email listings, etc. The savvy developer wants to provide you with one-stop searching. The search engines mentioned in this chapter will undoubtedly become more powerful, more reliable, and easier to use. They already seem to be becoming more similar to one another. But for now, at least, understanding the two broad classes of search engines should help you select the right tools and use them more effectively.

Directories Versus Search Engines

You can think of search engines as falling into two basic classes. We'll call the first group *directories*, while the second group is composed of *search engines* proper. Both of these types of search engines index a number of Web pages and let you search the indexed information by entering the word(s) to be queried. But while *that's all* that a regular search engine does, a directory additionally provides a catalog of the resources it indexes. This catalog is organized by subject matter, something like a library's subject card catalog. However, it's a lot briefer, and only the top level of the outline is initially displayed (in its entirety).

When you go to the Web site of a directory (e.g., Yahoo!), you'll find a list of subjects, such as News, Sports, Entertainment, Reference, Computers, Health, etc. Each of these subjects acts as a link to additional related resources available on the Web. You can narrow your search by selecting these subject links, which become more and more specific. Thus, if you select a Sports link, you would then view a page of sports-related topics/links from which to select. You might then choose a link to information about Football, Soccer, Baseball, Swimming, whatever. Again, you'd get an even more specific list of links related to your last choice. For example, if you chose Baseball, you might get a page of links to the Major Leagues, Minor Leagues, Spring Training, Scores and Stats, Negro Leagues, Women in Baseball, etc.

But a directory is more than this catalog of resources; remember, it's also a search engine. Thus, at any point in using a directory, you can search its database. As a matter of fact, you don't have to use the catalog feature at all. If you want, you can simply go to the directory's site and search the entire database, just as you would with a regular search engine. Or you can use the catalog-style links and search along the way; most directories let you limit a search to a particular subject area, if you want. If you're confident that what you're looking for would fall under a particular heading, limiting the search in this way certainly speeds things up and can greatly reduce the number of useless matches returned by the search.

Directories tend to have more limited databases than plain old search engines (though some directories are getting very powerful). This can be a plus or a minus, depending on your circumstances. If you want to browse around without a clear purpose, or if you want to research a subject in general, a directory is a great place to start. Also, it's less likely you'll turn up thousands of confusing matches when you use a directory.

However, when you want to find something that a directory search doesn't turn up, or when you want to do comprehensive research, you'll need to use a more conventional search engine, such as AltaVista. Most of them have a very great reach (i.e., they've indexed a huge number of Web documents, etc.). The downside of search engines is that you're very likely to turn up more matches than you want. Unless you're looking for a very distinctive or unusual word or words, it's not uncommon for a search to turn up thousands (or even millions!) of matching documents. In these cases, you *can* get lucky and find that the top-ranked documents are just what you had in mind. More often, you'll need to come up with alternate or additional search terms in order to narrow the results. (The query syntax for each of the major search engines is discussed later in this chapter; see the next chapter for additional tips on narrowing your search.)

In addition, if you have only a vague idea what you might want to find out there, the catalog feature may be useful—or it may lead you down the wrong paths. When you're not quite sure what you're looking for, a search engine can help you narrow your sights.

The bottom line about searching tools is that both directories and search engines can be very helpful, particularly if you coordinate them.

The Top Search Engines and Directories

This chapter does not pretend to cover every available search engine, but hopefully we've hit the high spots. There are a number of reasons to use one search engine over another: ease of use, size of the database(s) you can search, what other information resources are offered with it, and even how it looks. As a matter of fact, the way a search engine looks and feels will probably be as big a deciding factor for most users as any. And why not? It's a tool you may be relying on a lot.

Personally, I tend to use Yahoo! when I want a directory, and Infoseek when I want to do broader searching. Are these tools for everyone? Probably not. I like that Yahoo! is easy to use and easy to look at; it also cuts through a lot of the specious stuff a broader search is likely to turn up. I like Infoseek because its databases are as big as any of the major search engines (Excite, HotBot, and Lycos are of a similar scope), but its query syntax and matching algorithms really let you zoom in on the right results. And I like the way it looks.

Lately I've also gotten into using Excite, partly because it can generalize a query to search for related terms—a pretty cool feature. Excite also offers extensive Web reviews, a terrific NewsTracker service, and a number of customizable online "channels" for news and information in different categories. Excite City.Net provides travel information for a variety of locations worldwide.

HotBot is a pure search engine and it's very powerful. HotBot has a jazzier look than most—not surprising since it's affiliated with *Wired* magazine (**http://www.wired.com**). HotBot provides a user interface that lets you narrow a search somewhat by point-and-click (though you'll need to know the written syntax for some dimensions). It also tends to turn up a very high number of matches.

Lycos offers a number of resources in a straightforward layout. It offers a directory organized by subject, each topic linking to headlines and other related links. You can also access reviews of the "Top 5% Sites" on the Web, online "City Guides" (i.e., travel guides) for a number of locales, and Lycos sites for different countries (e.g., Germany, Sweden) in the native language. Lycos also lets you search for picture and sound files, as well as UPS tracking numbers. In addition, Lycos offers an advanced search engine called Lycos Pro, which provides a more elaborate syntax to help you narrow your search.

AltaVista is probably the purest search engine, without a lot of "site clutter"—and you can use it on a simple or a more advanced level. It also offers extensive help in narrowing your search.

A number of search engines let you search Usenet news; I prefer DejaNews for this purpose because that's all that it does, and it works as a pretty good news client as well, but it isn't as easy to use as it might be.

Basically, every search engine has its selling points. I've used any number of them. Researching some topics, I've used every one of them! Another factor to consider: the resources coupled with these tools, and the tools themselves, are changing all the time. And they're competing hard to provide you with one-stop information services. Even now there are great similarities in terms of the information they offer. In the future, they may be even more similar.

At this point in time, if you're a novice, it's hard to go wrong in starting with Yahoo!. Then experiment around with some of the bigger search engines. (Yahoo! now automatically calls on AltaVista for additional matches as well.)

There are a growing number of sites from which you can access several search engines; the next section, "Places to Find Them All," describes three of the most prominent. If you want to reach a particular search engine directly, use the URLs listed in Table 6–1.

Table 6-1: Popular Search Engines/Directories and Where to Find Them

Search Engine/Directory	URL
AltaVista	http://www.altavista.digital.com/
DejaNews	http://www.dejanews.com/
Excite	http://www.excite.com/
HotBot	http://www.hotbot.com/
Infoseek	http://www.infoseek.com/
Lycos	http://www.lycos.com/
NetGuide Live	http://www.netguide.com/
WebCrawler	http://www.webcrawler.com/
Yahoo!	http://www.yahoo.com/

Places to Find Them All

There are a number of sites from which you can access several of the most popular and powerful search engines and directories. The idea is that you can go to a particular URL and link to a number of different search engines from there. Generally, you can indicate what search engine you want to use and enter your search terms in a box provided on the central page, then your query is conveyed to the desired search engine.

Both Netscape and Microsoft offer Web sites that serve as repositories of search tools. Among the underdogs in this endeavor is MasterSite, an up-and-coming search smorgasbord.

Netscape's search tool page is currently at the URL:

```
http://home.netscape.com/home/internet-search.html
```

Since URLs come and go, remember that you can get to the right page by clicking on the Net Search button in the Netscape Navigator browser window. Figure 6–1 shows Netscape's search site. As you can see, Netscape's Net Search page provides links to prominent search engines/directories such as Lycos, WebCrawler, Excite, Yahoo!, and Infoseek (all of which are described in more detail later in this chapter). The Net Search page also offers access to a number of other searching services, including "white pages" and "yellow pages," for getting phone numbers, addresses, email addresses, etc., for people and organizations, respectively. (These kinds of tools are described in more detail in Chapter 7.)

Microsoft provides a proprietary searching tool called the Search Wizard, which lets you search Microsoft's considerable online resources. The Search Wizard page also links you to tools like AltaVista, Excite, Infoseek, Lycos, and Yahoo!. The current URL of the Search Wizard is **http://www.microsoft.com/search/default.asp**. However, you can also get there if you're using Microsoft Internet Explorer as your browser; simply click on the button labeled **Search the Net**.

MasterSite provides yet another central listing of search tools, at the URL **http://www.mastersite.com/**. MasterSite is really aiming for one-stop searching, and it's a site worth watching. Currently, it offers a number of the premier search

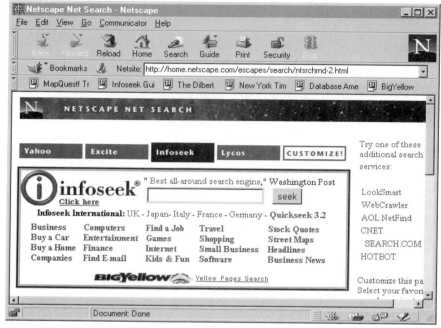

Figure 6–1: Netscape offers a gateway to a number of popular search tools

engines, as well as a few lesser ones (like SurfPoint, which is more of a Web surfer's companion). Like many of the search tools, MasterSite has added facilities to let you search white and yellow pages, email addresses, etc. Their home page also offers some extremely useful add-ons: you can directly query a dictionary, a thesaurus, and a book of quotations; or you can link to sites to look up Zip Codes, Congressional email addresses, international phone listings, additional dictionaries, telnet sites, software, and a number of other resources.

AltaVista

http://www.altavista.digital.com/

Digital Equipment Corporation's AltaVista is the quintessential search engine, providing a text box in which you can enter queries—without the other information offerings that are becoming typical of other search engines. This singularity of purpose can be either a minus or a plus, depending on your needs at the time. There are definitely moments when it's nice to get down to the business of searching, and AltaVista makes this pretty simple.

You can opt to search either the Web or Usenet news. Although AltaVista's Web database is purported to be a bit smaller (at least as of this printing) than those of Excite, Infoseek, HotBot, and Lycos, every one of my AltaVista searches has turned up a number of matches at least in the ballpark with the other tools.

If you search Usenet, you get links to the matched news articles as well as to the people who posted them. If you select a link to the sender, your browser should provide a window in which to compose an email message. Likewise, links to newsgroups should open up your browser's news program, so you can post articles.

The way AltaVista organizes its results makes them easier to peruse than the findings of many other search engines. At the bottom of each results page is a list of page numbers corresponding to the subsequent screensful of matches. You can skip to any page simply by clicking on its number. With most search engines, you're limited to scanning results in the order they are returned. But this device of AltaVista's makes it possible to jump from the first page of results to the twentieth if you want.

In addition to being straightforward and simple to use, AltaVista offers a product called LiveTopics that helps you narrow your searches as well as explore related topics. Since turning up more documents than you can handle seems inherent in searching, LiveTopics can be very useful.

You access LiveTopics on the page returned to you with your search results. The results appear near the top of the page; following the results you should see something like:

```
Overwhelmed by 2000000 documents? Let LiveTopics guide you!
```

If you can think of a better query on your own, you can search again. Or choose the appropriate interface to LiveTopics (Java-enabled, JavaScript-enabled, or text-only), and follow some simple steps to narrow your query.

Although LiveTopics can help bail you out after a messy query, your use of AltaVista will be much more efficient if you understand its query syntax upfront. The following sections outline both the searching parameters and syntax options.

A final note: AltaVista's search engine is used to power a number of other tools, including Yahoo! (described later in this chapter) and InfoSpace (described in Chapter 7).

AltaVista search parameters

If you use the online help for most search engines, you'll find that most of them classify some queries as simple and some as advanced. However, AltaVista is one of the few that makes you declare whether you're issuing a simple or an advanced query—and actually recognizes different syntax options for each type of query. You must choose the link **Advanced Query** in order to use the fancier syntax.

The following three sections explain the syntax rules that apply to each of these queries:

1. Both simple and advanced queries

2. Simple queries only

3. Advanced queries only

Regardless of the type of search, you can specify a couple of parameters. The text line above the box in which you enter your query terms includes two drop-down menus that let you specify:

- The database to be searched: the Web or Usenet. The Web is the default.

- The form (i.e, length, amount of detail) of the results: Standard, Compact, or Detailed. Standard is the default; it provides a summary of a few lines about each match.

If you're not familiar with drop-down menus, look for a box that contains a words or words followed by a small button. The words that appear are the current menu selections. You reveal the other menu items by clicking on the box; then select any item by clicking on that.

AltaVista syntax for both types of queries

Whether you're using the simple or advanced query box, AltaVista looks for each of the words you type without assuming a relationship between them. It also drops out common words like "a," "an," and "the." If you're looking for something esoteric, all of this may be fine, but in many cases you'll want to phrase a search to make it more exact. The following guidelines can help you phrase either a simple or advanced query:

- Surround your query in quotes if you want it to be treated as a single phrase, rather than a series of individual search terms. Punctuation marks between the words creates the same effect. Thus, the following examples are equivalent:

  ```
  "writing a cover letter"
  ```

  ```
  writing;a;cover;letter
  ```

  Note that creating a phrase is the only way to search for something that would otherwise be interpreted as a common word and thus dropped out of the search. For instance, you need to quote "vitamin A" or the "A" will get dropped:

  ```
  "vitamin A"
  ```

- Capitalize words only if you want a case-sensitive match. If a name consists of multiple words, also quote it (or use punctuation between the words). For instance:

  ```
  "To Kill a Mockingbird"
  ```

  A lowercase word matches any instances of the word containing one or more uppercase letters. Thus,

  ```
  mockingbird
  ```

  will turn up matches for the bird as well as the book. (You probably wouldn't want to phrase so loose a query.)

- Use an asterisk (*) as a wildcard to represent omitted letters in a word. This enables you to match variations of a word, or even match something you're not sure how to spell. The following query,

  ```
  bik*
  ```

  will match biking, bikes, etc.

- Use a special field syntax to limit searches to certain fields in Web documents (titles, URLs, hypertext links, hosts, anchors, etc.). The fields you can specify are: **anchor**, **applet**, **domain**, **host**, **image**, **link**, **object**, **text**, **title**, and **url**. Here's the basic syntax:

  field_name: *search_terms*

  - **anchor** matches hypertext links that include the specified text:

    ```
    anchor:"programming examples"
    ```

  - **applet** matches the name of a particular Java applet class (within an **<applet>** HTML tag), in this case *AnalogClock*:

    ```
    applet:AnalogClock
    ```

  - **domain** matches documents from the specified *top-level domain* (e.g., .**com**, .**edu**, etc.). Note that you don't have to include the "dot" (.) before the domain name:

    ```
    domain:edu
    ```

    (See Chapter 4, *Internet Addressing*, for more information about domain names.)

  - **host** searches the hostname portion of URLs. To find pages with URLs that include the hostname of O'Reilly & Associates, try:

    ```
    host:oreilly.com
    ```

    This will match documents at *www.oreilly.com, website.oreilly.com, software.oreilly.com*, etc.

  - **image** matches the specified text within HTML **<image>** tags:

    ```
    image:eiffel.gif
    ```

  - **link** matches documents that contain at least one link to a document with the specified text in its URL:

    ```
    link:redsox.com
    ```

  - **object** matches the name of a particular ActiveX object (within an **<object>** HTML tag), in this case a FutureSplash Control called *Future-Splash1*:

    ```
    object:FutureSplash1
    ```

- **text** matches documents that have the specified word(s) within the text proper. The following query should match documents containing references to Boston Red Sox shortstop Nomar Garciaparra.

  ```
  text:Garciaparra
  ```

  (Because this is an unusual last name, it is enough to come up with the right matches. However, this is very rare. More commonly, you'll need to supply a quoted phrase.)

- **title** matches documents with the specified word(s) in the title portion:

  ```
  title:"Baseball America"
  ```

- **url** matches any document with the specified word(s) in its URL:

  ```
  url:espnet.sportszone
  ```

- If you elect to search the Usenet news database (rather than the Web), you can limit searching to certain elements of news postings/articles. The basic syntax is the same as for the Web (given in the previous example). However, the news-specific special fields are: **from**, **keywords**, **newsgroups**, **subject**, and **summary**.

  - **from** matches text in the **From:** fields of article headers:

    ```
    from:val@oreilly.com
    ```

  - **keywords** matches articles in which the specified word appears in the associated keywords list (where applicable):

    ```
    keywords:cats
    ```

  - **newsgroups** matches articles posted or cross-posted to any newsgroup whose name includes the specified word(s). (Basically, this field name matches text in the **Newsgroups:** field in the article header.)

    ```
    newsgroups:sailing
    ```

  - **subject** matches text in the **Subject:** line of article headers:

    ```
    subject:boa.constrictor
    ```

  - **summary** matches articles in which the specified word(s) appear in the **Summary:** field of article headers (where applicable):

    ```
    summary:"Windows 95"
    ```

AltaVista syntax for simple queries only

In addition to the general syntax rules given in the preceding section, the following guidelines can be used for simple queries (the default):

- To specify that a word or phrase must appear in matched documents, put a plus sign (+) immediately before it:

  ```
  +"Boston Red Sox" +tickets
  ```

- To specify that a word or phrase *must not* appear in matched documents, put a minus sign (-) immediately before it:

```
+champagne -domestic
```

AltaVista syntax for advanced queries only

If you select the **Advanced** search link:

- You can use the "AltaVista Syntax for Both Types of Queries" (two sections back).

- You *can't* use the plus and minus sign notation that works for simple queries only.

- You *can* specify that certain elements must be included or excluded from the search by using the following shorthand terms: AND, OR, NEAR, and NOT. Note that the lowercase versions of these terms (i.e, **and**, **or**, **near**, and **not**) work just as well. Here's how to use each of the terms:

  - AND specifies that the elements listed before and after must both appear in matched documents:

    ```
    hotel AND "New York"
    ```

  - OR specifies that at least one of the terms must appear in matched documents:

    ```
    Beijing OR Peking
    ```

  - NEAR specifies that the two terms are within ten words of each other in matched documents. The following query also matches Franklin Delano Roosevelt:

    ```
    Franklin NEAR Roosevelt
    ```

  - NOT can be used on its own. The following query looks for documents that include "blowfish," but don't have "Hootie":

    ```
    NOT Hootie AND blowfish
    ```

  - AND is very frequently used with NOT, to specify that the term following must not appear in matched documents. Here is a Red Sox fan's query:

    ```
    "New York" AND NOT Yankees
    ```

- In addition, you can group elements using parentheses, as is done in mathematical equations. The following examples illustrate this type of syntax. This query matches documents containing both "vitamin C" and one of the pair "vitamin A" and "beta-carotene":

  ```
  ("vitamin A" OR "beta-carotene") AND "vitamin C"
  ```

  The query

  ```
  (NOT Hootie) AND blowfish
  ```

is equivalent to the previous "blowfish" example (i.e, you match documents with "blowfish" but not "Hootie").

To exclude *both* "Hootie" and "blowfish" from matched documents:

```
NOT (Hootie AND blowfish)
```

Remember that lowercase operands work too, so this is the same query:

```
not (Hootie and blowfish)
```

The following two queries are also equivalent:

```
Franklin near (Roosevelt or Mint)
```

```
(Franklin near Roosevelt) or (Franklin near Mint)
```

DejaNews: A Gateway to Usenet

http://www.dejanews.com/

DejaNews is a tool designed to let you search Usenet news, both past and present. You can also use it as a makeshift news client—to read and post articles. (For a more thorough discussion of DejaNews and the techniques you can use for searching, see Chapter 7.)

Excite: All the Fun, All the Time

http://www.excite.com/

In addition to one of the larger Web databases around, Excite provides a ton of news as well as reviews of Web sites. It's also heavy with other information resources, with a slightly higher emphasis on "fun stuff" than many of the other comparable sites. Among the information resources Excite provides are the following:

- The customizable "Channels by Excite." These pages are similar to the departments of an online magazine, with news and information on topics ranging from Arts & Entertainment to Health & Science, News, Politics, Health & Science, and Sports, etc. (If you've been an Excite user before, the Channels are the next generation of Excite Live!.)

The News channel links to stories gathered from hundreds of newspapers and magazines. Use Excite **NewsTracker** to search these sources.

"My Channel" (where your name can replace the *My*), which can be configured to provide the news, stock quotes, sports scores, television listings, weather, horoscopes, and favorite sites. It also provides an online calendar program you can use to remind you about upcoming events. From My Channel, check out the "fun" link where you can read comics, columnists (like Dave Barry), and amusing news stories, as well as access puzzles, games, soap opera updates, etc. (If these links aren't your idea of fun, remember that all of the Excite channels can be customized.)

- Web Guide—a directory of links organized by subject (e.g., Arts, Computing, Science, Education, etc.); this centers around Excite's Web reviews.

- Links to reference facilities like **People Finder**, **Yellow Pages**, **Email Lookup**, **Shareware**, **Maps**.

- Excite services for France, Germany, Sweden, and the United Kingdom.

- City.Net, Excite's database of information about more than 4000 cities worldwide.

- Download Excite Direct to have an Excite search box right on your browser window.

Excite search parameters

The Excite search engine works on two levels: typical keyword matching, and a more abstract level on which it interprets the sense of the keyword(s) and tries to find matches for the "concept" you intend. Thus, a search for the phrase

```
"finding a job"
```

also turns up links relating to employment, job hunting, etc. Since most topics are described in a variety of ways depending on the context, Excite's concept-based searching can come in very handy.

Once you have search results, Excite offers a couple of features that help you scan them more effectively. First, you can click on the link **View by Web Site**, to group all the links from the same site. Following each result, there is also a link called **More Like This**, which you can use to access similar results.

By default, Excite lets you search a database of World Wide Web documents. However, there are four alternative databases you can opt to search instead. Click on the link called Options to select one of these databases:

- The World Wide Web

- Current news stories

- The Excite Web Guide, which includes more than 80,000 recommended sites

- Usenet newsgroups

- City.Net

Excite query syntax

You can use the Excite search engine on a very basic level—simply by entering one or more keywords to match, or take advantage of Excite's more advanced searching capabilities, which require you to know a special syntax, to form more specialized queries.

On the basic level, Excite couldn't really be easier to use because basically *there is no syntax*. The "finding a job" example in the preceding section shows just how simple this level of searching can be.

However, like most search engines, Excite does provide some special syntax operators that help you home in on exactly the right information. You can use the following guidelines to phrase a search:

- To search for a phrase, enclose it in quotes:

    ```
    "Itchy and Scratchy Show"
    ```

- To specify that a word or phrase must appear in matched documents, put a plus sign (immediately) before it:

    ```
    +"Les Miserables" +"New York"
    ```

- To specify that a word or phrase *must not* appear in matched documents, put a minus sign (immediately) before it:

    ```
    +"talk show" -"Jerry Springer" -Geraldo
    ```

- To specify that certain elements must be included or excluded from the search, you can also use the following operators: AND, OR, and AND NOT. (Note that these terms *must be all in uppercase letters.*) You can also use parentheses to group search words and phrases. Here's are some examples:

    - AND specifies that the elements before and after must both appear in matched documents:

        ```
        Kermit AND "Miss Piggy"
        ```

        The following query will match documents that mention Kermit and either of his friends:

        ```
        Kermit AND ("Miss Piggy" OR "Big Bird")
        ```

    - OR specifies that at least one of the terms must appear in matched documents:

        ```
        ravioli OR dumpling
        ```

    - AND NOT indicates that the term following must not appear in matched documents:

        ```
        "Ronald Reagan" AND NOT Bonzo
        ```

HotBot: Souped-Up Searching

http://www.hotbot.com/

Wired, the funky, trendy magazine about the Internet, has its own equally funky search engine called HotBot. (Read the online version of the magazine by clicking the link **WIRED SOURCE.**) HotBot is more of a pure search engine than many of the other tools described in this chapter, most of which concentrate a number of other information resources at their sites. However, HotBot has one of the largest Web databases, it provides a lot of help in phrasing very specific searches, and it seems to turn up more matches than any other tool.

You can either enter a simple search that can be refined using four menus, or you can enter a more advanced search using a complex search syntax, a special user interface (called *panels*), or both of these techniques (for maximum flexibility). The next two sections describe the simple and advanced search parameters—explaining how you can use HotBot's interface (menus and panels) to refine your search. (If you're as sick as I am of getting search results in languages you don't understand, keep an eye out for ways to limit searching to a particular geographic area.) Then *HotBot Query Syntax* describes the language you can use (either alone or with the user interface) to phrase complex searches.

HotBot search parameters: simple (menus)

The top of the HotBot home page offers a simple interface for entering queries. The box in which you enter your search terms appears in the upper part of the page, to the lower-right of the SEARCH icon. Surrounding the search box are four labeled boxes; each of these corresponds to a menu that lets you set parameters for both the query and the results returned.

The current setting for each menu is displayed in the text box. You display the other menu choices by clicking the pointer on the Down Arrow button to the right of the text. The first menu lets you specify the database to search. The default, which appears in the text box, is "the Web." However, clicking the button to the right of "the Web" reveals a second database choice: Usenet News.

The second menu (to the right of the database menu) lets you specify the way your search terms should be matched with results:

- *All the words.* This default setting specifies that all of the terms you search for must appear in a document for it to be considered a match. Since an inclusive search is the default, you don't have to type any extra operators (like plus signs or AND) in order to match all of your terms.

- *Any of the words.* A more casual match.

- *The exact phrase.* (Surrounding your query in double quotes works just as well.)

- *The person.* Selecting this option tells HotBot to treat the words you type as the name of a person, and to match variations on that name. (Thus, Franklin Roosevelt would also match Franklin Delano Roosevelt.)

- *Links to this URL.* This is an unusual option that provides some interesting info. If you select this option and then search for a URL (such as http://www.oreilly.com), you can find out how many people are currently visiting that site. Pretty cool.

- *The Boolean expression.* Selecting this option enables the use of Boolean expressions (e.g., AND, OR, and NOT) for advanced searching. (Note that the options "all the words" and "any of the words" can serve in place of phrases containing ANDs and ORs.)

The third menu (below the search box) specifies how many search results to return per page; the default is 10. The menu reveals additional choices of 25, 50, 75, and 100.

Below this menu is the fourth menu, which lets you specify how detailed results should be. The default is "full descriptions," but you can also opt for "brief descriptions," or "URLs only."

HotBot search parameters: advanced (panels)

The HotBot home page has a series of *panels*, each of which offers a number of choices that let you narrow your search. However, the first time you go to the Hot-Bot site, you might well ask yourself, *what panels?* By default, only the heading of each panel appears on the page. You need to click on the heading in order to reveal the corresponding panel. These are the headings, which appear about halfway down the page on the left side:

- Modify

- Date

- Location

- Media Type

You can open all of the panels with one click on the link **Open All**, above the **Modify** heading.

The Modify panel lets you specify two search parameters. The first one states that the search terms "must," "should," or "must not" appear to have a match. The second one matches "the words," "the exact phrase," "the person," or "links to this URL." (The menus that accompany the simple search part of the page provide similar options. See the preceding section for explanations of what they do.)

The Date panel lets you limit matches to documents from a certain time period. The default is to match any date (Whenever). But you can limit matching to the last *x* number of days, months, or years. Or specify that matches must come "After" or "Before" a particular date.

The Location panel offers three options: AnyPlace, CyberPlace, and GeoPlace. A check in front of AnyPlace (the default) specifies the entire database be searched. You can check CyberPlace and then enter a domain name to limit the search to that domain (e.g., oreilly.com). GeoPlace lets you limit the search to domains from a particular geographic area (e.g., North America, Africa, Central America).

The Media Type panel offers another unusual way to narrow your search—to pages that include specific types of files. The choices are: Image, Audio, Video, Shockwave, Acrobat, VRML, JavaScript, VBScript, Java, ActiveX, and Extensions. (Use the final one to specify any file extensions you want.)

If you take the trouble to fill in any of these panels, and you'd like to save the settings for future searches, click on the link **Save My Settings**, near the bottom of the page. If you change these settings at any point during your session, you can also recover them by clicking on **Load My Settngs**.

HotBot query syntax

You can use the following syntax to phrase searches:

- Quote phrases you want to match exactly (or select "the exact phrase" from the second menu or the Modify panel).

- Use a plus sign (+) to specify that a term must appear; and a minus sign (-) to specify that a term *must not* appear. The following query should turn up references to the Rodgers and Hammerstein musical *Cinderella*:

    ```
    +Cinderella +musical -Disney -ballet
    ```

- If you select "the Boolean expression" from the second menu on the HotBot page, you can refine your search using AND, OR, and NOT (the symbols &, |, and ! do the same thing) and parentheses to group terms as in a math equation. For example:

    ```
    (amusement OR theme) AND park
    ```

- Preface search terms with special "meta words" to limit searches in a variety of ways. (Note that most of these restrictions can be achieved via the interface panels described in the preceding section.) Here's the basic syntax:

    meta_word: *search_terms*

The various meta words are described below:

- Use **domain** to limit searching to a particular domain (up to three levels deep):

    ```
    domain:oreilly.com
    ```

- Use **depth** to limit depth of returned documents:

    ```
    depth:4
    ```

- Use **linkdomain** to limit searching to documents containing links to the specified domain. The following phrase finds pages that link to Yahoo!:

    ```
    linkdomain:yahoo.com
    ```

- Use **linkext** to limit searching to documents that contain files with the specified extension. The following phrase finds pages that contain JPEG files:

    ```
    linkext:jpg
    ```

- Use **scriptlanguage** to search for pages that contain the specified programming language (acceptable values are JavaScript and VBScript):

    ```
    scriptlanguage:VBScript
    ```

- Use **newsgroup** with a complete newsgroup name to limit searching to that group:

    ```
    newsgroup:rec.pets.cats
    ```

- feature:*media_type* lets you limit searching to pages that include specific types of files. (Note that most of these types can also be specified using the Media Type panel described in the preceding section.) The valid *media_types* are: **embed** (plug-ins), **script** (embedded scripts), **applet**, **activex**, **audio** (many audio formats), **shockwave**, **acrobat**, **frame** (HTML frames), **table** (HTML tables), **form** (HTML forms), **vrml** (VRML files), and **image** (many graphic file types).

You can restrict results to documents last modified within certain dates. However, the syntax to do this is currently very limited. For now you're probably better off sticking with the Date panel described in the preceding section. If you're determined to try the syntax, see HotBot online help for instructions and updates.

Infoseek: Smarter Than the Average Search Engine

http://www.infoseek.com/

Infoseek is a terrific hybrid service that not only combines a powerful search engine with a directory but also throws in a ton of other information resources. From the Infoseek home page you can access the following:

- The "Web's largest directory."

- **Smart Info**, which links to white pages, yellow pages, email addresses, company profiles, stock quotes, investment information, a dictionary, thesaurus, maps and directions, Zip Codes, etc. (A service called **BigYellow** provides the phone and email listings; you can get to this via **Smart Info** or directly through the **Big Yellow** link.)

- **Premier News**, which links to stories gathered from sources like the *New York Times*, CNN, and the *Washington Post*.

- **Personalized News**, which links to customized television and movie listings, local weather, personal stock reports, etc. Infoseek has arrangements with a number of other info services to bring you some of these offerings. For example, MovieLink (**http://www.movielink.com**) and GIST Communications (**http://www.gist.com/**) provide the movie and TV listings, respectively. While for most of these resources you only have to supply your city, state, and Zip Code the first time you connect, note that you have to register for the free GIST service in order to get the complete (and customized) television listings for your area.

- UPS Service.

- Updates on Internet happenings (**NetClock Events**).

- Additional Infoseek sites intended specifically for users in France, Italy, Japan, and the United Kingdom (each in the country's native language, of course). And more to come.

- Infoseek's Quickseek software (which adds an Infoseek search box to your browser).

Infoseek isn't the only resource-heavy site, but a number of other features make it noteworthy.

First, the Infoseek query language is simpler than most. Perhaps even more importantly, the way that search terms are parsed (or interpreted) tends to result in matches with a high degree of accuracy. If you're more ambitious, Infoseek also offers an advanced query syntax that lets you search documents with pinpoint accuracy (e.g., match words in the URL, in links, etc.). Search parameters and syntax are explained in subsequent sections.

Second, Infoseek actually offers *two* search engines, each of which produces a different level of results. The default search engine is called Ultrasmart—it's what you get automatically when you connect to the Infoseek site. At the top level, Ultrasmart provides both a directory and a search box (in which you can enter queries). Then, when you request a search, you not only get a list of the links that match, but also mini-directory of "Related Topics" as well as "Related News" items. For instance, when I searched for "Yastrzemski" (as in Carl, former Boston Red Sox left fielder), I got not only hundreds of links to related pages that mention the Hall-of-Famer, but also a small directory with headings/links such as "Baseball," "Baseball in the U.S.," "Boston Red Sox," etc. (In this case, there were no related news items.) Ultrasmart's diversified search results are great if you want to do a combination of searching and browsing.

Another great feature of Ultrasmart: at the bottom of each results page is a box you can use to *search through the results only*, to narrow them down. While more search tools are offering ways to help you narrow your search, this search-within-the-search is among the best.

If you know exactly what you're looking for and want to get it fast, you can instead opt for a more concise search tool called Ultraseek. It's like Ultrasmart without the niceties—there are no directory features at any level, just results. Click on the Ultraseek button, below the Ultrasmart catalog on the home page, in order to hide the catalog and do streamlined searching.

Infoseek search parameters

For both Ultrasmart and Ultraseek, the default database to be searched is a database of World Wide Web documents. However, there are a number of alternative databases you can select instead. Below the box in which you enter your query is a drop-down menu with the default choice "the Web," followed by a small button. Clicking anywhere on the box displays the entire menu of databases choices:

- The Web
- Usenet Newsgroups
- News Wires
- Premier News
- Industry & Local News

- Email Addresses

- Company Profiles

- Web FAQs (i.e., Usenet's lists of Frequently Asked Questions)

Infoseek query syntax

After you select a database to search, you have to come up with search terms. Infoseek's query language allows for simple phrasing and very accurate matching. Currently, Infoseek is the only major search tool that will do the following:

- Recognize capitalized sequences of words automatically as proper names or titles (i.e., you don't have to surround the words with quotes).

- Search for variants of a particular term (i.e., if you search for "theater", you'll also match "theatre"; a search for "goose" will also turn up "geese").

In addition, while several search engines let you search for a phrase, Infoseek is one of the few that retains common words within a phrase. For instance, HotBot will strip the meaty phrase "may the force be with you" down to the bone—the single word "force"—before seeking any matches.

Use the following guidelines to phrase a search:

- Capitalize the names of people, places, organizations, etc. No quotes are necessary; Infoseek recognizes sequential capitalized words as a single name. Note, however, that when you capitalize a word, you force a case-sensitive match. Thus, you should never capitalize anything that normally wouldn't be. This is a useful query:

    ```
    Denver Broncos
    ```

    But this will match the words only if they appear in all caps:

    ```
    DENVER BRONCOS
    ```

    And this version doesn't tell Infoseek that the words are a name:

    ```
    denver broncos
    ```

    Instead it will match "denver" and "broncos" separately. You can turn up documents about the city of Denver, but also John Denver; the Broncos football team, but also Bronco Billy, bucking broncos, you name it.

- To search for multiple names, separate them with commas. For example:

    ```
    John Quincy Adams, Aaron Burr, Massachusetts
    ```

- When words must appear next to each other in matched documents, surround them with quotation marks or put hyphens between them:

    ```
    "writing a cover letter"
    writing-a-cover-letter
    ```

- To specify that a word or phrase must appear in matched documents, put a plus sign (immediately) before it:

  ```
  +Denver Broncos +tickets
  ```

- To specify that a word or phrase *must not* appear in matched documents, put a minus sign (immediately) before it:

  ```
  +blowfish -Hootie
  ```

- You can often turn up what you want by asking a question in plain language. The following query will get the information you want:

  ```
  What is the capital of Montana?
  ```

  The downside is that it also turns up millions of matches. The following query is much more precise:

  ```
  +Montana +capital
  ```

- To specify a second search—through the results of the first search—separate the terms for each search using the vertical bar symbol (|). For example, the following query first searches for the phrase "writing a cover letter"—then searches those results for the word "job":

  ```
  "writing a cover letter" | job
  ```

  (Phrasing a query like this is the fastest way to do "nested" searches. But remember that Ultrasmart also provides a search window at the bottom of each results page to let you search through the current results.)

- Use a special field syntax to search for all the pages at a particular Web site; or within certain fields in Web documents (titles, URLs, and hypertext links). The recognized field names are: **site**, **link**, **url**, and **title**. Here's the basic syntax:

    field_name: *search_terms*

  - Use **site** to search the site part of URLs. To find pages on the Web site of O'Reilly & Associates:

    ```
    site:oreilly.com
    ```

    This will match documents at **www.oreilly.com**, **website.oreilly.com**, **software.oreilly.com**, etc.

  - Use **link** to match the text of hypertext links within documents. The following query matches documents with at least one link (to a URL) containing **oreilly.com**:

    ```
    link:oreilly.com
    ```

  - Use **title** to match the title portion of documents. The following query matches documents with *Sports Illustrated* in the title:

    ```
    title:Sports Illustrated
    ```

- Use **url** to match text anywhere in a document's URL. The following query matches documents at the O'Reilly Web site that have something to do with their WebSite product:

```
+site:oreilly.com +url:website
```

Lycos: Stronger Every Day

http://www.lycos.com/

Lycos was Carnegie-Mellon University's entry in the search engine race, now gone independent. It also happens to be used by a number of other search engines—it's not uncommon to run across the words "powered by Lycos" at another site.

Once one of the most basic search tools, Lycos has recently gotten fancy, now providing an advanced search facility called Lycos Pro. Like many other search tools, Lycos Pro offers a number of syntactical operators to help you phrase complex searches. But Lycos Pro also offers a unique advantage: You can specify how results are ranked (and thus the order in which they are displayed). You need a Java-enabled browser to take advantage of this capability; more about this later.

Like most of the other available tools, the Lycos Web site provides not only a powerful search engine, but also a number of other information resources, including:

- Reviews of the **Top 5% Sites**

- A small Web directory, organized by topic

- A searchable database of sounds and pictures

- Yellow pages

- **PeopleFind**

- **StockFind**

- **Lycos City Guides**, travel guides for a variety of cities and countries (http://cityguide.lycos.com/)

- Lycos FindMachine software (which lets you use Lycos to search directly from your desktop, without running your browser)

- UPS Service

- News

- **Road Maps**

- Corporate profiles and information (**Companies Online**)

- Classified ads

Lycos parameters for basic search

Like most other search engines, Lycos searches the Web by default. But you can actually choose from a number of databases: The Web, Sounds, Pictures, Top 5% of sites (as judged by Lycos), Personal Home Pages (a fairly limited database), and

UPS Tracking Numbers. If you want to choose a custom search using Lycos Pro, there are additional parameters.

Lycos Pro search parameters

Choose **Lycos Pro** from the Lycos home page to access menus to set the following search options:

- *The database to search:* The Web; Sounds; Pictures; Top 5% of sites (as judged by Lycos); Personal Home Pages (a fairly limited database); UPS Tracking Numbers

- *How many terms to match:* match any term (the default); match all terms; match *x* terms (where *x* is an integer from 2-7)

- *How close the match should be:* loose (the default), fair, good, close, or strong

- *How many results to display per page:* 10 (the default), 20, 30, or 40

- *In what form to display results:* standard (the default), summary (shorter), or detailed

Lycos Pro results ranking

If your browser is Java-enabled, you can use "Lycos Pro with Java Power Panel." This version of Lycos Pro offers all of the parameters described in the preceding section. In addition, it has the Power Panel, a Java applet that contains some horizontal *tuners*, controls you can move from side to side using your pointer. These tuners let you specify which criteria Lycos Pro should use in sorting your results. There is a tuner for each of the following criteria:

- Match every word

- Frequency of words

- Appear in title

- Appear early in text

- Appear close together

- Appear in exact order

You can give a value for each of the criteria, from 0 to 100 (which correspond to "unimportant" and "very important," respectively). Moving the tuner all the way to the right gives it a value of 100; the left end is 0.

By default, "Match every word" has an importance of 100; all of the others have an importance of 50. That means that those documents that match every word will be ranked higher—and thus appear closer to the top of the results.

If it were very important to you that the words matched "appear close together," you could move that tuner over to the right. Then documents matching that criteria would be ranked highly in the results. Maybe you want words to appear in the title *and* close together—then you'd move both of those tuners towards 100. You get the idea.

Note that the control on each of the tuners looks like a gold handle. You can either drag it using the pointer or click elsewhere on the horizontal bar to make the handle move to that location.

Lycos basic query syntax

If you want to stick with the basic Lycos search facility, the queries are easy, involving these few guidelines:

- Be as specific as possible; more words are often better.

- To match an exact phrase, including a proper name, enclose it in quotation marks:

    ```
    "John Lennon"
    ```

- Use a plus sign 0+) to specify that a term must appear and a minus sign (-) to specify that a term *must not* appear. The following query should find references to the TV series M*A*S*H, while avoiding mashed potatoes and "The Monster Mash":

    ```
    +mash +Alda -potato -monster
    ```

    (No, that is not a terribly serious example.)

Lycos Pro advanced query syntax

If you're using Lycos Pro (with or without the Power Panel), you have many more syntactical operators at your disposal:

- Surround your query in quotes if you want it to be treated as a single phrase:

    ```
    "freedom of speech"
    ```

- Use a plus sign to specify that a term must appear, and a minus sign to specify that a term *must not* appear.

- Specify that certain elements must be included or excluded from the search, or fall within certain parameters by using the following shorthand terms: AND, OR, NOT, NEAR, NEARx, ONEAR, ONEAR/x, FAR, FAR/x, OFAR, OFAR/x, ADJ, ADJ/x, OADJ, OADJ/x, and BEFORE. Note that some of these terms have equivalent punctuation symbols. Here's how to use each of the terms:

    - AND specifies that the elements listed before and after must both appear in matched documents:

        ```
        walking AND calories
        ```

    - OR specifies that at least one of the terms must appear in matched documents:

```
"Bill Clinton" OR "Al Gore"
```

- The term following NOT cannot appear in matched documents:

```
Jackson NOT Michael
```

(Note that "Jackson AND NOT Michael" is equivalent.)

- NEAR finds documents in which the two terms appear within 25 words of each other:

```
Butte NEAR Montana
```

NEAR/x specifies that the two terms are within x words of each other. The following query specifies that Abbott and Costello no more than ten words apart:

```
Abbott NEAR/10 Costello
```

An O in front of either NEAR or NEAR/x specifies that the terms must appear in matched documents in the order they appear in the query. The following query looks for documents containing "Ted" and "Williams," in that order and no more than five words apart:

```
Ted ONEAR/5 Williams
```

- FAR finds documents in which the two terms are at least 25 words apart:

```
Hatfields FAR McCoys
```

FAR/x lets you specify a different number of words apart:

```
Hillary FAR/50 Bill
```

An O in front of either FAR or FAR/x specifies that the terms must appear in matched documents in the same order they appear in the query. The following query matches documents in which "Washington" and "Adams" appear in that order, at least 25 words apart:

```
Washington OFAR Adams
```

- ADJ specifies that the terms must appear next to each other (adjacent) in matched documents:

```
Mickey ADJ Mouse
```

ADJ/x matches documents in which the terms appear exactly x words apart. It's hard to imagine this would have any more than very limited usage; but here's an example:

```
Laurel ADJ/2 Hardy
```

An O in front of either ADJ or ADJ/x specifies that the terms must also appear in the document in the same order they appear in the query. The following query will match "Hardy and Laurel"—but not the order we'd expect:

```
Hardy OADJ/2 Laurel
```

- BEFORE specifies that the first search term must appear before the second one in any matched document:

```
Captain BEFORE Kirk
```

- In addition, you can group elements using parentheses, as is done in mathematical equations. The following examples illustrate this type of syntax. This query matches documents containing both "Katherine Hepburn" and one of the pair James Stewart and Cary Grant:

```
("James Stewart" OR "Cary Grant") AND "Katherine Hepburn"
```

NetGuide Live: Make Sense of the Web

http://www.netguide.com/

NetGuide Live is a search engine with the spin of a Web review. Billed as "Your Daily Guide To The Net," NetGuide reviews Web sites, announces live online events (like celebrity chat sessions), gives awards to outstanding online offerings, etc.

NetGuide's search engine by default lets you search a database of sites they've judged to be the "Best of the Web." This is a fairly sizeable database, and the ongoing reviews keep it growing. The text box in which you enter the words you want to search for is in the upper-right corner of the home page.

Below the search box, notice there are two labeled buttons. These buttons let you choose between the default "Best of the Web" search and a wider search of a "Comprehensive Web page index." If you click the button for the latter option, NetGuide acts more like a conventional search engine. Although its Web-wide database is more limited than many other search engines, it still seems to turn up a large number of good matches.

Unlike some of the fancier search engines, NetGuide's query syntax is simple: just enter one or more words you want to match. It doesn't understand anything tricky like ANDs or ORs, plus signs (+) or minus signs (-). However, you can use quotes to specify that words must appear together in the matched documents (e.g., "first amendment").

Another feature of the NetGuide home page is a brief catalog you can use to "Browse the Best of the Web." It's divided into sections like Arts & Culture, Education, Government & Law, etc. Between using this catalog and searching through the "Best of the Web" database, you should be able to keep up with many of the new offerings.

In keeping with the goal of one-stop searching, NetGuide also offers links to a number of sources of news and information, including CNN News, TechWeb News, BigBook Yellow Pages, and Four11 White Pages. There are also links to information about the Internet in general, a guide to New Sites, etc.

Finally, don't miss the link to NetGuide Magazine Online, or you can reach it directly at **http://techweb.cmp.com/ng/home/**.

WebCrawler: Sometimes Less Really Is More

http://www.webcrawler.com/

WebCrawler is a directory and search engine that helps you find some of the good stuff that might otherwise be obscured by the tangles of the Web. The emphasis is on reviewed sites. The WebCrawler site includes an extensive directory, not unlike Yahoo!'s.

WebCrawler's home page also offers online maps, assisted by MapQuest (http://www.mapquest.com); white page and email directories, powered by WhoWhere (http://www.whowhere.com); as well as extensive classified ads (they're free!). There are also links to DejaNews, Excite, and a number of other services.

Keep in mind that WebCrawler is *the* search engine to use if you're interested in Internet Relay Chat (covered in Part Eight of this book). The **Chat** link in the WebCrawler directory opens up an enormous library of chat-related resources, from software to gateways to reference material. Check it out.

WebCrawler's search engine is easy to use—plain language often works just fine. For example, the following query is perfectly acceptable:

```
hotels in Rome
```

If you want to come up with a fancier search phrase, WebCrawler also recognizes some syntactical operators, described two sections ahead.

When you use WebCrawler's search facility, the default format of the results is fairly simple, with the links for the top 25 matches (without descriptions) displayed at a time. These results are ranked with a percentage that corresponds to the level of relevance (100% is the highest possible relevance).

In a column to the right of the search results are some other links WebCrawler calls Shortcuts. Based on your query, the search engine comes up with some relevant Shortcuts gathered from the WebCrawler directory as well as their services section, which includes classified ads, an online music store, TV listings, weather, etc. If you put a city name in your query, the Shortcuts column will include links to weather and maps for that city and other related resources.

WebCrawler search results parameters

WebCrawler lets you set a few parameters that determine how results are displayed. In order for these options to work, your browser must support cookies. (See Chapter 1, *A Living Glossary of the Internet*, for more information about cookies.) You can specify the following options for the results page:

- Whether document titles alone or both titles and summaries are displayed

- The number of results displayed per page: 10, 25 (the default), or 100

- How you navigate through the results: with a "Next 25" button, a list of page numbers, result ranges (e.g., 1-25, 26-50), or Next and Previous buttons

WebCrawler query syntax

With WebCrawler, you can always try a simple query like this:

```
low calorie recipes
```

But a more refined search never hurts. The following rules apply:

- Match the exact phrase by putting it in quotes:

  ```
  "Masterpiece Theatre"
  ```

- Specify that certain elements must be included, excluded, or have a particular relationship to one another by using the following shorthand terms: AND, OR, NOT, NEAR, and ADJ. Here's how to use each of the terms:

  - AND specifies that the elements listed before and after must both appear in matched documents:

    ```
    software AND free
    ```

  - OR specifies that at least one of the terms must appear in matched documents:

    ```
    "Bob Hope" OR "Bing Crosby"
    ```

  - The use of NOT specifies that the search term following cannot appear in matched documents. The following query looks for documents that include "tuna," but don't have "salad":

    ```
    tuna NOT salad
    ```

  - NEAR/x specifies that the two terms are within x words of each other in matched documents. The following query matches any document in which "house" and "haunted" appear within ten words of each other:

    ```
    house NEAR/10 haunted
    ```

    Without the /x parameter, NEAR specifies that the two terms be next to each other in either order.

  - ADJ specfies that the two terms be next to each other in the given order:

    ```
    Christmas ADJ tree
    ```

- You can also group elements using parentheses in the style of math equations. The following query matches documents containing the words "Christmas" and "tree" next to each other, in that order, and "Santa":

  ```
  ("Christmas" ADJ "tree") AND Santa
  ```

Yahoo!

http://www.yahoo.com/

Yahoo! is a Web directory, perhaps the premier one. It's easy to look at and easy to use. It also has an ever-increasing array of services and features, which are summarized in Chapter 5.

There are two basic strategies for using Yahoo!:

- Follow links within the directory.

- Search the Yahoo! database (an index to the offerings found under the directory) and beyond (Yahoo! calls up AltaVista as well).

The best way to use Yahoo! is to take advantage of both of these capabilities.

If you're interested in a general topic that happens to be named in the top level of the directory, you might begin by selecting that link to see what offerings fall under it. Keep in mind, however, that the directory is many levels deep, and what you're looking for might not be at the top. A search should point you in the right direction. And a search is certainly the way to go if you're looking for something very specific.

The Yahoo! database is actually divided into four sections:

- Categories

- Web Sites

- News Headlines

- Net Events (i.e., chats, etc.)

When you use the Yahoo! search engine, results are divided by database section. Additionally, Yahoo! will use AltaVista to do a broader search of the Web. Near the top of each results page are links to the various groups of matches:

- Category matches

- Site matches

- News Headline Matches

- Net Events (chats, etc.)

- AltaVista Web Pages

Naturally, you may not get results in one or more of these sections.

The category matches section lists the parts of the Yahoo! directory that match your query. Each part of the directory is identified by the series of links that get you there from the top level (Yahoo! home page). A search for "recycling" turns up a whopping 14 category matches, of which the following are representative:

```
Yahoo! Category Matches    (1 - 14 of 14)

Business and Economy: Companies: Environment: Recycling

Society and Culture: Environment and Nature: Recycling

Regional: Countries: Canada: Business: Companies: Environment: Recycling

Regional: Countries: United States: Dependent Areas: Puerto Rico:
Business: Recycling
```

As with any directory, note that the same general topic often occurs under a number of different branches.

The site matches section of the results lists individual URLs from the Yahoo! database that match your query. Each URL is preceded by a "bullet" symbol. Above each URL appears the part of the directory under which the URL is classified. Our same search—for "recycling"—reveals 476 site matches, beginning with the following:

```
                 Yahoo! Site Matches    (1 - 6 of 476)

Business and Economy: Companies: Electronics: Recycling

     o Electronic Recycling - recycling and remarketing services.

Business and Economy: Companies: Health: Medical Equipment

     o B&B Recycling - recycling of medical parts.

Business and Economy: Companies: Industrial Supplies: Machinery and
Tools: Recycling

     o Recycling Equipment Guide - web guide to commerical, industrial,
       and agricultural chippers, grinders, and other recycling equipment.
```

(With 476 site matches, I should probably refine my search.)

The news headline section lists recent news stories that match your query. News stories are provided by Business Wire (**http://www.businesswire.com**).

The Net events section of the results lists upcoming chat sessions, RealAudio broadcasts, etc., that match your query.

Yahoo! also calls on AltaVista to do a wider search for your terms. Check out the AltaVista Web Pages link on the results page. Normally, category matches (and site matches, if there's room) appear on the first page of results. Note that if no category or site matches are turned up, the Alta Vista results appear on the first page.

Yahoo! search parameters

At the top level of the Yahoo! directory—the home page—all searches take place through the entire Yahoo! database. However, if you link to another level in the directory, you have the option of limiting your search to the corresponding part of the database. Toggle buttons below the search box let you choose between the entire database or the current section. For example, if I go to the **Sports** part of the directory, I can choose to "Search only in Sports."

To the right of each search box is a link labeled "Options." Selecting this link reveals some additional search parameters you can set. The most powerful option lets you specify the database to search:

* Yahoo! (the default)

* Usenet

* Email addresses

If you stick with the Yahoo! database, there are four additional options, each offering a number of mutually exclusive settings.

The first option lets you specify the "search method"—basically how the matching is done. Here are the choices:

- Intelligent default

- An exact phrase match

- Matches on all words (AND)

- Matches on any word (OR)

- A person's name

The default is—big surprise—"Intelligent default." This means that the search engine tries to match each word you enter and come up with something reasonable—just about what every search tool does if you don't provide any special parameters or syntax.

Some of the other parameters have equivalent syntactical operators. You can tell Yahoo! that you want to match the "exact phrase" by selecting that requirement from the options list or by putting the phrase in quotes. You can specify that words have to be matched by selecting the option "Matches on all words"—or by preceding each word with a plus sign (+). (The AND and OR used to explain two of the options are somewhat misleading; these words are not valid syntactical operators for Yahoo!.) The "person's name" option is unique; there's no other way to tell Yahoo! you've entered a person's name. However, there's no particular benefit either. Quoting a name should work as well.

The second parameter lets you specify the type of results you get first:

- Yahoo! Categories

- Web Sites

The default, "Yahoo! Categories," means you get category and then site matches (as explained in the preceding section). If you choose "Web Sites," site matches come first—but you can still get category matches by selecting the corresponding link on the results page.

The third search parameter lets you limit matches to those documents that have been added to the database within a particular time frame. You can tell Yahoo! to "Find only new listings added during the past": 3 years (the default), 6 months, 3 months, 1 month, 1 week, 3 days, or 1 day.

You can also specify the number of matches that are returned on each page of results (after the first page). The choices are: 20 (the default), 10, 50, and 100. Naturally, a page of 100 results will span several windows full.

Yahoo! query syntax

Yahoo!'s search syntax is actually pretty simple.

- Surround your query in quotes if you want it to be treated as a single phrase, rather than a series of individual search terms.

- Use an asterisk (*) as a wildcard to represent omitted letters in a word. This enables you to match variations of a word, or even match something you're not sure how to spell. The following query,

  ```
  writ*
  ```

  will match writing, writer, etc.

- To specify that a word or phrase must appear in matched documents, put a plus sign (immediately) before it:

  ```
  +"Carl Sagan" +Contact
  ```

- To specify that a word or phrase *must not* appear in matched documents, put a minus sign (immediately) before it. The following query turns up information about poison ivy the plant—not the Batman nemesis:

  ```
  +"poison ivy" -Batman
  ```

- Use a special field syntax to limit searches to certain fields in Web documents (specifically, titles or URLs). The fields you can specify are: **t** for title or **u** for URL. The basic syntax is:

  field_abbreviation: search_terms

  For example, the following query matches documents with "Songline Studios" in the title portion:

  ```
  t:"Songline Studios"
  ```

  To match any document with "cubs" in its URL:

  ```
  url:cubs
  ```

  This query finds a number of Web pages about the Chicago Cubs. (If there are Web pages out there about baby bears and lions or cub reporters, they might show up, too.)

CHAPTER 7

Finding People and Places

The Internet provides several search engines that are primarily intended to help you locate general information. However, many search engines also offer a way to search for basic information about people and places. And there are a number of utilities and sites geared entirely towards helping you find this kind of information.

Generally, this means finding email addresses, phone numbers, and street addresses (and even maps and directions to help get you there). Online listings that provide this kind of information about individuals are commonly called *white pages*, just like the books that provide individual phone listings. It's not surprising then that the online equivalent business listings are called *yellow pages*. There are even online *blue pages* that provide information about U.S. government offices.

What are the sources for such online listings? Many are drawn from conventional telephone resources. However, there are also services, such as one called Four11 (to suggest the 4-1-1 number you dial for telephone information), which also encourage people to register information about themselves with the service.

How extensive are the online listings? Is everyone in the country included in some kind of Big Brother database? No, but the listings are fairly extensive. My parents' telephone number and address are available online, and neither of them has ever used a computer, much less registered with an online service.

Does it make sense to log on to the Net just to find the phone number of a person or business in your area? Of course not. That's what telephone books and directory assistance are for.

Is this how Columbo would track down a missing person? No, he's way too smart. The online listings don't keep pace with people's moving around, and they don't include as many people as directory assistance does. I have friends who live within ten miles of here. They're listed in the phone book, but somehow they've managed to elude every online "people finder" I've tried. Go figure. Certainly it's always a better idea to call directory assistance for new listing information.

This chapter covers some of the tools and methods for getting some of the basic information about a person: their telephone number, street address, and email address. It will also show you where to look for phone numbers and addresses generally found in the yellow pages and blue pages.

Keep in mind that there is a big overlap among the services that provide this kind of info, as well as cooperation among them, and with the broader search engines described in Chapter 6, *Internet Directories and Search Engines*. For instance, Yahoo! (**http://www.yahoo.com/**) provides a link to white page listings, but it's actually a link to a separate service, Four11. Infoseek (**http://www.infoseek.com**) provides a wide range of information from phone and email listings to searching in a variety of categories, and even sending UPS packages. However, in order to search through phone numbers and email addresses, Infoseek calls on BigYellow (**http://www.bigyellow.com**), a service of Nynex. And, since BigYellow is primarily a yellow page service, their white page service is powered by Four11.

In practice, you won't care which databases are accessed by which service. You'll only care about getting the information. Still, if you keep your eyes open, you're bound to notice the incestuous way all of these services work.

In addition to the directories found on the Web, the current chapter also describes an older utility called *finger*, which can tell you information about a user on a UNIX system. You use *finger* to find out things like a user's login name (and thus their email address), whether they're currently logged in, etc. If the user in question has created special information files called *.plan* and *.project*, you can also read these. Although *finger* is not as widely used as it once was and it has a number of limitations, it can come in handy. There are also versions of the program for Windows.

A final note: There's a big difference between *finding* someone and *finding out about* someone. This book is not going to teach you how to snoop on someone, or even how to research the online activities of any private individual. If you want to look into a person's presence on the Internet, no one can stop you. Search engines don't care what words you search for, including names. But systematic searches like this raise very serious concerns about privacy. (For further discussion of online privacy, see the section "Authentication, Cookies, and Privacy" in Chapter 1, *A Living Glossary of the Internet*.)

Where to Begin?

The reality is that there are dozens and dozens of facilities that help you search for people and places on the Internet. You certainly won't benefit by knowing about that many tools. However, because it's never a sure thing that a particular search utility's database will provide a good match for your query, it's good to have a few options.

There are two common ways to approach the task of finding a person or place on the Net:

- Try the people finder, business finder, or other appropriate directory facility offered by your favorite search engine(s). A number of these are outlined in the section "How Net-Wide Search Engines Can Help," later in this chapter.

- Try a service intended specifically for these types of queries. See the section "Online Email and Phone Directories," later in this chapter, for a list of some of the more popular services.

Since many search engines go to a more specific directory service anyway, it really depends on where you want to be. I'm always using a search engine, so I'm more likely to start looking for phone numbers and addresses from there. If you have a preferred search engine, check out the description in "How Net-Wide Search Engines Can Help." You may never need to look further.

You also have the option of going directly to an information service that specializes in "people and places." There are many powerful ones, a number of which are mentioned in "Online Email and Phone Directories."

In any case, if you don't find what you're looking for with one tool, definitely try a few others. Even the larger listings have unpredictable omissions.

In This Case, Less Query Is Often More

OK, so you've read some of Chapter 6, *Internet Directories and Search Engines*. And you've become a search engine superjock, able to phrase complex queries in a flash. Good for you. Now—forget all that.

When you're searching through directories of phone numbers, street addresses, etc., giving more information about the person or organization sometimes impedes the matching process. For the most part, when searching for information about an individual, you're better off limiting your query to a last name, city (if you're absolutely sure), and state. If the name is a ubiquitous one, like *Martinez* or *Johnson*, you might want to add a first initial or name.

For yellow page listings, stick with a part of the name you're sure about. For instance, suppose you want to find one of the offices of a corporation named Acme Something-Or-Other. (They make rockets, ropes, dynamite, portable holes, and other tools that help you catch a road runner.) Unfortunately, Acme has many branches and subsidiaries in your area. There's an Acme Boobytraps, Acme Exploding Things, Acme Rotating Gizmos (ARG), Acme Exploding Things International, Acme Rabbit Tower (the corporate headquarters), and Acme Shmacme. But you don't know any of this. In fact, you don't know a whole helluva lot. It's just as well, because the first thing you should be searching for is just plain Acme. Include the name of the state—and throw in the name of the town if you're absolutely sure.

Email searches may be something of an exception, depending on how the directory is set up. Some directories return email addresses along with phone numbers and street addresses. Others require a separate search for email addresss. In the latter case, you generally need to give a last name, and, unless it's a very unusual last name, a first name or initial.

For any directory search (white pages, yellow pages, blue pages, etc.), if you can't find the listing you want, try variations on your query (leaning toward the side of less information); and, if that fails, try other services.

Why does less often translate to more in queries like these? The matching algorithms many of these services use do not leave much room for variation. If you're a bit off from what the database has, that can translate to being way off.

For instance, suppose you want to find out someone's phone number, and you happen to know many of the other pertinent facts about them (i.e., full name, address, city, state). You *can* give all of this information in your query. However, anyone who's opened a phone book knows that the listings don't follow an exact formula. Some people use only a first initial. Some married couples list themselves separately or under only one of their names. Street names are truncated. You get the picture. Since many of these online directories gather data from telephone companies, you can't count on the information in one of these databases being as reliable or complete as the information in your head.

Here's a case in point: I couldn't remember the phone number of a friend of mine in New York. Since I was at work and already running a browser, I decided to look online at BigYellow's white pages (which are actually driven by the Four11 service). I certainly know my friend's full name, as well as her husband's, and I even remembered their exact street address. But when I supplied most of this information (fictionalized here) in my query, BigYellow came up empty.

```
First Name: Catherine
Last Name: Pena
Street: Shadow Lane
City: Larchmont
State:  NY
```

Why? Well, it turned out that whatever source the database used listed only my friend's husband's name. From the search engine's side, the last name I gave matched the last name of *someone* in the same town, but the fact that there was no "Catherine" killed the whole thing.

Here's another typical problem: I live in the Boston area, and there are certain parts of the city (somewhat analogous to boroughs) that go by other names. But, technically, they're still part of Boston. One of these areas is Jamaica Plain. I can search for a friend of mine in JP, as it's called, if I list her city as Jamaica Plain. But an out-of-towner might easily give Boston as the city. Even though that's right, and the numbers of people in JP can be found in the Boston telephone book, most online services will not find the right information unless you give Jamaica Plain as the town.

Now, this is not to suggest that these services leave *no* room for variation. If you do give a first name and the person is actually listed by first initial only, most services are smart enough to return the listing anyway.

Four11 has made some noteworthy advances in this department, offering an option called "SmartNames," which automatically matches common variations on a first name. Thus, if you give Bob, it will also look for Robert. But it couldn't match up Francis with Frank, and it doesn't seem to know what to do with last name variations like Riley, Reilly, and Reilley.

What I Use (Editor's Note: Like I Care)

In order to write a book like this, I've had to test a lot of different programs, visit many sites, etc. Still, like many people, I tend to have my favorite sites and preferred set of tools. I'm primarily interested in function, but I'm also very influenced by a sort of general "fit" with my taste and what interests me. This is my roundabout way of saying that, although I'm going to recommend a few different search tools here, there are plenty of other very good ones, many of which might be better for you.

For searches involving people and places, I use the following:

- The general search engines Infoseek, Excite, and WebCrawler

- The specific services BigYellow, Infospace, and Four11

- Yahoo! (powered by Four11) to find email addresses (the Four11 database seems to have the the biggest reach in this department)

For more information about these and other services, see the following two sections.

How Net-Wide Search Engines Can Help

Most of the Net-wide search engines covered in Chapter 6 can help you find phone numbers, email and street addresses, maps of a location, etc. For some search engines, this help comes from proprietary sources, but more often a site will simply link to more specialized services that provide this kind of information. Here's an overview of the "people and place" resources made available through the major search engines:

Excite (http://www.excite.com/)

From the home page, try **People Finder**, **Email Lookup**, **Yellow Pages**, and **Maps**.

From **Yellow Pages**, you can access directories of toll free numbers, government blue pages, and other yellow page services (BigYellow, and Switchboard Business Search, and World Pages International).

From **People Finder**, you can access similar services (Four11, Lookup USA People Directory, Switchboard People Search) as well as a page linking to a number of *International Directories*.

The **Email Lookup** page links to similar services, including Bigfoot, Four11 Email Directory, and Internet Address Finder.

The **Maps** link lets you access maps of both domestic and international locales. You can also get a map for any U.S. address with City.Net's interactive map facility.

Infoseek (http://www.infoseek.com/)

There are three relevant links on the home page: **Find Businesses**, **Find People**, and **Find Email**. All of the information is actually provided by BigYellow, a very strong directory service. In addition, from the **Find People** and **Find Email** links, you can access: 800 and 888 numbers (provided by AT&T); a number of international phone directories (also BigYellow) for regions in six continents; city, state, and federal government phone listings (provided by Infospace); area codes (AmeriCom); and Zip Codes (the U.S. Postal Service).

Lycos (http://www.lycos.com/)

Never one to be left behind, Lycos' **PeopleFind** link uses the powerful Infospace directory service. You can do yellow page searches, courtesy of GTE Yellow Pages. **Road Maps** are also available. Lycos' **Companies Online** lets you search for information about companies with a Web presence, including URLs and email addresses (as well as the more conventional statistics like company size, structure, stock price, etc.).

WebCrawler (http://www.webcrawler.com/)

If you link to **Reference**, then **Phone Books**, you can access many different white page and yellow page facilities, including some for Canada, Europe, Australia, and other locations.

After choosing the link **Reference**, select **Email Addresses** to access appropriate search services (many of which overlap with the **Phone Books** section); you can also find sites that provide free email services for individuals.

Yahoo! (http://www.yahoo.com/)

One of Yahoo!'s better searching capabilities is not immediately obvious. If you click on the **options** link, next to the Search box and button, you'll see that you can opt to search a database of email addresses.

For email, white pages, and yellow pages, Yahoo! actually calls upon the Four11 service (described in the next section). At this stage of the game, the Four11 database is just about the best email address database around. If you opt to use it from Yahoo!, note that you have to select **options**, and then click the **email** option, before searching.

In order to use the email search facility, supply the person's first name (or initial) and last name. If you're not sure if someone goes by the first name Francis or Frank, you might try Fran (or F). The search engine should then match both Francis and Frank. (A SmartNames option takes care of some of the more common variations on first names. Thus, Bob will match Robert.)

Yahoo!'s **People Search** (white pages) is also a Four11 service, while their **Yellow Pages** is powered by Vicinity Corporation (**http://www.vicinity.com/**).

Online Email and Phone Directories

There are a number of sites whose primary service is to provide online phone, street, and email listings, for both individuals and organizations. Many of these extend their reach beyond the U.S. to Canada, Europe, and Australia. A lot of the mainstream search engines use these directories to provide their users with these type of services.

There are *a lot* of these directories on the Net. Here's a list of some of the more popular ones:

AT&T Toll Free Internet Directory (http://www.tollfree.att.net/)

The name says it all: an online 800 and 888 directory.

Bigfoot (http://www.bigfoot.com/)

The name is cute—but its status as one of the largest databases of email addresses and white page listings is a better reason to step on over.

BigYellow (http://www.bigyellow.com/)

More than 16 million yellow page listings, with a link to international directories, plus email listings (courtesy of Four11) and an Internet directory called BigTopics.

Four11 Directory (http://www.four11.com/)

The first stop for email address listings, Four11 (that's "4-1-1") provides an online directory of millions of email addresses. At one time, Four11 relied on people registering their addresses, but they've clearly found other ways to hunt them up. The database includes some very old addresses—which are listed as such—for some friends of mine.

For those who might not be inclined to make their email address public, Four11 also offers an interesting privacy option. You can register for a private mailbox at Four11. Then someone can search for your name and reach you at this private mailbox, without finding out your actual email address. The private mailbox forwards messages to your email address. It's basically like a two-way email mirror. You can see them, but they can't see you.

You can also get the typical yellow page, white page, and blue page (government) listings.

Infospace (http://www.infospace.com/)

They call themselves "The Ultimate Directory," which may be a slight exaggeration, but there are still a large number of valuable resources here: personal phone numbers, street addresses, and email addresses; business yellow pages, corporate executives, and government listings at all levels; fax and toll-free numbers; and maps and directions to located addresses. This service seems great at locating non-Internet information about individuals (telephone numbers and addresses, for instance), but it's rather weak at tracking down email addresses.

The Official U.S. Government Blue Pages
(http://www.bp.fed.gov/)

This online listing is the government's own attempt at a comprehensive blue pages service. The goal is to provide info on the local, city, state and federal levels, but so far it mostly covers federal agencies and representatives located in certain U.S. cities. This will undoubtedly be improved.

U.S. Postal Service Zip+4 Code Lookup
(http://www.usps.gov/ncsc/)

Get the long-format Zip Code for any address in the U.S.—or the five-digit code, for that matter.

WhoWhere (http://www.whowhere.com/)

Yellow pages, white pages, email listings, government sites, toll free numbers, home pages, etc.

World Pages (http://www.worldpages.com/)

Business finder, people finder, government finder, email. Emphasis on yellow pages for places around the world. Also travel resources.

Yellow Pages Online (http://www.ypo.com/)

More than 18 million U.S. business listings and counting.

Zip2 (http://www.zip2.com/)

More than 16 million U.S. business listings, with a cool interface that lets you search by name, category, city, near a particular address, or even by clickable maps.

Finger: Finding Users on UNIX Systems

At one time, the *finger* program was one of the hotter technologies to find out something about a user on another (or even your own) system. Although the *finger* program is only good for finding users on UNIX systems, it still flourishes in many corporate and academic settings. It seems especially good for finding the email addresses of students and university staff. Thus, the following command (using the UNIX version of *finger*) helped me locate the address of a friend of mine who's in grad school at Cornell:

```
% finger walsh@cornell.edu

[cornell.edu]
Information from Cornell's Network Identity Directory...
-------------------------------------------------------
```

```
Your query returned   1 match  :

Name:          Andrea M Walsh              Nickname:
Send Email To:  amw14@cornell.edu
Campus Phone:
Campus Address:
Local Phone:
Local Address:
Project:
```

As you can see, the system's output leaves room for a lot more information. This configuration is site-specific—not every site will provide the same output. Traditionally, *finger* provides info such as:

- A user's full name

- Email address

- Whether they're currently logged in or when they last logged in

- When they last read email

- Whatever information they've chosen to share with you in two *finger*-specific files called *.plan* and *.project* (which generally live in their *home* directory)

  Customarily, a user's *.plan* file lets others know what they're up to these days; while *.project* contains notes about a specific project. But the contents are really up to the user.

If you're a Windows user and you're interested in the kind of information *finger* can provide, there are plenty of windows-based versions of the program. Try searching at **http://www.winsite.com/**.

CHAPTER 8

Accessing Libraries and Other Resources with Telnet

Telnet is an older Internet utility that lets you log on to remote computer systems. Basically, a Telnet program gives you a character-based terminal window on another system. You get a login prompt on that system. If you're permitted access, you can work on that system, just as you would if you were sitting next to it.

Traditionally, Telnet has been used by people who have logins on remote systems and want to do serious work there. I frequently use the UNIX *telnet* program at work. When I'm logged on to our primary system, I Telnet over to another one of the networked computers to access certain files.

But Telnet has some additional uses that are more relevant to people who are exploring the Internet. Most notably, you can use Telnet to connect to thousands of catalogs at libraries around the world. This capability is wonderful for anyone doing serious research. Imagine being able to find out which books in your particular discipline are available at a number of specialty libraries in remote locations—all while you plug away at your desk.

There are also many other resources made available via Telnet. The U.S. government likes to distribute information that way. You can also access information about weather, music, finances, business, the stock market, entertainment, you name it.

This chapter introduces some of the resources available via Telnet. We'll also take a look at one of the common Telnet programs for Windows and go through the process of visiting some typical Telnet sites.

Telnet Resources on the Internet

In the age of the World Wide Web, Telnet sites are not very high in people's consciousness. Nor, in most cases, should they be. Who wouldn't rather get their online weather report over the Web, complete with illustrations of the sun and rain clouds, when the alternative is a stuttering terminal screen? But Telnet can't be overlooked because it is currently just about the only way to access thousands of library catalogs remotely.

You can also use Telnet to connect to a number of NASA databases, as well as bulletin board services, and freenets.

Telnet also comes in handy as an interface to a search facility called *Archie*. Archie is a system that helps you locate files on anonymous FTP servers (described in Chapter 17, *FTP and File Transfer*). Archie can be very slow, and it's also somewhat exacting as far as what constitutes a match. But Archie can also be useful, particularly if you can set it running and come back to it after it's had a while to search.[*]

Many other Telnet resources are duplicated by some Web site or other. You can definitely get loads of weather reports, stock reports, financial information, etc., on the Web. And it sure looks better than the character output of a Telnet application.

One of the best places to find out about available Telnet resources of all kinds is the Web site of a shareware program called *hytelnet*:

    http://library.usask.ca/hytelnet/

Developed by Peter Scott, who's affiliated with the library at Berkeley University, *hytelnet* can help you access just about any Telnet resource out there. The program also exists for a variety of platforms (including DOS, Windows, UNIX, and Macintosh), and there's a great deal of support. To get the software, select the link "About HYTELNET?" at the preceding URL, or go directly to:

    http://www.lights.com/hytelnet/

Peter Scott also runs a mailing list that provides updates about which Telnet resources become available and which resources disappear. You can subscribe by sending an email message to the address:

    listserv@library.berkeley.edu

Leave the Subject line blank, and put the following text in the body:

    subscribe hytelnet *your_first_name your_last_name*

For more information about *Mailing Lists*, see Chapter 11.

The *hytelnet* Web site itself is a veritable library of Telnet resources. You can look up the appropriate address for libraries all over the world, as well as the right login name and port to use. The same level of information is available for Archie servers, bulletin boards, NASA, etc. Check it out.

---

[*] Of course, Web search engines are very likely to turn up information that will lead you to the proper FTP site too. And they are definitely faster than our old buddy Archie. But there's no guarantee a Web search will turn up the exact name or path of any file on an FTP server, either.

Telnet for Windows

Telnet is a *helper application* that is commonly installed on many personal computers along with Windows. You may already have a Telnet client. On my PC, Telnet lives under *c:\windows*. The easiest way to find Telnet on your PC is to select Run from the Start menu, then enter "telnet" in the Run dialog, and hit Return. If there's a Telnet application in your path, it will be run for you.

If Telnet isn't in your path, the Run dialog won't find it, and the next thing to do is to search for "telnet" using your Windows Explorer or File Manager. If you still come up empty, and using Telnet interests you, it's easy to get a freeware version. (See Chapter 20, *Helper Applications*, for more information.) Or you might consider getting the *hytelnet* shareware program (see the previous section).

I have a simple Telnet client that was installed with Windows 95. Telnet is not a complicated facility, and the Windows client isn't fancy by any means, but it does provide some handy menus. Whichever version of Telnet you end up using, the principles are pretty much the same. The current section shows how to log on to a remote Telnet server using this basic Windows client.

Figure 8–1 shows the initial Telnet window.

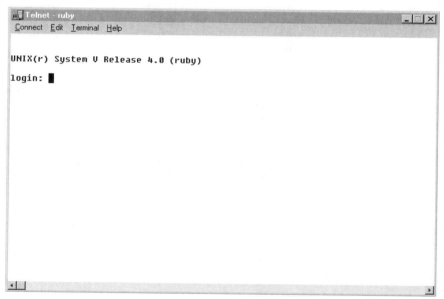

Figure 8–1: Telnet for Windows

To connect to another computer, you use the following menu sequence:

Connect menu → **Remote System** . . .

This opens a dialog box, in which you enter the address of a Telnet server:

```
Host Name: address
Port: telnet
Term Type: vt100
```

Notice that you can also specify a port to connect to, as well as the type of terminal you want Telnet to emulate. The default port of "telnet" and default terminal "vt100" will do in most cases. When you hear about a Telnet site on the Net, pay attention to whether there is another port number specified. Sometimes you'll also read about an alternate terminal type up front. Or you may get a help message when you connect to the Telnet site.

Within the connection dialog box, there's an arrow to the right of each choice; clicking on this arrow reveals a pull-down menu of other choices. Once you connect to a host, the address of the host will be available on this menu. This address will also appear on the **Connect** menu, so that you can go directly to the site the next time.

When you initially connect to a Telnet site, you may be automatically logged on to the system, or you may get a login prompt. The login name you should use varies from system to system. Whatever advance information you have about the site should include it. A login name might be *library*. Often it's something specific to the server—for example, many Archie servers want you to use the login *archie*. But the required login name might be just about anything. (The *hytelnet* site can tell you the right login name for a gazillion Telnet servers. Sometimes the system login prompt at the Telnet server will even include this information.)

Note that the **Connect** menu also has items that let you **Disconnect** and **Exit** the program; the Alt+F4 keyboard shortcut also exits the Telnet client.

Suppose we fill in the connection dialog to log on to Weather Underground. (We can get the address from **http://www.lights.com/hytelnet/**.)

```
Host Name: downwind.sprl.umich.edu
Port: telnet
Term Type: vt100
```

Telnet displays the following welcome screen:

```
---------------------------------------------------------------------------
*
*                          University of Michigan
*
*                           WEATHER UNDERGROUND
*
---------------------------------------------------------------------------
*
*
*                  comments: ldm@cirrus.sprl.umich.edu
*
*
*
*  This information available on the web at
*    http://www.wunderground.com
*
*
* With Help from:  The National Science Foundation supported Unidata
*                  Project
*                  University Corporation for Atmospheric Research
```

```
*                 Boulder, Colorado  80307-3000
*
*
*
*   NOTE:----------> due to heavy load, this service will be
*                    unavailable at times. Try connecting to
*                    one of these machines:
*
*                    telnet rainmaker.wunderground.com
*
*                    telnet um-weather.sprl.umich.edu 3000
*
------------------------------------------------------------------
*        This service is for educational and research purposes only.
*
*        Commercial, for-profit users should contact feed.
------------------------------------------------------------------

Press Return for menu, or enter 3 letter forecast city code:
```

I hit Return to get their menu of options:

```
                 WEATHER UNDERGROUND MAIN MENU
                 *****************************
                 1) U.S. forecasts and climate data
                 2) Canadian forecasts
                 3) Current weather observations
                 4) Ski conditions
                 5) Long-range forecasts
                 6) Latest earthquake reports
                 7) Severe weather
                 8) Hurricane advisories
                 9) National Weather Summary
                10) International data
                11) Marine forecasts and observations
                12) Ultraviolet light forecast
                13) K-12 School Weather Observations
                14) Weather summary for the past month
                 X) Exit program
                 C) Change scrolling to screen
                 H) Help and information for new users
                 ?) Answers to all your questions
                   Selection:

          Enter 3-letter city code: BOS
```

I went out on a limb and guessed that BOS was the code for Boston. I got the following report:

```
Weather Conditions at 10 AM EDT on 25 MAY 97 for Boston, MA.
Temp(F)    Humidity(%)    Wind(mph)    Pressure(in)    Weather
==================================================================
  54          N/A         EAST at 8       29.87        light rain

EASTERN ESSEX-EASTERN NORFOLK-EASTERN PLYMOUTH-SUFFOLK-
INCLUDING THE CITIES OF...GLOUCESTER...LYNN...SALEM...BOSTON...
QUINCY...COHASSET...PLYMOUTH
1056 AM EDT SUN MAY 25 1997

 THIS AFTERNOON...PERIODS OF RAIN. A THUNDERSTORM POSSIBLE TOWARD
EVENING.  HIGH 60 TO 65. SOUTH WIND 10 TO 20 MPH.
```

```
TONIGHT...PERIODS OF RAIN ENDING BY MIDNIGHT.  A THUNDERSTORM
POSSIBLE IN THE EVENING. LOW 50 TO 55. WIND BECOMING NORTH 10 TO
15 MPH. CHANCE OF RAIN 80 PERCENT.
MEMORIAL DAY...PARTLY SUNNY. HIGH NEAR 65.


                  ***********************
                  State extended forecast
                  ***********************
EXTENDED FORECAST...
   Press Return to continue, M to return to menu, X to exit:
```

You get the idea. Terminal output like this is not terribly easy to read, and you can't scroll it. But Telnet sure comes in handy when you want to find just that obscure book.

Accessing a Library Catalog

Suppose for a moment that you're a paleontologist-in-training (or maybe just one of the millions of movie-goers who are having *Jurassic Park* fantasies). You've told your academic advisor that you're going to write a crackerjack dissertation on dinosaur eggs. Only now you're having trouble hunting up information about them. Telnet to the rescue!

Searching library catalogs is Telnet's forte—and there are libraries all over the world accessible via Telnet. From the *hytelnet* site (described earlier in this chapter), I get the address and login info for the Telnet server at the American Museum of Natural History (in New York).

The *hytelnet* site tells me:

* The Museum's server is *nimidi.amnh.org*.

* The login I'm supposed to use is *library*.

* I don't need a password—once I've given the login name, hitting the Return key will get me onto the system.

Here's the initial screen I got:

```
                        Nimidi
3.2.1                                       Introduction

------------------------------------------------------------------
The Voyager Online Public Access Catalog (OPAC) allows staff and
patrons perform complex searches of USMARC-based records. Type a
question mark (?) at any time for more information.



------------------------------------------------------------------
Search                                      Help?
                                            Exit

Type selection and press ENTER: .
```

A letter in each command was highlighted to indicate that you could issue the command using this single letter. I typed S for search and got the search screen:

```
                    Nimidi
                                          Search
Selection
- - - - - - - - - - - - - - - - - - - - - - - - - - - - - - - - - - - - - - -
                       Subject

                       Author

                       Title

                       Keyword

                       Journal Title

                       Call Number

                       Course Reserve

                       Other Searches

- - - - - - - - - - - - - - - - - - - - - - - - - - - - - - - - - - - - - - - - - -
   Help?
   Exit

Type selection and press ENTER: .
```

The first letter of each search option was highlighted, with the exception of R for (course) reserve. I typed S for Subject and then entered the subject of dinosaurs. (Yeah, I could have searched for dinosaur eggs right off the bat. But I'm not a very good student.) Here are the results of the search for *dinosaur*:

```
                              Nimidi
   Search request: Subject = dinosaurs
   Search results: 62 entries found

Headings Index

- - - - - - - - - - - - - - - - - - - - - - - - - - - - - - - - - - - - - - - - - - -
   Select  Titles  Heading
      1.      74    Dinosaurs
      2.       5    Dinosaurs.
      3.       1    Dinosaurs Africa.
      4.       1    Dinosaurs Arizona Petrified Forest National Park.
      5.       1    Dinosaurs Bibliography.
      6.       1    Dinosaurs Canada.
      7.       1    Dinosaurs Canada, Western Juvenile literature.
      8.       1    Dinosaurs Catalogs and collections Canada.
      9.       1    Dinosaurs Catalogs and collections New York (State) New York.
     10.       1    Dinosaurs Catalogs and collections United States.
     11.       1    Dinosaurs China.
     12.       1    Dinosaurs China Pictorial works.
     13.       2    Dinosaurs China Szechwan Province.
     14.       1    Dinosaurs Collectibles United States Directories.
- - - - - - - - - - - - - - - - - - - - - - - - - - - - - - - - - - - More > - - - - - - - - -
   Search             # of Heading              Help?
                                     Page Down   Exit

Type selection and press ENTER: ....
```

Nope. Not what I wanted. I advance to the next page of results by typing D for Down.

```
                              Nimidi
Search request: Subject = dinosaurs
Search results: 62 entries found


Headings Index

------------------------------------------------------------------------
Select  Titles   Heading
  15.      1     Dinosaurs Colorado.
  16.      1     Dinosaurs Colorado Dinosaur Ridge.
  17.      1     Dinosaurs Congo (Brazzaville) Likouala Region.
  18.      6     Dinosaurs Congresses.
  19.      4     Dinosaurs Dictionaries.
  20.      1     Dinosaurs Dictionaries.
  21.      1     Dinosaurs East (U.S.)
  22.      2     Dinosaurs Eggs
  23.      2     Dinosaurs Encyclopedias.
  24.      1     Dinosaurs Evolution.
  25.      4     Dinosaurs Exhibitions.
  26.      4     Dinosaurs Gobi Desert (Mongolia and China)
  27.      1     Dinosaurs Gobi Desert (Mongolia and China) Exhibitions.
  28.      1     Dinosaurs Identification.
------------------------------------------------- < More > ---------
Search                # of Heading        Page Up
  Help?
                                          Page Down
  Exit

Type selection and press ENTER: ....
```

Ta-da! Two whole books about dinosaur eggs. I am all set. I enter 22, the number corresponding to the dinosaur eggs entry.

```
                              Nimidi
Search request: Subject = dinosaurs
Search results: 2 entries found

Titles                                                       Index

------------------------------------------------------------------------
Select  OPAC Subject Headings   TITLE                AUTHOR
  1.    Dinosaurs Eggs          Contribution a l'etu  Penner, Morris Michael
  2.    Dinosaurs Eggs          Dinosaur eggs and babi Carpenter, Kenneth, 19

------------------------------------------------------------------------
Search     Headings    # of Title        Help?

                                         Exit
Type selection and press ENTER: ....
```

Oh, well. One of the books is in French, and I'm no better a linguist than I am a paleontologist. So, I take a look at a more complete listing for the book in English by entering its number (2).

```
                              Nimidi
Search request: Subject = dinosaurs
Displaying 2 of 2 entries                 Holdings Display
```

```
------------------------------------------------------------------------
     Dinosaur eggs and babies / edited by Kenneth Carpenter, Karl F. Hirsch,...

  Title:              Dinosaur eggs and babies /
  Primary Material:   Book
  Publisher:          Cambridge ; New York, NY, USA : Cambridge University
                         Press, 1994.

  Location:           Main Stacks

  Call Number:        QE862.D5 D455 1994

  Number of Items:    1
  Status:             Not Charged

------------------------------------------------------------------------
  Search      Headings     Full Record              Previous Record  Help?
              Titles                                               Exit

 Type selection and press ENTER: .
```

Now I'm set. I can disconnect from the library's Telnet site by typing x, and I'll see if I can get ahold of that book.

PART IV

Email and News

CHAPTER 9

Why Email and News

This section of the book deals with two services that are available via the Internet: electronic mail and Usenet news. These services are actually very distinct. So, why are we putting them together? Basically because they both have to deal with online communication. Furthermore, the applications that Netscape and Microsoft have created to deal with mail and news treat these services as two sides of the same coin. And there's some sense in this.

If you're familiar with mail and news, you may be skeptical. These are not services you can confuse with one another.

Just about everyone with Internet access has used email. You already know what it's about. You know how handy it can be. In fact, email is virtually indispensible to a fairly wide population.

A lot of email is sent between individuals, but it can also be used to let people conduct a group discussion. This may simply involve sending messages to a bunch of your friends, your department at work, an entire school, whatever. The term *mailing list* is used to refer to a list of people to whom mail from other people on the list is sent. Many mail programs let you create an *alias* for a list of email recipients. When group discussions via email have many participants, a more formal mailing list becomes necessary, often with automated distribution, subscription, etc. There are literally thousands of such mailing lists currently in operation, on a wide range of topics.

Usenet news is another service that allows for distributed discussion. If you've never encountered Usenet, it's hard to appreciate what it's like. Basically, Usenet is composed of thousands of groups of people who share ideas online. These *newsgroups* are organized by subject. Each newsgroup is run something like a bulletin board service, with people posting messages that everyone who *subscribes* to the group can read and respond to. (Subscribing is a very loose business; basically, it just involves telling your newsreading program that you want to see that group.)

Some newsgroups conduct very professional and formal discussions of serious topics; others are like online clubs of people with the same hobby or passion. There's a lot of enthusiasm, sharing of valuable help and ideas, and unexpected camaraderie. There's also a lot of confusion, controversy, and downright belligerence. You really have to experience Usenet for a while—and sample different groups—to get a full picture.

Email and news are completely different services. They're also very different in character. You probably know—at least superficially—most of the people with whom you exchange email (unless you're sending it to a very large mailing list). In Usenet, people initially know only superficial details about each other: names, email addresses, organizations, etc. They have to rely on the content of each other's news *postings* to get an idea what people are like. The facelessness of Usenet sometimes encourages people to say things they might otherwise think better of. In many groups, in fact, it's a free-for-all.

What email and news do have in common is that they both let you communicate with other people online. In both cases you can compose and send messages. Email is delivered to one or more recipients. News messages are posted so that anyone who subscribes to the group can read them. Both mail and news also allow you to read messages sent by other people. In fact, many of the functions you want to perform with an email program, you also want to accomplish with news.

This logic is not lost on the premier Internet software companies. Both Netscape Communicator and Microsoft Internet Explorer come with modules that let you participate in email and Usenet news. And, although mail and news are clearly distinct services, for both products, the mail and news applications are closely related.

MSIE includes applications called Internet Mail and Internet News. Their primary application windows look very much alike. They are each coupled with a similar set of subwindows. Certain menu items, buttons, and other controls are limited to one or the other application, but there is more overlap than not.

In the case of Netscape Communicator, the email module, Messenger, and the news modules, Collabra Discussions, are even more intertwined. In fact, they are really more like a single application. You use one window to manage both your email folders and Usenet newsgroups. It's called the Message Center. You use a single window, called a Message List window, to list the headers of messages, whether they're from a mail folder or a newsgroup. You can view individual messages from the folder or group in the same window, too. Certain functions may be enabled or disabled, depending on whether you're working with mail or news. But the application windows don't change—only their content varies.

The current section of this book explains some of the things you might want to know about email. Chapter 10, *Email Strategies and Survival Tips*, discusses a number of these topics, including addressing conventions, message handling, sending attached files, and email netiquette.

Chapter 11, *Mailing Lists*, deals with the use of email for distributed discussions and gives you an idea of the kinds of lists to which you can subscribe.

This section also introduces Usenet news, including the newsgroup hierarchy, how to get oriented to and survive in the sometimes oddball Usenet culture, how to track down information in old news postings, etc. (See Chapter 12, *Getting Along in Usenet*, for details.)

Finally, this section deals with email and news applications, specifically:

- Netscape Messenger (mail) and Collabra Discussions (news). Although these applications have different names, the same basic windows are used for each—only the content changes. Thus, in order to avoid a lot of redundancy, we're dealing with both applications in a single chapter. Chapter 13, *Netscape Messenger and Collabra Discussions*, provides an overview of Messenger/Collbra, with tips and tricks for using them, as well as an extensive reference to features and customization.

- Microsoft's Internet Mail and Internet News. These are also very similar to one another, but there are separate windows for each. Chapter 14, *MSIE Internet Mail*, deals with Internet Mail, including tips and a reference; while Chapter 15, *MSIE Internet News*, does the same for Internet News.

CHAPTER 10

Email Strategies and Survival Tips

Electronic mail (email) is one of the most basic network services. You don't even have to be on the Internet to use it. There are a number of networks from which you can launch a message that will be routed where you want it to go. Nowadays, everyone and her mother has email. Just ask a number of my coworkers who exchange email with their moms all the time.

Email has become integral to communication in many businesses and other organizations, from schools to the government. Millions of people exchange email with their bosses, coworkers, teachers, and fellow students. You can even send email to your Congressional Representative, Senator, or the President of the United States. (Don't hold your breath waiting for more than a canned reply though.) Email is also a good, economical way to touch base with friends (and even family) who are a toll call away.

This chapter takes a quick look at email addressing, as well as some issues you might want to consider in choosing an email name. We'll also take a quick look at *signature files*, which many people append to their email messages (and Usenet news) in order to convey information like their email address and phone number.

Although sending and receiving email is extrememly simple, if you've never done it, there are a few parameters you should understand. We'll review the basics of filling in a message header to send it to the right people. There are also a number of ways to deal with the email messages you get. For one thing, the various ways you can reply to a message can be a bit confusing. We'll consider some of the common mail-handling options.

Although email can be very useful, like any purely written form of communication, it has some serious limitations as well. The current chapter discusses some of the pitfalls of communicating via email, along with some suggestions for making yourself understood.

In trying to solve all of people's informational needs, both Netscape and Microsoft provide email programs along with their higher profile browsing programs.

Netscape Communicator 4.0 includes a module called Netscape Messenger, while Microsoft Internet Explorer 3.0 includes the aptly named Internet Mail. See Chapter 13, *Netscape Messenger and Collabra Discussions*, for an overview of Netscape's mail and Usenet news applications, with a quick reference to the various operations you can perform. Chapter 14, *MSIE Internet Mail*, provides a quick reference and overview for that system.

The current chapter, however, covers the special topic of attaching files to your email messages, using both Netscape Messenger and MSIE's Internet Mail.

Email Addresses

Email addresses commonly take this form:

> *username@hostname*

Here are a number of typical email addresses (well, almost typical):

```
Walter.Cronkite@cbs.com
president@whitehouse.gov
santa@npole.org
einstein@princeton.edu
mencken@aol.com
```

Not all hostnames are this simple, and some usernames are downright unfriendly. If CompuServe provides your email service, you'll get a number instead!

There are also a few smaller networks that require a syntax other than the *name@address* format. If the intended recipient gets mail on one of these networks, you'll have to find out his/her exact address. (Sometimes the person will put this information in their *signature* file, described later in this chapter.) But the address format we've called typical pretty much is.

When you choose a login name for email purposes, you might want to pick a "portable" name, that is, a name that you're likely to be able to use if you move your email account to another hostname. For example, if you have a common first name, there's a good chance someone else is already going to be using that as their email name. If you're a Jane, John, Mary, etc., you might want to consider using your last name, a first initial and last name, or even just initials (popular in the nerd world).

Signature Files

When you receive an email message, you can often find the person's proper email address among the message's header lines. Here's a doctored version of a header from a friend of mine (who is not named either Vicki or Friend):

```
Date: Fri, 30 May 1997 11:37:55 -0400
To: val@oreilly.com
From: "Vicki Friend" <vfriend@nfx.net>
Subject: Norfolk Tides update
```

There may be no Vicki Friend, but if there were, it would be easy to see that her email address is **vfriend@nfx.net**.

Unfortunately, some message headers get garbled en route, as the message is passed among different servers. That's where so-called *signature* files can help. A signature file is a short text file you can append to mail messages (and Usenet news postings) to let people know something about you. Often this information is limited to basic facts like email address, full name, etc. You might include your business name, home or work address, phone and FAX numbers, etc.

Putting your email address in a signature file makes sure people to whom you send messages can reach you back. For business purposes, it's nice to be able to give people some relevant phone numbers and addresses. You might think twice before including personal data like home address and phone number, though.

While signature files were devised for these practical purposes, they've also taken on an element of fun. Many people include quotations and even art drawn using ASCII characters. After all, people are fairly anonymous on the Net, and a signature file provides a canvas (albeit tiny) on which you can express yourself a bit.

However, netiquette dictates that signature files should be kept to a few lines—four or five tops. Long sig files (as they're called) waste time and disk space. They also waste money since many people pay for their connect time.

So, when creating a signature file, use the following guidelines:

- Supply your name and email address.

- Give it a little panache if you want.

- Keep it short and to the point.

The following signature files serve all of these purposes:

```
Jack Nicklaus                          nicklaus@masters.com
"The more I practice, the luckier I get." -Me



\\\\\\\\\\\\\\\\\\\\\\\\\\\\\\\\\\////////////////////////////
Wile E. Coyote, Genius                 coyote@acme.com
                     "That's all folks . . ."
////////////////////////////////////\\\\\\\\\\\\\\\\\\\\\\\\\\\


        /\/\
       ^o  o^   Cat Ballou
       -->T<--   cat@hoosegow.gov
         -       Sioux City, Wyoming  -"Where We Hang 'Em High"
   ___o0O___0Oo___


$$$$$$$$$$$$$$$$$$$$$$$$$$$$$$$$$$$$$$$$$$$$$$$$$$$$$$$$$$$$$$$$$$$$$
H. Ross Poirot                      poirot@orient.express.com
Billionaire Sleuth    Call me when you do somethin' stupid, aw right?
$$$$$$$$$$$$$$$$$$$$$$$$$$$$$$$$$$$$$$$$$$$$$$$$$$$$$$$$$$$$$$$$$$$$$
```

On a Windows system, your signature file can be called anything and stored anywhere, but you'll have to tell your mailer the filename and the directory in which it resides. For Netscape Messenger and MSIE Internet Mail, use the options/preferences dialog. Customization for Netscape Messenger and other Communicator modules is described in Chapter 2, *Netscape Navigator.* See Chapter 14 for more information about customizing MSIE Internet Mail.

In a UNIX environment, the signature file should be called *.signature* and should be kept in the user's home directory. Having a *.signature* file on a UNIX system does not guarantee your mailer will use it, however. Some mailers may require you to specify its use in another *.config* file. Check the documentation for your mail program, or ask your system administrator.

An Email Primer

The ins and outs of sending and getting email are just about second nature to anyone who's used it for a while. If you're new to email, there are a few nuances you should know about.

Sending Messages

Depending on the mail program you use, you may have a few options as to whom you send messages to and how. Generally, you can specify the recipients by entering their email addresses in the proper fields of the message *header.*

Typically, all messages have a "To" field in which you enter the email address(es) of the primary recipient(s); there's no reason this can't be a list of people. For many mailers, you can separate multiple names with a space; some accept commas as well, but check your mailer's documentation.

Next in the header usually comes a "Subject" line, the contents of which are entirely up to you. It's polite to jot down a phrase that will clue recipients in to the message's content. (Note that when you're communicating with a mailing list administration program, you should leave the Subject line blank; see Chapter 11, *Mailing Lists,* for more information.)

Here comes the potentially tricky part: many mailers allow you to send copies of the message. Generally, this *carbon copy* feature (often abreviated cc) is intended to be used to send the message to people who aren't among the primary recipient(s)—but whom you'd like to make aware of its contents. People commonly copy themselves on messages as well, to keep a record of their communications. Some mailers are actually set up to keep copies of all your outgoing messages in a particular folder—or will let you specify that option.

Generally, when you send mail to a group of people, all of their addresses appear in the the header lines of the mail when it's received. So, everybody who gets the mail knows who else got it too. However, some mailers provide an extra copy feature called a *blind carbon copy* (abbreviated bcc). When you send a blind carbon, this information doesn't appear in the message headers sent to the other recipients. They don't know about the person who got the blind copy—and that's the idea. Personally, this option's clandestine nature bugs me. The only time I use it is to send a copy to myself—when I'm too embarrassed to admit that I'd want to keep a copy of such a silly message.

When filling out the address fields of your messages, keep in mind that most of the state-of-the-art mailers also have an *address book* feature. An address book is basically a file in which you can store frequently used email addresses and also abbreviated versions of them (known as *aliases*). Hypothetically, you should be able to fill in the various email addresses in a message header by selecting the addresses from an address book dialog box. If you define aliases in your address book, you can use these in the header, rather than typing the full addresses. Both Netscape Messenger and MSIE Internet Mail provide address book features. (See Chapters 13 and 14 for tips on using them.)

Handling Incoming Messages

Most email programs give you the option of handling your incoming mail in a number of ways. Even the simplest program lets you save messages on your system. Friendlier mailers allow you to create different *folders* or *mailboxes* in which to store both incoming and outgoing messages. You should also be able to save messages to files elsewhere on your system and send messages directly to the printer.

Almost any mailer will also let you forward a message you've received to another address. In Windows-based email programs, typically you would click a Forward button or select a Forward item specifying that you want to forward a message. This generally opens up a subwindow in which the text of the forwarded message appears. Most mailers will somehow signal that a message is being forwarded. Sometimes the header will say so. The text of the forwarded message may also be preceded by a line that identifies it. For example:

```
To: val
Subject: (Fwd) "50 Things" series; good opp'ties here
Content-Type: text/plain; charset=us-ascii
Mime-Version: 1.0
Status: RO

--- Forwarded mail from lamb@oreilly.com (Linda Lamb)

[FORWARDED MESSAGE WOULD APPEAR HERE]
```

Commonly, the text of a forwarded message is indented and preceded by right angle brackets. The source may also be identified, as in the following:

```
Date: Sat, 31 May 1997 11:19:19 -0700
From: joe@surfers.net (Joe Surfer)
To: Multiple recipients of list <baseball-chat@plaidworks.com>
Subject: Re: Pittsburgh Pirates

At 09:21 AM 5/29/97 -0700, Angela Ramirez wrote:
>As a Pirates fan, I have to hope that spirit
>can prevail over spending money in today's sports market.
>
>But it's a long shot.

[Joe's comments follow]
```

(Note that it's not practical—or considerate—to quote an entire long message using angle brackets. Use only key excerpts.)

Once you have a forwarded message in a composition window, you can type in the address, edit the message, etc., before sending.

There are also a couple of standard ways to reply to a message. You can send a return message to:

- The sender of the original message only

- The sender and everyone else who received the original message

There are usually commands or buttons that let you choose one of these reply options. Naturally, however, you can then edit the header lines to send your reply to anyone you like. (You may want to reply to a *partial* list of the original recipients.)

Mail Filtering

One way to make the disposition of your incoming mail easier is to set up *mail filters*. With mail filtering, you tell the mailer what to do with incoming messages that match certain criteria. For instance, you might create a filter that deletes all the messages with the words "you're fired" in the Subject line (only kidding). Or, you can specify that messages from your mother get saved in a particular folder.

(See Chapter 13 to learn how to filter mail with Netscape Messenger. Chapter 14 gives the lowdown on filtering with MSIE Internet Mail.)

Tips for Email Users

If you try telling a friend a funny story in email, you'll quickly appreciate some of the limitations of communicating in type. The most obvious one is that you can't use any vocal inflection to indicate that this part is suspenseful, or this is a surprise, somebody's mad, there are two voices here, this is the silly part, whatever. And you can't indicate any of this by shrugging your shoulders, raising an eyebrow, smiling, or clapping a hand to your forehead either. All of the nonverbal clues we readily employ in other forms of communication are missing.

The result is that miscommunications tend to abound in email. Naturally, it's easier when you know the other person well, but that isn't always the case. Even when you know someone, it's difficult to convey humor, irony, etc. Simple brevity can be mistaken for rudeness, or even anger. (As you might imagine, things are even worse in Usenet news, where the relative anonymity of participants encourages missed meanings and liberates people to be a lot nastier than they would be in person.) Some people think of email as a casual statement that doesn't commit them to anything, while others think it's been typed in stone.

Sounds kind of hopeless, doesn't it? Well, things aren't really all that bad. A simple way you can clarify your meaning in email is to use so-called *smileys* (also known as *emoticons*). A smiley is a little picture created with a few keyboard keys of a smiling face turned on its side. There are actually a huge number of variations on the basic smiley to suggest all kinds of different emotions. Here are a few popular ones:

```
:-)  smile
:-(  frown
;-)  wink
:-|  straight face
:-o  surprise!
```

Smileys are a concrete way of saying "I'm kidding," "I'm sad," or whatever—without coming out and saying it. Certainly a well-placed winking smiley can let someone know you're joking.

Personally, I'm not terribly fond of smileys. They seem hokey and overused. But there are times when even I will resort to a smiley—particularly in news postings—just to make sure my meaning is clear. I generally opt for the subtler two-symbol version:

> :)

Actually, it's not that difficult to write email messages that don't cause misunderstandings or come back to haunt you. But it does take a little effort. Here are some guidelines that should help:

- Be polite in what you say. Address people in an appropriate and respectful manner. Take the time to say please and thank you. Sign your name. Don't take liberties. You know how to be polite.

- Also be a polite email user:

    - Don't nest tons of forwarded messages in a single message. Cut things down to the relevant parts.

    - Don't include long signature files. The convention is to keep it to four or five lines, tops.

    - If you want to be very considerate, keep your messages within fairly narrow margins, so they can be included in other messages more easily.

- Consider your audience. In email to strangers or acquaintances, be sure to spell things out. If you know someone well, naturally you have a lot more latitude.

- Reread your messages to make sure they make sense. (It's a good idea to pay some attention to grammar and spelling, too.)

- Don't write anything you want to keep private. Once it's out there in email, system administrators have access to it, and savvy hacker types can get at it too. Some companies may even monitor employees' email. (Not mine though! ;-)

- Don't write anything you'll regret later. If you're in a snit, cool off for a while before replying.

- Don't fan the "flames" other people start—that is, don't let yourself get dragged into an email brawl.

Handling Spam (Junk Email)

If you're new to the Internet, you may think of spam as something that comes in a can. However, in the context of electronic communications, the term spam is used to refer to any messages that people perceive as valueless and annoying, particularly those sent to a large number of recipients. This includes Usenet news postings without much substance or credibility that are posted to multiple newsgroups. However, more commonly, spam refers to email you get from people or systems unknown, often with the intent of selling you something you don't want. In other words, spam is junk email.

Big deal, you say? I get *real* junk mail at home by the bushel, you say? People's attitudes about spam seem to range from "I just delete it" to "I will track down these evil spammers and hit them with a large rubber mallet!" Why are some people so upset about spam? Well, can you imagine getting supermarket circulars, clothing catalogs, and charity solicitations *with postage due?*

It doesn't cost much to send junk email. A single message can be routed to thousand of recipients in a flash. But there are costs incurred by the systems that route the junk messages (which Net-wide get up into the millions per day!), and also costs incurred by the recipients. If you're an individual who's paying for a Net connection by the hour or minute, you're paying to receive spam.

In addition, an absolutely staggering volume of spam is circulated on a daily basis. This represents a tremendous waste of bandwidth that could, and arguably should, be used for better purposes. Of course, I'm sure my friendly neighborhood mail carrier would rather deliver a few birthday cards than tote sixty pounds of catalogs a day.

Some people are so outraged by the waste that there are rumblings in the U.S. for anti-spam legislation. However, the last time I checked, part of the First Amendment looked suspiciously like "freedom of spam." If the right to disseminate pornography is protected, the right of each and every citizen to spam at will seems pretty safe too. Also, even if an anti-spam law squeaked through the U.S. legislature, the Net is an international phenomenon. A worldwide anti-spam treaty? Seems like we should take care of nuclear and chemical weapons first.

OK, I've finally tipped my hand. When it comes to spam, I'm an "I'll just delete it" kind of person. But if you're someone who's fed up with spam, there are some steps you can take to make your spam encounters less frequent and more tolerable. First let's see what we're up against.

Inside Spam

If you've ever received spam, you undoubtedly know it. From the looks of my mailbox, Sunday would appear to be Spam Day. (But the junk actually arrives on any day ending in "y".)

```
tools@cybercrap.com       Sun Aug 24 18:51   62/2577   Power tools for webmaster
suchamess@nerdworld.com   Sun Aug 24 18:54   68/3293   $ Make Extra Cash $
91245222@nolife.com       Sun Aug 24 18:58  184/7876   FREE CASH GRANTS
25723212@yeahright.net    Sun Aug 24 19:54   57/2956   MAKE MONEY FROM HOME
```

```
junkman@infinitebull.com   Sun Aug 24 23:34    90/3791   FINALLY : A Financial New
Sysop@nightmare.COM        Sun Aug 24 23:44    232/21864 ** Financial Freedom **
```

Each of these messages is an advertisement, which may or may not be for a legitimate product or service; spam is sometimes used to con people out of money. It
may also be used as a soap box, a way to beg for money, whatever. (To be fair,
some people may receive ads, speeches, etc., that they'll be happy to get. One
person's spam is another person's sirloin, you might say—if you were really grasp-
ing for a joke.)

I've changed the names of the senders of these messages to protect the guilty—
actually to keep the guilty from suing us. However, this is probably an unneces-
sary precaution because most of the people sending you spam don't want you to
know exactly who they are.

The companies whose products and services are advertised via spam often con-
tract the actual spamming out to those who do it for a living. These so-called
spammers want you to call the phone number contained in the email ad, or write
away for the product advertised—but they don't want you to reach them by return
email. They don't want you to tell them to leave you alone—even if their messages say you can do that. More about this in the next section.

How do you get on a spammer's list? It's hard to say. If you actively participate in
Usenet newsgroups or mailing lists, you make your email address public. You
might register with an online service that makes your address a matter of public
record, or even sells their subscriber lists. There are also lots of white page directories of email addresses out there. Evidence suggests the spammers have tapped
into the subscriber lists of many of the large Internet Service Providers. As a matter
of fact, if you have an account with one of these, you should consider yourself
spam bait.

The bottom line is that it's hard to take advantage of what's on the Net without
running the risk of your address being used for spam. And you can speculate
about how your address has made the spammers's lists, but you'll probably never
know for sure. You'll only see the spam hit the fan.

Anti-Spam Measures

There are a number of measures you can take to protect yourself from spam.
Some require quite a bit more effort than others. No combination of measures is
foolproof. The only way to make sure you don't get any spam at all is not to have
an email account. But there are way to reduce your spam.

Some spam messages will actually say something like: "If you don't want to be
included in future mailings, return a message to this address, and put the word
REMOVE in the Subject line." The trouble is that, in many cases, the spammers
don't mean it. In fact, if you ask to be removed, they may simply take this as proof
that your email address is active—that someone's actually using it. In other cases,
when you try to reply to a spam message, you'll find that your reply can't be
delivered. The return email address isn't valid. This is no accident.

Many spammers are experts at shielding themselves from people who would complain about receiving the junk email. Often, a spam message will have a bogus

header, so you can't simply send a complaint back. In some cases, the spammer will use a disposable account to send out the spam. If you want to take the trouble to examine the list of systems through which the message was routed, you can complain to the postmasters at those addresses—but this is not a trivial task. (Although I'm fairly spam-tolerant when it comes to my own mailbox, I definitely see the merits of system administrators making their sites more spam-resistant.) The "Stop Spam FAQ" (http://www.mall-net.com/spam/spamfaq.html) goes into great detail about what's involved.

Filter out spam

What simpler measures can you take to avoid spam? Well, the easiest thing you can do is to set up some mail filters. (Both Netscape Messenger, described in Chapter 13, and MSIE Internet Mail, described in Chapter 14, provide fairly simple mechanisms for filtering mail.) For instance, as my sample spam messages from the previous section indicate, I get a lot of spam that makes the wild assumption that I'm interested in new and different ways to make money. While I must admit these particular spammers are onto something—using interest in money as a common denominator for a mass mailing—like Lucy and Ethel, I prefer to come up with my own money-making schemes.

To deal with this kind of spam, I can set up some filters that look for words like "money," "financial," "cash," and even a dollar sign ($), and specify that these messages be deleted. As a more prudent alternative, I might want to have the filter instead save this alleged spam in a special folder. Then I can look through it periodically and make sure no legitimate email messages got filtered out with the spam. This is a little more work, but it saves me from missing messages with "I owe you money" or "Big rai$e for you!" in the Subject. If you choose to put spam aside in this way, you'd want to go through it regularly and purge the real garbage.

If you notice that you're getting multiple spam messages from the same address, you can also set up filters according to the sender of the message. However, no matter what criteria you use to come up with filters, there's some work involved. And there's always the chance of more spam, on new topics, and from new sources.

If you're lucky, you'll find that most of your spam centers around a few subject areas, and you'll be able to filter it effectively. If filtering isn't enough, and you find yourself being circled by vultures at the end of the spam trail, the next steps to consider are changing your email address or getting a second address.

Change address or use two addresses

Like moving to a new house, changing your email address is not without hassle. You'll have to make sure your friends and business associates get your new address. You might consider having the mail that is sent to your old address (which unfortunately may include spam) forwarded to your new address for a transition period. This will give you time to inform the right people about your new address, and make sure you don't miss any mail in the meantime.

Of course, even if you take your first email address out of commission, the more you use your new address, the more likely the spam-mongers will get ahold of it too. If you're on a true anti-spam crusade, you can additionally get and maintain a second email account. Then use one account for your public dealings (e.g., to register for online services, to post to Usenet, etc.) and one for private communications. The account you use in public is the one that's likely to get spammed, while (hopefully) the private account will remain relatively clear.

In the ideal situation, whoever is providing your email service would let you have two addresses and not charge you a thing. However, the odds of this happening aren't very great. If you have an email account through an employer, school, or other organization, they may give you a second email address to help you avoid spam. But if you get email through a pay service, such as an Internet Service Provider, most likely they'll ask you to pay for a second address.

Luckily, there are a number of companies that provide basic email services, many of them for free. Getting an account with one of these services may help you avoid spam—but spam avoidance is actually a side benefit of the primary objective of these services, which is to make people's email portable. If your email address is at some third-party service, your mail can either be forwarded to you wherever you want, or accessed at the service from wherever you are. You can move around all you like, without ever having to tell anyone a new address.

When you sign up for one of these email accounts, you'll have to come up with a login name. The rest of your address will be the domain name of the email company, or one of many different domain names they offer. Thus, you might have an address like *buddy@writeme.com*.

When you're choosing an email service, it's important to find out how mail sent to you at this address will be handled. Some companies do no more than forward the mail to your current address. This is basically useless for spam avoidance, unless you maintain two email addresses *in addition to* the service address.

It's more practical to choose a service that lets you maintain a mailbox on their server. While a number of services will expect you to pay to have a mailbox, there are some companies offering free mailboxes. Here are some of the services that provide both email accounts and mailboxes for free (as of this writing):

MailCity (http://www.mailcity.com/)
> MailCity is a Web-based mail service that lets you access your email from any location using a Web browser. You can also attach files and GIF images directly to MailCity messages, as well as view attachments you receive. MailCity can give you so much for free because they're supported by advertising.

MailExcite (http://www.mailexcite.com/))
> Like most search engines, Excite (described in Chapter 6, *Internet Directories and Search Engines*) is trying to serve all your information needs. MailExcite is their variation on MailCity.

hotmail (http://www.hotmail.com/)

Another Web-based email service. Participate in email from anywhere, using only a browser.

GoPlay (http://www.goplay.com/)

The GoPlay Network offers free services like Web-based email, as well as online personals, greeting cards, and other playful things.

About File Attachments

Most of the "smarter" mail programs, including the Netscape and MSIE mailers, make it relatively easy for you to attach files to messages and receive attached files with your incoming mail. How a file is attached to a mail message depends on its *format*. A number of formats are listed in Chapter 16, *File Types and Extensions*, but there are two broad categories into which all of these formats fall:

* ASCII—plain text

* Binary—compiled data such as graphics, programs, word processor files, etc.

Table 16-1 lists some of the more common file types, organized by the filename suffix(es) generally used to identify them. Check out the ASCII/Binary column to determine the classification of each file type.

When you want to convey an ASCII file along with a mail message (or Usenet news posting), you can actually just paste it into the body of the message. However, it isn't very practical—or polite—to include very large text files (e.g., PostScript) within mail messages. Also, binary files can't pass through regular email channels as is.

Luckily, a facility called MIME (Multimedia Internet Mail Extensions) allows you to convey files as attachments; i.e., they are transferred along with mail messages, but separately. Both the MSIE and Netscape mail programs support MIME.

When you attach a file that's in a binary format, MIME *encodes* it before sending. (While a binary file can't simply be mailed like text, a MIME-encoded file can be.) Then, presuming the recipient's mailer supports MIME, the file will be *decoded* on the other side—that is, converted back to its original (usable) format. You're not limited to attaching binary files in this manner. It's also appropriate to attach large text files—so that the entire text doesn't appear in the body of a single message.

Since UNIX systems traditionally have had their own character-based mail programs, UNIX has its own encoding and decoding utilities. The most popular of these are *uuencode* and *uudecode*. If you're using one of the older mailers, like *mailx*, before you mail a binary file, you *uuencode* it—to convert it to ASCII text. Then the recipient has to use *uudecode* to convert the file back to its original binary format. Obviously, this puts the burden of preserving the file on the sender and recipient. If the recipient works in a Windows environment, *uuencode* has been until recently a less practical encoding method. However, the latest version of the WinZip file compression/archiving program does handle uuencoded files.

If a file you want to attach (whether binary or ASCII) is very large, before you attach it, you should also *compress* it. There are a number of tools that compress files, some of which are discussed in Chapter 19, *File Compression and Archiving*. You may also receive files in compressed format. Chapter 19 also describes how to uncompress files using some of the popular utilities.

File Attachments Made Simple

The best strategy for dealing with file attachments is to use a smart, friendly, MIME-compatible mailer like Netscape Messenger or MSIE Internet Mail. Both of these programs make it very simple to attach files and even easier to receive them.

You should also try to find out what kinds of attachments the recipient can handle at the other end. Work out the best way to convey the file between you.

Attaching and receiving files with MSIE Internet Mail

When you tell Internet Mail you want to send a New Message (see Chapter 14), you'll get a composition window labeled New Message Dialog. If you want to write a message, do so as usual in the composition area.

The dialog's **Insert** menu includes two items that let you include files with your mail message:

- **Text File** specifies that the file should be included as part of the message proper. This is only advisable for text files that aren't very long.

- **Attachment** tells the mailer to send the file separately and to use the appropriate MIME encoding to make sure it gets transferred without being garbled.

Before you attach the file, you need to know whether the file is in a binary or ASCII format. If you're not sure, check Table 16-1. Then, to attach the file, select the appropriate menu option. Unless the file is a fairly short text file, you're going to select **Attachment**.

Regardless of whether you select **Text File** or **Attachment**, a dialog is displayed to let you specify the name of the file. A breeze.

There are even easier ways. If you want a text file to be transferred in the body of a message, you can paste it in. If you want a file to accompany a message as an attachment proper, you can actually drag the icon for the file into the composition area of the window.

Whenever you specify a file attachment—using either the **Attachment** menu or by dragging it in—the icon representing the file will appear in the lower pane of the message window, as in Figure 10-1.

Now what? Well, if the file is a text file, you're done. You can send the message. However, for binary files, you have to tell Internet Mail to use MIME or *uuencode* to encode the file for transfer.

The **Format** menu on the message window has a **Settings . . .** item. If you select that, you'll open a dialog in which you can specify the type of encoding:

- MIME
  - None (i.e., no encoding)
  - Quoted Printable
  - Base 64
- uuencode

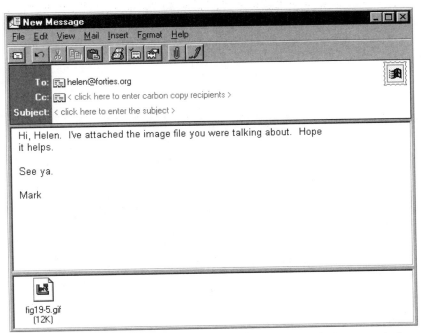

Figure 10-1: Attached file appears in lower pane of outgoing message window

Quoted Printable and Base 64 are two common MIME encoding schemes. In terms of picking an encoding method, the only thing you need to care about is whether the person on the other end will be able to handle attachments in that format. Select *uuencode* to send the message to someone on a UNIX system who you know wants that type of encoding. If you go with MIME, base 64 may be a slightly more common format that more people will be able to handle.

Once you specify an encoding method, you can send the message. The attachment will be conveyed with it. The recipient's mail program may automatically decode the file, or they may have to employ a utility for that purpose.

You'll be grateful to be using Internet Mail when you're on the receiving end of an attached file. If the file was sent using either type of MIME encoding or uuencoding, Internet Mail should convert the file back to its original format for you when it arrives.

When a message with an attachment arrives, a small paperclip symbol appears to the left of its entry in the Internet Mail list pane. When you view the message, the paperclip symbol will also appear in the upper-right corner of the viewing pane.

If you click on the paperclip, a small text box is displayed containing the name and size of the file. Click on the text box to access the file. You'll get a dialog asking whether you want to open the file or save it to disk.

If you know what the file is and you have the software to handle it, you might want to open it on the spot. Or, you can save it and figure out how to handle it later. If the file made it with its filename extension intact, you should be able to figure out what it is and what kind of program you'll need to read/view/play it. (See Chapter 16 for more information.)

If the file's a mystery, you may find a clue at the top of the file itself. Or, you may have to contact the sender.

Attaching and receiving files with Netscape Messenger

Netscape Messenger also makes handling file attachments very simple. When you tell Netscape Messenger you want to send a New Message (see Chapter 13), you'll get a Message Composition window, as displayed in Figure 10–2.

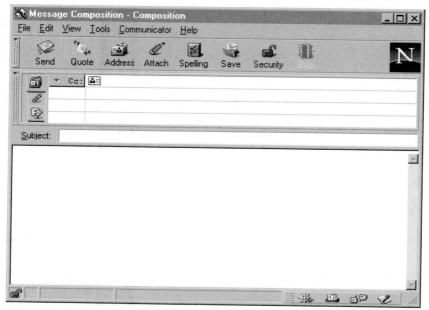

Figure 10–2: Message Composition window (Messenger)

If you want to write a message, do so as usual in the composition area. The **Attach** button on the window's Message toolbar reveals a menu with two items that let you include files with your mail message:

- **File**... opens a dialog in which you can specify any local file to be attached to the current message.

- **Web Page**... opens a dialog in which you can enter a URL, specifically to attach a Web page.

In the former case, when you specify a file in the dialog, the name of the file appears in the composition window, in the so-called *addressing area*. (See Chapter 13.) The addressing area has three overlapping tabs; the middle one, with the red paperclip symbol, is where attached files get listed. Once you name a file in the dialog, an icon and its name appear on this attachments tab. If you don't want to bother with menus and such, you can actually drag a file icon onto this area, and it will be treated as an attachment. Note that the tab has to be on top for this to work; click on the paperclip to raise the attachments tab to the front of the addressing area.

The default encoding for attachments is MIME. If you're sending a binary file, and you think the recipient can handle a MIME attachment, you're all ready to send the file.

However, the third tab in the addressing area reveals some message-sending options. Among the options is the following:

```
Uuencode instead of MIME for attachments
```

Check the box in front of this option to specify that attached files be encoded with *uuencode* instead of MIME. Once you're satisfied with the encoding method, you can send the message. The attachment will be conveyed with it. The recipient's mail program may automatically decode the file, or they may have to employ a utility for that purpose.

The **Web Page**... item on the **Attach** button's menu lets you do something pretty cool—actually mail a Web page. All you have to do is supply the URL in the resulting dialog. Depending on what mailer the recipient is using, she may have to save the HTML document and then try to view it. But if the recipient is using Netscape Messenger, the Web page will actually appear in the message viewing window!

Which brings us to the topic of receiving file attachments. Netscape Messenger makes this very easy. If the file was sent using MIME encoding or uuencoding, Netscape Messenger should convert the file back to its original format for you when it arrives.

When you receive attached files Messenger is equipped to display (such as text files and HTML documents), the mailer will automatically show them in the message body. You don't have to do a thing in order to access them.

When you view a message to which one or more files are attached, the body of the message will have a paperclip symbol in the upper-right corner. If you click on this symbol, the viewing window will be divided horizontally into two panes. The lower pane will display icons corresponding to the attached files.

You can access a file by clicking on its icon. You'll get a dialog asking whether you want to open the file or save it to disk.

If you know what the file is, and you have the software to handle it, you might want to open it on the spot. Or you can save it and figure out how to handle it later. If the file made it with its filename extension intact, you should be able to figure out what it is, and what kind of program you'll need to read/view/play it.

If the file's a mystery, you may find a clue at the top of the file itself. Or you may have to contact the sender.

CHAPTER 11

Mailing Lists

While much of the group discussion on the Net takes place by way of Usenet newsgroups, there are email-only forums as well. *Publically accessible mailing lists* allow people with common interests to receive and share information via electronic mail. While some mailing lists exist simply to disseminate information on a particular topic, most lists allow people to conduct a group discussion about the subject in question.

The way a mailing list works is that you first *subscribe* to it by sending a fairly simple email message to an address set up for list administration. This may be the address of a program (if the list is automated) or a person (if it's not). Some mailing lists are actually getting their own Web sites; thus, you might be able to subscribe by filling out a form at the list's Web site. Once you're subscribed, you participate in the discussion by sending messages to a second address, set up to forward mail to the entire group. You'll also receive email messages from other list participants via this address.

Note that while many lists require you to subscribe before sending mail to the group, some will distribute messages from nonsubscribers. Also, some lists require you to have certain professional credentials or affiliations in order to subscribe, although these are in the minority. The source you use to find out about the mailing list (some of which are covered later in this chapter) will include details like this.

For each mailing list there is generally an *owner* (sometimes more than one) who is responsible for managing the list. This owner may also *moderate* the discussion, as is done in certain Usenet newsgroups. A moderator reviews messages sent to the list and may choose to exclude messages that seem to be outside the focus of the mailing list. If the number of subscribers to a mailing list gets so large that disseminating the discussion by email becomes impractical, the subscribers may try to launch a Usenet newsgroup instead.

There are a few commonly used list management programs. The ways you manage your subscription may vary slightly, depending on the administration program.

However, there are also many similarities among programs. Whether a mailing list is managed by a program or a person, subscribing and participating tends to be very simple. As a matter of fact, with more than 7500 available mailing lists (and counting), the hardest part may be finding the lists that suit your interests.

This chapter introduces some lists (to give you an idea of the wide range of offerings) and provides guidelines for finding a list that interests you. It also covers the basics of getting on and participating in a mailing list (both automated and not). Finally, the chapter gives the syntax of some of the more advanced commands recognized by various mailing list administration programs. You can mail these commands to a list's administration address to affect your subscription and request various services.

From Aardvark Lovers to ZZ Top Fans

Mailing lists are like Usenet newsgroups in more than one respect: not only do they provide a way for discussions to take place online, the subject matter for these discussions run the widest possible gamut. With thousands of mailing lists, including the ridiculous, the absolutely serious, and everything in between, the current chapter can't possibly cover it all. However, just to give you an idea, this section introduces a number of mailing lists. This seemingly random list has actually been chosen deliberately—to illustrate the randomness of what's out there.

Please be aware that, although the juxtaposition of some ultra-serious with some silly groups may imply disrespect to the former, there is no such intention. We just want to give people an idea of the range of available mailing lists.

The list is excerpted and adapted from the comprehensive list of publically accessible mailing lists, copyright by Stephanie de Silva. Consult the PAML document for additional info about any of these lists. (The next section explains how you can access the complete list.)

AfricaW

An unmoderated forum to support the struggle of African women for social progress in Africa and in the world at large and to discuss matters of mutual concern. The term "African women" shall include women of the African diaspora, and the list aims to promote their solidarity with the women of Africa.

ALZHEIMER

For caregivers, clinicians, researchers, students, or anyone interested in learning more about Alzheimer disease and related disorders.

Austrian People's Party

The Austrian People's Party is offering its press releases (in German) via a mailing list. In German.

California Kayak Friends (CKF)

For the California Kayak Friends, kayakers in Southern California and Nevada.

Mayberry

For discussion of TV shows featuring Andy Griffith, including *The Andy Griffith Show* and *Mayberry RFD*.

MISSINGKIDS

Discussion forum for information, programs, services, research, and general networking for those people interested in, involved with, or affected by, the issue of missing children, child abduction, kidnapping, and runaway children. (This is not a place to list missing children. It is a place to locate individuals, agencies, and programs, to assist and guide you in this task.)

NAAAP-Chicago

To inform subscribers about the many joint projects with Asian American community service groups, professional organizations, and university student groups events sponsored by NAAAP-Chicago.

NYC Sushi Dining Group

Planning for monthly group dinners at top NYC area sushi restaurants.

Radiodrama

Discussion of all aspects of modern radio drama.

Roach-L (aka The Raunchy Roach Show)

This mailing list distributes the comic strip of the same name (by Hollywood cartoonist Butch Berry) in the form of GIF files (sent as MIME attachments). The main character is a Roach with his own televsion show.

Spider-Man

Discussion of Spider-Man, his allies, enemies, family, etc.

Steely Dan (aka Walter Becker & Donald Fagen)

In-depth discussion of the work of Walter Becker, Donald Fagen, and other musical artists associated with Steely Dan.

Stephen King

Discussion of Stephen King and his books.

THUMPER

Single-cylinder motorcycle owner's mailing list.

tiger-list

Discussion about Tiger Woods, the professional golfer.

trektrade

Where Star Trek memoribilia collectors meet.

UK-RADIO

Discussion about broadcast radio in the U.K.: BBC National and Local Radio, Independent National Radio, ILR, satellite, and the pirates.

Unicycling

Discussion of all aspects of unicycling: learning to ride, learning new skills, where to buy a unicycle, where you can ride with others. There is also a bidirectional gateway between the Unicycling Mailing List and the Usenet newsgroup *rec.sports.unicycling*.

Email and News

unix-peripherals

Discussion of new technology and changing regulations regarding UNIX peripherals with specific emphasis on terminals, printers, networking, data communications, and bar code equipment.

Vampire-L

Dedicated to the White Wolf Role-Playing game, "Vampire." Those who may be interested in the subject but are not familiar with the game itself are also invited to join.

veggie-list

Discussion of issues pertaining to vegetables and other edible plants. Common topics: vegetable garden design, propagation, cool season and warm season corps, natural and chemical fertilizers, when to plant seeds, container gardening, vegetable storage and canning, soil preparation, water techniques, and pest and plant diseases.

vintage

Discussion of vintage clothing and costume jewelry of all eras. How to find such clothing and jewelry, where to buy it, how to judge its quality, how much to pay for it, how to wear it, etc.

The Weird Science Society Mailing List

An open, public forum for the Weird Science Society, an organization devoted to promoting amateur scientific research and experimentation, especially in areas of unusual, or unconventional sciences and technologies.

White House

Discussion of the German band Bobo In White Wooden Houses.

WLREHAB (Wildlife Rehabilitation Mailing List)

To serve the needs of wildlife rehabilitators and those interested in wildlife. Open to discussion of all areas of wildlife rehabilitation (i.e., the care of injured and orphaned wildlife with the ultimate goal of releasing healthy animals back into the wild). The list subscribers also run an animal placement service and a newsletter exchange list.

WOODS (WOOD, WOODY)

Discussion of issues of importance to these families or surname studies, including genealogy.

Finding the Right List

With more than 7500 mailing lists (and counting), pinpointing the list or lists you want might easily be a nightmare. There is a comprehensive list of all the groups, called the PAML (for Publically Accessible Mailing Lists). It's maintained by Stephanie da Silva, who has copyrighted it but has generously agreed to let us use excerpts for illustration purposes.

The complete PAML is available at the FTP site *rtfm.mit.edu.* (More about this shortly.) However, as you might imagine, this is one massive document. Currently, it's broken up into 20 (!) sizeable files. Luckily, a company called NeoSoft (with the support of ListServe.com) has put a searchable version of the PAML on the Web at:

```
http://www.NeoSoft.com/internet/paml/
```

Click on the **Search** link at the bottom of the page to access a search engine for the list. There's also an **Index** link, which lets you choose between an index organized by mailing list name and an index organized by subject.

I went straight for the Search page and hunted up several mailing lists that discuss various aspects of baseball: a general list, team-specific lists, one about minor league baseball, baseball history, etc. I could also have gone to the subject index and clicked on the **baseball** link. When you get down to a single list that interests you, the PAML provides general information about the list, which should include something about how to subscribe.

If you prefer, you can also retrieve the PAML from the FTP site **rtfm.mit.edu**. If you log in via anonymous FTP (see Chapter 17, *FTP and File Transfer*), you can find the parts of the PAML in either of the following directories:

```
/pub/usenet/news.answers/mail/mailing-lists
/pub/usenet-by-group/news.lists.misc/
```

The first directory has an advantage: the files are named *part01* through *part20*. In the second directory, the files have names like this:

```
Publicly_Accessible_Mailing_Lists,_Part_01_20
```

(Although FTP lets you rename files en route, it's simpler just to retrieve the bunch of short filenames using FTP's **mget** command, as follows.) Once you're logged in to *rtfm.mit.edu* via anonymous FTP, the following commands will retrieve all the files:

```
ftp> cd /pub/usenet/news.answers/mail/mailing-lists
ftp> prompt
Turn off interactive prompting.
ftp> mget part*
```

See Chapter 17 for more information.

Keep in mind that the list is huge! If you don't want the whole thing, be aware that the mailing lists are in alphabetical order. So, if you want the ZZ Top mailing list, it's a good bet that the information will be in *part20*.

Mailing List Basics

There are three important things to know in order to participate in a mailing list:

- How to subscribe

- How to send messages to and receive messages from the list

- How to get off the list

Subscribing to a Mailing List

Whatever source you consult to find out about mailing lists there will be some basic information about the list, usually including how to subscribe. This information is important. Although there are some fairly common ways to deal with mailing lists of different kinds, there are also a number of exceptions. So, the first guideline is to depend on whatever information the list owners are distributing about their list.

If the basic information you find about a list doesn't include instructions on subscribing, it will include an email address you can write to for information. Generally, the word "help" in the body of the message is sufficient to get you a substantial reply with all of the instructions you'll need.

With just about everything in the world moving onto the Web, it's no surprise that a lot of mailing lists are getting their own Web page. Whether a list has a Web page is the kind of information you can get from the list of Publically Accessible Mailing Lists, described earlier in this chapter. If a mailing list is on the Web, there's a good chance that you can actually subscribe from there by filling in a form. However, for lists that don't support this kind of interface or for those who prefer to work entirely through email, the current section explains what you'll need to know.

Many of the publically available mailing lists are managed by programs, which are referred to generically as *list servers* or *listservs*. The generic name *listserv* is actually taken from the specific name of one of the more popular programs. Among the other popular programs are *listproc* and *majordomo*. A listserv program responds to a discrete set of commands that you send to the list's admin mailing address. You use these commands to affect your subscription. Though you'll often be sending a single command to a list's admin address, keep in mind that you can send multiple commands in one message when necessary. (There are a couple of such cases in the next section.)

With automated lists, generally the email address from which you send your subscription request is the address to which the messages from the mailing list will be sent. It's also the only address from which the list will accept your mail. (Lists run by the *majordomo* program are an exception—rather than relying on the header of your message to get your email address, *majordomo* lets you specify an address *within* your subscription request.)

While programs run a large percentage of mailing lists, some lists are actually run by people. Some of these lists may still require you to follow a certain format in wording administrative requests. However, for many a courteous note will do. Check out the list of Publically Available Mailing Lists for the particular guidelines for any mailing list.

Regardless of who or what is managing a mailing list, there are generally two relevant addresses:

- The address of the listserv program or administrator for the particular list; you use this address to email requests regarding your subscription (e.g., subscribe, unsubscribe, suspend subscription for a period of time, send help info, etc.).

- The address of the mailing list itself; email sent to this address is forwarded on to all subscribers.

A brief caution: *Don't send administrative mail to the address for the list itself.* In other words, if you want to do some business, like unsubscribing from the list, make sure you send mail to the admin address. It's a common error to send such requests to the mailing list address—then they get passed on to all the participants. This really seems to bug a lot of people.

When a person is running a mailing list, the admin address might be just about anything, but in many cases it takes this form:

```
listname-request@hostname
```

For example:

```
fun-talk-request@greattime.org
```

When a listserv program is running the list, the administrative email address takes the form

```
listserv_program@hostname
```

where *listserv_program* is the admin software (e.g., *listserv, listproc, majordomo*), and *hostname* is the computer from which the list is run. Here are some typical mailing list admin addresses:

```
listserv@acme.com
listproc@cornell.edu
majordomo@aspca.org
```

To subscribe to a mailing list, you need to send the request to the admin email address.

For lists that are run by people, for subscription guidelines consult any information you have about the list. Some lists, like the Gulf Area Sea Paddlers (or GASP!) still ask you to follow a certain syntax. To subscribe to this list for sea kayakers in the Gulf of Mexico and the Caribbean, you'd send a message to the address *gasp-request@lists.intelenet.net* and put the word *subscribe* in the body of the message.

However, you can subscribe to many of the lists run by people just by sendng a polite note like this one:

```
From: val@oreilly.com
To: fun-talk-request@greattime.org
Subject: Please subscribe me to fun-talk
Hi. Would you please add my name to the fun-talk mailing
list?

Thanks!

Val Q.
```

For lists that are run by programs, commands (such as subscription requests) need to follow a syntax specific to the program. As a general rule, you should place commands in the body of the message and leave the subject line blank. (Some listserv programs will choke on a subject line.)

To subscribe to a mailing list run by *listserv* or *listproc*, send a message with the body text:

```
SUBSCRIBE [listname] your_first_name your_last_name
```

Since some servers will run more than one list on a particular host, it's a good idea to name the list in your subscription request. A mailing list called *cintired* (about the Cincinnati Reds) is run by *listserv*. The following message requests a subscription for their longtime manager, Sparky Anderson:

```
From: sparky@world.std.com
To: listserv@miamiu.acs.muohio.edu
Subject: [leave it blank]
subscribe cintired Sparky Anderson
```

For *listproc*, the command to subscribe is the same. Here's the request I sent to get myself on the *baseball-chat* mailing list:

```
From: val@oreilly.com
To: listproc@plaidworks.com
Subject:
subscribe baseball-chat Val Quercia
```

For lists run by *majordomo*, you don't have to include your name, but you may optionally include the email address at which you want to receive list mail. The following message requests a subscription to the list *spider-man* (discussion of the superhero):

```
From: val@oreilly.com
To: majordomo@icc.nwark.com
Subject:
subscribe spider-man val@oreilly.com
```

When you request a subscription (or actually issue any request to the admin address), you should receive a confirmation message back. The initial message you receive upon subscribing generally includes all you'll need to know to manage your subscription and participate in the discussion, often including guidelines for what's appropriate. *Save this message* for future reference.

Sending and Receiving List Mail

Every mailing list has an address that serves in effect as the list's mailbox. When you send a message to this address, the message is forwarded to the entire list of subscribers. The address generally takes this form:

```
listname@hostname
```

Thus, to send mail to the *baseball-chat* list, I address it to:

```
baseball-chat@plaidworks.com
```

If you think that's easy, receiving mail from the list is even easier. Your mailbox simply fills up with it. Therein lies a potential problem. Some of these lists get an incredible amount of traffic.

If your mailbox runneth over with mailing list messages, check the initial message you got from the list to see if they offer a *digest* option. Some lists will save up messages and send you a bunch, concatenated into a single message that is commonly known as a *digest*. Some digests are compiled weekly and some daily, depending on the nature and amount of information involved.

If your list offers a digest form, you can send a message to the admin address requesting to receive your mail that way. For *listserv*, mail the following line to the admin address to turn on the digest option:

```
SET [listname] DIGEST
```

Turn off the digest option like this:

```
SET [listname] NODIGEST
```

For *listproc*, you can receive your mail in digest form by sending the message,

```
SET [listname] MAIL DIGEST
```

and turn off digest form by sending the message:

```
SET [listname] MAIL ACK
```

The *majordomo* program treats the digest form and the regular form of a mailing list as separate lists. So, in addition to subscribing to the digest form, you also need to unsubscribe to the regular list:

```
To: majordomo@thathost.com
Subject:

subscribe myfavelist-digest
unsubscribe myfavelist
```

If you decide you want to go back to the non-digest form, you'd again have to send two requests:

```
To: majordomo@thathost.com
Subject:

unsubscribe myfavelist-digest
subscribe myfavelist
```

Getting Off a Mailing List

If you decide you no longer want to be included on a mailing list, it's simple to get your name off. For person-run lists, check the documentation on the list. Some may require a message with the body "unsubscribe." But many will happily remove your name if you simply write "Please take me off the list. Thanks a lot."

For automated lists, the command to keep in mind is also "unsubscribe." For *listserv* and *listproc* send a message to the list's admin address, and put the following in the body of the message:

```
unsubscribe [listname]
```

The same line should work for *majordomo*, unless you subscribed under a different email address.

In that case, you'll need to tell the program that address:

```
unsubscribe [listname] [email_address]
```

listserv alternately accepts:

```
signoff [listname]
```

Every time you make a change to your mailing list subscription, you should get an acknowledgment by email. Thus, when you unsubscribe, you should get a message confirming you're off the list.

Quick Reference to Common Mailing List Commands

The various listserv programs recognize a number of commands you can mail to the list's administrative address to affect your subscription and request various services. Depending on the listserv's capabilities, you may be able to suspend the mail you receive from the list, obtain a list of other subscribers, etc.

This section covers some of the more useful commands for the mail admin programs *listserv, listproc,* and *majordomo.* For the sake of completeness, we've thrown in the commands to subscribe, unsubscribe, and receive the list in digest form, covered earlier in this chapter. Table 11–1 provides the listserv commands; Table 11–2 lists the listproc commands; Table 11–3 displays the majordomo commands.

Table 11–1: listserv Commands

Function	Command Syntax
Subscribe	SUBSCRIBE [*listname*] *firstname lastname*
Unsubscribe	UNSUBSCRIBE [*listname*] or SIGNOFF [*listname*]
Request digest form (when available)	SET [*listname*] DIGEST
Cancel digest form	SET [*listname*] NODIGEST
Temporarily suspend mail from list	SET [*listname*] NOMAIL
Restart suspended mail	SET [*listname*] MAIL
Get a list of other lists managed by the same server	LISTS

Table 11–1: listserv Commands (continued)

Function	Command Syntax
Get a list of all *listserv* lists	LISTS GLOBAL
Get a list of all *listserv* lists that include the specified string	LISTS GLOBAL */string*
Get a list of subscribers	REVIEW [*listname*] F=MAIL
Get a list of subscribers, sorted by name	REVIEW [*listname*] BY NAME F=MAIL
Get a list of subscribers, sorted by country	REVIEW [*listname*] BY COUNTRY F=MAIL
Get a list of archive files (if any) for the list	INDEX [*listname*]
Retrieve an archive file	GET *filename* [*filetype*] [*listname*] F=MAIL

Table 11–2: listproc Commands

Function	Command Syntax
Subscribe	SUBSCRIBE [*listname*] *firstname lastname*
Unsubscribe	UNSUBSCRIBE [*listname*]
Request digest form (when available)	SET [*listname*] DIGEST
Cancel digest form	SET [*listname*] NODIGEST
Temporarily suspend mail from list	SET [*listname*] MAIL POSTPONE
Restart suspended mail	SET [*listname*] MAIL ACK SET [*listname*] MAIL DIGEST
Get a list of other lists managed by the same server	LISTS
Get a list of subscribers	RECIPIENTS [*listname*]

Table 11–2: listproc Commands (continued)

Function	Command Syntax
Get a list of archive files (if any) for the list	INDEX [*listname*]
Retrieve an archive file	GET [*listname*] *filename*

Table 11–3: majordomo Commands

Function	Command Syntax
Subscribe	SUBSCRIBE [*listname*] [*email_address*]
Unsubscribe	UNSUBSCRIBE [*listname*] [*email_address*]
Request digest form (when available)	SUBSCRIBE *listname*-DIGEST UNSUBSCRIBE [*listname*] (Need both commands)
Cancel digest form	UNSUBSCRIBE *listname*-DIGEST SUBSCRIBE [*listname*] (Need both commands)
Temporarily suspend mail from list	N/A
Get a list of other lists managed by the same server	LISTS
Get a list of subscribers	WHO [*listname*]
Get a list of archive files (if any) for the list	INDEX [*listname*]
Retrieve an archive file	GET [*listname*] *filename*

CHAPTER 12

Getting Along in Usenet

Usenet is not a network in the sense that the Internet is. It's actually a part of the traffic that occurs over the Internet. Usenet is like a worldwide conversation, or more accurately, thousands of conversations, that take place among users online. Usenet communications happen in the context of groups of users interested in the same subject. There are literally thousands of these "newsgroups" accessible via the Internet. Newsgroup communications are also carried over other networks and channels, including UUCP (UNIX to UNIX Copy).

You participate in a newsgroup by sending (or "posting") "articles" or "messages," and by reading other people's postings. These postings happen sequentially—like on an electronic bulletin board—not all at once, as in a real conversation. (The online equivalent of an actual conversation happens in "chat" groups. Part Eight discusses Internet Relay Chat, the mainstay of chat networks.) When a series of postings ensue from an initial one, the particular sequence is known as a message *thread*.

There are newsgroups for people interested in various types of hardware and software, branches of science, sports, the arts, travel, health, whatever. Each newsgroup is named to identify the subject area of its discussion, using a somewhat unfriendly hierarchical naming scheme. The section "Newsgroup Naming Scheme," later in this chapter, explains the naming conventions as well as some of the more common classifications.

You are not limited to the number of newsgroups you read or contribute to—except by your schedule. However, keep in mind that most news servers limit the size of the "newsfeed" they provide (i.e., make only certain groups available, or expire articles quickly). The sheer (and ever-growing) number of groups necessitates this. However, highly trafficked groups—those with a lot of postings—will generally be available.

Some newsgroups have one or more "moderators" who judge whether postings are appropriate to the group. Moderators can exclude postings at their discretion. They may also maintain one or more files of frequently asked questions, though

177

these so-called FAQs (pronounced "F-A-Qs" or "fax") may also be maintained by other interested group participants.

In unmoderated newsgroups, anything goes—at least in theory. However, as in any social context, if you act rudely or inappropriately, you may be called on it.

Naturally, you don't have to be out of line to get into a Usenet conflict. Misunderstandings and simple disagreements can—and do—flare up all the time. In fact, the difficulties you might experience in communicating by email—the inexpressiveness of words without vocal or facial expression—may be ten times more severe with news. Why? Well, partly because it's a free-for-all. Anyone can respond to anyone else. Also because of the sheer number of participants. And because most of these people don't know each other (at least initially) from a hole in the wall.

A disagreement that escalates into the Usenet equivalent of a brawl is generally called a *flame war*. The nasty messages that comprise it are called *flames*. When you send one, you're *flaming* the recipient. You get the idea.

To complicate matters even further, the facelessness of news seems to breed tactlessness and rudeness, even from people who may be quite agreeable in person. There's a "netiquette" to news participation, and some knowledge of it should minimize difficulties you may have. The section "Tips for Usenet Participants," later in this chapter, provides some basic guidelines and help in seeking additional information.

For the most part, netiquette isn't much more than common courtesy. But in addition to being polite in your communications, avoid computer-related rudeness, such as including long signature files (that cost money to download) and posting binary files to groups other than *alt.binary* and its subgroups. It's appropriate to read a group for a while to understand the tenor and scope of the conversations— some groups welcome novices, other groups can be downright hostile. Reading the FAQ always helps; most groups post the FAQ from time to time, but you can also post a message asking where you can get a copy. There are also Web and FTP sites at which many FAQs are available. (See Chapter 5, *Landmark Sites and Other Resources*, for more information.)

Newsgroup Naming Scheme

Usenet uses a hierarchical naming scheme, not unlike that used for Internet domain names (See Chapter 4, *Internet Addressing*.) Newsgroups have a name composed of at least two parts, divided by periods (or "dots"); the first part generally classifies the group's interest by type, geographic location, etc. For instance, groups beginning with the syllable *rec* deal with subjects that are generally considered recreational; groups beginning with *comp* discuss computer-related topics; the *alt* hierarchy encompasses a wide range of "alternative" newsgroups (outside of Usenet proper).

There are also prefixes to distinguish groups geared toward a particular city, region, or country. For example, *boulder* introduces groups focusing on the Colorado city, *ba* refers to the San Francisco Bay area, *ne* is New England, *de* refers to groups originating in Germany, etc.

Some schools and colleges have their own newsgroups. Look for first syllables like *harvard*, *mit*, (Massachusetts Institute of Technology), *uwash* (University of Washington), *mcgill* (McGill University), *tamu* (Texas A&M University), and *ucsc* (University of California, Santa Cruz).

There are also more proprietary prefixes, like *ora* for O'Reilly & Associates, my employer and the publisher of this book. Bitstream, Inc., has its own (*bit*) as well.

The first part of each newsgroup name lets you quickly classify it under a general subject area. Additional name components more clearly define the newsgroup.

In some cases, the second name component represents a subcategory of the first component. For instance, under *misc* is a category called *invest*. Then under *invest* are a number of groups concerned with various dimensions of investment. *misc.invest.canada* is a group for people who might be interested in making investments in Canada, while *misc.invest.funds* provides general information about possible investment funds. Both groups fall under the top-level category *misc* and the second-level category *invest*.

Keep in mind that group names can get very long. Group organizers try to make the names as specific as possible. Thus, there are newsgroup names with as many as four or more components. For example, the group *rec.collecting.sport.baseball*) deals with collecting baseball memorabilia, which as a hobby has been classified under the recreational part of the Usenet tree.

Following are descriptions of some of the most common top-level newsgroup hierarchies and the types of groups you're likely to find in them.

Business-related topics | biz

This part of the Usenet tree includes groups interested in business in general, company-specific groups, and groups relating to employment. Groups that begin with *biz* allow advertising within the group, while the rest of Usenet frowns on it.

Typical Groups: *biz.dec*, *biz.jobs*, *biz.jobs.offered*, *biz.marketplace*, *biz.oreilly*, *biz.sco*.

Computer- and engineering-related topics | comp

There are hundreds of groups under the *comp* hierarchy. Among the subhierarchies are: *ai* (artificial intelligence); *databases*; *infosystems*; *lang* (programming languages); *mail* (email applications); *os* (operating systems); *protocols*; *society* (social reprecussions of computers); *sys* (hundreds of groups covering most computer systems); etc.

Typical Groups: *comp.ai.games*, *comp.lang.c++*, *comp.lang.java*, *comp.laptops*, *comp.forsale.computers*, *comp.os.ms-windows*.

---

misc	*Miscellaneous groups*
	This part of the hierarchy is an umbrella for whatever groups don't really fit anywhere else. While some of these groups cover topics that are unique in news (e.g., *misc.kids*), some merely offer a different slant on subjects dealt with in other parts of the news hierarchy. For example, while the *comp* branch of news includes *comp.forsale.computers*, *misc* offers *misc.forsale.computers*.
news	*Topics relating to Usenet and the newsgroups*
	While many of these groups simply distribute facts and statistics about news, this is the home of the important group *news.newusers.questions*, which helps new Usenet participants get oriented. The group *news.software* discusses news-reading programs.
rec	*Recreational interests and hobbies*
	Among the larger subhierarchies are *rec.sport*, *rec.music*, and *rec.arts*. Beyond these parts of the tree are groups dealing with a wide variety of hobbies and interests, from bicycles to woodworking, travel, boats, pets, bird watching, and even beer.
	Typical Groups: *rec.arts.movies*, *rec.arts.startrek.**, *rec.sport.basketball*, *rec.pets.cats*, *rec.humor*.
sci	*Topics relating to science*
	Not for the faint of heart when it comes to nerdly matters, the groups in the *sci* branch range from weird science to science in education to the most arcane technical pursuits.
	Typical Groups: *sci.astro*, *sci.math*, *sci.chem*, *sci.materials*, *sci.fractals*, *sci.cryonics*, *sci.edu*.
soc	*Topics relating to society, social life, etc.*
	This is a fairly diverse hierarchy, encompassing groups focused on social issues and society, cultures the world, and just plain socializing. The huge *soc.culture* subhierarchy has 133 branches and counting.
	Typical Groups: *soc.feminism*, *soc.culture.african-american*, *soc.adoption*, *soc.culture.mexican*, *soc.veterans*, *soc.politics*, *soc.personals*.

Chat-type groups	*talk*

A free exchange of ideas is the general spirit of the *talk* hierarchy. (Flames abound here.) *talk.politics* has a number of branches.

Typical Groups: *talk.environment, talk.christianity, talk.politics.mideast, talk.politics.animals, talk.drugs.*

Alternative newsgroups	*alt*

Alternative groups are actually considered to exist outside the realm of Usenet proper. While you must follow a strict set of guidelines to create a newsgroup under the Usenet umbrella, group creation under the *alt* hierarchy is a free-for-all. Thus, there are many oddball groups, as well as many specious or just plain stupid ones. There are also plenty of legitimate groups who want a different venue, or who don't have the readership to merit a full-fledged Usenet group.

Typical Silly Groups: *alt.bellybutton.lint, alt.tupperware.eat.it.up.yum, alt.barney.die.die.die.*

Typical Legitimate Groups: *alt.adoption, alt.censorship, alt.personals, alt.music.karaoke, alt.radio.pirate, alt.cars.*

Email and News

Getting Oriented

Usenet can be a scary virtual place. Every time you get into a new newsgroup, you have to assess the territory. What's appropriate for this discussion? What are the people like? If I ask such-and-such, how will people react? Will I get flamed?

Whether you're walking for the first time into a new crowd, a new neighborhood, or a new newsgroup, it's smart to scope things out before you start shooting your mouth off. Different newsgroups have climates almost as diverse as different neighborhoods of New York City. Some are almost as dangerous to the sensitive of heart.

Here's a lousy-case scenario. You jump into a new newsgroup. You quickly decide to post a question or comment. A number of other participants view your remarks as, um, well, stupid. They post flames telling you what a jerk you are. You apologize profusely. But it's too late. You slink away into Usenet oblivion, to live a lonely, miserable existence, with only flesh-and-blood friends who show up in person, and no electronic friends at all. Boo hoo. You also can't get the information you asked about in the first place.

If you're new to Usenet or to a particular group, there are a number of approaches that should help you get your feet wet (rather than drown in the process):

- Read a group for a while before posting anything. Get to know the scope and tenor of the discussion so you can gauge what's appropriate.

- If you're not sure what's appropriate, post your questions to the group *news.newusers.answers*. This is a calm, understanding, and supportive environment in which you can basically ask any dumb question you have and get a reasonable answer. This group is primarily intended for Usenet newbies.

- Find out if the group you're interested in has an FAQ list (frequently asked questions). The FAQ is intended to answer the most common queries posted to the group. Reading the FAQ upfront will save you from posting one of these questions and being told to go and read the FAQ. (Not that that's such a terrible thing.) More about FAQs in the next section.

- Once you start participating, use reasonable netiquette. Most of that is no more than common sense, but there's a "Netiquette Primer for Usenet Participants" later in this chapter.

Just the FAQs

Many newsgroups maintain a list of frequently asked questions, or FAQs. Some groups will even have multiple FAQs, each with a different focus. For instance, some of the newsgroups having to deal with pets will have FAQs about general care issues, training your pet, general health, specific health problems, etc.

Some FAQs present helpful information concisely, and you'll be thrilled to have them. Some are long and full of arcane detail, and you'll want to pull your hair out immediately. But if you get ahold of a group's FAQ, read it in at least a cursory fashion because it can help you on a couple of levels. First, it can give you some insight about the atmosphere within the group, the level of discussion, etc.

Second, it can stop you from posting a question that's been asked hundreds of times before. Some groups take the reposting of a commonly asked question well, and participants answer it happily no matter how often it crops up. In some groups, participants may bark "read the FAQ!" at you. You might be helped, you might be ignored, you might just be flamed, who knows. If you have a question, it can only work in your favor to check the FAQ before posting. Of course, if your question involves a pressing matter, just go ahead and wing it.

FAQs are usually posted to the newsgroup periodically, but you don't have to wait. Many FAQ files are archived at the FTP server *rtfm.mit.edu.* Go to the directory:

```
/pub/usenet-by-group/
```

This directory has subdirectories named for most Usenet groups. Thus, I can get into the directory,

```
/pub/usenet-by-group/rec.pets.cats/
```

---

and retrieve the various FAQs about cats. See Chapter 17, *FTP and File Transfer*, for more about FTP. Or use the following URL to access the archives using your browser:

```
ftp://rtfm.mit.edu/pub/usenet-by-group/
```

The FAQ files are also archived (in compressed form) at:

```
ftp://ftp.uu.net/usenet/news.answers/
```

You can access FAQs in HTML form and search through them at "Search FAQs," a service of Oxford University:

```
http://www.lib.ox.ac.uk/search/search_faqs.html
```

Netiquette Primer for Usenet Participants

There are plenty of Usenet participants who treat each other with respect and consideration. And still many others who could use a good scolding from Miss Manners for their rampant disregard of common courtesy. People insult each other. Flame wars abound.

Some groups are far more inclined towards politeness than others. *rec.pets.cats* is a very polite group. Groups that discuss professional interest tend to be fairly calm. But where the discussion centers around passionate opinion, the flames can really fly.

I once saw a "prototypical flame" in some newsgroup or other. It went something like this:

```
Dear Stupid [Bleep]:

My thing is SO superior to your thing that I don't even know how you
can call your thing a thing.  Get the [bleep] out of this group,
you [bleep]ing stupid [bleep].

And the same goes for your mother.

P.S. [Bleep] yourself and die!
```

I'm afraid this template flame is not too far-fetched. There's something about communicating via an electronic medium that unleashes people's more arrogant and insolent tendencies.

That's not to say there isn't a lot of polite discussion out there, too. You can be a nice Usenet participant by following some basic rules of netiquette:

- If you're not sure whether a question is appropriate to a particular group, consult the group's FAQ (if there is one) before posting.

- Don't post the same message to multiple groups (i.e., cross-post) without a good reason. Remember that some people will be reading multiple groups about the same subject—and they don't want to read your message over and over.

- Don't tack on long signature files; some people have to pay for their net connection.

- Use common courtesy in phrasing your messages.

- If you feel inclined to write something in the heat of the moment, cool off for a while before posting.

- If you must get into a dispute with someone else, take the discussion out of the group and into email.

DejaNews: A Usenet Search Engine

If you participate in, or simply monitor, even a single highly trafficked newsgroup, you know how difficult it is to keep up with the discussion or to pinpoint the postings you really want to read. DejaNews can help. DejaNews is a searchable Usenet news archive. The developers call it "the biggest and the best" of its kind, and they seem to be right. You can access the news database, as well as many other news-related resources, at the URL:

```
http://www.dejanews.com/
```

While a number of Internet-wide search engines (see Chapter 6, *Internet Directories and Search Engines*) allow you to search Usenet, DejaNews is designed specifically for that purpose. Thus, DejaNews provides many more search options (explained two sections from now) specifically geared towards helping you refine a search through news. One of the most important options lets you specify a search through recent news postings (the default) or through older archives (dating back to 1995).

When you search for a particular term or terms, DejaNews searches its database to find postings that include them. The results include links to the text of the various postings, from which you can access other postings (if any) in the same message thread.

Not only does DejaNews let you search through postings, you can also use it to figure out what newsgroups are likely to discuss particular topics. This is very handy when you're looking for the right group to match a certain interest.

You can read the postings that match your search at the DejaNews site—just as you would from your own news program. If you register as a DejaNews user (it's free), you can also post news, using a simple form interface.

DejaNews also provides a number of resources for new Usenet participants, including a discussion of the newsgroup hierarchy, an overview of the things you can do with DejaNews, netiquette information, and a glossary of news-related terms. From the home page, click the **New Users** link to access many of these resources. The site will also lead a newbie through the process of reading and posting news.

DejaNews Search Mechanics

The DejaNews home page includes two mutually exclusive boxes you can click on to specify the basic kind of search you want to do. The choices:

- Find Articles (i.e., search for individual Usenet postings that include the search terms; this is the default)

- Find Newsgroups (i.e., search for newsgroups that tend to mention these terms in discussions)

I selected "Find Newsgroups" and then searched for groups that mention the C++ programming language. The search turned up the following eight newsgroups:

```
Confidence    Newsgroup
   99%        comp.lang.c++
   88%        ba.jobs.offered
   61%        misc.jobs.offered
   45%        misc.jobs.contract
   20%        biz.jobs.offered
    9%        comp.lang.c
    9%        tw.bbs.comp.language
    7%        alt.jobs
```

The "Confidence" rating gauges the likelihood of the particular group discussing my search topic, based on the number of matches.

The default type of search—through individual postings—yields a list of the messages that match the query, which can be from any newsgroup in the archive. My off-the-cuff search for "catnip" turned up a bizarre 901 matches. Twenty matches are returned on a page. Here are the first ten I got (doctored to protect the privacy of nipheads everywhere):

```
Date     Scr      Subject                Newsgroup             Author

1. 97/05/28 027 Re: CATNIP?????         rec.drugs.misc        Celtic@spam.net
2. 97/05/28 027 Re: CATNIP?????         alt.drugs.psychedel   faked9de37@aol.com
3. 97/05/27 027 CATNIP?????             rec.drugs.misc        little@man.com
4. 97/05/28 026 Re: Catnip and kitten?  rec.pets.cats.healt   jude@vista.com
5. 97/05/28 026 Catnip and lions        alt.fan.lion-king     mcleary@thornu.edu
6. 97/05/28 026 catnip and catmint      rec.gardens           "Dr. Love"
7. 97/05/27 026 Rabbits & catnip        rec.gardens           dmartin@sinatra.org
8. 97/05/27 026 Re: Catnip and kitten?  rec.pets.cats.healt   socks@whitehouse.org
9. 97/05/27 026 Re: CATNIP???           rec.drugs.misc        stoned@anytime.com
10. 97/05/27 026 Re: Catnip and kitten? rec.pets.cats.healt   val@oreilly.com
                         .
                         .
                         .

Get next 20 matches
```

Within the results, the "Scr" column (for "Score") rates each posting as to the closeness of the match, with the best matches at the top of the list. If the number of matches extends beyond 20, click on the link **Get next 20 matches** to view the next batch.

Each line of the results includes two links:

- The Subject entry links to the text of the posting.

- The Author entry links to a special "Author Profile," which is basically a summary of this person's recent Usenet participation. (From a privacy standpoint, this information is a little disturbing. However, you can turn up the messages someone's posted just by searching for their name—and many other search engines let you search Usenet postings as well.)

If you click on the Subject link, your browser will load the text of the message, including header lines. From that point, if the message was part of a discussion thread, you can access the related messages by clicking on the Subject line in the message header. You can also access the "Author Profile" by clicking on the From line in the header, or an email address in the person's *.signature* file (if any).

If you want to post news from DejaNews, the system requires you to register or to send an email message to confirm each posting. Since the latter proposition is a drag and it's fast and painless to register, why not register? If you click on the **Post** link, you'll be able to access the link to register. All you need to supply is your email address. You'll get further instructions by email, instructing you to use your browser to go to a particular URL. This will enable your own private "cookie," a security mechanism that makes sure no one else posts news from DejaNews using your email address. See Chapter 1, *A Living Glossary of the Internet*, for more information about cookies.

DejaNews Search Options

The basic DejaNews search involves entering one or more search terms in the box intended for them.

However, DejaNews also offers a so-called "power search," which allows you to specify a number of parameters for the search. Click on the **Power Search** link to set these options. The following is a list of the available options with their possible settings; note that you can check one setting per option:

```
Keywords matched:      All                   Any
Usenet database:       Current               Old
                       (e.g., 4/12/97 to Now)  (e.g., 3/19/95 to 4/12/97)
Number of matches
(per page):            25                    50            100
Search results detail: Concise               Detailed
Search results format: Listed                Threaded
Sort by (per page):    Score                 Newsgroup     Date
                       Author                Subject
Article date bias:     Prefer new            Prefer old
Article date weight:   Some                  Great         None
```

The defaults options for the power search are:

```
Keywords matched: All
Usenet database: Current
Number of matches (per page): 25
Search results detail: Concise
Search results format: Listed
```

```
Sort by (per page):  Score
Article date bias:  Prefer new
Article date weight:  Some
```

One of the more interesting options is the one that lets you specify an "Old" version of the "Usenet database." Being able to search some of the older articles can come in pretty handy. You might also consider having results returned with messages in the same thread kept together (for "Search results format," select "Threaded").

In addition to these basic options, DejaNews lets you create a custom *query filter*, which is basically just a list of additional parameters to match. Select the **Query Filter** link from the power search page. The query filter lets you limit your search to the following:

```
Newsgroup(s)
Dates
Author(s)
Subject(s)
```

It's easy to fill out the query filter form. The online help also includes sample query filters. You click separate buttons to Create or Clear the filter.

CHAPTER 13

Netscape Messenger
and Collabra Discussions

Included with Netscape Communicator are modules called Netscape Messenger and Netscape Collabra Discussions that let you read and send electronic mail and Usenet news, respectively. The current chapter covers the version of the programs distributed with Communicator 4.01 and installed on a Windows platform. If you are using another version, or running these modules on another platform, some of the functions, menu items, key commands, etc., may vary.

This chapter provides the following:

- An overview of Messenger and Collabra, with a look at the various windows you'll use to read, send, and manage mail and news messages

- A guide to some of the less obvious, and more useful, program features— things you might not immediately realize you can do

- A quick reference to the various actions you can perform using Netscape Messenger and Collabra (For each action, the charts in this chapter list the menu items, keyboard shortcuts, and toolbar buttons and other window features you can use to perform the action.)

You might also be interested in customizing these modules. Note that Netscape Communicator lumps together Preferences for the Navigator, Messenger, Collabra, and Composer modules into a single dialog. This dialog is accessible from any of the modules using the **Edit → Preferences** menu sequence (or the keyboard shortcut Alt+E, E). For a reference to these Preferences, see the final section of Chapter 2, *Netscape Navigator*.

A Look at Netscape Messenger and Collabra

Although Netscape Communicator's email and news applications are technically separate, in practical terms they look like a single package. Whether you're using mail or news, the linchpin of message management is a window called the Message Center, pictured in Figure 13–1.

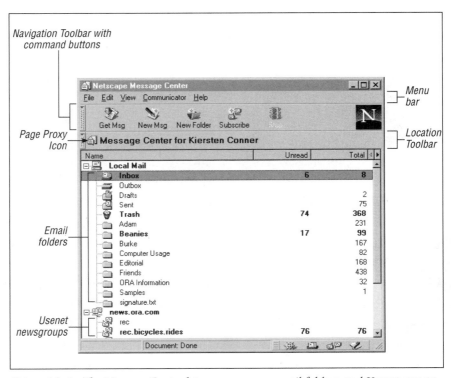

Figure 13–1: The Message Center lets you manage email folders and Usenet groups

The Message Center is like a directory manager for your email folders and Usenet newsgroups. Within the window is a directory tree of your email folders as well as a tree that corresponds to your Usenet news server. If you expand the news tree, you'll see the newsgroups to which you are currently subscribed. There is also information about the number and size of messages in each folder/newsgroup.

Double-clicking on a folder or newsgroup name in the Message Center opens up that folder or group in another window called a Message List window. The Message List displays a list of the message headers for the particular folder/group.

You can set up the Message List window to have a single viewing pane, which shows the header list, or to open up a lower pane, in which you can view individual messages. If the Message List window is one pane, when you select a message to read, it is displayed in a separate Message List window (which differs slightly in available menu options, etc.). Figure 13–2 shows a Message List window that is a single pane. Figure 13–3 shows a Message List window with a split pane; note that the bottom part displays the text of the message whose header is selected in the top part.

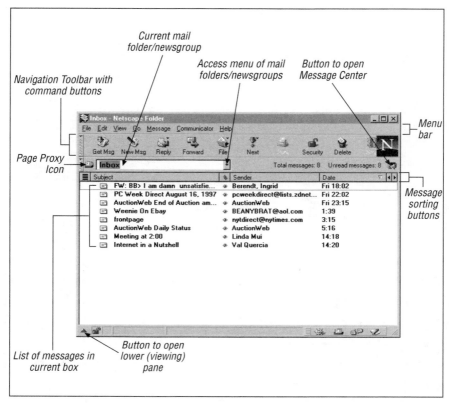

Figure 13–2: Single-pane Message List window shows headers for folder/newsgroup

Keep in mind that, like the Message Center, the Message List window serves both email and Usenet news functions. While the previous illustration shows the mail incarnation, it's simple to switch the window to view news at any time. Notice the part of the toolbar that displays the name of the current folder. This is actually a menu from which you can select any of your mail folders or subscribed newsgroups. The selected folder/group replaces the one currently displayed in the Message List window.

This ability to switch between folders and between mail and news in a single window is very useful. It's also very necessary if you're using the default configuration of Messenger and Collabra—because there can only be one Message List window open at a time. However, this feature is configurable. The section "Tips, Tricks, and Hidden Stuff," later in this chapter, covers how to do this, how to work with window panes, and a number of other program features.

The other window you'll encounter in using email and news is the window you'll get when you ask to create a new mail or news message. This window, aptly called a Composition window, appears in Figure 13–4.

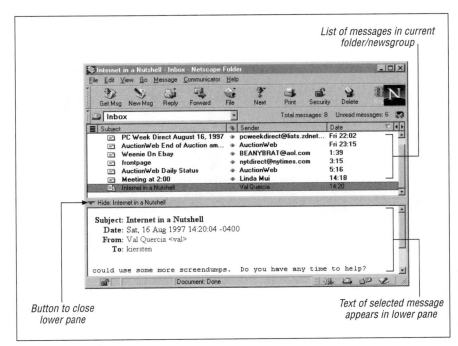

List of messages in current folder/newsgroup

Button to close lower pane

Text of selected message appears in lower pane

Figure 13–3: Split the Message List pane to view messages in lower pane

Tips, Tricks, and Hidden Stuff

Like the other Communicator modules, Netscape Messenger and Collabra Discussions are designed to work intuitively. Making note of the command buttons on the navigation toolbar and glancing around at the various menus should help you figure out pretty quickly the basic functions you'll need to know.

But even easy-to-use programs like these have their subtleties. The following sections describe some of the features that may not be entirely obvious but certainly can come in handy. These may be functions you haven't noticed or alternative ways to perform functions you already know about. The more you play with these and the other Communcator modules, the more likely you are to turn up tricks of your own.

Working Offline

If you pay for your Internet connection, the ticking clock can be fairly significant. In order to help save you connect-time charges, all of the Messenger and Collabra windows let you take your act offline. The **File** menu on every window has a toggle that lets you **Go Offline** and then **Go Online** again. (Of course, when you go offline with any of the Communicator modules, you still have to disconnect from your Internet service to actually save money.)

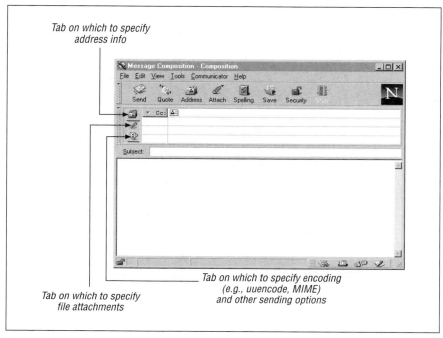

Tab on which to specify
address info

Tab on which to specify encoding
(e.g., uuencode, MIME)
and other sending options

Tab on which to specify
file attachments

Figure 13–4: Requesting a new mail or news message opens a Composition window

Generally, you'll want to download mail and news, and then go offline to read messages, compose your own, etc. When you ask to go offline, you'll be prompted as to what messages the program should go get for you first. The default is all your new mail and news. You can opt to exclude either (or both, if you suspect you have no new messages). You'll also be asked if the program should send any messages you've composed that haven't been sent yet. The default is to send them.

When you compose messages offline, all send functions become, in effect, "queue for later delivery." Then when you ask to go back online, you'll be prompted again as to whether to send the queued messages as well as to download whatever new messages have accumulated for you on the remote server. The default is to send everything you've saved for later and to get all your new messages.

Using Panes in the Message List Window

The Message List window displays the list of messages in the current mail folder or newsgroup. You can choose to configure the Message List window in either of two ways:

- A single pane displaying only the list of message headers. When you select a message to read, a second Message List window opens up to display it.

- Two panes, an upper pane containing the list of message headers, and a lower pane displaying the contents of the current (highlighted) message.

When you have a single pane, notice a small Up Arrow button appears in the lower-left corner of the window. You can open up a lower pane by clicking on the Up Arrow button.

When the lower pane is open, a small down arrow appears above and to the left of it (on the divider between the upper and lower panes). Next to the arrow is the word "Hide." You click on this arrow to close the lower pane.

Note that the View menu offers a toggle called Hide/Show Message that closes/opens the message pane as well.

Although there is no Preference setting to determine the number of panes, the modules will remember whichever configuration you choose and use it during your next session.

Opening/Raising Message Center from Message List

In the Message List window, notice the mysterious green arrow button under the Netscape logo (in the upper-right part of the window). The arrow wraps back around on itself, resembling a belt, and this wrapping back is a key to its function. You use the arrow button to cycle back to the Message Center window. If the Message Center window isn't running, it will be opened for you. If the Message Center is already open, clicking on the circular arrow raises the Message Center window to the front of the display.

Organizing Folders in the Message Center

Within the Message Center window, there are five default folders:

- *Inbox:* where your new mail shows up.

- *Outbox:* mail that's queued to be sent later. This happens if you tell Messenger to go offline, and then try to send messages; however, even when the program's online, you can accomplish the same thing by choosing **Send Later** from the **File** menu in the Composition window.

- *Drafts:* messages you've saved in the Composition window (using the **Save Draft** option of the **File** menu, or Ctrl+S).

- *Sent:* copies of messages you've sent.

- *Trash:* messages you've deleted from one of the other folders.

The default folders are listed first in the Message Center window. Then come any folders you've created (**File** → **New Folder** . . .)—these are listed alphabetically.

You're pretty much stuck with the default folders and their locations in the Message Center, but you can create and organize your own folders to your heart's content.

Folders can be nested, just as in any directory structure. By default, a new folder gets created under whatever folder is highlighted in the Message Center; if none is highlighted, the new folder appears one level below "Local Mail," which represents to your mail directory.

You can drag and drop the symbols that represent folders to change their relationship to one another. For instance, if you drag the symbol for a folder called "January" onto the symbol for an "Inventory" folder, January becomes a subfolder of Inventory. You can also move a folder into another folder by using the menu sequence **View** → **Move Folder**, and then select the folder name from the displayed menu.

To move a folder to the top of the hierarchy, drag and drop it on the symbol for the mail directory, "Local Mail."

To change a folder's name, highlight it, and then select **Rename Folder...** from the **File** menu.

Hide or Show the Various Toolbars

As with Navigator, you have the option of displaying or "hiding" most of the toolbars on your Messenger and Collabra windows. If you don't tend to use the offerings on a particular toolbar, closing it can save you some screen space. You can always open it again, if the need arises.

Each of the windows that compose the mail and news modules has two toolbars that can be closed. The Message List and Message Center windows both have a navigation toolbar (with command buttons) and a location toolbar (with the name of the folder/group or the message heading). The Message Composition window has a message toolbar (with command buttons) and an addressing area (that can also be closed).

At the left side of each of these toolbars is a *tab* you can click on to close the bar. When the bar is open, the tab is vertical, with a small down arrow at the top. When you use the tab to close the bar, the tab takes on a horizontal orientation. You can click on the horizontal tab to open the toolbar again.

You can also open and close toolbars using various options on the **View** menu of each window.

Location Toolbar Provides Folder/Group Menu

Here's a good reason not to hide a location toolbar. In a Message List window that is open to a particular folder/group, the location toolbar displays the folder/group name (e.g., Inbox, *rec.pets*, etc.). The down arrow at the right end of the name field indicates that this field on the location toolbar is actually a menu. Click anywhere on the name field to display the menu, as shown in Figure 13-5. This menu lists all of your mail folders and all of the newsgroups to which you have subscribed. You can switch the Message List window over to another folder or group by selecting it from the menu.

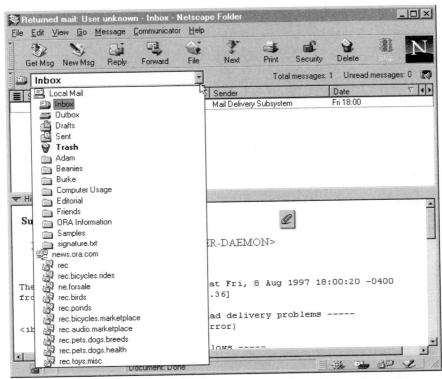

Figure 13–5: Message List location bar provides menu of folders and newsgroups

You can also open whichever folder or group is highlighted in the Message Center by hitting the Return key, typing Ctrl+O, or by selecting **Open Folder** from the File menu.

A Separate Window for Each Folder

By default, Netscape Messenger and Collabra let you have only one Message List window open at a time showing folder/group headers. In other words, you can't have a Message List window listing Inbox headers and one listing *rec.pets* news postings at the same time.

If you'd like to have different windows open to different folders/groups, you can specify a program Preference to that effect:

1. Open up the Preferences dialog by selecting **Preferences** from the **Edit** menu (or using the keyboard shortcut Alt+E, E).

2. Under "Category:" select "Mail & Groups."

3. Toggle off the preference "Reuse message list (thread) window." (The box in front of it should *not* contain a checkmark.)

If you want to go back to using a single message list window to display headers, go back through the procedure and check the preference on again.

A Separate Window for Each Message

When the Message List window containing message headers is a single pane, you view the contents of an individual message in a separate Message List window. By default, each subsequent message you view is displayed in the same window. That means you can't look at more than one message at the same time.

Netscape Messenger has a preference setting that lets you view multiple messages simultaneously. Follow Steps 1 and 2 from the previous section. Then toggle off the preference "Reuse message window."

Subscribing to Newsgroups

Both the Message Center and Message List windows offer a **Subscribe to Discussion Groups** item on the **File** menu; this item opens a dialog in which you can subscribe and unsubscribe to Usenet newsgroups. The dialog appears in Figure 13–6.

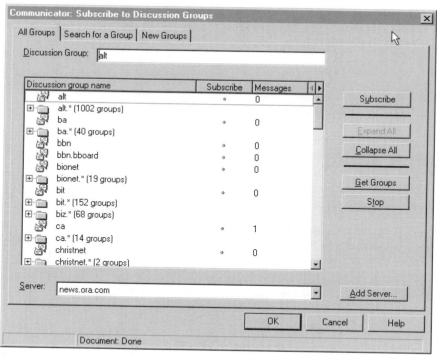

Figure 13–6: Use dialog to view newsgroup hierarchy and select groups

The dialog has three sections, each accessible using one of the "tabs" that appear at the top. The first tab, titled "All Groups," lists all of the newsgroups available on your current news server. Generally the top-level newsgroup names appear in "collapsed" form; you have to expand a branch yourself by clicking on the plus sign to the left of it.

When you find a group to which you want to subscribe, you can either select it and click the dialog's Subscribe button, or click on the small dot that appears after the group name, under the Subscribed column. This dot is a toggle that lets you subscribe and unsubscribe to the group; if you're subscribed, a checkmark will appear instead.

Rather than look through the entire hierarchy, you can instead open the second tab of the dialog, titled "Search for a Group." Enter some part of a group name in the text box near the top of the dialog, and then hit Return or select the Search Now button. Matching group names are displayed in the box below, as shown in Figure 13-7.

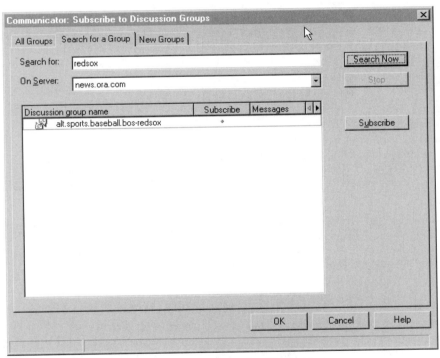

Figure 13-7: Searching for a group name makes life simpler

I can subscribe to any group the search turns up by clicking on the dot in the Subscribe column or by using the Subscribe button.

There are a few ways to unsubscribe from a group. The simplest way is to delete the group name from the Message Center list of folders/groups. If you have the Subscription dialog open, you can unsubscribe to a group by toggling off the checkmark in the Subscribed column. Also, when you highlight the name of a group to which you are subscribed, any Subscribe button in the dialog becomes an Unsubscribe button. How convenient.

Whatever you do in the Subscribe/Unsubscribe dialog, you have to OK your choices using the button of that name at the bottom of the box.

Undeleted Messages Appear at the End of the Current Folder

If you delete a message and then immediately undo it (**Edit** → **Undo**, or Ctrl+Z), the message is put back in the folder—but it appears as the last message.

Undoing Versus Redoing

In the Composition window, the undo function is a toggle. You can undo an edit. Invoking undo again, redoes what you did before the first undo. *Right*, you're thinking. *What the heck is she talking about?* Here's an example. Suppose I open a Composition window (Ctrl+M) and type in some message text:

```
Hi there. How are you?
```

Then I decide that's not the way I want to begin my message. So I use Ctrl+Z to undo what I've just done—in this case, undo means delete what I just wrote. So, I'm back to an empty text area. Then I reconsider—that wasn't really such a bad opening. So I use Ctrl+Z again, and the text is put back. I can keep toggling between this silly line and no line by entering Ctrl+Z until I make up my mind. But I can't make other changes until I do; Ctrl+Z will always toggle the last edit.

So, what's this "redo" business about? Well, in the Message Center and Message List windows, there is an additional function that's used with undo. Suppose I delete a message from my Inbox, but then I'm sorry. The standard undo (**File** → **Undo**, or Ctrl+Z) will bring back the deleted message. But if I change my mind *again*—I really want to delete the message after all—I have to use **Redo** (on the same menu) or its shortcut, Ctrl+Y. For some reason, in the Message Center and Message List windows, **Undo** is not a toggle. Instead, **Redo** *undoes the undo*.

The Top Keyboard Shortcuts

If you check out the reference pages for Messenger and Collabra functions (later in this chapter), you'll see that there's a keyboard shortcut (or accelerator) for just about every one. However, many of these shortcuts are just the keys that let you access the various menus items. For instance, you can undo an edit with the menu sequence **Edit** → **Undo**. The key sequence "Alt+E, U" does the same thing because Alt+E brings up the **Edit** menu, and then U invokes the **Undo** item.

For the most commonly used functions, there are true keyboard shortcuts, many of which require the use of the Ctrl key. Table 13–1 summarizes those common functions and the keyboard shortcuts for them. Note that some of these functions may not work in every window that makes up the Messenger and Collabra modules. Also remember that these are Windows-specific shortcuts. However, some of them may still apply if you're working in a UNIX or Macintosh environment.

Table 13-1: Keyboard Shortcuts for Common Functions

Function	Shortcut
Address book	Ctrl+Shift+2
Bookmark, add	Ctrl+D
Bookmarks, edit	Ctrl+B
Close (window)	Ctrl+W
Copy (selected text)	Ctrl+C
Cut (selected text)	Ctrl+X
Delete (message/folder)	Del
Exit (program)	Ctrl+Q
Find text in message	Ctrl+F
Find text again	Ctrl+G
Font, make larger	Ctrl+]
Font, make smaller	Ctrl+[
Forward message	Ctrl+L
Forward message with quoting (>)	Ctrl+Shift+L
Get New Messages	Ctrl+T
Go back one folder/group	Alt+←
Go forward one folder/group	Alt+→
Help info	F1
Interrupt download	Esc
Mark all messages as read	Shift+C
Mark message as read	M
Mark message as unread	U
Mark messages received up until *date* as read (default is current date)	C
New Browser Window	Ctrl+N
New Composer Window	Ctrl+Shift+N
New Message	Ctrl+M
Next Message	Shift+N
Next Unread Group	G
Next Unread Message	N
Next Unread Thread	T

Table 13-1: Keyboard Shortcuts for Common Functions (continued)

Function	Shortcut
Open Browser	Ctrl+1
Open Folder	Ctrl+O
Open Inbox	Ctrl+2
Open Message Center	Ctrl+Shift+1
Paste (last cut/copied text)	Ctrl+V
Previous Message	Shift+P
Previous Unread Message	P
Redo (last Undone edit)	Ctrl+Y
Reply to newsgroup	Ctrl+D
Reply to sender	Ctrl+R
Reply to sender and newsgroup	Ctrl+Shift+D
Reply to sender and other recipients	Ctrl+Shift+R
Save message in file	Ctrl+S
Select all	Ctrl+A
Send now	Ctrl+Enter
Undo (last edit)	Ctrl+Z

Creating Personal Toolbar Links to Folders, Message Center

Many Communicator module windows have a handy little tool known as a Page Proxy icon, which is introduced in Chapter 2. Both the Message Center window and Message List window (when it's open to a folder/group) have this icon, which represents the URL of the window and can be found at the left end of the location toolbar. Within the Message List window, the icon symbol reflects whichever folder or newsgroup the window is open to. For instance, the Inbox icon is a box of letters.

You can drag the Page Proxy icon from the location toolbar and drop it to create a link that will bring up the window. Perhaps the best use of this strategy is to create one or more links on the Netscape Navigator personal toolbar (also described in Chapter 2).

Why bother when it's so easy to switch between modules? Well, normally when you switch from Navigator to Messenger, you go directly to your Inbox. From there, you can switch to any mail folder. But you might prefer to have a link on the Navigator personal toolbar that takes you directly to one or more of your other folders.

This strategy can also let you access newsgroups more quickly. In order to get into a newsgroup from Navigator, you normally have to go through the (Messenger/Collabra) Message Center, then open a group. A link can let you go directly to a particular newsgroup without having to deal with the Message Center. Hypothetically, you could have Navigator personal toolbar links to let you access a number of different folders and/or newsgroups quickly. (Of course, the toolbar is only so big. ;-)

Likewise, the Message Center has an icon on its location toolbar. You can also drag this onto Navigator's personal toolbar, for a quick link. However, since it's fairly easy to open the Message Center using a menu item (**Communicator → Message Center**) or keyboard shortcut (Ctrl+Shift+1), this isn't very useful.

Message Sorting

Whether you're working with email messages in Messenger, or Usenet news messages in Collabra, you have different options as to how the entries should be sorted in the Message List window.

By default, messages are sorted by date, with the latest headers at the end of the list. (This is called *ascending order*; more about that shortly.) Each message header has several components, most notably Subject, Sender, and Date. Notice that these names appear as titles above the list pane. This is partly to help you see what's what, but also to give you the option of sorting another way—the titles are actually buttons.

For instance, if you click on the Subject title, the messages with the same Subject line will be grouped together; the groups will be put in alphabetical order. However, within each Subject group, the messages will still go from oldest to newest. (An even fancier way to keep related messages together involves *threading*, explained in the next section.)

You might play with the sorting method for a number of reasons. Rather than search through the headers within a folder (**Edit → Search Messages**), maybe you can find what you want by sorting your messages according to Sender? This groups messages from each person/source and then organizes the groupings alphabetically.

Note that you can re-sort at any time. If you mess around with the order, you can get fairly close to the original organization by clicking on Date.

The title buttons over the list pane aren't the only way to sort. You can invoke all of the possible sorting options using the **View** menu. Choose the **Sort** item to reveal a menu of sorting possibilities. On the menu, primary sorting methods appear above a horizontal line; they are mutually exclusive. Regardless of what primary sorting method you choose (date, subject, whatever), you can additionally choose between the default ascending order (oldest to newest) and descending order (newest to oldest). These options appear below the line on the menu.

Note that there are a lot more sorting options on the menu than the message header lines—and the titles over them—suggest. In reality, each message header actually has a lot more components than the default layout shows. You may not ever need or want to look at these components, but there is a way to scroll over to see them.

Notice the tiny left and right arrow buttons at the right end of the sorting buttons. The right arrow button lets you show additional columns of header info, and provides a sorting button over each. However, the default layout of the list pane will work for most people.

Working with Message Threads

Whether you're reading mail or news, you can opt to have messages organized by *thread*. This means that related messages appear together, with followups indented below the email or news message to which they apply. Messages can be nested a number of layers deep.

In order to have messages displayed in this way, you have to request *threading*. Notice the tiny button above and to the left of the list pane; it looks like a miniature outline. Click that button to organize messages in the current folder/newsgroup by thread. You can also select **by Thread** from the **Sort** menu (under the **View** menu). Figure 13–8 shows a Message List window open to the newsgroup *rec.ponds*; in this window, threading is turned on. A symbol that looks like a spool of thread, with a down arrow below it, appears to the far left of the first message in a thread. A plus sign following the spool indicates that the thread is "collapsed"; i.e., only the heading for the original message is displayed. Click on the plus sign to "expand" the thread, and to reveal all the follow-up messages. When a thread is expanded, a minus sign appears in front of it.

It's easy to highlight and work with an entire thread. With any message in the thread highlighted, type Ctrl+Shift+A. This expands and highlights the thread. (You can instead expand the thread by clicking on the plus sign; then click on the spool to highlight the entire thread.)

While the thread is hightlighted, you can open up each of the messages, each in its own Message List window, by hitting Return. (You can also use a Netscape's mysterious popup menu. Click the second pointer button on the spool; then select **Open Message** from the menu.)

You can save the entire thread in a single file by selecting **Save As** . . . from the **File** menu.

You can also copy the thread to another folder (**Message** → **Copy Message**), delete it (email only), etc.

In Collabra (news) only, you can specify that a thread be "ignored" or "watched." This is mostly for your own tracking purposes. When *only the first message* in a thread is highlighted, typing the letter "k" classifies the thread as Ignored. In front of an ignored thread appears a small international negation symbol (that's the red circle with the diagonal line through it). Typing "w" classifies the thread as one to be Watched. An eyeglass symbol is the clue. Use "k" or "w" a second time to turn

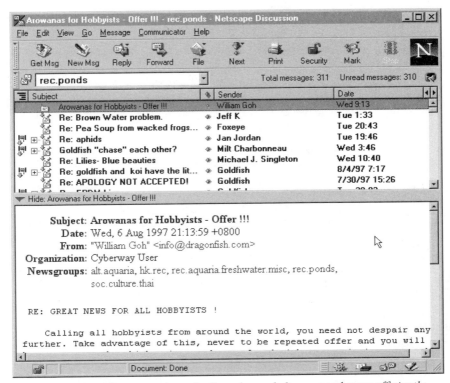

Figure 13–8: Displaying messages in threads can help you read more efficiently

off their respective settings. (You can also set this status using the **Ignore Thread** and **Watch Thread** items on the **Message** menu.)

Classifying a thread as watched or ignored lets you fine-tune how you view your messages. Select **Messages** from the **View** menu to check out your options. The **Messages** submenu has four mutually exclusive viewing options above a horizontal line. You can choose to view any of the following categories of messages:

- New

- Threads with New

- Watched Threads with New

- All

Choosing **Watched Threads with New** redisplays the list pane so that only those "watched" threads that also have new messages are listed. You can switch back to viewing **All**—or any of the other categories—at any time.

On the same **Messages** menu is a single item below the line: an **Ignored** toggle. To display messages you've tagged as "ignored," toggle this item on. To hide "ignored" messages, toggle it off.

Using the Address Book

Netscape Messenger and Collabra make it easy to create and use an address book—a file in which you can save the email addresses you use most frequently and come up with shortcuts (*aliases*) for them.

When you receive mail from someone, you can add their address to your address book by selecting **Add to Address Book** from the **Message** menu; below this selection, you need to specify either to add just the **Sender** of the message or the sender and **All** recipients.

When you select either option, you get a dialog box in which the basic address book information has already been written for you (see Figure 13–9).

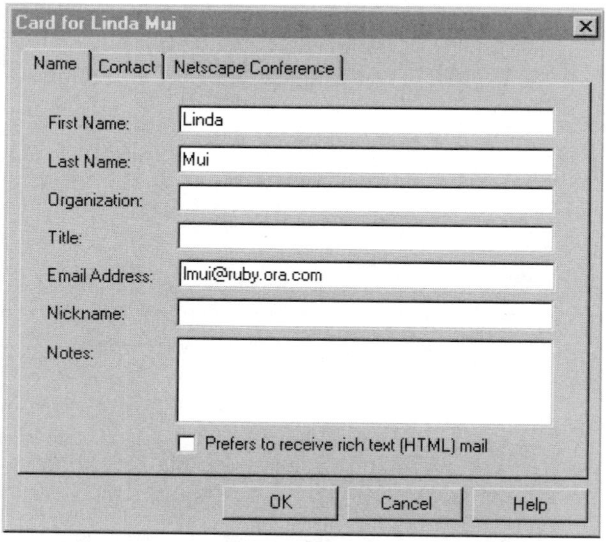

Figure 13–9: There's a card of information for each person in the address book

You can fill in additional information on the three tabs of the dialog, including their business or organization, street addresses, and phone numbers. It's often a good idea to create a "Nickname," which is an alias you can use in place of a person's full email address.

If you asked to put the sender and all recipients of a message in your address book, when you OK the information in the initial card dialog, you'll get another dialog for the next person on the list.

You can also create new entries from scratch, remove entries, etc., in a special Address Book window. Select **Address Book** from the **Communicator** menu, or use the keyboard shortcut Ctrl+Shift+2 to open the window (a typical one of which appears in Figure 13–10). Note that you can search for a particular name using the text box titled "Type in the name you are looking for."

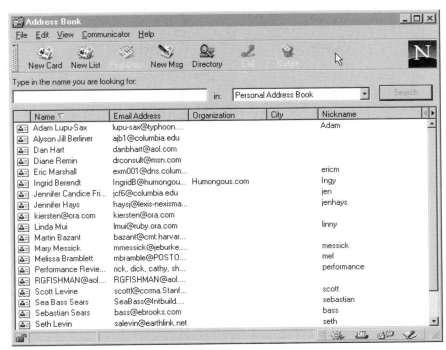

Figure 13–10: Address book window

The default data to search is the Address Book itself. But your box containing "Personal Address Book" is actually a menu. The other menu choices are white and yellow page directories like Four11. So, you can actually search for someone's email address on the Net, and then add it directly to your Address Book.

Email Addresses from Address Book Are Completed for You

Chapter 2 explains how Navigator will try to match URLs you enter and complete them for you, if they match a URL from your browsing history. Similarly, Messenger/Collabra will try to complete email addresses for you by matching what you're typing against your Address Book.

Filtering Mail Messages

You use a mail filter to specify that if a message meets certain criteria, it will be handled in a particular way. For example, if there's a lot of email about parking circulated at your office and you don't own a car, you might create a filter that deletes messages with "parking" in the header. Or, you might want to save messages about a certain subject or from a certain person in a particular folder. Whatever. Setting up filters like these can make it a lot easier to manage your email.

Netscape Messenger's **Edit** menu offers an item called **Mail Filters**, which opens up a dialog you can use to create and manage your own filters. Select the New button in the Mail Filters dialog to open up another box, titled Filter Rules (see Figure 13–11).

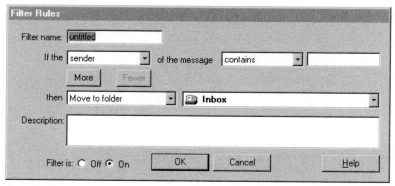

Figure 13–11: Specify mail filters using dialog

You use the Filter Rules dialog to specify what you want a filter to do. This is actually pretty simple. The first thing to do is simply to name the filter—just to give you a way to identify it and work with it later. Provide a name in the text field near the top of the dialog.

Then there are a number of additional fields, most of which must be filled in using menus—so you don't have to be a filter whiz or anything. Our figure can't show all the menu options, but here's a text summary:

```
If the subject    of the message    contains        [whatever text you enter]
       sender                       doesn't contain
       body                         is
       date                         isn't
       priority                     begins with

then   Move to folder
       Delete
       Change priority
       Mark read
       Ignore thread
```

You need to select an item from every menu, as well as enter the text that triggers the filter. For example:

```
If the body of the message contains marketing
then Delete
```

Naturally, your choices have to make sense in context. The following choices wouldn't do anything useful:

```
If the sender of the message is full of it
then Delete
```

This is better:

```
If the sender of the message is Howard Stern
then Delete
```

If you choose **Move to folder**, you'll get an additional menu of folder names. Likewise, selecting **Change priorities** gives you another menu from which to select a level of priority.

You can create as many filters as you like. The top-level dialog lets you edit or delete existing filters. It also lets you specify the order in which filters are invoked. If you get into using filters, you might want to devise some that are meant to be used in sequence. For instance, you might want to first delete messages from Wacky Joe, and then save those having to do with an interest that you and Joe happen to have in common.

Messenger and Collabra Quick Reference

The following pages provide a reference to the various ways you can perform Netscape Messenger and Collabra Discussions functions. Keep in mind that this reference is based on the version of the programs shipped with Netscape Communicator 4.01 and installed on a Windows platform. If you're using another version of the programs, or are running them on another platform, certain functions, menu commands, keystrokes, etc., may vary.

Within the reference, under each function heading, the ways you can perform the function are listed in the following order:

- Menu items

- Keyboard shortcuts

- Buttons and other browser window features

Note that some functions are only available in certain windows of the mail/news modules. For example, you can save a draft of a message you're writing in the Composition window (**File** menu → **Save Draft**, or Ctrl+S). However, this function doesn't mean anything in the other two Messenger/Collabra windows (Message Center and Message List).

For each function entry, assume that it is available for all of the module's windows unless there is a note to the contrary.

Address book
add sender to
(Message List only)
    Message → Add to Address Book
        → Sender
    Alt+M, A, S
add sender and recipients to
(Message List only)
    Message → Add to Address Book
        → All

Alt+M, A, A
edit (Message List only)
    Communicator → Address Book
    Ctrl+Shift+2
    Alt+C, A
use addresses in outgoing message
(Composition window only)
    File → Select Addresses
    Alt+F, T
    Address button

Addressing Area (Composition window only)

hide/show

    View → Hide/Show Addressing Area

    Alt+V, A

    Toggle using tab on left of bar

view Address(es)

    Click on Cardfile tab

view Attachments

    Click on Paperclip tab

view Options

    Click on Checkmarks tab

Attachments

attach Address Book card (Composition window)

    File → Attach → Address Book Card

    Alt+F, A, A

    Attach button → Address Book Card

attach file (Composition window)

    File → Attach → File

    Alt+F, A, F

    Attach button → File

attach My Address Book card (Composition window)

    File → Attach → My Address Book Card

    Alt+F, A, M

    Attach button → My Address Book Card

attach Web page (Composition window)

    File → Attach → Web Page

    Alt+F, A, W

    Attach button → Web Page

open (Message List only)

    File → Open Attachments → select attachment

    Alt+F, A

    Click on icon for attached file

show as links (Message List only)

    View → Attachments → As Links

    Alt+V, A, L

show inline (Message List only)

    View → Attachments → Inline

    Alt+V, A, I

view for outgoing message (Composition window)

    View → Attachments

    Alt+V, H

    Paperclip tab in Address Area

Back, display one folder/group (Message List only)

    Go → Back

    Alt+←

    Alt+G, B

Browser window

open/raise

    Communicator → Navigator

    Ctrl+1

    Navigator button on Component Bar

open new

    File → New → Navigator Window

    Ctrl+N

    Alt+F, N, N

    Navigator button on Component Bar

Categories, hide/show Message List

    View → Hide/Show Categories

    Alt+V, C

Character set, specify for outgoing message (Composition window only)

    View → Encoding → choose character set

    Alt+V, E, down arrow to character set, Return

Close current window (See also Exit)

    File → Close

    Ctrl+W

    Alt+F, C

Composer, open new window

    File → New → Blank Page

    Ctrl+Shift+N

    Alt+F, N, P

    Composer button on Component Bar

Copy
> *message(s) to folder*
> *(Message List only)*
> > Messages → Copy Message →
> >   select folder
> > Alt+M, C, folder number
> *selected text*
> > Edit → Copy
> > Ctrl+C
> > Alt+E, C

Customize mail/news
> Edit → Preferences
> Alt+E, P

Cut selected text
> Edit → Cut
> Ctrl+X
> Alt+E, T

Delete
> *folder (Message Center only)*
> > Edit → Delete Folder
> > Delete key
> > Drag folder icon onto Trash
> >   folder icon
> *message (Message List only)*
> > Edit → Delete Message
> > Delete key
> > Alt+E, D
> > Delete button
> *newsgroup from Message Center*
> *(i.e., unsubscribe)*
> > Edit → Delete Discussion Group
> > Delete key
> > Alt+E, D
> *text (Composition window only)*
> > Edit → Delete
> > Delete key
> > Alt+E, D

Download
> *interrupt (n/a in Composition win-*
> *dow)*
> > View → Stop Loading
> > Escape key
> > Alt+V, S
> > Stop button
> *mail or news (selected folder/group)*
> *(n/a in Composition window)*

File → Get Messages → New
> Ctrl+T
> Alt+F, G, N
> Get Msg button
news for all groups
> expand news server entry in Mes-
>   sage Center (when online)
news for current group
(Message Center only)
> File → Get Messages → New
> Ctrl+T
> Alt+F, G, N
> Get Msg button

Email address
> *view for outgoing message*
> *(Composition window only)*
> > View → Address
> > Alt+V, D
> > Cardfile tab in Address Area

**Encoding (e.g., MIME, uuencode),
view/set for outgoing message**
> *(Composition window only)*
> > View → Options
> > Alt+V, O
> > Options tab in Addressing Area

Exit program (See also Close)
> File → Exit
> Ctrl+Q
> Alt+F, X

File attachments
> *See Attachments*

**Filters, create/edit mail (n/a in Compo-
sition window)**
> Edit → Mail Filters
> Alt+E, L

Find
> *message header*
> *(n/a in Composition window)*
> > Edit → Search Messages
> > Alt+E, M
> *text in current message*
> *(n/a in Message Center)*
> > Edit → Find in Message
> > Ctrl+F

Alt+E, F
text again
(n/a in Message Center)
    Edit → Find Again
    Ctrl+G

Flagged message (Message List only)
display first
    Go → First Flagged Message
    Alt+G, F
display next
    Go → Flagged Message
    Alt+G, G
display previous
    Go → Previous Flagged Message
    Alt+G, G

Folder(s)
compress
(n/a in Composition window)
    File → Compress Folders
    Alt+F, D
create new
(n/a in Composition window)
    File → New Folder
    Alt+F, W
    New Folder button (Message Center)
delete selected
(Message Center only)
    Edit → Delete Folder
    Delete key
move back to previous
(Message List only)
    Go → Back
    Alt+←
    Alt+G, B
move forward to next
(Message List only)
    Go → Forward
    Alt+→
    Alt+G, W
move one into another
(Message Center only)
    View → Move Folder → select folder
    Alt+V, M, folder number
    Drag one folder into other
open (from Message Center)
    File → Open Folder

Ctrl+O
Alt+F, O
Double-click on folder name
open (from Message List)
    Select folder from pulldown menu on Location toolbar
properties, edit
(n/a in Composition window)
    Edit → Folder Properties
    Alt+E, S
rename (Message Center only)
    File → Rename Folder
    Alt+F, R

Font
make larger (Message List only)
    View → Increase Font
    Ctrl+]
    Alt+V, F
make smaller (Message List only)
    View → Decrease Font
    Ctrl+[

Forward
display one folder/group (Message List only)
    Go → Forward
    Alt+→
    Alt+G, W
message (Message List only)
    Message → Forward
    Ctrl+L
    Alt+M, D
    Forward button
message quoted (>)
(Message List only)
    Message → Forward Quoted
    Ctrl+Shift+L
    Alt+M, Q

Headers
length of displayed
(Message List only)
    View → Headers → All, Normal, or Brief
    Alt+V, D, (A, N, or B)

Images
show
(Message List only)

View → Show Images
Alt+V, W

Interrupt download (n/a in Composition window)
View → Stop Loading
Escape
Alt+V, S
Stop button

Mail account, manage
Edit → Manage Mail Account
Alt+E, N

Mark
all messages as read (Message List only)
Message → Mark → All Read
Shift+C
Alt+M, M, A
selected message(s) as read (Message List only)
Message → Mark → as Read
M
Alt+M, M, R
seleced message(s) as unread (Message List only)
Message → Mark → as Unread
U
Alt+M, M, U
thread as read (Message List only)
Message → Mark → Thread Read
Alt+M, M, T

Message(s)
compose new
File → New → Message
Ctrl+M
Alt+F, N, M
New Msg button (n/a in Comp window)
copy to folder (Message List only)
Messages → Copy Message → select folder
Alt+M, C, folder number
display all (Message List only)
View → Messages → All
Alt+V, M, A

display ignored threads (Message List only)
View → Messages → Ignored
Alt+V, M, I
display next (Message List only)
Go → Next Message
Shift+N
Alt+G, N
down-arrow
display next flagged (Message List only)
Go → Next Flagged Message
Alt+G, L
display next unread (Message List only)
Go → Next Unread Message
N
Alt+G, U
display only new (Message List only)
View → Messages → New
Alt+V, M, N
display threads with new (Message List only)
View → Messages → Threads with New
Alt+V, M, T
display watched threads with new (Message List only)
View → Messages → Watched Threads with New
Alt+V, M, W
mark as read (Message List only)
Message → Mark → as Read
M
Alt+M, M, R
mark as unread (Message List only)
Message → Mark → as Unread
U
Alt+M, M, U
open in separate window (Message List only)
File → Open Message
Alt+F, O
Double-click header in Message List
save in Drafts folder (Comp window only)
File → Save Draft
Ctrl+S
Alt+F, S

Save button
save in file (n/a in Message Center)
File → Save As
Ctrl+S
Alt+F, S
save in folder (Message List only)
Message → File Message →
choose folder
Alt+M, L, folder number
File button, select folder
send later (Composition window)
File → Send Later
Alt+F, L
send now (Composition window)
File → Send Now
Ctrl+Enter
Alt+F, D
Send button
source, show
View → Page Source
Alt+V, U
update message count
(Message Center only)
File → Update Message Count
Alt+F, U

Navigator Personal Toolbar
Add link to Message Center or Message List
Drag page proxy icon from Message Center or Message List onto Navigator Personal Toolbar

New Message
File → New → Message
Ctrl+M
Alt+F, N, M
New Msg button (n/a in Comp window)

News (See also Message)
add server (Message Center)
File → New Discussion Group Server
Alt+F, G
compose new message
(for group(s) selected in Message List or Message Center)
File → New → Message

Ctrl+M
Alt+F, N, M
New Msg button
change server
(Message Center only)
File → New Discussion Group Server
Alt+F, G
open Message Center to access
Communicator → Collabra Discussion Groups
Ctrl+3
Alt+C, D
Collabra button on Component Bar

Newsgroup (See also Subscribe/ unsubscribe)
manage
Edit → Manage Discussion Group
Alt+E, O
open (Message Center)
File → Open Discussion Group
Ctrl+O
Alt+F, O
Double-click group name in Message Center
open (Message List)
Select name from menu on Location toolbar

News server, add (Message Center)
(See also Preferences)
File → New Discussion Group Server
Alt+F, G

Next, display (Message List only)
category
Go → Next Category
Alt+G, C
flagged message
Go → Next Flagged Message
Alt+G, L
message
Go → Next Message
Shift+N
Alt+G, N
down-arrow
newsgroup

Go → Next Group

Alt+G, X

unread message

Go → Next Unread Message

N

Alt+G, U

unread category

Go → Next Category

Alt+G, C

unread newsgroup

Go → Next Unread Group

G

Alt+G, D

unread thread

Go → Next Unread Thread

T

Alt+G, T

Offline, take mail/news

File → Go Offline

Alt+F, I

Open

Inbox and receive new mail

Mail button on Component Bar

Inbox without receiving new mail

Communicator → Messenger
Mailbox

Ctrl+2

Alt+C, then M

Double-click folder name in Message Center

other Communicator module

Communicator → item corresponding to window on last
part of menu

Alt+C → number corresponding
to window

Page specs, view

(Message List only)

View → Page Info

Alt+V, I

Pane, Message List viewing

close

View → Hide Message

Alt+V, G

Down arrow button above pane,
on left

open

View → Show Message

Alt+V, G

Up arrow button below pane, on
left

Paste last cut/copied text

as is

Edit → Paste

Ctrl+V

Alt+E, P

preceded by angle brackets (>)
(Composition window)
(See also Reply)

Edit → Paste as Quotation

Alt+E, Q

Preferences, edit mail/news

Edit → Preferences

Alt+E, P

Previous, display (Message List)

flagged message

Go → Flagged Message

Alt+G, G

message

Go → Previous message

Shift+P

Alt+G, P

unread message

Go → Previous Unread Message

P

Alt+G, S

Properties

edit for mail folder
(n/a in Composition window)

Edit → Folder Properties

Alt+E, S

edit for newsgroup
(n/a in Composition window)

Edit → Discussion Group Properties

Alt+E, S

Redo last undone edit

(n/a in Composition window)

Edit → Redo

Ctrl+Y

Alt+E, R

Refresh Message List window
    View → Refresh
    Alt+V, H

Reload Message List window
    View → Reload
    Alt+V, R

Reply
    include previous message in
    (Composition window only)
      File → Quote Original Text
      Alt+F, Q
      Quote button
    to newsgroup
    (Message List only)
      Message → Reply → to Group
      Ctrl+D
      Alt+M, R, G
      Reply button → to Group
    to sender of mail
    (Message List only)
      Message → Reply → to Sender
      Ctrl+R
      Alt+M, R, S
      Reply button → to Sender
    to sender of mail and all recipients
    (Message List only)
      Message → Reply → to Sender
        and All Recipients
      Ctrl+Shift+R
      Alt+M, R, A
      Reply button → to Sender and All
        Recipients
    to sender and newsgroup
    (Message List only)
      Message → Reply → to Sender
        Group
      Ctrl+Shift+D
      Alt+M, R, U
      Reply button → to Sender and
        Group

Save message
    in Drafts folder (Composition win-
    dow only)
      File → Save Draft
      Ctrl+S
      Alt+F, S

      Save button
    in file (n/a in Message Center)
      File → Save As
      Ctrl+S
      Alt+F, S
    in folder (Message List only)
      Message → File Message →
        choose folder
      Alt+M, L, folder number
      File button, select folder

Search through
    message headers
    (n/a in Composition window)
      Edit → Search Messages
      Alt+E, M
    text in current message
    (n/a in Message Center)
      Edit → Find in Message
      Ctrl+F
      Alt+E, F
    yellow pages/white pages
      Edit → Search Directory
      Alt+E, Y

Select all (folders, groups, text)
    (n/a in Message List)
      Edit → Select All
      Ctrl+A
      Alt+E, A

Send
    message now (Composition window)
      File → Send Now
      Ctrl+Enter
      Alt+F, M
      Send button
    message later (Composition window)
      File → Send Later
      Alt+F, L
    messages saved for later
    (n/a in Composition window)
      File → Send Unsent Messages
      Alt+F, M

Signature
    view for outgoing message
    (Composition window only)
      View → Options
      Alt+V, O

Sort messages by date or sender, etc.
(Message List only)
   View → Sort → choose sorting method
   Alt+V, O, choose sorting method
   Click on appropriate header over message list (e.g., Subject)

Source, view message
(Message List only)
   View → Page Source
   Alt+V, U

Spell check (Composition window only)
   Tools → Check Spelling
   Alt+T, S
   Spell button

Stop download (n/a in Composition window)
   View → Stop Loading
   Escape
   Alt+V, S
   Stop button

Subscribe/unsubscribe to newsgroup(s) (See also Delete)
edit subscription list (n/a in Composition window)
   File → Subscribe to Discussion Groups
   Alt+F, B
   Subscribe button (Message Center)
subscribe to new group (n/a in Composition window)
   File → New Discussion Group
   Alt+F, W
unsubscribe to selected group(s) (Message Center)
   Edit → Delete Discussion Group
   Delete
   Alt+E, D

Thread
display next unread thread (Message List only)
   Go → Next Unread Thread

   T
   Alt+G, T
mark as read
(Message List only)
   Message → Mark → Thread Read
   Alt+M, M, T

Toolbar(s), hide/show
Addressing Area (Composition window only)
   View → Hide/Show Addressing Area
   Alt+V, A
   Toggle using tab on left of bar
Location (n/a in Composition window)
   View → Hide/Show Location Toolbar
   Alt+V, L
   Toggle using tab on left of bar
Message (Composition window only)
   View → Hide/Show Message Toolbar
   Alt+V, M
   Toggle using tab on left of bar
Navigation (n/a in Composition window)
   View → Hide/Show Navigation Toolbar
   Alt+V, N
   Toggle using tab on left of bar

Trash folder
empty (Message Center only)
   File → Empty Trash Folder
   Alt+F, Y

Undo last edit
(See also Redo)
   Edit → Undo
   Ctrl+Z
   Alt+E, U

Unscramble news (Message List)
   View → Unscramble (ROT13)
   Alt+V, B

Email and News

Wrap lines

in Composition window

    View → Wrap Long Lines on
        Send

    Alt+V, W

in Message List window

    View → Wrap Long Lines

    Alt+V, P

CHAPTER 14

MSIE Internet Mail

Included with Microsoft Internet Explorer is a module called Internet Mail, a versatile email program with a clean and simple interface. Unlike many similar tools, Internet Mail is not over-programmed—in other words, it doesn't have tons of functionality buried too deeply for you to find it.

This chapter discusses the version of Internet Mail included with MSIE 3.02. If you're using a different version of the program, keep in mind that certain functions, menu commands, keystrokes, etc., may vary.

First, the chapter provides a quick overview of the Internet Mail module and its component windows. The chapter then discusses some of the neater features you might not notice at first glance. Finally, the chapter provides a quick reference to the various actions you can perform with this module. For each action, the reference pages list the menu items, keyboard shortcuts, and toolbar buttons and other window features you can use to perform the action.

In order for you to be able to make sense of some of the shortcuts covered in the quick reference section, the overview section includes illustrations of the basic module windows and subwindows, with prominent features labeled. As with most MSIE features, you can get a message about a feature's purpose by placing the pointer over it (when the focus is on that window). Use this "mini-help" information to supplement the information provided in the tables.

If you participate in Usenet news (discussed in Chapter 12, *Getting Along in Usenet*), you'll also want to check out MSIE's Internet News program. Internet News has a number of features in common with Internet Mail, including similar windows and a number of the same functions. You can even initiate certain functions across modules (e.g., you can ask to send a new mail message when you're running news). To learn about *MSIE Internet News*, see Chapter 15.

Internet Mail Components

Internet Mail has a basic application window, pictured in Figure 14–1.

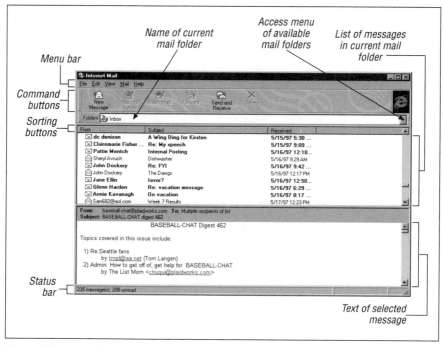

Figure 14–1: Primary Internet Mail window

By default, this window is divided into two panes: the top pane lists the messages in the current folder; the bottom pane, called the Preview Pane, shows the contents of the current message. (The **View** menu lets you change the number and arrangement of the panes, if you want.)

You can read your mail in the Preview Pane or open the current message in a separate window, using the **Open** command on the primary module's **File** menu; double-clicking on the entry for the message in the Internet Mail list pane does the same thing. For the sake of clarity, we'll call these subwindows Read windows—but there's no official name for them. A typical Read window appears in Figure 14–2. Note that you can have as many of these Read windows open as you like, or you can read one message after another into the same window by using the Next and Previous buttons on the window's toolbar (see illustration). The window's **View** menu also offers the items **Next Message** and **Previous Message**.

Before you read a message, the listing for the message in the Internet Mail window is preceded by a small envelope icon. After you read it, the icon changes to an open envelope. (There are also commands to change the read/unread status of a message.)

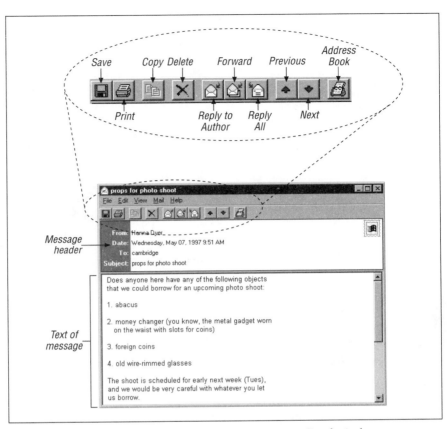

Figure 14–2: You can read a mail message in a separate Read window

The final window you'll be dealing with is a Write window, which opens up when you select a command to compose a message (e.g., the New Message toolbar button). When you open a Read or Write window like the one in Figure 14–3, you'll notice that its titlebar reflects its contents/purpose. For example, if you select the New Message button to open a Write window, the Write window will be labeled "New Message." If the message you're composing is a reply, the titlebar of the Write window will reflect the Subject line of the message to which you're replying, etc. Similarly, the titlebar of a Read window generally contains the Subject line of the message. (If there's no Subject line, the words "New Message" are used.)

Tips for Using Internet Mail

Internet Mail is a very straightforward application. But there are some useful features you may not notice right away. The following sections highlight some of these functions.

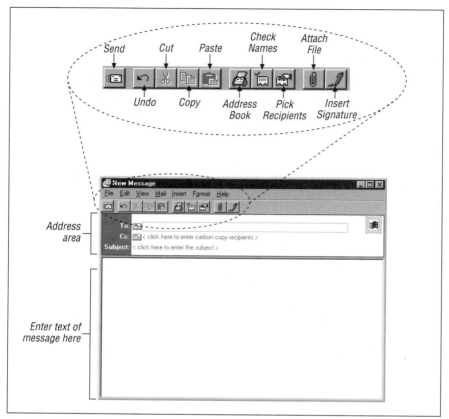

Figure 14–3: Compose and send messages from the Write window

Use Email Offline to Save Money

You can read and compose mail without being connected to the Internet. Internet Mail is set up to send and receive mail only when you request it (the Send and Receive button on the toolbar is one way). The messages you compose are saved in an Outbox folder until this happens. Copies of sent messages go into a Sent Items folder (unless you specify otherwise using the **Options** dialog).

If you're using an intermittent Internet connection, it's a good idea to connect to the Net (specifically to your mail server) to download new mail (and perhaps send mail you've composed offline); then disconnect, and read and write messages at your leisure. You can reconnect when you want to send and receive mail again.

You need to supply incoming and outgoing mail server names when you config-ure Internet Mail. If you ever need to change them, they live on the Server tab in the Options dialog (**Mail** menu → **Options** item).

Change Folders Using Pulldown Menu on the Toolbar

If you take a look back at Figure 14-1, you'll notice that the name of the current mail folder (Inbox) is displayed in a text box in the lower part of the toolbar. The arrow on the far right of the box indicates that it's actually a pulldown menu. Click anywhere in the box to display the menu, which lists your available mail folders (see Figure 14-4).

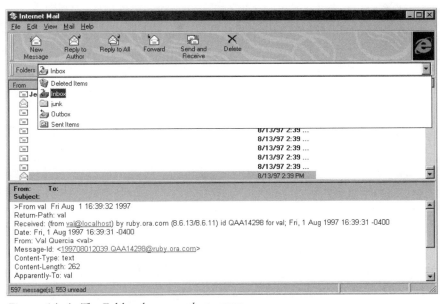

Figure 14–4: The Folders box reveals a menu

You can open another folder in the window by selecting it from the menu. The figure shows four default folders, which have the following purposes:

- Deleted Items

- Inbox

- Outbox

- Sent Items

There's also one folder that I created—called *junk*.

The messages you delete get moved to Deleted Items. In the default configuration, deleted mail lives there indefinitely. Internet Mail does offer an option that causes the Deleted Items folder to be emptied when you exit the program. Select **Options** from the **Mail** menu; then select the Read tab at the top of the dialog, and toggle the option on. (It's the last one on the page.) Then click the Apply button at the bottom of the dialog; close the dialog with the OK button.

The Inbox is where your new mail is stored when it arrives, of course. The "Sent Items" folder keeps copies of the messages you send. (This is a default of another option; you can toggle it off if you don't want to keep copies of your messages; see the Send tab in the Options dialog.)

When you create a new message and tell the Write window to send it (using Alt+S, or **Send Message** on the **File** menu), the message is put in a folder called the Outbox. Remember, in this environment, "send" actually means "queue to send when I say **Send and Receive**." (There are a number of ways to say this, including a toolbar button and the Ctrl+M keyboard shortcut.)

View a Message in a Separate (Read) Window

In the default configuration of Internet Mail, whichever message you select in the upper pane is displayed in the lower Preview Pane. If you'd prefer to look at a message in a separate Read window, double-click on its header line in the Internet Mail window.

You can also opt to close the Preview Pane. The *Preview Pane* item on the **View** menu reveals a submenu of three possible layouts. The first item, **None**, closes the Preview Pane entirely. **Split Horizontally** restores the default layout. Or, you can opt to have side-by-side panes: **Split Vertically**.

If you close the Preview Pane—leaving only the message headers in the Internet Mail window—you still have to double-click on a header in order to open it in a Read window.

Ways to Sort Your Mail

In Internet Mail, email message headers have three components, which correspond to the columns above the message list: who sent it (the From column), the subject of the message (Subject column), and the date (Received column). By default, mail appears in your Inbox sorted by the date received. You can instead choose to sort by the sender or subject by clicking on the corresponding column title. (The **View** menu also offers a **Sort By** submenu with three mutually exclusive choices: **From**, **Subject**, and **Received**.)

Regardless of which of these sorting methods is active, there is an additional sorting factor that applies: messages are either listed oldest to newest (*ascending* order) or newest to oldest (*descending* order). In the default Inbox, the newest messages appear at the bottom of the list, that is, in *ascending* order. You can switch to descending order using the **Sort By** submenu.

Using the Address Book

Like any good mailer, Internet Mail lets you save email addresses you use frequently and also to create shortcuts (commonly called aliases) you can use in place of the entire address. Select **Address Book** from the **File** menu in any of the module windows in order to create, edit, or view address book entries. A fairly skimpy Address Book appears in Figure 14–5. This is actually the Address Book on my friend Linda's PC, which I'm using for testing purposes. (You might notice

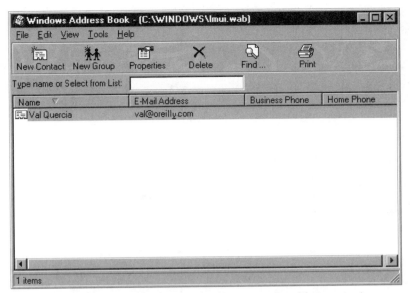

Figure 14–5: Address Book window with one measly address: mine!

the pathname of the Address Book file at the top of the window; the "lmui" is Linda's username.)

In order to create a new entry in the Address Book, I can use the New Contact button (**File → New Contact** or Ctrl+N works, too). This opens a Properties window in which you can specify lots information about the person.

The first page or tab of information, titled Personal, lets you supply information for the most basic Address Book entry: name, email address, nickname (alias), etc. Figure 14–6 shows this first page. You have to supply the following:

- Either a "Nickname" or regular name ("First" is enough, but you can enter "Middle" and "Last" if you want your mail to display the full name)

- An address in the "E-mail Addresses" box

Suppose I want to add an entry for my friend Uta who gets her email through America Online. Suppose again that her address is UNOwen@aol.com. I'd put "uta" in the "Nickname" field and "UNOwen@aol.com" in the "Email Addresses" box, and then click on the Add button (or type Alt+A) to create the entry.

The additional pages/tabs in the Properties dialog let me store a lot more information about my friend, things like where she lives, where she works, phone and fax numbers for both locations, the URL of her Web page, and whatever general notes I want to enter. If I supply a business and/or home phone number, the primary Address Book window will include that with her entry.

Once I'm done filling out information for a particular "contact," clicking OK takes me back to the Address Book window, where the new entry information is

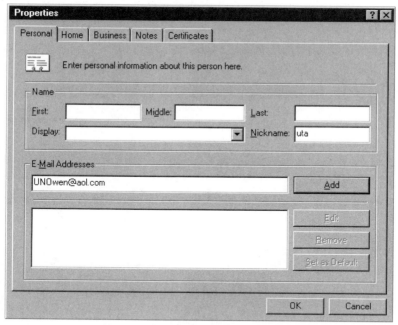

Figure 14–6: Supply information about a person to add them to your Address Book

displayed. (It's worthwhile to take note of the New Group button in the Address Book window; this lets you create an alias for multiple people in your book.)

OK, so I create some Address Book entries. When do I use them? Well, I can use a nickname on the "To" line of a mail message I'm writing, and Internet Mail will expand the nickname to match the more complete address saved in the Address Book.

If I can't remember someone's address, the Composition window's **Mail** menu offers an item called **Choose Recipients**, which lets you select names from the address book. The Select Recipients dialog appears in Figure 14–7. Select the name or names from the left side, and then select "To" or "CC" (carbon copy) on the right. (You can actually specify names for both.) Then click OK to go back to the Composition window. Ta-da. The names you picked appear on the outgoing message's header lines.

Keyboard Shortcuts for Common Functions

The reference pages for Internet Mail functions (later in this chapter) list a keyboard shortcut (or accelerator) for just about every function. However, many of these shortcuts are just the keys that let you access the various menu items. For instance, you can open a Write window by selecting **New Message** from the **Mail** menu; "Alt+M, N" does the same thing because the Alt+M key opens the **Mail** menu, and then **N** invokes the **New Message** item. However, since this is a func-

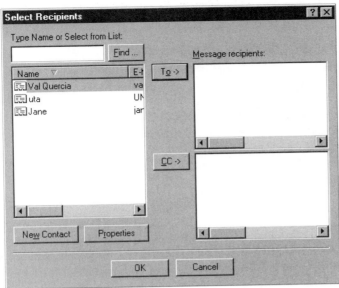

Figure 14–7: When writing email, you can choose recipients from the Address Book

tion most people will want to use all the time, the developers have created a shorter, more legitimate accelerator, namely, Ctrl+N.

For the most commonly used functions, there are true keyboard shortcuts, many of which require the use of the Ctrl key; Table 14–1 summarizes those common functions and the keyboard shortcuts for them. Note that some of these functions may not work in every window in Internet Mail.

Table 14–1: Keyboard Shortcuts for Common Functions

Function	Shortcut
Check names in header of outgoing message against address book	Ctrl+K
Close window	Alt+F4
Copy (selected text)	Ctrl+C
Cut (selected text)	Ctrl+X
Delete selected message(s)/text	Ctrl+D
Find again	F3
Find message/text	F3
Forward message	Ctrl+F
Help	F1
Mark as read	Ctrl+Enter

Table 14-1: Keyboard Shortcuts for Common Functions (continued)

Function	Shortcut
Mark as unread	Ctrl+Shift+Enter
New message	Ctrl+N
Next message	Ctrl+>
Open selected message	Ctrl+O
Previous message	Ctrl+<
Print selected message(s)	Ctrl+P
Reply to all	Ctrl+Shift+R
Reply to author	Ctrl+R
Select all	Ctrl+A
Send and receive mail	Ctrl+M
Send message (i.e., queue to send with Send & Receive function)	Alt+S
Undo last text edit	Ctrl+Z

Specifying and Using a Signature File

Among Internet Mail's customizable options is a way to specify a signature file, which you can append to outgoing mail. Select **Options** from the **Mail** menu; then click on the tab labeled Signature at the top of the Options dialog.

You specify what the signature should be in the top half of the dialog:

- No signature (the default)

- Text you enter in the dialog

- A file whose pathname you provide

Click in front of your choice and then provide additional information (e.g., the text of your signature or the name of a signature file elsewhere on your system). In Figure 14–8, someone's chosen to enter their signature in the dialog. The lower half of the Signature page lets you specify when Internet Mail should include your signature. The default is to use it for all outgoing messages (first toggle), except "replies and forwards" (second toggle).

If you don't want to use a signature for all outgoing messages, turn off the first toggle (the second one goes off with it). Then if you want to include a signature with a particular message, you just have to request it explicitly. The Composition window lets you add a signature to a message you're writing by selecting **Signature** from the **Insert** menu.

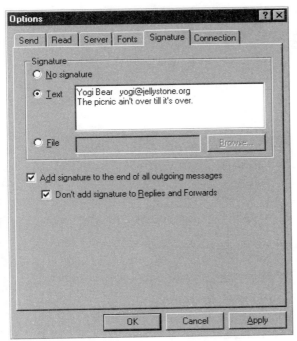

Figure 14–8: Signature from the U.S. Park Service

Setting Up Mail Filters

With mail filtering, you tell the mailer what to do with incoming messages that match certain criteria. For instance, you might create a filter that saves all the messages you get from your boss in a particular folder, or all the messages with a certain word or words in the Subject line, whatever.

Internet Mail's filtering function is called **Inbox Assistant**. Select **Inbox Assistant** from the **Mail** menu. You'll get a window similar to the one in Figure 14–9. The initial window lists the filters you create; ours is empty. To create one, I begin by clicking on the Add button (Alt+A works too), which opens a Properties window (see Figure 14–10). The upper half of the window lets you specify what criteria a message has to meet to be detected by the filter; the lower half specifies how messages that meet those criteria should be handled. In terms of criteria, you must provide information for at least one field, but you can use additional fields if you like. The default action to take when a filter finds a particular message is to delete the message—or specifically to move the message to the *Deleted Items* folder. However, the "Move To:" field is actually a menu of folders; besides Deleted Items, the menu will include any folder you've created (e.g., my *junk* folder is on my menu).

In practice, you might use a filter in the following way. Suppose there's a lot of mail circulated in my company about our basketball team (this is pretty hypothetical because we don't have one)—and I have no interest in this. These messages

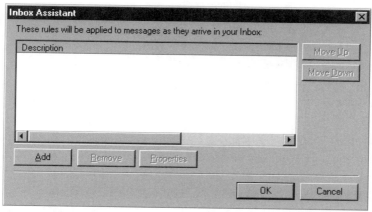

Figure 14-9: Inbox Assistant

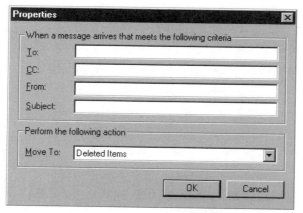

Figure 14-10: Properties subwindow lets you specify what you want the filter to do

all have "basketball" in the Subject line—so I enter it in the Subject line of the Properties dialog. When I click OK, I've created a filter that deletes messages with "basketball" in the Subject. The Properties dialog is closed, and the new filter is listed in the initial Inbox Assistant window, as in Figure 14-11. You can create as many filters as you like. The checkbox in front of the filter description lets you turn it off and on, without wiping it off the list (use the Remove button or Alt+R to do that). The Properties button lets you edit the filter.

You can rearrange the order of the filters—and thus the order in which they are applied—using the Move Up and Move Down functions. This allows you to use filters in combination.

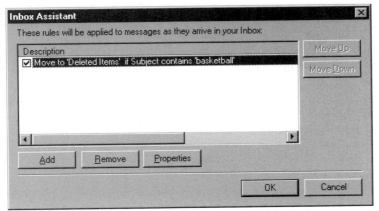

Figure 14–11: Newly created filter appears in Inbox Assistant window

Sending a Message in HTML Format

The **HTML** item on the **Write** menu allows you to send a message in HTML format. When you select this item, additional editing options become available on the **Format** menu. The Write window is also modified to include a special HTML editing toolbar, as illustrated in Figure 14–12. This feature lets you retain HTML formatting in the email you send. This is a fun feature, but keep in mind that not every mailer can display HTML files. Keep your audience in mind.

Quick Reference to Internet Mail

The following pages provide a reference to the various ways you can perform Internet Mail functions. Keep in mind that this reference is based on the version of Internet Mail shipped with MSIE 3.02. If you're using another version of the program, certain functions, menu commands, keystrokes, etc., may vary.

Within the reference, the functions are organized alphabetically. Under each heading, the ways you can perform the function are listed in the following order:

- Menu items

- Keyboard shortcuts

- Buttons and other window features

Note that some functions are only available in certain windows of the mail program. For example, you can attach a file to an outgoing message (in a Write window). But this function doesn't mean anything when you're viewing message headers in the primary Internet Mail window or when you're reading mail (in a separate Read window).

For each function entry, assume that it is available for all of the module's windows unless there is a note to the contrary. In cases where a function applies to only one of the three window types, the valid window will be listed below the function

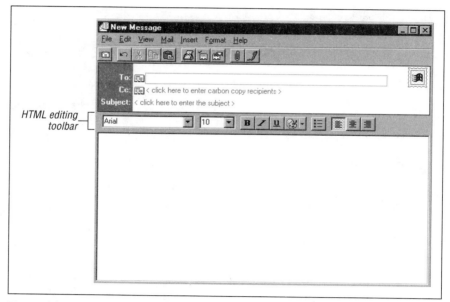

HTML editing toolbar

Figure 14–12: Internet Mail lets you edit and send HTML files

name. If the function applies to two of the three types, the note will say that the function is not applicable (i.e., *n/a*) to the third type.

While the reference pages cover most of the bases you'll care about, there may be some minor features—particularly in the Read and Write windows—that haven't gotten as much attention. Keep in mind that you can always get additional information using the "mini-help" facility (i.e., placing the pointer over a feature to get a short description of what it does).

Following the function reference is a shorter reference to the various Internet Mail customization options.

About Mail and News
Help → About Microsoft Mail and News
Alt+H, M

Address book
import entries from another (e.g., Netscape's)
(Internet Mail only)
File → Import → Address Book . . . (select book from list)
Alt+F, I; select book
open (n/a Read window)
File → Address Book . . .
Alt+F, B

Address Book toolbar button
(Write window only)

Alignment, modify in outgoing message
(Write window only)
(HTML must be selected from Format menu)
Format → HTML → Align
Alt+O, H, A

Attach file
separately (Write window only)
Insert → File Attachment
Alt+I, F

Insert File button
Drag file icon into window
(text file) within body of message
(Write window only)
Insert → Text File
Alt+I, T
Copy and paste text into window

Best of the Web (Internet Mail only)
Help → Microsoft on the Web →
Best of the Web
Alt+H, W, B

Bullets, use in outgoing message
(Write window only)
(HTML must be selected from Format menu)
Format → HTML → Bullets
Alt+O, H, B

Close window
File → Close
Alt+F4
Alt+F, C
Close button on frame

Columns in List Pane, customize
(Internet Mail only)
View → Columns . . .
Alt+V, C

Copy
message to other folder
(Internet Mail only)
Mail → Copy to → Choose folder
Alt+M, C, use arrow keys to high-
light folder, hit Return
selected text
Edit → Copy
Ctrl+C
Alt+E, C
Copy button on toolbar (Read
and Write windows only)

Cut selected text
(Write window only)
Edit → Cut
Ctrl+X
Alt+E, T
Cut button on toolbar

Delete current message
(n/a in Write window)
File → Delete
Ctrl+D
Alt+F, D
Del key (Read window only)
Delete button on toolbar

Encoding/MIME, change manually
(Write window only)
(Note that attachments should be handled automatically)
Format → Settings . . .
Alt+O, S

Folder
compact (to save disk space)
(Internet Mail only)
File → Folder → Compact
(choose folder name or All
Folders)
Alt+F, F, O; highlight folder using
arrow keys or type A for All;
hit Return
create (Internet Mail only)
File → Folder → Create
Alt+F, F, C
delete (Internet Mail only)
File → Folder → Delete (choose
folder from menu)
Alt+F, F, D; highlight folder using
arrow keys; hit Return

Font, modify in outgoing message
(Write window only)
(HTML must be selected from Format menu)
Format → HTML → Font . . .
Alt+O, H, F
HTML editing toolbar has choices
for font style, type, size, and
color

**Forward message (n/a in Write win-
dow)**
as attachment
Mail → Forward as Attachment
Alt+M, A

separately
    Mail → Forward
    Ctrl+F
    Alt+M, F
    Forward button

Frequently Asked Questions
(Internet Mail only)
    Help → Microsoft on the Web →
        Frequently Asked Questions
    Alt+H, W, Q

Get new mail
(Internet Mail only)
    Mail → Send and Receive
    Ctrl+M
    Alt+M, S
    Send and Receive button

Help
online support
(Internet Mail only)
    Help → Microsoft on the Web →
        Online Support
    Alt+H, W, S
topics
    Help → Help Topics
    F1
    Alt+H, H

Home page, open in browser
(Internet Mail only)
    File → Start Page
    Alt+F, A

HTML format, send message in
(Write window only)
(see also Font, Alignment, Bullets)
    Format → HTML
    F1
    Alt+O, H

Language in which to view/compose messages
    View → Language → Select from
        list
    Alt+V, G, select language

Messages
import from another mailer

(Internet Mail only)
    File → Import → Messages . . .
        (select mailer; currently only
        Exchange)
    Alt+F, I, M, select mailer
mark as read (for auto-marking, see
    Internet Mail Options)
(Internet Mail only)
    Edit → Mark as Read
    Ctrl+Enter
    Alt+E, E
export to another mailer
(Internet Mail only)
    File → Import → Messages . . .
        (select mailer; currently only
        Exchange)
    Alt+F, E, M, select mailer
properties, display
    File → Properties
    Alt+F, R

Microsoft
home page
(Internet Mail only)
    Help → Microsoft on the Web →
        Home Page
    Alt+H, W, H
Product news
(Internet Mail only)
    Help → Microsoft on the Web →
        Product News
    Alt+H, W, P
send feedback to
(Internet Mail only)
    Help → Microsoft on the Web →
        Send Feedback
    Alt+H, W, D

Move message to other folder (including trash)
(Internet Mail only)
    Mail → Move to → Choose folder
    Alt+M, V, use arrow keys to high-
        light folder, hit Return

New message, open Write window to compose
    Mail → New Message
    Ctrl+N
    Alt+M, N *(Internet Mail and Read*

window)
Alt+M, M *(Write window)*
New Message toolbar button
(Internet Mail only)

News, open Internet
(Internet Mail only)
File → Read News
Alt+F, N

Next message, view
(n/a in Write window)
View → Next Message
Ctrl+>
Alt+V, N
Next button (Read window only)

Open current message in Read Window
(Internet Mail only)
File → Open
Ctrl+O
Alt+F, O
Double-click message title in List
pane

Options, specify mail customization
(see Internet Mail Options)
Mail → Options
Alt+M, O

Paste last cut or copied text
(Write window only)
Edit → Paste
Ctrl+V
Alt+E, P
Alt+E, U
Paste button

Preview pane
hide/show
(Internet Mail only)
View → Preview Pane → None
Alt+V, V, N
hide/show header info
(Internet Mail only)
View → Preview Pane → Header
Information
Alt+V, V, D
split horizontally

(Internet Mail only)
View → Preview Pane → Split
Horizontally
Alt+V, V, H
split vertically
(Internet Mail only)
View → Preview Pane → Split
Vertically
Alt+V, V, V

Previous message, view
(n/a in Write window)
View → Previous Message
Ctrl+<
Alt+V, P
Previous toolbar button in Read
window

Print current message
(n/a in Write window)
File → Print
Ctrl+P
Alt+F, P
Print button in Read window

README file (Internet Mail and News)
Help → Read Me
Alt+H, R

Refresh window
(Internet Mail only)
View → Refresh
Alt+V, R

Reply
to all
(n/a in Write window)
Mail → Reply to All
Ctrl+Shift+R
Alt+M, L
Reply to All button
to author
(n/a in Write window)
Mail → Reply to Author
Ctrl+R
Alt+M, U
Reply to Author button

Save message in file
(n/a in Write window)
File → Save As . . .
Alt+F, S (Internet Mail)
Alt+F, A (Read window)

Search
the Web (in MSIE window)
(Internet Mail only)
File → Search the Web
Help → Microsoft on the Web →
Search the Web
Alt+F, H
Alt+H, W, W
through message headers
(Internet Mail only)
Edit → Find Message . . .
F3
Alt+E, F
through message headers again
(Internet Mail only)
Edit → Find Next
F3
Alt+E, X
through message text
(n/a in Internet Mail)
Edit → Find . . .
F3
Alt+E, F
through message text again
(n/a in Internet Mail)
While Find is dialog open (see
search through message text),
keep hitting Return

Select all text
Edit → Select All
Ctrl+A
Alt+E, A

Send
mail (queued to go out)
(Internet Mail only)
Mail → Send and Receive
Ctrl+M
Alt+M, S
Send and Receive button
message (or queue to send)

(Write window only)
File → Send Message
Alt+S
Alt+F, M
Send button on toolbar

Signature file, attach
(Write window only)
(must first specify sig file under
Internet Mail Options)
Insert → Signature
Alt+I, S
Insert Signature button

Software, download free Microsoft
(Internet Mail only)
Help → Microsoft on the Web →
Free Stuff
Alt+H, W, F

Sort messages (Internet Mail only)
by ascending/descending order
View → Sort By → Ascending
Alt+V, S, A
by date received
View → Sort By → Received
Alt+V, S, R
by From field
View → Sort By → From
Alt+V, S, F
by Subject field
View → Sort By → Subject
Alt+V, S, B

Status Bar, hide/show
(Internet Mail only)
View → Status Bar
Alt+V, B

Toolbar hide/show
View → Toolbar
Alt+V, T

Undo last text edit
(Write window only)
Edit → Undo
Ctrl+Z
Alt+E, U
Undo button on toolbar

Internet Mail Options

You can set a number of options that determine how Internet Mail looks and operates. All of these preferences are set using the Options dialog box, which is displayed using the menu sequence:

```
Mail → Options
```

Or the keyboard shortcut:

```
Alt+M, and then O
```

Within the Options dialog, the various preferences are organized on six overlapping tabbed windows, which look something like file folders. The tabs reveal the following categories:

- Send
- Read
- Server
- Fonts
- Signature
- Connection

The following pages provide an index to Internet Mail's customization options. Under each option heading, you'll find the possible settings, the default(s) (if any), and the appropriate tab on which to find/set it.

Character set (language) in which to display
Central European, Cyrillic, or
Western European
Default is Western European
Fonts tab

Connection
Type to use
LAN; manual; or modem;
default given at setup
Connection tab
Dial-up connection number (with modem only)
Default given at setup
Connection tab
Disconnect when finished sending/receiving (modem only)
Off by default
Connection tab

Color of text (Write window)
Black by default

Fonts tab

Font, display
Fonts tab

Mailer
Make Internet Mail default
On by default
Send tab

Messages
Check for new every x minutes
On by default; 10 minutes
Read tab
Divide those larger than x KB
Off; 60 when on
Send tab
Empty Deleted Items folder on exit
Off by default
Read tab
Mark as read after previewing x seconds
On by default; 5 seconds

Read tab
Play sound when messages arrive
On by default
Read tab
*Save copies of outgoing (in Sent
Items folder)*
On by default
Send tab
Send immediately
Off by default
Send tab
Send in HTML format
Off by default
Send tab
Send in text format
On by default
Send tab

Password
User's
Default given at setup
Server tab
Use secure authentication
Off by default
Server tab

Replies
Include original message in
On by default
Send tab
Quote original with x character
On by default; > character
Send tab

Selecting text
Auto select entire word
On by default
Send tab

Send messages immediately
Off by default
Send tab

Servers
Incoming mail (SMTP)
Default given at setup
Server tab
Outgoing mail (POP3)
Default given at setup
Server tab

Signature
Append to all outgoing messages
On by default (if sig specified)
Signature tab
Don't use sig in replies and forwards
On by default (when sig is speci-
fied)
Signture tab
*No sig; or text of sig entered in
Options dialog; or sig file from sys-
tem*
No sig is default
Signature tab

Sound, play when new mail arrives
On by default
Read tab

User account for mail server
User's email address
Name given to setup wizard is
default
Server tab
User name to display
Name given to setup wizard is
default
Server tab
User name/password for login
Info given to setup wizard is
default
Server tab

CHAPTER 15

MSIE Internet News

Internet News is MSIE's Usenet news module. Although news is a completely different service from electronic mail, Internet News actually looks and works a lot like MSIE's Internet Mail application (described in Chapter 14, *MSIE Internet Mail*). Both applications share a clear and to-the-point interface, coupled with a bunch of more advanced features. You can also initiate certain functions across modules (e.g., you can open the mailer from the news application).

First, the current chapter provides a quick overview of the Internet News module, including illustrations of the basic window and subwindows, with prominent features labeled.

The chapter then discusses some of the ways you can make Internet News work for you—including a number of the less obvious features. Note that a few of these tips are very similar to some given for Internet Mail in Chapter 14. In cases where the information is redundant, we've kept the current descriptions short and referred you back to Chapter 14.

Next, the chapter provides a quick reference to the various actions you can perform with this module. For each action, the reference pages list the menu items, keyboard shortcuts, and toolbar buttons and other window features you can use to perform the action.

In order to make sense of some of the shortcuts, you may have to refer back to the illustrations at the beginning of the chapter. As with most MSIE features, you can also get a message about a feature's purpose by placing the pointer over it (when the focus is on that window). Use this "mini-help" information to supplement the information provided in the reference pages.

Internet News Components

Internet News has a basic application window, pictured in Figure 15-1.

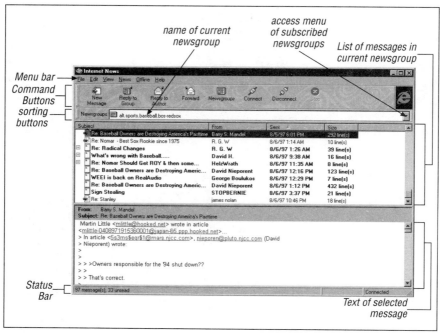

Figure 15-1: Anatomy of Internet News

By default, this window is divided into two panes: the top pane lists the messages in the current newsgroup; the bottom pane, called the Preview Pane, shows the contents of the current message. (The **View** menu lets you change the number and arrangement of the panes, if you want.)

You can read your news in the Preview Pane or open the current message in a separate window, using the **Open** command on the primary module's **File** menu; double-clicking on the entry for the message in the Internet News list pane does the same thing. As in the case with Internet Mail, we'll call the subwindows in which you view news postings Read windows, and the subwindows in which you compose news messages Write windows. Typical Read and Write windows appear in Figure 15-2 and Figure 15-3, respectively. Also like Internet Mail, you can have as many Read windows open as you like to look at news, or you can read one message after another into the same window by using the Next and Previous buttons on the window's toolbar (see illustration). The window's **View** menu also offers the items **Next Message** and **Previous Message**.

Before you read a news posting, the listing for the message in the Internet News window appears in bold type. Once you've read the message, the listing appears in a lighter type. Preceding the entry for each message in the list is an icon that

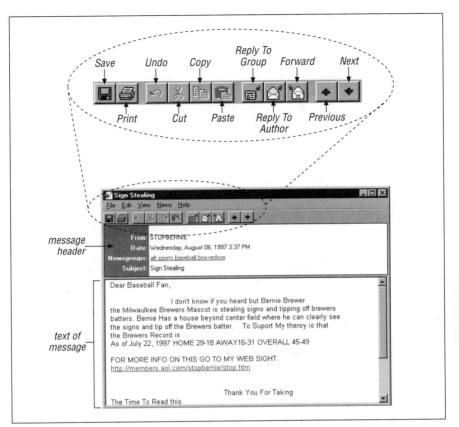

Figure 15–2: You can read a news posting in a separate Read window

gives you a clue as to its status. The particular icons are not terribly intuitive. There are a four basic icons, which you can interpret based on the following principles: yellow means the message has not been read; white means the message has been read; a pushpin means both the header and body of the message have been downloaded; no pushpin means only the header is immediately available.

Icon Symbol	What It Means
Yellow page with pushpin	Unread message and header both available in local memory.
Yellow page without push-pin	Unread message, currently with header only in local memory.
White page with pushpin	Read message and header both available in local memory.

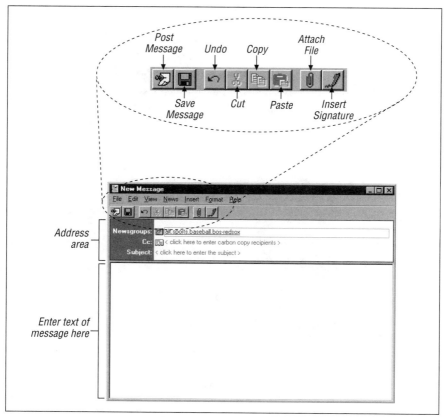

Figure 15-3: Compose and post news from the Write window

Icon Symbol	What It Means
White page without push-pin	Read message, currently with header only in local memory.

If you don't have color, remember that the listings for unread messages appear in bold type, while read messages appear in lighter type. As with the mail module, there are commands to change the read/unread status of a message.

There are two additional icons that appear when messages are organized by *thread*. When threading is in effect (the default), related messages are displayed together, with follow-ups indented under the original message and connected to it. Threading makes the list pane in the Internet News window resemble a file system directory tree. A single message thread is either "collapsed," so that only the heading for the original message is displayed, or "expanded" (like a file folder) to reveal all the follow-up messages. The symbol that represents a collapsed message thread is a plus sign; a minus sign indicates that the thread has been expanded (and thus all messages in the thread are visible).

The final window you'll be dealing with is a Write window, which opens up when you select a command to compose a news message (e.g., the New Message toolbar button). The "Newsgroups" field in the message header should reflect the current newsgroup name, if any (i.e., if a newsgroup is highlighted in the primary Internet News window). When you open a Read or Write window, you'll notice that its titlebar reflects its contents/purpose. For example, if you select the New Message button to open a Write window, the Write window will be labeled "New Message." If the news message you're composing is a follow-up to another posting, the titlebar of the Write window will reflect the Subject line of the message to which you're responding, etc. Similarly, the titlebar of a Read window generally contains the Subject line of the message. (If there's no Subject line, the words "New Message" are used.)

Both the Read and Write windows have their own menus, buttons, and other features. Many of these are referenced in the Internet News quick reference table (in the following section). However, since the table's primary emphasis is on the main Internet News application window, you may need to supplement the information for the subwindows using the "mini-help" facility (i.e., placing the pointer over a feature to get a short description of what it does).

Getting the Most Out of Internet News

Internet News has a number of useful features that may not immediately jump out at you. Some of them are described in the following sections.

While some of these interesting features apply to news only, keep in mind that some of them are also available in the similar Internet Mail application. In these cases, we'll highlight differences where they exist, but otherwise we'll refer you back to the appropriate sections in Chapter 14.

Newsgroups and News Folders

The Internet News window can be opened to a particular newsgroup or to one of three news-specific folders:

- Outbox—where news you've composed offline waits until it is posted (using the **Offline** menu → **Post and Download**, or Alt+O, P).

- Posted Items—copies of the news you've posted. (Saving posted news articles to this folder is the default, but you can turn off this feature using the Send tab in the Options dialog. See "Internet News Options" later in this chapter.)

- Saved Items—copies of news messages you've saved using the menu sequence **File** → **Save** (or Alt+F, S). This Save function works in all the module windows. Thus, you can save articles you read and also those you write.

These folders, along with the newsgroups to which you are currently subscribed, appear on a menu that is accessible from the "Newsgroups" box on the titlebar. Click anywhere on the box to open the menu, as in Figure 15–4.

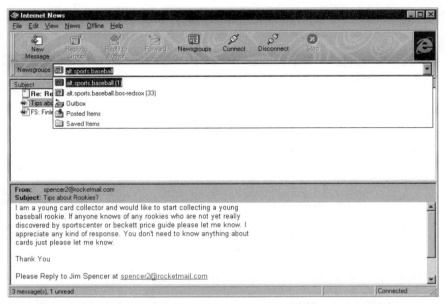

Figure 15–4: You can switch between newsgroups and folders using pulldown menu

The name of the current group (*alt.sports.baseball*) is displayed in the "Newsgroups" text box. The menu shows this group and another one to which I am subscribed, followed by the news folder names. (The number in parentheses following each newsgroup name is the number of unread articles that are available.) I can have the Internet News window display a newsgroup or folder by selecting its name from the menu.

Reading and Writing News Offline

Just like Internet Mail, Internet News is designed to let you download news and then read it (and compose your own news messages) "offline." This is intended to benefit people with intermittent Internet connections, especially those who pay to dial in to an ISP or other service. When you first run Internet News, it will look for your news server to download news articles. (If you're not connected to the Net at the time, you can get connected, and then click on the Connect button on the Internet News toolbar. This tells the program to look for news to download.)

Once you've downloaded news, you can tell Internet News to disconnect from the news server by clicking the Disconnect toolbar button. (The **File** menu also offers **Connect** and **Disconnect** items.) Then you can hang up your Internet connection, and read and write news messages on the cheap.

When you write a news article while Internet News is offline, requesting that the article be posted (Alt+S, or **File** → **Post Message**) actually just queues it to be sent later. (A dialog box will inform you of this.) Queued articles are saved in the Outbox folder until you **Connect** again, or select **Post and Download** from the **Offline** menu. (In either case reconnecting also posts the news that's been waiting in your Outbox.)

While you're not connected, note that you can use various items on the **Offline** menu to mark messages for downloading. These will be transferred to your system the next time you connect.

Subscribing, Unsubscribing, and Checking Out Newsgroups

You can open up a dialog box in which to subscribe to and unsubscribe from newsgroups, to peruse group names, or to read groups without subscribing to them. Ctrl+W is the fastest way to open this dialog, but you can also select **News-groups** from the **News** menu. The initial dialog typically contains an alphabetical list of the groups available on your news server, as shown in Figure 15–5. (As it happens, the groups that appear first in the alphabetical list are on the politically controversial side. I hope no one writes to me about it.)

Email and News

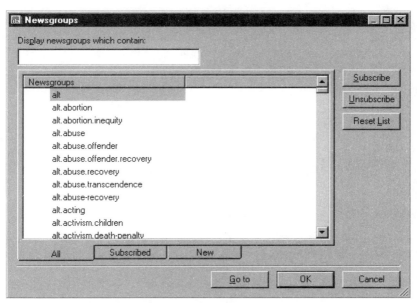

Figure 15–5: Subscribe to or just preview newsgroups using dialog

You can scroll down the list of newsgroups. If you know what you're looking for, the box at the top of the dialog lets you search for groups containing whatever text you enter. Figure 15–6 shows the results of my search for "birds." Note that you don't have to do anything after you enter text in the search box—not even hit

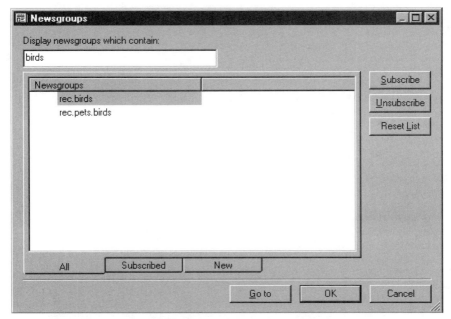

Figure 15–6: Search for newsgroup names

Return. The dialog matches what you type as you type. (To go back to the original list, clear the box.)

When you find a group that interests you, you can either subscribe to it (which means the program will make it accessible automatically every time you read news), or you can just read it on the spot without subscribing.

When you're subscribed to a group, a newspaper icon will appear in front of the newsgroup name on the list. When the dialog is open, either of the following actions will subscribe you to a group:

- Double-click on the newsgroup name

- Select the name(s) and then click on the Subscribe button (or type Alt+S)

You then need to click on the OK button at the bottom of the dialog to close it and go back to Internet News. Any groups you've added should appear on the "Newsgroups" menu.

You can also use the dialog simply to read a group without subscribing. To do so, select the name and then click on the "Go to" button at the bottom of the dialog (Alt+G works too). This closes the dialog and opens the Internet News applications to the selected group. If you decide you want to subscribe, you can select **Subscribe to this Group** from the **News** menu in the Internet News window. If you haven't done this by the time you quit out of the group, another dialog will ask you if you want to subscribe at that time.

Notice also that the Newsgroups dialog has additional tabs that show "Subscribed" and "New" groups. Click on these tabs to view those groups. Obviously, it's easier to edit your subscription list from this tab.

You can unsubscribe from the group that's currently displayed in the Internet News window by selecting **Unsubscribe from this Group** from the **News** menu, or you can unsubscribe from any group(s) using the Newsgroups dialog. Open the dialog (Ctrl+W) and then do the following:

- Double-click on the name(s) of the group(s) to remove from the subscription list.

- Select the name(s) of the group(s), and then click on the Unsubscribe button (or use Alt+U).

Again, you need to click OK to close the dialog and implement the changes.

View a Message in a Separate (Read) Window

In the default configuration of Internet News, whichever message you select in the upper pane is displayed in the lower Preview Pane. If you'd prefer to look at a message in a separate Read window, double-click on its header line in the Internet News window.

You can also opt to close the Preview Pane. The **Preview Pane** item on the **View** menu reveals a submenu of three possible layouts. The first item, **None**, closes the Preview Pane entirely. **Split Horizontally** restores the default layout. Or, you can opt to have side-by-side panes by choosing **Split Vertically**.

If you close the Preview Pane—leaving only the message headers in the Internet News window—you still have to double-click on a header in order to open it in a Read window.

Keyboard Shortcuts for Common Functions

The reference pages for Internet News functions (later in this chapter) list a keyboard shortcut (or accelerator) for just about every function. However, many of these shortcuts are just the keys that let you access the various menus items. For the most commonly used functions, there are true keyboard shortcuts, many of which require the use of the Ctrl key; Table 15–1 summarizes those common functions and the keyboard shortcuts for them. Note that some of these functions may not work in every window in Internet News.

Table 15–1: Keyboard Shortcuts for Common Functions

Function	Shortcut
Check names in header of outgoing message against address book	Ctrl+K
Close window	Alt+F4

Table 15–1: Keyboard Shortcuts for Common Functions (continued)

Function	Shortcut
Copy (selected text)	Ctrl+C
Cut (selected text)	Ctrl+X
Find message/text	F3
Find again	F3
Forward message	Ctrl+F
Help	F1
Mark all as read	Ctrl+Shift+A
Mark as read	Ctrl+Enter
Mark as unread	Ctrl+Shift+Enter
Mark thread as read	Ctrl+T
New message to newsgroup	Ctrl+N
Next message	Ctrl+>
Open selected message	Ctrl+O
Post news	Alt+S
Previous message	Ctrl+<
Print selected message(s)	Ctrl+P
Reply to author	Ctrl+R
Reply to newsgroup	Ctrl+G
Select all	Ctrl+A
Undo last text edit	Ctrl+Z

Specifying and Using a Signature File

A signature file is a short bit of information about you that can be appended to news postings (and email messages). MSIE actually allows you to have different signature file specifications for mail and news.

If you want to set up a signature for Internet News, begin by selecting **Options** from the **News** menu; then click on the tab labeled Signature at the top of the Options dialog.

You specify what the signature should be in the top half of the dialog:

- No signature (the default)

- Text you enter in the dialog

- A file whose pathname you provide

Click in front of your choice and then provide additional info (e.g., the text of your signature or the name of a signature file elsewhere on your system).

The lower half of the Signature page lets you specify when Internet News should include your signature. The default is to use it for all outgoing messages (first toggle), except "replies and forwards" (second toggle).

If you don't want to use a signature for all outgoing messages, turn off the first toggle (the second one goes off with it). Then if you want to include a signature with a particular message, you just have to request it explicitly. The Composition window lets you add a signature to a message you're writing by selecting **Signature** from the **Insert** menu.

Refer to Chapter 14 for more complete information.

Ways to Sort Your News

In Internet News, message headers have four components that correspond to the columns above the message list: the Subject of the message, who sent it (the From column), the date Sent, and the Size in number of lines. By default, news appears in each group sorted by the date received, with the most recent messages at the bottom of the list. You can instead choose to sort by the sender, subject, or size, by clicking on the corresponding column title. (The **View** menu also offers a **Sort By** submenu with four mutually exclusive choices: **Subject**, **From**, **Sent**, and **Size**.)

Regardless of which of these sorting methods is active, there is an additional sorting factor that applies: messages are either listed oldest to newest (*ascending* order) or newest to oldest (*descending* order). By default, the newest messages appear at the bottom of the list, that is, in *ascending* order. You can switch to descending order using the **Sort By** submenu.

Using the Address Book

Internet Mail and Internet News share an address book. The **Address Book** item on the **File** menu lets you open it from either application. You may want to add addresses gathered from Usenet to your address book. Chapter 14 gives more complete information about setting up your address book.

However, be aware that it's easy to add the addresses of people who post news to your address book. First, open the news article in its own window by double-clicking on its entry in the Internet News window (Ctrl+O also opens a highlighted message). Then, in the Read window, select **Add Sender to Address Book** from the **File** menu. Follow the rest of the instructions in Chapter 14 to create a complete address book entry for this person.

You can also grab address book info to add to outgoing news messages. When would you do this? Well, you might post news to a group and email a copy of the message to one or more people. The Internet News Write window lets you post news and email the same message. The first header line in the Write window is for "Newsgroups"; you can put email addresses under "CC:" (for carbon copy).

Within the Write window, you can access address book entries for the carbon copy line by selecting **Choose Recipients** from the **News** menu. This opens a Select Recipients dialog. Select the name(s) on the left, then use Alt+C or the "CC:" button to specify that they should be added to the carbon copy field of the outgoing message. You need to click OK at the bottom of the dialog to go back to the Write window, where the names of the selected recipients will appear. See Chapter 14 for more details.

Posting News in HTML Format

As in the case of Internet Mail, Internet News lets you edit and post messages in HTML format. To enable this feature, choose **HTML** from the Write window's **Format** menu. When you select this item, additional editing options become available on the **Format** menu. The Write window is also modified to include a special HTML editing toolbar, as illustrated in Chapter 14.

Keep in mind, however, that it may be less practical to post HTML files than to mail them—simply because there are many older newsreaders that can't display files in this format.

Quick Reference to Internet News

The current section serves as a quick reference to the various actions you can perform with Internet News. Keep in mind that this reference is based on the version of Internet News shipped with MSIE 3.02. If you're using another version of the programs, certain functions, menu commands, keystrokes, etc., may vary.

The following reference pages list the various functions you can perform using Internet News. The pages are organized alphabetically by function, with each function followed by the menu items, keyboard shortcuts, and toolbar buttons and other window features you can use to perform the function.

Note that some functions are only available in certain windows of the news program. For example, you can attach a file to an outgoing message (in a Write window). But this function doesn't mean anything when you're viewing message headers in the primary Internet News window or when you're reading news (in a separate Read window).

For each function entry, assume that it is available for all of the module's windows unless there is a note to the contrary. In cases where a function applies to only one of the three window types, the valid window will be listed below the function name. If the function applies to two of the three types, the note will say that the function is not applicable (i.e., *n/a*) to the third type.

While the reference pages cover most of the bases you'll care about, there may be some minor features—particularly in the Read and Write windows—that haven't gotten as much attention. Keep in mind that you can always get additional information using the "mini-help" facility (i.e., placing the pointer over a feature to get a short description of what it does).

Following the function reference is a shorter reference to the various ways you can customize Internet News, using the **Options** dialog.

About Mail and News
> Help → About Microsoft Mail and News
> Alt+H, M

Address book, access
> *(Internet News only)*
> File → Address Book . . .
> Alt+F, B

Alignment, modify in outgoing message
> *(Write window only)*
> *(HTML must be selected from Format menu)*
> Format → HTML → Align
> Alt+O, H, A

Attach file separately
> *(Write window only)*
> Insert → File Attachment . . .
> Alt+I, F
> Insert File button
> Drag file icon into window

Best of the Web
> *(Internet News only)*
> Help → Microsoft on the Web → Best of the Web
> Alt+H, W, B

Bullets, use in posting
> *(Write window only)*
> *(HTML must be selected from Format menu)*
> Format → HTML → Bullets
> Alt+O, H, B

Clean up news files
> *(Internet News only)*
> File → Clean Up Files . . .
> Alt+F, F

Close window
> File → Close
> Alt+F4
> Alt+F, C

> Close button on frame

Columns in List Pane, customize
> *(Internet News only)*
> View → Columns . . .
> Alt+V, C

Connect to news server
> *(Internet News only)*
> File → Connect
> Alt+F, N
> Connect button

Copy selected text
> Edit → Copy
> Ctrl+C
> Alt+E, C
> Copy button (Read, Write windows only)

Customize news
> *(n/a in Write window)*
> News → Options . . .
> Alt+N, O

Cut selected text
> *(Write window only)*
> Edit → Cut
> Ctrl+X
> Alt+E, T
> Cut button

Disconnect from news server (saves connect charges)
> *(Internet News only)*
> File → Disconnect
> Alt+F, I
> Disconnect button

Download
> *new messages*
> *(Internet News only)*
> Online → Post and Download
> Alt+O, P
> *selected message*
> *(Internet News only)*

Email and News

Click on list entry
multiple selected messages (must be disconnected)
(Internet News only)
　　Highlight (Ctrl+click), then
　　　　Offline → Mark Message for
　　　　Download; then Offline → Post
　　　　and Download
　　Alt+O, M; then Alt+O, P

Encoding/MIME, change manually
(Write window only)
(note that attachments should be handled automatically)
　　Format → Settings . . .
　　Alt+O, S

Find text in message
(n/a in Internet News)
　　Edit → Find . . .
　　F3
　　Alt+E, F

Followup, post to newsgroup
(n/a in Write window)
　　News → Reply to Newsgroup
　　Ctrl+G
　　Alt+N, G
　　Reply to Group button

Font, modify in posting
(Write window only)
(HTML must be selected from Format menu)
　　Format → HTML → Font . . .
　　Alt+O, H, F
　　HTML editing toolbar has choices
　　　　for font style, type, size, and
　　　　color

Forward posting in email
(n/a in Write window)
　　News → Forward
　　Ctrl+F
　　Alt+N, F
　　Forward button

Frequently Asked Questions
(Internet News only)
　　Help → Microsoft on the Web →

Frequently Asked Questions
　　Alt+H, W, Q

Header, toggle additional fields
(Write window only)
　　View → Full Headers
　　Alt+V, H

Help
online support
(Internet News only)
　　Help → Microsoft on the Web →
　　　　Online Support
　　Alt+H, W, S
topics
　　Help → Help Topics
　　F1
　　Alt+H, H

Home page, open in browser
(Internet News only)
　　File → Start Page
　　Alt+F, G

HTML format, post article in
(Write window only)
(see also Font, Alignment, Bullets, Plain text)
　　Format → HTML
　　F1
　　Alt+O, H

Language in which to view/compose messages
　　View → Language → Select from
　　　　list
　　Alt+V, G, select language

Mail, open Internet
(Internet News only)
　　File → Read Mail
　　Alt+F, M

Mark (only works when you're not connected; otherwise, highlighting downloads messages)
all messages for download
(Internet News only)
　　Online → Mark All for Download
　　Alt+O, A

---

selected message(s) for download
(Internet News only)
  Online → Mark Message for
    Download
  Alt+O, M
thread for download
(Internet News only)
  Online → Mark Thread for
    Download
  Alt+O, T

Message(s)
Download selected message(s)
(Internet News only)
  Click on entry for message in List
    Pane
mark all as read
(Internet News only)
  Edit → Mark All as Read
  Ctrl+Shift+A
  Alt+E, L
mark selected as read (see Thread)
(Internet News only)
  Edit → Mark as Read
  Ctrl+Enter
  Alt+E, E
mark as unread
(Internet News only)
  Edit → Mark as Unread
  Ctrl+Shift+Enter
  Alt+E, N
open selected in Read Window
(Internet News only)
  File → Open
  Ctrl+O
  Alt+F, O
  Double-click list entry for mes-
    sage in List Pane
properties, display
  File → Properties
  Alt+F, R

Microsoft
home page
(Internet News only)
  Help → Microsoft on the Web →
    Home Page
  Alt+H, W, H
Product news
(Internet News only)

Help → Microsoft on the Web →
    Product News
  Alt+H, W, P
send feedback to
(Internet News only)
  Help → Microsoft on the Web →
    Send Feedback
  Alt+H, W, D

Newsgroups
select for download (can be non-
  subscribed)
(Internet News only)
  Online → Mark Newsgroups . . .
  Alt+O, N
select groups to post to
(Write window only)
  News → Choose Newsgroups . . .
  Alt+N, N
view/edit subscription list
(Internet News only)
  News → Newsgroups . . .
  Ctrl+W
  Alt+N, W
  Newsgroups button

Next
message, view
(n/a in Write window)
  View → Next Message
  Ctrl+>
  Alt+V, N
  Next button (Read window only)
unread message, view
(n/a in Write window)
  View → Next Unread Message
  Alt+V, M
unread thread, view
(n/a in Write window)
  View → Next Unread Thread
  Alt+V, E

**Open current message in Read Win-
dow**
  (Internet News only)
  File → Open
  Ctrl+O
  Alt+F, O
  Double-click list entry for mes-
    sage in List Pane

Options, set news customization
(see Internet News Options)
(n/a in Write window)
    News → Options . . .
    Alt+N, O

Paste text (Write window only)
    Edit → Paste
    Ctrl+V
    Alt+E, P
    Paste button

Plain text, post article in (see also HTML)
(Write window only)
    Format → Plain Text
    Alt+O, P

Post
article (once you've finished writing)
(Write window only)
(see also Post new article)
    File → Post Message
    Alt+S
    Alt+F, M
    Post button
new article to group (i.e., open Write window)
(n/a in Write window)
    News → New Message to Newsgroup
    Ctrl+N
    Alt+N, N
    New Msg button (Internet News only)
queued articles
(Internet News only)
    Online → Post and Download
    Alt+O, P

Preview Pane
hide/show header info
(Internet News only)
    View → Preview Pane → Header Information
    Alt+V, V, D
hide/show; split horiz or vert;
(Internet News only)
    View → Preview Pane; then 3 mutually exclusive choices: None, Split Vertically, Split Horizontally
    Alt+V, V, one of: N, V, H

Previous message, view
(n/a in Write window)
    View → Previous Message
    Ctrl+<
    Alt+V, P
    Previous button (Read window only)

Print current message
(n/a in Write window)
    File → Print . . .
    Ctrl+P
    Alt+F, P

Read
mark all messages as
(Internet News only)
    Edit → Mark All as Read
    Ctrl+Shift+A
    Alt+E, L
mark selected message(s) as
(Internet News only)
    Edit → Mark as Read
    Ctrl+Enter
    Alt+E, E
    Click on entry for message in List Pane
mark thread as
(Internet News only)
    Edit → Mark Thread as Read
    Ctrl+T
    Alt+E, T

README file (Internet Mail and News)
    Help → Read Me
    Alt+H, R

Refresh window (Internet News only)
    View → Refresh
    Alt+V, R

Reply
to author (by mail)
(n/a in Write window)

News → Reply to Author
Ctrl+R
Alt+N, U
Reply to Author button
to newsgroup
(n/a in Write window)
News → Reply to Newsgroup
Ctrl+G
Alt+N, G
Reply to Group button
to newsgroup and author
(n/a in Write window)
News → Reply to Newsgroup and
Author
Alt+N, E

Save message
in file
File → Save As . . . (Internet
News and Read windows only)
Alt+F, A
Save button on toolbar (Read and
Write windows only)
in Saved Items folder
File → Save Message
Alt+F, S

Search
for text in message
(n/a in Internet News)
Edit → Find . . .
F3
Alt+E, F
the Web (in MSIE window)
(Internet News only)
File → Search the Web
Help → Microsoft on the Web →
Search the Web
Alt+F, H
Alt+H, W, W

Select all text (in current pane)
Edit → Select All
Ctrl+A
Alt+E, A

Signature file, attach
(Write window only)
*(must first specify sig file under
Options)*

Insert → Signature
Alt+I, S
Insert Signature button

Software, download free Microsoft
(Internet News only)
Help → Microsoft on the Web →
Free Stuff
Alt+H, W, F

Sort messages (Internet News only)
*by ascending (default) or descend-
ing order*
View → Sort By → Ascending
Alt+V, S, A
by date sent
View → Sort By → Sent
Alt+V, S, S
by From field
View → Sort By → From
Alt+V, S, F
by size
View → Sort By → Size
Alt+V, S, Z
by Subject
View → Sort By → Subject
Alt+V, S, B
by thread
View → Sort By → Group Mes-
sages by Thread
Alt+V, S, G

Start page, open in browser
(Internet News only)
File → Start Page
Alt+F, G

Status bar, hide/show
(Internet News only)
View → Status Bar
Alt+V, B

Stop download
(Internet News only)
File → Stop
Alt+F, T
Stop button

Subscribe/unsubscribe
(Internet News only)

News → Newsgroups
Ctrl+W
Alt+N, W

Subscribe to current group
(Internet News only)
News → Subscribe to this Group
Alt+N, S

Thread
expand/collapse current
(Internet News only)
View → Expand/Collapse
Alt+V, X (to expand)
Alt+V, L (to collapse)
Click on thread symbol
group messages by
(Internet News only)
View → Sort By → Group Messages by Thread
Alt+V, S, G
mark selected as read
(Internet News only)
Edit → Mark Thread as Read
Ctrl+T
Alt+E, T

Toolbar hide/show
View → Toolbar
Alt+V, T

Undo last edit
(Write window only)
Edit → Undo
Ctrl+Z
Alt+E, U
Undo button

Unmark messages for download
(Internet News only)
Online → Unmark for Download
Alt+O, U

Unread, mark messages as
(Internet News only)
Edit → Mark as Unread
Ctrl+Shift+Enter
Alt+E, N

Unscramble (ROT13)
(Internet News only)
Edit → Unscramble
Alt+E, U

Unsubscribe from current group
(Internet News only)
News → Unsubscribe from this Group
Alt+N, S

View
all messages
(Internet News only)
View → All Messages
Alt+V, A
unread messages only
(Internet News only)
View → Unread Messages Only
Alt+V, D

Internet News Options

You can set a number of options that determine how Internet News looks and operates. All of these preferences are set using the Options dialog box, which is displayed using the menu sequence:

```
News → Options
```

Or the keyboard shortcut:

```
Alt+N, and then O
```

Within the Options dialog, the various preferences are organized on six overlapping tabs, which look something like file folders. The tabs reveal the following categories:

- Send

- Read

- Server

- Fonts

- Signature

- Advanced

The following pages provide an index to Internet Mail's customization options. Under each option heading, you'll find the possible settings, the default(s) (if any), and the appropriate tab on which to find/set it.

Character set (language) in which to display
>Central European, Cyrillic, or
>>Western Eurpoean
>Default is Western European
>Fonts tab

Color of text (Write window)
>Black by default
>Fonts tab

Compact files
>*When there is x percent wasted
>space*
>20 by default
>Advanced tab

Download x headers at a time
>On by default; 300 headers
>Read tab

Font, display
>Fonts tab

News messages
>*Check for new every x minutes*
>On by default; 10 minutes
>Read tab
>*Delete x days after downloaded*
>On by default; 5 days
>Advanced tab
>*Don't keep read messages in cache*
>On by default
>Advanced tab
>*Divide those larger than x KB*
>Off; 60 when on
>Send tab
>*Download x headers at a time*
>On by default; 300 headers
>Read tab
>*Mark as read after previewing x seconds*
>On by default; 5 seconds
>Read tab
>*Mark all messages as read when
>exiting group*

Off by default
Read tab

Play sound when messages arrive
On by default
Read tab

Save copies of outgoing (in Posted Messages folder)
On by default
Send tab

Send in HTML format
Off by default
Send tab

Send in text format
On by default
Send tab

Threads, auto-expand
Off by default
Read tab

Newsgroup(s)

Notify user of new groups
On by default
Read tab

Mark all messages as read when exiting group
Off by default
Read tab

Start in named group
Off by default; if on, must also specify group
Read tab

Newsreader

Make Internet News the default
On by default
Send tab

Password

User's
Default given at setup
Server tab

Use secure authentication
Off by default
Server tab

Preview Pane, show messages in
On by default
Read tab

Replies

Include original message in
On by default
Send tab

Quote original preceded by x character
On by default; > character
Send tab

Selecting text (Auto select entire word)
On by default
Send tab

Server(s), news
Default given at setup
Server tab

Signature

Append to all outgoing messages
On by default (if sig specified)
Signature tab

Don't use sig in replies and forwards
On by default (when sig is specified)
Signature tab

No sig; or text of sig entered in Options dialog; or use sig file from system
No sig is default
Signature tab

Threads, auto-expand
Off by default
Read tab

User account for news server

User's email address
Name given to setup wizard is default
Server tab

User name to display
Name given to setup wizard is default
Server tab

PART V

File Handling

CHAPTER 16

File Types and Extensions

Files exist in many different formats, or types. At the general level, files are commonly classified by broad categories, such as text, video, audio, graphic images, applications, etc. However, within each of these categories are a number of more specific types, each of which can be identified by a particular filename extension.

The following table lists some of the more common file formats, organized by filename extension. A file called *house.gif* has the extension *.gif.* As the table indicates, this means it is an image file in GIF format.

Many file types also have an additional classification known as *MIME type*. MIME (Multipurpose Internet Mail Extensions) is a facility that allows for the electronic transfer of complex data files. MIME-compliant mailers, such as MSIE Internet Mail and Netscape Messenger, provide for such transfers. (See Chapter 10, *Email Strategies and Survival Tips*, for more information.)

Browsers also access a file's MIME type in order to know how to handle it. Just about any browser can display a GIF or JPEG image. But if a browser comes upon a file format it can't handle, it will ask you if you want to save the file on your computer. You can expand the number of MIME types your browser can handle by installing additional applications (e.g., helper applications, plug-ins) that the browser can call upon to open particular types of files. See Chapter 20, *Helper Applications*, and Chapter 21, *Plug-ins and ActiveX Controls* , for more information.

Note that among file types there is an even more basic distinction: all files are either ASCII (composed of text characters) or binary (compiled data—readable only by a program). This particular distinction is especially significant if you're going to transfer a file—by FTP, email, Usenet news, etc.

Ext	MIME type(s)	Binary/ ASCII	Description/How to use the file
.ai	application/postscript	A	PostScript viewer
.aif(f), .aifc	audio/aiff,r audio/x-aiff	B	Sound player
.art, .arx	image/x-jp	B	First Publisher Clip Art
.au	audio/basic	B	Sound player; MSIE; Navigator w/ plug-in
.avi	video/avi	B	Windows video file; video player; MSIE Navigator w/ plug-in
.bmp	image/x-MS-bmp	B	Psp file; Microsoft Paint
.c		A	C source code file
.dbm		B	Database file
.dll		B	Dynamic link library; (Windows 3.x, OS/2)
.doc	application/msword	B	MS Word
.eps	application/postscript	A	Encapsulated PostScript; PostScript viewer
.exe	application/x-msdownload	B	Self-extracting file or executable
.fac		B	USENIX FaceSaver file
.gif	image/gif	B	GIF image file; Browser or picture viewer
.gz	application/x-gzip	B	gunzip (UNIX decompress)
.h		A	Header file
.hlp		A	Help information
.hqx	application/mac-binhex40	B	Mac BinHex Archive
.htm, .html	text/html	A	HTML doc; browser
.ice	x-conference/x-cooltalk	B	Cooltalk file
.jpg, .jpeg, .jpe, .jfif, .pjpeg, .pjp	image/jpeg	B	JPEG image; browser or picture viewer
.man		A	Manual page file
.mid		B	MIDI player; MSIE; or Netscape w/ plug-in

Ext	MIME type(s)	Binary/ ASCII	Description/How to use the file
.mov	video/quicktime	B	MSIE (w/ Quicktime ActiveX control); or Netscape w/ QuickTime plug-in
.movie	video/x-sgi-movie	B	Silicon Graphics movie
.mpg, .mpe, .mpeg .m1v .mp2 .mpa	video/mpeg	B	MPEG video player
.msw		B	Microsoft Word fi
.pbm	image/x-portable-bitmap	B	Portable bitmap image
.pcd	image/x-photo-cd	B	Kodak photo CD image
.pdf	application/pdf	B	Portable Document Format; Acrobat
.pgm	image/x-portable-graymap	B	Portable graymap image
.pic		B	Macintosh QuickTime bitmap image
.pl	application/x-perl	A	Perl source file
.png	image/x-png	B	Portable network graphics bitmap image
.pnm, .rpnm	image/x-portable-anymap	B	Portable anymap image
.ppm	image/x-portable-pixmap	B	Portable pixmap image
.ps	application/postscript	A	PostScript viewer
.qt	video/quicktime	B	QuickTime movie; QuickTime or plug-in
.ra, .ram	audio/x-pn-realaudio	B	RealAudio file; browser w/ RealAudio capability or plug-in
.ras	image/x-cmu-raster	B	Rasterfile graphic image
.rgb		B	RGB image file
.rtx	text/richtext	A	Rich Text Format; Microsoft Word
.sea		B	Self-extracting archive (Mac); execute to unpack

Ext	MIME type(s)	Binary/ ASCII	Description/How to use the file
.shar		A	UNIX shell archive; unshar command
.sig		A	Signature files
.sit		B	Stuffit archive (Mac)
.snd	audio/basic	B	Digitized sound file; music player; browser w/ sound plug-in
.tar		B	UNIX tape archive; unarchive using tar
.tar.gz		B	tar archive compressed with gzip; decompress and untar
.tar.Z		B	tar archive on which compress has been run; decompress and untar
.tif(f)	image/tiff	B	TIFF image;image viewer
.txt	text/plain	A	ASCII text file
.uu, .uue		A	uuencoded file; uudecode
.vmf	Internet Wave/audio	B	Internet Wave.
.vpc	application/x-virtual-places	B	Virtual Places (VPLACES)
.wav audio/wav	audio/x-wav	B	Waveform audio file
.wp		B	WordPerfect text file
.wrl, .wrz	x-world/x-vrml	B	VRML 3D Geometry file; browser w/ VRML plug-in
.xbm		B	X bitmap image
.xll	application/vnd.ms-excel	B	MS Excel file; MS Excel or browser w/ Excel plug-in
.xpm		B	X pixmap image; picture viewer
.xwd		B	X window dump file; xwud
.Z	application/x-compressed	B	UNIX uncompress
.zip	application/x-zip-compressed	B	Decompress using WinZip

CHAPTER 17

FTP and File Transfer

The term FTP is used in a number of different, though interrelated, senses. First, FTP refers to the *File Transfer Protocol*, which defines a method for transferring files from one computer to another over a network. A computer that stores files for transfer using this protocol is called an *FTP server* or *FTP site*.

Anonymous FTP is a method whereby FTP servers allow the general public to access files. Someone connecting to an FTP site via anonymous FTP does not need an account on that system, a special password, or any other specific permissions. You simply log in with the username *anonymous* and give your email address in place of a password. You can then download (i.e., transfer a copy of) files from the FTP site to your own computer. When a public FTP site has a lot of traffic, the administrators may make the same resources available at one or more additional *mirror sites*.

By far the most common use of FTP is to use anonymous FTP to download files from a public server. However, keep in mind that FTP also works in the other direction—that is, you can *upload* files from your computer onto an FTP server. In order to do this, you must have the appropriate permissions on the remote system. In many cases this means having a private user account, with your own login name and password. However, on many UNIX FTP servers there is a directory called */incoming*, which is intended to be a repository of files from people on the outside. Anyone can dump pretty much anything into an */incoming* directory.

There are a number of programs (or *clients*) that let you copy files to and from FTP sites. These programs are commonly named *ftp*, or some variation thereof (e.g., WS_FTP is an FTP program for Windows). There are two basic classes of FTP clients: programs that use a command-line interface and programs that use a point-and-click interface.

Both the UNIX *ftp* program and the MS-DOS FTP client work by way of a command-line interpreter, which recognizes a number of special commands that you enter at an **ftp>** prompt. (In some Windows environments, you can also enter FTP commands in an MS-DOS window, at the DOS command-line prompt.) This chapter explains how to use some of the more common FTP commands in a typical anonymous FTP session. For information about all of the commands, see Chapter 18, *FTP Command Reference*.

Among the more popular point-and-click programs is WS_FTP, which runs on Windows systems. Rather than enter commands, you use buttons and dialog boxes. If you're running Windows on your computer and you use FTP a lot, WS_FTP may be the best way to go. The current chapter covers when you can use WS_FTP, where to get it, and (basically) how it works.

In certain circumstances, you may need to request that files be sent to you via email. There are a number of FTP email gateways. You can access them using a service called **ftpmail**, described later in this chapter.

Keep in mind that, while FTP clients are ideally the way to go if you're going to transfer multiple files, you can actually use a Web browser as a limited FTP client. A Web browser lets you connect to an FTP site and download one file at a time, as explained in the following section.

Accessing FTP Files Using a Web Browser

Not everyone who explores the Internet will need to use an FTP program. A World Wide Web browser also works as an FTP client, allowing you to download one file at a time. Note, however, that you can't upload files using a browser.

To connect to an FTP site using a browser, supply a URL of the form:

```
ftp://ftp_server/pathname/
```

For example, the following URL connects you to our old favorite, the O'Reilly & Associates FTP server, and puts you in the */pub* directory:

```
ftp://ftp.oreilly.com/pub/
```

When you use a Web browser, the contents of an FTP server look like a table of contents, in which each file is represented by both by an icon and text name (see Figure 17–1). As in many environments, a folder icon represents a directory, and a page represents an individual file. Often there will be a written description of the type of file, but not always.

Both icons and filenames are links that let you navigate around the FTP file system. You click on a folder or name to open a directory, etc. When you click on a filename or page icon, if the browser can handle the file type, the file will be displayed in the browser window. You can then use your browser's "save file" command to download a copy to your computer. If your browser doesn't understand the file type, it should ask you if you want to save the file directly to your disk.

Although this is a perfectly fine way to download small HTML and other ASCII files as well as image and sound files your browser can read, it's not that practical a way of downloading binary files (particularly large ones) on a regular basis. If you need to grab a lot of files from FTP servers, you should definitely get a program intended for that purpose.

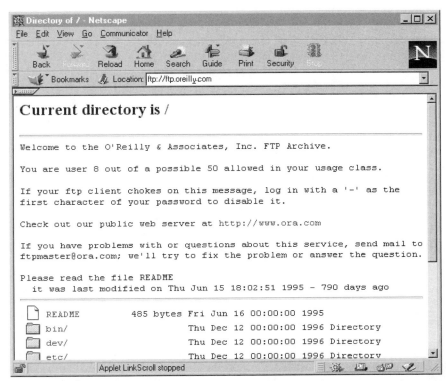

Figure 17–1: How an FTP file system looks in browser window

Of course, you *are* intended to use your browser to download software, graphics, etc., from Web sites (i.e., using the HTTP protocol, rather than FTP).

Before You Use FTP

Before we get into some sample FTP sessions, let's take a look at some of the FTP clients you might use, depending on your environment, as well as some basic concepts behind FTP file transfers. While the current chapter cannot hope to describe every procedure for every possible FTP client, understanding some of these concepts should help you use your client to accomplish what you want.

Which FTP Program?

Depending on your computer's operating system and the type of Internet connection you have, there are different options as to the FTP program you use. Table 17–1 lists some of the FTP programs available with certain types of connections. Select a program that's appropriate for your operating system.

Table 17–1: Some FTP Programs, Depending on Net Connection and OS

Internet Connection Method	Possible FTP Clients
SLIP or PPP account	UNIX: *ftp*; DOS and Windows: MS-DOS FTP; Windows only: WS_FTP, CuteFTP; etc. In some Windows environments, you can also enter FTP commands in an MS-DOS window (at the DOS command-line prompt). Mac: Fetch.
UNIX Shell Account	UNIX *ftp* client.
America Online, CompuServe, etc.	Each of these services offers a proprietary FTP module with a point-and-click interface (similar to WS_FTP). However, if you install the appropriate Winsock, you should also be able to use WS_FTP.

AOL's and CompuServe's FTP clients don't look exactly like WS_FTP, but they work along the same principles. Before you use these or other FTP programs, you should familiarize yourself with the following concepts.

FTP File Transfer Concepts

Whether you're using a friendly Windows-based FTP client with a point-and-click interface or a version of FTP that requires you to type in special commands, the concepts involved in transferring files are the same. Understanding these concepts, along with some general terminology, should help you figure out most any FTP program.

The first step in transferring files using FTP is to *connect* to a remote FTP server, or *open* the connection. If you use WS_FTP, when you first run the program, you get a dialog box titled "FTP Client Connect to . . . " in which you can select or enter the names of remote hosts, your login name, password, etc. Command-line FTP programs recognize the command **open**, which takes the name of the FTP server as an argument, as in:

```
ftp> open ftp.x.org
```

The introduction to this chapter gives a basic description of the concept of anonymous FTP. There are a number of public FTP servers that let you log in using the name *anonymous*; you're then expected to give your email address at a password prompt so the administrators can have some idea of who's doing what at their site.

With WS_FTP, you specify your username and password, as well as the FTP host to connect to, in a dialog box, and then click OK to establish the connection.

Public FTP servers generally limit the number of anonymous users who can be logged on at any one time. Thus, during heavy user traffic, you may be refused a connection. If you're not allowed to log in, see if the system message mentions any *mirror sites*, alternative servers from which you can access the same resources.

As you might expect, you're very limited as to what you can do as an anonymous FTP user. Generally, you can look around in the local file directories to see what's available for downloading. In order to do accomplish this, you can change from one directory to another, you can list the contents of the various directories, and you can download one or more of the publically accessible files (i.e., copy files from the remote server to your own computer). If the remote system has an *incoming* directory, you can deposit files from your computer; you can also disconnect from the server, but that's about it.

FTP is much more powerful if you're transferring files between two computers on which you have your own user account. If you have the appropriate permissions on the remote system, you can upload files from your computer, create directories on the remote system, etc.

In the terminology commonly associated with command-line FTP programs, to download files from the remote server to your local computer is to *get* them. Similarly, when you upload files from your computer to a remote FTP server, you *put* the files on the server. The **get** and **put** commands let you download and upload a single file at a time; **mget** and **mput** transfer multiple files simultaneously. Keeping **get** and **put** operations straight in your head is probably the hardest part of using FTP.

With WS_FTP, you request file transfers by highlighting the name(s) of the file(s) to copy on one side of a dialog box, and the directory in which to put them on the other side of the box. Then you click on a button decorated with either a left or right arrow, to specify the direction of the transfer. The section on WS_FTP, later in this chapter, gives you a clearer picture.

At the end of an FTP session, you need to disconnect from the remote host. Both the **close** and **disconnect** commands exit the current connection and return you to the **ftp>** prompt; both **bye** and **exit** will exit a connection (if any) and quit FTP altogether. WS_FTP has a Close button to exit the connection and an Exit button to quit the application.

Typical Anonymous FTP Session (Command-Line)

Follow these steps for a standard anonymous FTP session:

1. Start your FTP program. For the UNIX version, type the *ftp* command; for the DOS version under Windows 95, select Run from the Start menu, then enter "ftp" in the Run dialog, and hit Return; or select *Ftp.exe* from the *c:\windows* directory.

2. To connect to the FTP server, type the following command at the **ftp>** prompt:

   ```
   ftp> open server_name
   ```

On a UNIX system or using the DOS-based FTP client, you can combine steps one and two by typing this command:

```
% ftp server_name
```

at a system prompt. The following command opens a connection with the FTP server of O'Reilly & Associates:

```
% ftp ftp.oreilly.com
```

3. Once you're connected, the FTP server will prompt for your login name and password. Use **anonymous** for your login; then type your email address at the password prompt. (Naturally the password will not appear.)

```
Connected to amber.oreilly.com.
220 amber.oreilly.com FTP server (Version wu-2.4.2-academ[BETA-13](1) Thu
                              Apr 10 01:30:45 EDT 1997) ready.
Name (ftp.oreilly.com:val): anonymous
331 Guest login ok, send your complete e-mail address as password.
Password:
230 Guest login ok, access restrictions apply.
ftp>
```

4. Once you're logged in, you can change to the directory from which you want to download files. For example:

```
ftp> cd pub/archives
```

If you don't know where files might be, poke around in the directory structure. The **ls** command lists the contents of the current directory; **dir** gives a listing complete with file size, permissions, etc.

```
ftp> ls
200 PORT command successful.
150 Opening ASCII mode data connection for file list.
lost+found
README
bin
dev
etc
incoming
outgoing
pub
intl
private
published
usr
226 Transfer complete.
91 bytes received in 0.0095 seconds (9.4 Kbytes/s)
ftp>
```

If you **cd** around, you can check where you are at any time by using **pwd** (print working directory). (In order to get around in this fashion, you should know something about the directory structure on UNIX systems. Ask someone, or check out a guide like *Learning the UNIX Operating System*, published by O'Reilly & Associates.)

5. If you still can't figure out what files you want or where they are and there's an available README file, download it:

```
ftp> get README
200 PORT command successful.
150 Opening ASCII mode data connection for README (485 bytes).
226 Transfer complete.
local: README remote: README
497 bytes received in 0.0028 seconds (1.8e+02 Kbytes/s)
ftp>
```

Take a look at the copy of the README file on your own system; it should give you an idea what the FTP site offers. If you think the README file is short enough to view in one windowful, you can instead direct it to standard output (*stdout*):

```
get README -
```

This scrolls the contents of README by your window while you're still connected to the FTP server. (If the file is long, obviously this is impractical.)

For the purposes of our example, let's say you want to download a file called *viola.gz* in the directory */pub/www/viola*. First you change to that directory:

```
ftp> cd /pub/www/viola
250 CWD command successful.
```

Then you list its contents (**dir** produces a detailed list):

```
ftp> dir
200 PORT command successful.
150 Opening ASCII mode data connection for /bin/ls.
total 5006
-rw-r--r--   1 303     100           2389 Apr 14  1995 README
-rw-r--r--   1 303     100             69 Apr 14  1995 README.binary
drwxr-xr-x   2 303      61            512 Oct 20  1995 old
drwxr-xr-x   2 303      61            512 Oct 20  1995 screenDumps
-rw-r--r--   1 303     100        1127884 Apr 14  1995 viola-3.3.tar.gz
-rw-r--r--   1 303     100         933473 Apr 14  1995 viola.gz
-rw-r--r--   1 303      61         921118 Dec 19  1994 violaIntro.ps
-rw-r--r--   1 303      61         155635 Dec 19  1994 violaIntro.ps.gz
-rw-r--r--   1 303     100        1930297 Apr 14  1995 vw.gz
226 Transfer complete.
616 bytes received in 0.7 seconds (0.87 Kbytes/s)
```

6. Once you target the file(s) you want, you need to specify what FTP transfer mode to use. (.Ref t , later in this chapter, lists a number of common file types and the transfer mode they require.) The *.gz* suffix indicates that *viola.gz* is a compressed file, which requires binary mode:

```
ftp> binary
200 Type set to I.
```

(If you use FTP much, you'll undoubtedly encounter files that have been compressed in a variety of ways. In order to handle them effectively, see Chapter 19, *File Compression and Archiving*.)

7. Then you can retrieve the file using the **get** command. (It's a large file, even in its compressed form, so the transfer takes some time.)

```
ftp> get viola.gz
200 PORT command successful.
150 Opening BINARY mode data connection for viola.gz (933473 bytes).
226 Transfer complete.
local: viola.gz remote: viola.gz
933473 bytes received in 1.8e+02 seconds (5.2 Kbytes/s)
ftp>
```

Note that FTP allows you to rename your copy of a retrieved file. This comes in handy when you already have a file by that name on your system and you don't want to overwrite it. To specify a new name for the copied file, give it as a second argument. The following command copies the remote file *viola.gz* to the local filename *viola2.gz*:

```
ftp> get viola.gz viola2.gz
```

The default directory in which retrieved files are saved depends on your environment. See the description of the **get** command in Chapter 18 for more information. If you want to retrieve multiple files at once and they all require the same transfer mode, you can use the **mget** command:

```
ftp> mget file1 file2 file3
```

(Normally you'll be prompted to confirm the transfer of each file. Use the **prompt** command first to suppress this.)

8. Once your file transfers are complete, you can disconnect from the FTP server (but retain the FTP prompt):

```
ftp> close
221 Goodbye.
ftp>
```

Or disconnect and also quit the FTP application:

```
ftp> bye
221 Goodbye.
val@ruby 75%
```

Once you're back on your own computer, the downloaded file should be there.

During an anonymous FTP session, you can also upload files (using **put** or **mput**) to an */incoming* directory. However, you'll need a login account (as well as the appropriate permissions) on the FTP server to do much else. Those issues are between you and the system administrator at the FTP site. If you're not allowed to do something, FTP will let you know. Chapter 18 lists all of the valid commands.

Binary or ASCII Files?

When you transfer a file using an FTP program, it's necessary to specify the *mode* of transfer, based on the type of file you want to copy. FTP has two commonly used modes: *binary* (also called *image*) and *ASCII*. ASCII mode is used to transfer text files; binary mode is used to transfer compiled data files, such as executable programs, graphic images, audio files, etc.

The way you specify the transfer mode for a particular file depends on the FTP program. Command-line FTP utilities (e.g., UNIX *ftp*, MS-DOS FTP) recognize the commands **binary** (or **image**) and **ascii**. An FTP client with a point-and-click interface may have a button or buttons you click on to set the mode. WS_FTP has mutually exclusive buttons to choose either ASCII or binary transfer.

Since ASCII format is generally the default mode, if you're using a command-line version of FTP, you should be able to transfer text files without running a mode-setting command. However, if you want to download another type of file, you'll need to run the **binary** command first.

You want to avoid transferring binary files in ASCII mode—the copies you get will be garbled and useless. Keep in mind, however, that FTP sites that provide software files may be configured to make binary mode the default. When you connect to a site at which binary transfer is the default mode, you may get a message to that effect as part of the system greeting.

Table 17–2 lists a number of common file types and the appropriate transfer mode for them.

Table 17–2: Common File Types and FTP Transfer Modes

File	Mode
Text file	ASCII, by definition
Spreadsheet	Probably binary
Database file	Probably binary, possibly ASCII
Word processor file	Probably binary (e.g., *.doc*, *.fm*), possibly ASCII (e.g., *.rtf*, *.mif*)
Program source code	ASCII
Electronic mail message	ASCII
PKzip'ed file	Binary
Backup file	Binary
Compressed file	Binary
Binhexed or uuencoded[a] file	ASCII
Tar archive	Binary
Executable file	Binary
PostScript (laser printer) file	ASCII
WWW (HTML) document	ASCII
Picture files (e.g., GIF, JPEG, MPEG)	Binary
Audio files (e.g., WAV, AU)	Binary

a. **uuencode** is a UNIX utility analogous to BinHex for DOS and Windows systems. UNIX users frequently use it to encode binary files in an all-ASCII representation, which makes them easier to transfer correctly.

For more detailed information, see Chapter 16, *File Types and Extensions*, and Chapter 19.

A Friendlier FTP for Windows: WS_FTP

If you're working in a Windows environment, and you need to transfer files on a regular basis, get yourself a free and friendly FTP program, such as WS_FTP.[*] WS_FTP works using a point-and-click interface, with dialog boxes, file boxes, scrollbars, buttons, and all the features people tend to like about Windows. The best part of using WS_FTP is that you'll never have to learn the dozens of FTP commands detailed in Chapter 18.

You can download a version for either Windows 3.1 or Windows 95 using your Web browser. Go to the URL:

```
http://huizen.dds.nl/~johnr/softplaz/
```

Select the version of WS_FTP you want and then click the Download button.

If you don't want to use a browser, you can use your command-line DOS version of FTP to **get** the file from **gatekeeper.dec.com**. (The pathname of the file is **/pub/micro/msdos/win3/winsock/ws_ftp32.zip**.) Transferring a file using binary mode is described in the section "Typical Anonymous FTP Session (Command-Line)," earlier in this chapter. Then unzip the compressed file (as described in Chapter 19), and install it.

The first time you start WS_FTP, you'll get a "Session Profile" dialog (pictured in Figure 17–2) in which you can enter an FTP server name and other session parameters. Click in front of the Anonymous Login box for an anonymous FTP site, and then enter **anonymous** in the User ID field and your email address in the Password field. (If you want, you can also specify the directories to access on both the Local PC and the Remote Host, in two fields near the bottom of the window.) Click the Save button to save this profile information for future FTP sessions. Then click the OK button to initiate an FTP session using the settings in the Profile dialog. Assuming the remote FTP server accepts the connection, the WS_FTP window proper opens, as in Figure 17–3. The left pane of the window displays the contents of the local directory; the right pane displays the contents of the remote directory. The name of each appears at the top of their respective panes. Unless you specified directories in the Session Profile dialog, the local directory will be whichever one you were in when you initiated the session; the remote directory will (generally) be the top-level (root) directory (represented by /). The contents of each directory are divided by a horizontal line, with subdirectories above and files below.

To change directories, click on the name and then click the ChgDir button. To select a file for transfer, click on its name. Choose the transfer mode by clicking in front of ASCII, Binary, or L8 (L8 is a synonym for *tenex*; see Chapter 18 for more information), which appear below the directory panes. Then click on one of the arrow buttons located between the panes to transfer the file. The left arrow downloads files from the remote to the local system (in effect, performs a **get** operation); the right arrow uploads files from the local to the remote systems (a **put**).

---

[*] There are additional Windows FTP clients out there as well. For instance, CuteFTP exists in shareware and freeware forms. WS_FTP Pro is a fancier version of WS_FTP, but you have to pay for it.

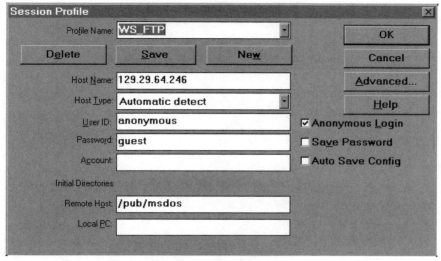

Figure 17–2: WS_FTP Session Profile dialog

One of WS_FTP's better features is that it actually lets you preview a file's contents before you transfer it. While the name is highlighted, select the View button.

The .netrc File: Auto-login and Macro Definitions

If you're using the *ftp* client on a UNIX system, you can create a file that stores both your anonymous login information for any number of FTP servers and also any macros you define. (Macros are scripts that let you run a sequence of FTP commands.)

You should create this file, called *.netrc*, in your home directory. This is the basic format of the file:

```
machine ftp_server login login_name password email_address
```

Here's an excerpt from my *.netrc* file:

```
machine ftp.uu.net login anonymous password val@oreilly.com
machine gatekeeper.dec.com login anonymous password val@oreilly.com
machine rtfm.mit.edu login anonymous password val@oreilly.com
```

When your *.netrc* file contains an entry for a particular server, you don't have to type your name (**anonymous**) and password (i.e., your email address) when you connect via FTP. User authentication happens automatically.

Use *.netrc* to store entries for all the anonymous FTP servers you frequent. However, remember that the *.netrc* file is only intended to contain anonymous FTP information. *Never put your actual password in a .netrc file.*

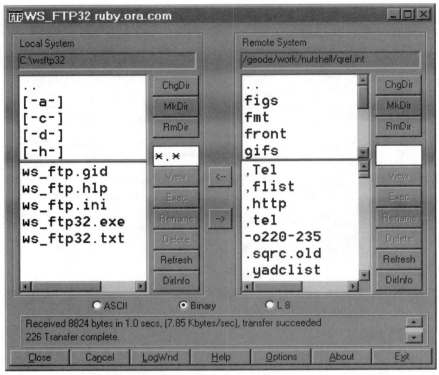

Figure 17–3: WS_FTP window lets you transfer files

If you're using WS_FTP, you can save login information by using a special Session Profile dialog. For more information, see the section "A Friendlier FTP for Windows: WS_FTP," earlier in this chapter.

Chapter 18 explains how to define and use macros, under the description of the *macdef* command. You can define a macro at the FTP prompt, using the **macdef** command. However, any macro you define during a particular session is lost when you exit FTP. You can save macros from one session to another by putting them in your *.netrc* file.

When you define a macro in your *.netrc*, it has to be associated with a particular FTP server. You place a **macdef** command at the end of a line that establishes your login for that server. Give as an argument the name you want to use to invoke the script. Then give the FTP commands you want the script to run on subsequent lines. A blank line signals the end of the macro. In the following example I've defined a macro called *mymac*, which does the following:

- Sets the transfer mode to binary

- Toggles off interactive prompting (Normally, FTP asks you to confirm each file transfer when you're copying multiple files at once.)

```
machine ftp.x.org login anonymous password val@oreilly.com macdef mymac
binary
prompt

machine ftp.uu.net login anonymous password val@oreilly.com
machine gatekeeper.dec.com login anonymous password val@oreilly.com
machine rtfm.mit.edu login anonymous password val@oreilly.com
```

The *mymac* macro sets up my session to perform **mget** operations (multiple file transfers). When I'm connected to the *ftp.x.org* server, I can invoke the macro using the $ command:

```
ftp> $ mymac
binary
200 Type set to I.
prompt
Interactive mode off.
```

To understand all this better, read about the **macdef**, **$**, **prompt**, and **mget** commands in Chapter 18.

FTP By Email

For people who don't have the time to wait around for an FTP transfer, or who might not have the right program, it's possible to request that files be emailed to you. A number of computers act as **ftpmail** servers. Such a server is an FTP application gateway—you send email to it requesting files from any FTP server, and the **ftpmail** server retrieves the files and mails them to you.

Here are a number of **ftpmail** servers, organized by location:

Europe	United States
ftpmail@doc.ic.ac.uk	ftpmail@ftpmail.bryant.vix.com
ftpmail@ftp.luth.se	ftpmail@sunsite.unc.edu
ftpmail@ftp.uni-stuttgart.de	ftpmail@ftp.uu.net
ftpmail@grasp.insa-lyon.fr	ftpmail@ftp.shsu.edu
ftpmail@ieunet.ie	

Taiwan	Australia
ftpmail@flight.cn.nctu.edu.tw	ftpmail@cs.uow.edu.au

Most **ftpmail** servers recognize a limited set of commands, many of which are similar to standard command-line FTP syntax. The email you send to an **ftpmail** server must contain the sequence of commands to retrieve the file(s) you want. Suppose, for instance, you want a copy of the health care FAQ put together by the *rec.pets.cats* newsgroup. You've read in the newsgroup (or on the Web) that the FAQ (called *health-care*) lives on the FTP server at **rtfm.mit.edu**, in the directory **/pub/usenet/news.answers/cats-faq/**

You can send an email message to an **ftpmail** server with the necessary commands to **get** the file, as in the following example. (Note that whatever you put in the Subject line is for your reference only; it isn't interpreted by **ftpmail**.)

```
To: ftpmail@ftpmail.bryant.vix.com
Subject: Cat health care FAQ
```

connect rtfm.mit.edu	*Connect to the FTP server*
chdir /pub/usenet/news.answers/cats-faq/	*Change to the right directory*
get health-care	*Retrieve the file*
quit	*Exit FTP*

Some **ftpmail** servers may have limitations as to what commands they recognize. You can get a list of what commands are available for a particular server by sending a message with the word "help" in the body.

Note that (as with any command-line FTP program) the burden of specifying the transfer mode is on you. Thus, if you want to retrieve a binary file, you need to put the **binary** command before any **get**. (For more information about transfer modes, see the section "Binary or ASCII Files?," earlier in this chapter.

The following list gives the commands recognized by the server *ftpmail@-ftpmail.bryant.vix.com*. Different servers may offer a different set of commands:

help
> Requests that a help message be sent by email.

reply *email_address*
> Tells the server to whom to send the response. This is optional and defaults to the user's email address.

connect *hostname* [*username* [*password*]]
> Establishes an FTP connection with the specified host. The default username is *anonymous*, and the default password is your email address. (Note that some **ftpmail** servers also have a default FTP host they access; see the site's help info.)

chdir *pathname*
> Changes directory to the specified *pathname*. (On some servers, only one **chdir** command can be used per session.)

ls [*pathname*]
> Requests a short listing of the contents of *pathname*. Default pathname is the current directory.

dir [*pathname*]
> Requests a long listing of the contents of *pathname*. Default pathname is the current directory.

index *term*
> Requests that the server's index be searched for the specified term. (Not available on all servers.)

ascii
> Changes the transfer mode to ASCII (commonly the default).

binary
> Changes the transfer mode to binary.

get *file*
> Requests that a file be retrieved and mailed back.

chunksize *size_in_bytes*

Splits files into parts of the specified size for mailing. The default is 64000 bytes.

compress

Specifies that binary files should be compressed (Lempel-Ziv encoding) before they are emailed back. You must specify **binary** first.

compact

Specifies that binary files should be compacted (Huffman encoding) before being emailed back. You must specify **binary** first.

uuencode

Specifies that binary files should be converted to uuencode format before mailing. You must specify **binary** first.

quit

Signals the end of the **ftpmail** commands; this is especially important if you have a *.signature* file at the end of your message.

Remember that some servers will recognize a different set of commands. There are even **ftpmail** servers, such as the one at Dartmouth College, that only works for the files on the server itself. Rely on the help information a site provides to sort out your options.

CHAPTER 18

FTP Command Reference

While the preceding chapter explains what the File Transfer Protocol and FTP utilities are about, this chapter is a quick reference to the commands recognized by certain FTP programs. Both the UNIX *ftp* and the MS-DOS FTP programs work using a command-line interpreter; it recognizes a number of special commands that you enter at the **ftp>** prompt. This chapter outlines the commands these versions of FTP recognize and the guidelines for using them.

Keep in mind that, even if your version of FTP offers all of the listed commands, whether a particular command works depends upon the level of permission you have to access the remote file system. If you connect to an FTP server using anonymous FTP, for instance, you should be able to copy files back to your own system (using FTP's **get** or **mget** command). This makes sense since anonymous FTP is intended to make files available to the public.

However, in most cases you won't be allowed to copy anything from your system to the remote one, even though FTP provides commands that can do that (**put** and **mput**). The notable exception is that most UNIX FTP servers provide a directory called */incoming* in which anyone can leave files. However, someone who's logged on to a remote system as an anonymous FTP user doesn't have the proper permissions to change any other part of that file system.

On the flip side, if you connect to a remote FTP server on which you have your own account—and log in using your username and password—you may have permission to deposit files, change the file system, etc. A number of FTP commands are only useful if you have write permission on the remote system.

In the command reference section of this chapter, there isn't always a distinction made between those that are useful in most circumstances and those that require special permissions. A little common sense should tell you what's possible. If that doesn't work, FTP returns messages regarding the outcome of the commands you issue. The descriptions of many of the commands include examples of usage, including typical system messages. FTP will let you know when your commands succeed. The command interpreter will also prompt you for necessary arguments if you omit them. Rely on FTP's messages to confirm you're using the utility properly.

FTP Command-Line Options (UNIX)

If you're running *ftp* on a UNIX system, you can establish certain behaviors of the command interpreter by initially running *ftp* with one or more options. For example, the following command starts *ftp* in debugging mode and also connects to the FTP server *ftp.x.org*:

```
% ftp -d ftp.x.org
```

Let's take a brief look at the command-line options you can use with the UNIX *ftp* program.

-d   Enables debugging mode (i.e., *ftp* prints more system info).

-g   Disables filename globbing (i.e., filename expansion).

-i   Turns off interactive prompting during multiple file transfers.

-n   Specifies no auto-login upon initial connection. If auto-login is not disabled, *ftp* checks the *.netrc* file in the user's home directory for an entry describing an account on the remote machine. If no entry exists, *ftp* prompts for the user's login name and password on the remote machine. (The default login name is the user's login on the local machine.)

-v   Turns on verbose mode (i.e., *ftp* shows all responses from the remote server, as well as data transfer statistics). This option is on by default if *ftp* is running interactively with its input coming from the user's terminal.

FTP Commands

The following commands should work at the FTP command prompt (ftp>), regardless of whether you're running UNIX *ftp* or an MS-DOS FTP program.

? [command]	?
Prints a message explaining the use of an FTP command. If no argument is given, FTP prints a list of the recognized commands. A synonym for **help**.	

! [command]	!
If no *command* is given, invokes an interactive shell *on the local machine*. For example, the following sequence opens an interactive shell on the machine **ruby**; the user then runs the *du* command to summarize disk usage in the current directory on the local machine.	

```
ftp> !
val@ruby 26% du
```

$\rightarrow$

| ! | ```
1       ./RCS
1       ./ps
212     .
val@ruby 27%
``` |
|---|---|
| ← | |

Enter an EOF (i.e., end-of-file sequence; generally Ctrl-D) to exit the shell and return to the FTP prompt.

If ! is issued with a *command* argument, *command* is run as a shell command on the local machine; when the shell command exits, you're automatically returned to the FTP prompt. Thus, the following command also runs *du* on the local machine and automatically returns you to the FTP prompt:

```
ftp> du
1       ./RCS
1       ./ps
293     .
ftp>
```

Note that there is no way to run a shell on the remote machine, nor should there be (for security reasons).

| $ | ## $ macro [args]
Executes the script called *macro*; *macro* must first be defined using the **macdef** command, either at the **ftp>** prompt, or in the user's *.netrc* file (see Chapter 17, *FTP and File Transfer*). Arguments are passed to the macro unglobbed (i.e., without filename expansion).

See the **macdef** command for an example defining a macro called **mymac**, which specifies **binary** transfer mode and turns off interactive prompting for multiple file transfers. You use the following command to run a macro such as **mymac**:

```
ftp> $ mymac
binary
200 Type set to I.
prompt
Interactive mode off.
ftp>
``` |
|---|---|

| account | ## account [password]
In some cases, once you've successfully logged on to a remote system, that system may require an additional password before granting access to certain resources. First you must supply the name of the account; if you did not supply the password as argument, the system will prompt for it (in a non-echoing input mode). |
|---|---|
```

```
ftp> account
Account: nutshell
331 Password required for Account nutshell.
Passwd:
ftp>
```

account

append *local_file* [*remote_file*]

append

Appends the *local_file* to a file on the remote machine. If *remote_file* is not specified, the name of the *local_file* is used (subject to alteration by any prior **ntrans** or **nmap** command issued in the current session).

```
ftp> append stuff morestuff
200 PORT command successful.
150 Opening ASCII mode data connection for morestuff.
226 Transfer complete.
local: stuff remote: morestuff
25 bytes sent in 0.0011 seconds (23 Kbytes/s)
ftp>
```

ascii

ascii

Specifies that data should be data transferred in ASCII format; this is (commonly) the default. See also **binary**. (Table 17-2 in Chapter 17 lists the FTP transfer modes for a number of common file types.)

```
ftp> ascii
200 Type set to A.
ftp>
```

bell

bell

When toggled on, causes a bell to sound after each file transfer command is completed. Off by default.

```
ftp> bell
Bell mode on.
ftp>
```

binary

binary

Specifies that data should be transferred in "EBCDIC image" format. You need to specify **binary** before you can use FTP to transfer any compiled data files (e.g., graphic and audio files, program data, etc.).

```
ftp> binary
200 Type set to I.
ftp>
```

$\rightarrow$

binary ←	See also the **ascii** and **type** commands. (Table 17-2 in Chapter 17 lists the FTP transfer modes for a number of common file types.)
bye	**bye** Ends the FTP session with the remote server and/or exits the FTP program. Typing an end-of-file character (generally Ctrl-D) accomplishes the same thing. A synonym for **quit**. ``` ftp> bye 221 Goodbye. val@local 66% ```
case	**case** Toggles remote filename case mapping during **get** and **mget** commands. When case is on, remote filenames with all letters in uppercase are written in lowercase when copied to the local directory. The default setting for case is off. ``` ftp> case Case mapping on. ftp> ``` With case mapping turned on, when we **get** the file called *TEST* from the remote system, the copy on the local system is automatically named *test*. Both the local and remote filenames appear in the fourth line of this output, immediately following the "Transfer complete" message. ``` ftp> get TEST 200 PORT command successful. 150 Opening ASCII mode data connection for TEST (16 bytes). 226 Transfer complete. local: test remote: TEST 17 bytes received in 0.0019 seconds (8.7 Kbytes/s) ftp> ``` Note that FTP does not inform you if the newly chosen name will overwrite another file on the local system.
cd	**cd** *remote_directory* Changes the working directory on the remote machine to the specified directory. The following example changes the remote directory to a directory called *test* (which is a subdirectory of the current working directory): ``` ftp> cd test 250 CWD command successful. ftp> ```

cdup

Changes the remote machine's working directory to its parent directory; like issuing the command:

```
cd ..
```

at a system prompt

```
ftp> cdup
250 CWD command successful.
ftp>
```

close

Ends the FTP session with the remote server, and returns the user to the command interpreter (**ftp>** prompt). (Note that the commands **bye** and **quit** additionally exit the FTP command interpreter.) When you disconnect from a remote server, any macros that have been defined for that session are erased. (Use the *.netrc* file described in Chapter 17, to define macros across sessions.)

```
ftp> close
221 Goodbye.
ftp>
```

cr

During a network ASCII type file transfer (see **ascii**), individual records are denoted by a RETURN/LINEFEED sequence. The **cr** command toggles the stripping of embedded carriage returns during an ASCII-type retrieval. When **cr** is on (the default), RETURN characters are stripped in order to conform with the UNIX standard of a single LINEFEED as record delimiter.

On non-UNIX remote hosts, records may contain single LINEFEED characters. However, when a network ASCII type transfer is made, a LINEFEED character may be distinguished from a record delimiter only when **cr** is off.

```
ftp> cr
Carriage Return stripping off.
ftp>
```

debug

Toggles debugging mode. Off by default.

```
ftp> debug
Debugging on (debug=1).
ftp>
```

$\rightarrow$

debug ←	When debugging is on, the FTP program prints each command sent to the remote machine, preceded by the string --->. Thus, if you specify debugging mode when you request a connection to a remote server, your username and password are printed: ``` % ftp -d ftp.uu.net Connected to ftp.uu.net. 220 ftp.UU.NET FTP server (Version wu-2.4(4) Mon Jan 6 13:57:37 EST 1997) ready. ---> USER anonymous 331 Guest login ok, send your complete e-mail address as password. ---> PASS val@oreilly.com 230- 230- Welcome to the UUNET archive. ``` (Note that you can also enable debugging on the *ftp* command line using the **-d** option. See the section "Options," earlier in this chapter.)
delete	**delete** *remote_file* Deletes *remote_file* (i.e., the named file on the remote machine). Obviously, you must have adequate permissions for the remote file and directory. Therefore, if you're using an anonymous login, this command is only useful in removing files from the *incoming* directory. The **delete** command can be more widely used if you have an account on the remote machine. ``` ftp> delete myoldfile 250 DELE command successful. ftp> ```
dir	**dir** [*remote_directory*] [*local_file*] Prints a listing of the contents of *remote_directory*, and optionally places the output in *local_file*. If no remote directory is specified, the current working directory on the remote machine is assumed. If no local file is specified, or *local_file* is standard input (-), output is sent to the terminal. To list the current working directory on the remote machine and copy the list to the local file named *rdirlist*, do the following: ``` ftp> dir . rdirlist 200 PORT command successful. 150 Opening ASCII mode data connection for /bin/ls. 226 Transfer complete. local: rdirlist remote: . 768 bytes received in 0.0022 seconds (3.4e+02 Kbytes/s) ```

disconnect

A synonym for **close**.

```
ftp> disconnect
221 Goodbye.
ftp>
```

form *[format_name]*

Sets the carriage control format subtype of the representation type to *format_name*. Since the only valid *format_name* is **non-print**, and the non-print subtype is the default, this command does no more than elicit a status message.

get *remote_file [local_file]*

Retrieves *remote_file* and stores it on the local machine. Note that you can give - as the local filename to write file on standard output (*stdout*); this is especially useful for displaying the contents of README files.

```
ftp> get README -
```

The directory in which retrieved files are saved is generally referred to as the *local directory*. On a Windows 95 system, retrieved files are put in the directory *c:\windows\desktop* by default. On a UNIX system, the local directory is the current directory in the shell from which you issued the *ftp* command. Before you **get** files, you may want to change the local directory using the **lcd** command.

You can get multiple files at once using the **mget** command.

Be sure to specify **binary** mode before retrieving binary files. For more information, see the **binary** command earlier in this chapter, and the section "Binary or ASCII Files?" in Chapter 17.

If a *local_file* name is not specified, the file is given the same name it has on the remote machine, subject to alteration by the current **case**, **ntrans**, and **nmap** settings. The current settings for representation type (see **type**, **ascii**, **binary**, and **tenex**), file structure (see **struct**), and transfer mode (see **mode**) are used while transferring the file.

glob

Toggles filename expansion, or globbing, for **mdelete**, **mget**, and **mput** commands. If globbing is turned off, filenames are taken literally. Globbing is on by default. (Note that you can also disable globbing on the *ftp* command line using the **-g** option.

→

glob ←	See the section "Options," earlier in this chapter.) Globbing for **mput** is done as in *sh(1)*. For **mdelete** and **mget**, each remote filename is expanded separately on the remote machine, and the lists are not merged. Expansion of a directory name may be radically different from the expansion of a filename. The exact result depends on the remote operating system and FTP server and can be previewed by issuing the command: `ftp> mls remote_files -` Note that **mget** and **mput** are not meant to transfer entire directories.

hash	**hash**
	
	Toggles hashmark (#) printing for each data block transferred. For each data block (8192 bytes) transferred, a hashmark (#) is also printed. Off by default. When toggled on, hashmark printing helps you monitor the progress of a transfer.
	
	`ftp> hash`
	`Hash mark printing on (8192 bytes/hash mark).`
	`ftp> put bigthings`
	`200 PORT command successful.`
	`150 Opening ASCII mode data connection for bigthings.`
	`###################`
	`226 Transfer complete.`
	`local: bigthings remote: bigthings`
	`134072 bytes sent in 0.12 seconds (1.1e+03 Kbytes/s)`
	`ftp>`

help	**help** *[command]* Prints a message explaining the use of an FTP command. If no argument is given, the FTP program prints a list of the recognized commands. A synonym for the ? command.

lcd	**lcd** *[directory]*
	
	Changes the working directory on the local machine. If no directory is specified, the user's home directory is used. The following example changes to the *bitmaps* subdirectory of the current directory (*/home/val*):
	
	`ftp> lcd bitmaps`
	`Local directory now /home/val/bitmaps`
	`ftp>`

ls *[remote_directory | -al] [local_file]*

Prints an abbreviated listing of the contents of a directory on the remote machine. If *remote_directory* is left unspecified, the current working directory is used. If no local file is specified, or if - is given for *local_file*, the output is sent to the terminal.

The **-a** option lists all entries, including those that begin with a dot (.); normally dot files are not listed. The -l option lists each file in long format, giving mode, number of links, owner, group, size in bytes, and time of last modification. If the file is a special file, the size field instead contains the major and minor device numbers rather than a size. If the file is a symbolic link, the filename is printed followed by and the pathname of the referenced file.

The following example shows there are two files (*myfile* and *todo*) in the *stuff* subdirectory of the current directory:

```
ftp> ls stuff
200 PORT command successful.
150 Opening ASCII mode data connection for file list.
stuff/myfile
stuff/todo
226 Transfer complete.
remote: stuff
26 bytes received in 0.0012 seconds (21 Kbytes/s)
ftp>
```

---

macdef *macro_name*

Allows the user to define a macro. Subsequent lines are stored as the macro *macro_name*; a null line (consecutive NEWLINE characters in a file or RETURN characters from the terminal) terminates macro input mode. There is a limit of 16 macros and 4096 total characters in all defined macros.

You can use **macdef** to define a macro either at the **ftp>** prompt or in your *.netrc* file. Macros defined on the command line remain defined until a **close** command is executed. When a macro is defined in a *.netrc* file, it must be defined for use on a particular FTP server.

The macro processor interprets the dollar sign (**$**) and the backslash (****) as special characters. A **$** followed by a number (or numbers) is replaced by the corresponding argument on the macro invocation command line. A **$** followed by an "i" signals that macro processor that the executing macro is to be looped. On the first pass, **$i** is replaced by the first argument on the macro invocation command line; on the second pass, it is replaced by the second argument; etc. A **** followed by any char-

macdef ←	acter is replaced by that character. Use the backslash to prevent special treatment of the dollar sign. The following macro, called **mymac**, defined at the **ftp>** prompt, specifies **binary** transfer mode and turns off interactive prompting for multiple file transfers. Note you must enter a blank line to signal the end of the macro. ``` ftp> macdef mymac Enter macro line by line, terminating it with a null line binary prompt ftp> ``` The same macro can be defined in a user's *.netrc* file; see Chapter 17 for more information. To run the macro, use the **$** command, described earlier in the current chapter.
mdelete	**mdelete** *remote_files* Deletes multiple files on the remote machine. If interactive prompting is on (the default), the FTP program will prompt the user to verify that each *remote_file* is to be deleted. You can turn off prompting using the **prompt** command. ``` ftp> mdelete lon* mdelete london? y 250 DELE command successful. mdelete longdist? y 250 DELE command successful. ftp> ```
mdir	**mdir** *remote_directories local_file* Similar to **dir** except multiple remote directories may be specified. Prints a listing of the contents of multiple remote directories, and writes the listing to *local_file*. Note that both arguments are required; if either or both are omitted, the user is prompted for them. If interactive prompting is on (the default), the FTP program will prompt the user to verify that the last argument is indeed the target local file for receiving **mdir** output. See also **mls**.
mget	**mget** *remote_files* A **get** command for multiple files. By default, **mget** does wildcard expansion (see **glob**) of the *remote_files* and does a **get** for each filename thus produced. Resulting filenames are then processed according to **case**, **ntrans**, and **nmap** settings.

The directory in which retrieved files are saved is generally referred to as the *local directory*. On a Windows 95 system, retrieved files are put in the directory *c:\windows\desktop* by default. On a UNIX system, the local directory is the current directory in the shell from which you issued the *ftp* command. Before you **mget** files, you may want to change the local directory using the **lcd** command.

Be sure to specify **binary** mode before transferring binary files. For more information, see the **binary** command earlier in this chapter, and the section "Binary or ASCII Files?" in Chapter 17.

If prompting is turned on (the default), the user is asked to confirm (**y** for yes) or disallow (**n** for no) each file to be transferred with **mget**. Thus, you may want to disable prompting before transferring multiple files; see **prompt**.

```
ftp> mget foot*
mget football.ans? y
200 PORT command successful.
150 Opening ASCII mode data connection for football.ans (1369 bytes).
226 Transfer complete.
local: football.ans remote: football.ans
1411 bytes received in 0.0026 seconds (5.3e+02 Kbytes/s)
mget football.quiz? y
200 PORT command successful.
150 Opening ASCII mode data connection for football.quiz (2718 bytes).
226 Transfer complete.
local: football.quiz remote: football.quiz
2792 bytes received in 0.0039 seconds (7.1e+02 Kbytes/s)
ftp>
```

mkdir *directory_name*

Creates a directory on the remote machine; requires write permission on the remote system.

```
ftp> mkdir work
257 MKD command successful.
ftp>
```

mls *remote_files local_file*

Similar to **ls** except that multiple remote files may be specified. **mls** allows you to list multiple files on the remote system and to save the listing in a file on the local system (*local_file*). Note that both arguments are mandatory; if either or both are omitted, the user is prompted for them. In the following example, **mls** is used to list files from two directories on the remote system (the current working directory, represented by a period, and a directory called *mystuff*) and to write that output to a file called *list* on the local system. If interactive prompting is on (the default), the FTP

$\rightarrow$

mls ←	program will prompt the user to verify that the last argument is indeed the target local file for receiving **mls** output. (See **prompt**.) ```\nftp> mls . mystuff list\noutput to local-file: list? y\n200 PORT command successful.\n150 Opening ASCII mode data connection for file list.\n226 Transfer complete.\nlocal: list remote: .\n178 bytes received in 0.0021 seconds (84 Kbytes/s)\n200 PORT command successful.\n150 Opening ASCII mode data connection for file list.\n226 Transfer complete.\nlocal: list remote: mystuff\n21 bytes received in 0.00059 seconds (35 Kbytes/s)\nftp>\n```
mode	**mode** *[mode_name]* Sets the transfer mode to *mode_name*. The only valid *mode_name* is **stream**, which corresponds to the default stream mode. Since the current implementation supports only **stream**, and requires that it be specified, this command does no more than elicit a status message. ```\nftp> mode mymodedude\nWe only support stream mode, sorry.\nftp>\n```
mput ~	**mput** *local_files* A **put** command for multiple files. By default, **mput** does wild-card expansion (see **glob**) of filenames in *local_files* and does a **put** for each file in the resulting list. Resulting filenames will then be processed according to **ntrans** and **nmap** settings. Be sure to specify **binary** mode before transferring binary files. For more information, see the **binary** command earlier in this chapter, and the section "Binary or ASCII Files?" in Chapter 17. If prompting is turned on (the default), the user is asked to confirm (**y** for yes) or disallow (**n** for no) each file to be transferred with **mput**. Thus, you may want to disable prompting before transferring multiple files; see **prompt**. ```\nftp> mput lon*\nmput london? y\n200 PORT command successful.\n150 Opening ASCII mode data connection for london.\n226 Transfer complete.\nlocal: london remote: london\n8316 bytes sent in 0.025 seconds (3.3e+02 Kbytes/s)\n```

```
mput longdist? y
200 PORT command successful.
150 Opening ASCII mode data connection for longdist.
226 Transfer complete.
local: longdist remote: longdist
3142 bytes sent in 0.0089 seconds (3.4e+02 Kbytes/s)
ftp>
```

nmap [*inpattern outpattern*]

Sets or unsets the filename mapping mechanism. If no arguments are specified, the filename mapping mechanism is unset. If arguments are specified: remote filenames are mapped during **put** and **mput** commands issued without a specified remote target filename and local filenames are mapped during **get** and **mget** commands issued without a specified local target filename.

nmap is useful when connecting to a non-UNIX remote host with different filenaming conventions. The mapping follows the pattern set by *inpattern* and *outpattern*. *inpattern* is a template for incoming filenames (which may have already been processed according to the **ntrans** and **case** settings). Variable templating is accomplished by including the sequences *$1, $2, . . . $9* in *inpattern*. Use a backslash (\) to prevent this special treatment of the dollar sign (**$**) character. All other characters are treated literally, and are used to determine the **nmap** *inpattern* variable values.

For example, with an *inpattern* of **$1.$2** and the remote filename *mydata.data*, **$1** would have the value *mydata*, and **$2** would have the value *data*.

The *outpattern* determines the resulting mapped filename. The sequence **$1, $2, . . . $9** is replaced by any value resulting from the *inpattern* template. The sequence **$0** that is replaced by the original filename. Additionally, the sequence [*seq1,seq2*] is replaced by *seq1* if *seq1* is not a null string; otherwise, it is replaced by *seq2*. For example, the command

```
nmap $1.$2.$3 [$1,$2].[$2,file]
```

would yield: the output filename *myfile.data* for input filenames *myfile.data* and *myfile.data.old*; *myfile.file* for the input filename *myfile*; and *myfile.myfile* for the input filename *.myfile*. SPACE characters may be included in *outpattern*, as in the example:

```
nmap $1 | sed "s/ *$//" > $1
```

NOTE: Use the backslash (\) character to prevent special treatment of the dollar sign (**$**), left bracket ([), right bracket (]), and comma (,) characters.

ntrans	**ntrans** *[inchars [outchars]]*
	Sets or unsets the filename character translation mechanism. If no arguments are specified, the filename character translation mechanism is unset. If arguments are specified: characters in remote filenames are translated during **put** and **mput** commands issued without a specified remote target filename and characters in local filenames are translated during **get** and **mget** commands issued without a specified local target filename.
	ntrans is useful when connecting to a non-UNIX remote host with different filenaming conventions. Characters in a filename that match a character in *inchars* are replaced with the corresponding character in *outchars*. If the character's position in *inchars* is longer than the length of *outchars*, the character is deleted from the filename.
	Only 16 characters can be translated when using the **ntrans** command under FTP. Use the **case** command if you need to convert the entire alphabet.
open	**open** *server [port]*
	Requests a connection to the specified FTP server. (You can also do that from the UNIX command line by issuing the *ftp* command with *server* as argument.) If the optional port number is given, the FTP program will attempt to contact the server at that port.
	If the auto-login option is on (default setting), the FTP program will also attempt to automatically log the user in to the FTP server.
| | ```
ftp> open geode
Connected to geode.oreilly.com.
220 geode FTP server (Version wu-2.4(1)
        Fri Oct 13 08:07:08 EDT 1995) ready.
Name (geode:val):
331 Password required for val.
Password:
230 User val logged in.
ftp>
``` |
	(Note that you can disable auto-login on the *ftp* command line using the **-n** option. See the section "Options," earlier in this chapter.)
prompt	**prompt**
	Toggles interactive prompting during multiple file transactions (**mget**, **mput**, and **mdelete**). If prompting is turned on (the default), the user is asked to confirm (**y** for yes) or disallow (**n** for no) each file to be acted upon. If prompting is turned off, any
```

mget or mput will transfer all files, and any **mdelete** will delete all files.

```
ftp> prompt
Interactive mode off.
ftp>
```

(Note that you can also disable interactive prompting on the *ftp* command line using the -i option. See the section "Options," earlier in this chapter.)

proxy *ftp_command*

Once you've connected to a primary FTP server (i.e., control connection), the **proxy** command allows you to connect to a secondary server (control connection) and then transfer files between the two. From the first connection, run the **open** command via **proxy**, to establish the secondary control connection. For example:

```
ftp> proxy open geode.oreilly.com
```

Once connected to the secondary server, enter the command

```
ftp> proxy ?
```

to see what FTP commands are executable there. Then use **proxy** to execute FTP commands on the secondary server.

The following commands behave differently when prefaced by the **proxy** command:

- **open** will not define new macros during the auto-login process.

- **close** will not erase existing macro definitions.

- **get** and **mget** transfer files from the host on the primary control connection to the host on the secondary server.

- **put**, **mputd**, and **append** transfer files from the host on the secondary server to the host on the primary server.

Third-party file transfers depend upon support of the PASV command by the server on the secondary server.

put *local_file [remote_file]*

Copies a local file onto the remote machine. You can copy multiple files at once using the **mput** command. Be sure to specify **binary** mode before transferring binary files. For more information, see the **binary** command earlier in this chapter, and the section "Binary or ASCII Files?" in Chapter 17.

→

File Handling

put ←	If *remote_file* is left unspecified, the local filename is used (after processing according to any **ntrans** or **nmap** settings) in naming the remote file. The transferred file retains the current settings for representation type, file structure, and transfer mode.
pwd	**pwd** Prints the name of the current working directory on the remote machine. ``` ftp> pwd 257 "/home/val" is current directory. ftp> ```
quit	**quit** Ends the FTP session with the remote server and/or exits the FTP program. Typing an end-of-file character (generally Ctrl-D) accomplishes the same thing. A synonym for **bye**. ``` ftp> quit 221 Goodbye. val@local 66% ```
quote	**quote** *arg1 arg2* . . . Sends the arguments specified, verbatim, to the remote FTP server. A single FTP reply code is expected in return. (The **remotehelp** command displays a list of valid arguments.) **quote** should be used only by experienced users who are familiar with the FTP protocol.
recv	**recv** *remote_file [local_file]* A synonym for **get**.
remotehelp	**remotehelp** *[command_name]* Requests help from the remote FTP server. If a *command_name* is specified, help information is requested about the particular command.
rename	**rename** *name1 name2* Renames the file *name1* on the remote machine to have the name *name2*. Obviously this is only possible with adequate permissions on the remote machine. Here's a successful case:

```
ftp> rename 50things fifty
350 File exists, ready for destination name
250 RNTO command successful.
ftp>
```

rename

reset

Clears the reply queue. This command resynchronizes command/reply sequencing with the remote FTP server. Resynchronization may be necessary following a violation of the FTP protocol by the remote server.

reset

rmdir *directory_name*

Deletes a directory on the remote machine; permission on the remote machine necessary.

```
ftp> rmdir junk
250 RMD command successful.
ftp>
```

rmdir

runique

Toggles storing of files on the local system with unique filenames; off by default. If a file already exists with a name equal to the target local filename for a **get** or **mget** command, a *.1* is appended to the name. If the resulting name matches another existing file, a *.2* is appended to the original name. If this process continues up to *.99*, an error message is printed, and the transfer does not take place. The generated unique filename will be reported. *runique* will not affect local files generated from a shell command.

runique

File Handling

send *local_file [remote_file]*

A synonym for **put**.

send

sendport

Toggles the use of PORT commands. By default, the FTP program will attempt to use a PORT command when establishing a connection for each data transfer. The use of PORT commands can prevent delays when performing multiple file transfers. If the PORT command fails, FTP will use the default data port. When the use of PORT commands is disabled, no attempt will be made to use PORT commands for each data transfer. This is useful when connected to certain FTP implementations that ignore PORT commands but incorrectly indicate that they have been accepted.

sendport

status	**status**
	Shows the current status of the FTP program. The following status message reflects typical defaults:
| | ```
ftp> status
Connected to geode.oreilly.com.
No proxy connection.
Mode: stream; Type: ascii; Form: non-print; Structure: file
Verbose: on; Bell: off; Prompting: on; Globbing: on
Store unique: off; Receive unique: off
Case: off; CR stripping: on
Ntrans: off
Nmap: off
Hash mark printing: off; Use of PORT cmds: on
ftp>
``` |
| struct | **struct** *[struct_name]* |
| | Sets the file structure to *struct_name*. The only valid *struct_name* is **file**, which corresponds to the default file structure. Since the current implementation only supports file and requires that it be specified, the **struct** command does no more than elicit a status message. |
| | ```
ftp> struct mystructure
We only support file structure, sorry.
ftp>
``` |
| sunique | **sunique** |
| | Toggles the storing of files on the remote machine under unique filenames; off by default. The remote FTP server must support the **STOU** command for successful completion. When on, the remote server will report the unique name. |
| | ```
ftp> sunique
Store unique on.
ftp>
``` |
	See the **runique** command for information on the unique filename scheme.
tenex	**tenex**
	Sets the representation type to that needed to talk to TENEX machines. See also **type**.
| | ```
ftp> tenex
200 Type set to L (byte size 8).
ftp>
``` |

trace

Toggles packet tracing; not currently implemented. (The -t command-line option, intended to enable packet tracing, isn't implemented either.)

type *[type_name]*

Sets the representation type to *type_name*. The valid type names are **ascii** for network ASCII, **binary** or **image** for image, and **tenex** for local byte size with a byte size of 8 (used to talk to TENEX machines). If no type is specified, the current type is printed. The default type is network ASCII.

```
ftp> type image
200 Type set to I.
ftp>
```

Note that the **ascii**, **binary**, and **tenex** commands are the equivalent of **type ascii**, **type binary** (or **type image**), and **type tenex**.

user *username [password] [account]*

Lets you identify yourself to the remote FTP server. If the server requires *password* and/or *account* and you don't supply them, the FTP program will prompt for them. If an *account* is specified, an account command will be relayed to the remote server after the login sequence is completed (if the remote server did not require it for logging in). Unless the FTP program is invoked with auto-login disabled, this process is done automatically on initial connection to the FTP server.

verbose

Toggles verbose mode, in which all of the FTP server responses are displayed to the user; includes statistics regarding the efficiency of each completed file transfer. On by default if FTP's commands are coming from a terminal, and off otherwise. (Note that you can also enable verbose mode on the *ftp* command line using the -v option. See the section "Options," earlier in this chapter.)

CHAPTER 19

File Compression and Archiving

Suppose you download some files from an anonymous FTP site (see Chapter 17, *FTP and File Transfer*) that provides a lot of free software. Since software files are generally pretty large, the administrator at the FTP site has *compressed* them. Compressed files can be transferred more quickly, which saves you some time and trouble in downloading. But what do you do with the compressed files when you get them? How do you convert them back to a useable form?

There may also be times when you'll be the one preparing files for someone else. For instance, what happens when you want to send a large file by email? Chapter 10, *Email Strategies and Survival Tips*, describes how to attach files to email messages using the Netscape and MSIE mailers. You have to consider factors like whether the file is in ASCII or binary format in order to know how to attach it. But you should also consider the size of the file. If a file is very large, you may want to compress it before attaching it to a mail message.

This chapter is intended to help answer these and other related questions.

There are a number of tools that compress files. For Windows, WinZIP and the older PKzip (a DOS program) are common. The Macintosh has Stuffit. UNIX has a few compression alternatives, among them *compress* and *gzip*.

Now, what if you want to mail a whole bunch of big files at once? What if an FTP site administrator wants to make it easy for you to download a whole directory tree in one swoop? Well, for most platforms, there's also a way to *archive* files. Archiving involves taking a group of files—perhaps even an entire directory tree—and combining them into a single file.

As luck—and a certain amount of foresight—would have it, Windows and Mac compression tools commonly archive files and compress them simultaneously. In fact, there isn't even a distinction made between a single compressed file and a compressed group of files—they're both archives.

By contrast, the more flexible UNIX environment has separate tools for file compression and archiving. The most popular archiving utility is *tar* (which comes from UNIX *tape ar*chive). First, an archive is created; then it is compressed.

Keep in mind that most compressed/archived file formats are *binary*. As explained in Chapter 10, files in binary format can't simply be emailed as is. They need to be encoded for transfer, and then decoded on the other end, to preserve the original format. If you're using MSIE's or Netscape's latest mail programs, you can specify that a file be sent along with a message as an *attachment*, and automatic MIME encoding is done for you. While a binary file can't simply be mailed like text, a MIME-encoded file can be. Ideally, the recipient's mailer will also support MIME, and the mailer will *decode* the file at the other end. Voila!

If you don't have a mailer that can encode files for you, you'll have to use another program. In UNIX environments, for instance, the *uuencode* and *uudecode* facilities are used to convert a binary file to ASCII text (for transfer purposes) and back again. If you're using an older mailer, such as *mailx*, before you mail a binary file (such as a compressed file), you need to convert it to ASCII with *uuencode*. Then the recipient has to use *uudecode* (or some equivalent) to convert the file back to its original binary format.

In Macintosh environments, Stuffit archive files need to be encoded with a utility called BinHex. Most versions of Stuffit will actually perform BinHex encoding if you request it.

Now, you may well be asking yourself, "When am I supposed to care about all this?" Well, here's your answer:

- When you want to attach a large or complicated file or files to an email message (e.g., binary files, a directory structure, PostScript or other long text files, etc.)

- When you receive email with attached files that require decoding, unpacking, decompression, etc.

- When you download compressed and/or archived files (e.g., using FTP) from the Internet

This chapter shows you some of the ways you can archive and/or compress files, depending on your environment. For UNIX systems, we'll additionally cover how to use *uuencode* and *uudecode* to turn binary files into ASCII for transfer purposes. Since you're liable to receive archived, compressed, and encoded files in the mail, as well as via FTP sites, the chapter will also explain how to convert them back to their original formats.

A general note: Whenever files are transferred, there are issues as to whether the person on the receiving end has the right tools to deal with the files in the format they get them. If you're preparing files for transfer, try to make sure the intended recipient can handle them. It's always reasonable to ask somebody what works for them before you go to the trouble of compressing.

Relevant File Formats

The filename suffix should provide a clue as to the utility used to compress, archive, and/or encode a file you receive. Table 19–1 displays the suffixes and how they're created.

Table 19–1: Compressed, Archived File Formats

File Suffix	How Created	How to Recover Original
.zip	WinZip, PKzip	same
.Z	UNIX compress	uncompress program
.gz	UNIX gzip (compression)	gunzip
.tar	UNIX tar archive	tar, zcat
.uu	uuencode	uudecode
.hqx	BinHex	same (or Stuffit with BinHex capabilities)
.sit	Stuffit	same

WinZip: File Compression/Archiving for Windows

There are plenty of free sources of WinZip. Any search engine should help you locate one. WinZip is transferred as a self-extracting archive (with a *.exe* extension). Simply opening the file will unpack its contents and get you the executable WinZip program. Here are some things you should know before you use it.

As far as WinZip is concerned, there's no difference between a compressed file and an archive of files. There are simply one-file and multiple-file archives, respectively. This factor, along with WinZip's interface, makes it fairly easy to use. WinZip archives have a *.zip* filename extension.

Since WinZip thinks only in terms of archives, that's the language we're going to use here. But keep in mind that we're compressing/uncompressing files.

The recently released WinZip 6.2 can also decode files encoded with *uuencode* (UNIX), *BinHex* (Mac), as well as three forms of MIME encoding (base64, plain/text, and quoted printable).

To Make a WinZip Archive

In order to create an archive:

1. Select **New Archive** from the WinZip **File** menu to open the New Archive dialog (the Ctrl+N shortcut does the same thing).

a. In the dialog, select a drive and directory in which to create the archive. (Use the **drives** menu to select another drive. Navigate the file system using the folder button with the up arrow; if you'd rather, you can create a new folder using the standard Windows button intended for this purpose.)

b. Enter the name to be used for the archive in the "File name:" box.

c. Click OK. The Add dialog is opened.

2. Use the Add dialog to select the file(s)/folder(s) to archive.

a. In the Add dialog, go to the desired folder. Open the folder if you want to archive its contents; they will be displayed in the dialog.

b. Highlight the name(s) of the file(s)/folder(s) you want to archive. The name(s) appear in the "File name:" box. You can type the name(s) in this box instead.

3. Click the Add button. The archive is created.

You're returned to the original WinZip window, which displays information about the newly created archive, including the size in bytes and the packed size. The "ratio" is how big the compressed file is compared to the original.

If you'd rather not deal with menus and (as many) dialogs, you can also create an archive by dragging and dropping files and/or folders into the primary WinZip window. Each time you add an item in this manner, a Drag and Drop dialog will be opened. Name the archive you want to create or append to in the "Add to Archive:" box. You can drag and drop as many items as you want and add them via this same dialog process.

You can also use the Add button in the main window to add to an existing archive.

Unpacking a WinZip Archive

Whether you're talking about a single archived file or a whole directory packed into a single archive, the unpacking process is simple:

1. Click on the Open Archive button. (You can instead select **Open Archive** from the **File** menu, or use the Ctrl+O keyboard shortcut.)

2. In the resulting Open Archive dialog, navigate to the folder that has the archive to be unpacked. Select the filename of the archive, or type it into the Filename box at the bottom of the window.

3. Double-click the archive name, or select and click Open. (Alt+O works too.)

4. The dialog is closed and the contents of the archive are displayed in the main WinZip window. But you still have to unpack it.

5. To extract the files from the archive, use the Extract button or the keyboard shortcut Ctrl+E. (You can also go to the **Actions** menu and select **Extract**.) This opens the Extract dialog.

6. Enter the name of the folder to "Extract to:" on the left side of the Extract dialog. (You can either type it in or use the Directories/Drives list on the right to navigate to the proper place.)

7. Click the Extract button in the dialog to finish the process. The contents of the archive should be in the folder you specified.

Note that you can choose to extract specific files rather than the entire archive. The Extract dialog has mutually exclusive settings for "all of the files" and "selected files." But you can also just select the items you want to unpack in the primary WinZip window, and then invoke the Extract function. The Extract dialog assumes you want to unpack only the selected items and chooses the "selected files" option for you.

UNIX File Compression and Archiving

In a typical UNIX environment, there are a number of ways to do just about everything. In fact, it might be harder to figure out what programs to use than to actually use them. We'll take a look at some of the more widely used utilities:

- The *compress* and *gzip* compression programs and their opposite partners, *uncompress* and *gunzip*

- The *tar* archiving utility

- *uuencode* and *uudecode*, which are used to convert binary files to ASCII (to allow their transfer) and back again

compress and gzip

Two compression utilities commonly available on UNIX systems are *compress* and *gzip*. The *g* in *gzip* stands for *GNU*, a free version of UNIX developed by the Free Software Foundation.

Both of these programs have the command-line syntax:

```
program file_to_be_compressed
```

For example:

```
gzip chapter1
```

Or

```
compress chapter1
```

Files created with the *compress* program have a *.Z* suffix; *gzip*ped files end with *.gz*.

Uncompressing these files is just as easy. The uncompress alternatives are called *uncompress* and *gunzip*, respectively. Note that you don't have to enter the suffix of the compressed file on the command line. For example:

```
gunzip chapter1
```

Or

```
uncompress chapter1
```

Since compressed files are in binary format, if you want to send them through email, they have to be encoded. If you're mailer won't do that for you, use *uuencode*, described later in this chapter.

tar Archives

Suppose I want to put all the source files for this book on an FTP site. I might want to create a single archive of all the files. The *tar* utility is commonly used to create archives in UNIX environments. *tar* command-line syntax is not terribly friendly. But it isn't terribly tricky either.

Use the *c* option to create the archive and *f* to specify that the archive be saved in a file. The name you supply following the options becomes the archive filename. Then additional arguments tell *tar* what goes in the archive. The following command would create a tar archive named *mybook.tar*, containing the entire subdirectory *inut*:

```
tar cf mybook.tar inut/*
```

Since *tar* archives are usually very large, I want to compress the resulting file,

```
compress mybook.tar
```

which produces a file called *mybook.tar.Z*.

If you download a *tar* archive, there's a good chance it will also be compressed. To unpack a compressed *tar* archive, you can either:

* Uncompress the file and then use *tar* to unpack it.

* Use a program called *zcat* to uncompress and then pipe the output directly to *tar*.

The following sequence would unpack the archive I just made:

```
uncompress mybook.tar          Note that uncompress assumes the .Z suffix

tar xf mybook.tar
```

The *zcat* program uncompresses a file and sends the results to standard output. This allows you to uncompress and untar on a single line. When you run *tar* with the *f* option and also use a dash (–) as the filename, *tar* reads from standard input:

```
zcat mybook.tar.Z | tar xf -
```

If you add the *v* option to *tar*, it will tell you each file it packs or unpacks. (The *v* stands for verbose.)

Like any compressed file, a compressed *tar* file needs to be encoded in order to be sent through email. If your mailer won't do that for you, *uuencode* will.

uuencode and uudecode

Binaries won't survive the emailing process in the proper format, but you can convert binary files to ASCII text files temporarily—just to facilitate transfer. The most common way to do this on a UNIX system is the *uuencode* program. To *uuencode* the compressed *tar* file created in the previous section, type:

```
uuencode mybook.tar.Z mybook.tar.Z > mybook.tar.Z.uu
```

Notice the unusual syntax. The source filename is given twice—the second instance is used as a label within the encoded file. (You can actually use any text for that label, but the filename makes the most sense.)

You need to provide both a source filename and a destination filename. Note that I'm giving the *uuencoded* file a *.uu* suffix, which is the convention. However, if I then send the file in mail, the recipient can save it under any name she likes; it's still easy to recover the original format. Suppose the person calls it *mailarch*. She could recover the files put into the *tar* archive using the following sequence:

```
uudecode mailarch
```

```
uncompress mybook.tar.Z
```

```
tar xf mybook.tar
```

Macintosh StuffIt Does It All

The Macintosh environment may not be quite as popular as it once was, but they still know how to make things easy for users, as the various incarnations of the StuffIt utility prove. As in the Windows environment, compression and archiving are considered to be one in the same. StuffIt archives have a *.sit* extension; files that have been archived are said to have been Stuffed.

One of the latest versions of the program, StuffIt Deluxe 4.0, has a lot of muscle. If you're running Macintosh System 7, you can even configure it to compress a file automatically when you add the *.sit* suffix and to uncompress it when you remove the suffix. This is a pretty cool feature. But regardless of whether you're using a souped-up or older version of StuffIt, the the basic compression/archiving operations are fairly standard.

Keep in mind that if you want to transfer StuffIt archives, you will additionally have to encode them. (Archive files are in binary format, which won't survive being emailed, etc.) The most common encoding method for the Mac is a program called BinHex (sort of the Mac equivalent of uuencode). As foresight would have it, StuffIt can actually BinHex the archive files you make, too.

StuffIt does not discriminate when it comes to platforms. It can actually emulate UNIX *compress* and *uncompress, uuencode* and *uudecode,* and *tar,* as well as Windows zipping/unzipping programs, etc.

StuffIt may also come with some smaller helper apps, like StuffIt Expander, a program that lets you drag and drop in an archive and expands it for you.

Many StuffIt commands are available both on menus and on a special command panel (which features a series of buttons).

Following are some general guidelines to follow in using StuffIt Deluxe 4.0 to create and unpack archives. If you're using an older version of StuffIt, the specifics may be different, but the principles should be the same.

Making an Archive (Stuffing)

Here's how to make a StuffIt archive:

1. Select **New** from the **File** menu. (The Fan-N shortcut works too.)

2. In the resulting dialog, name the archive. The default name is *Archive.sit.* Then click on the New button or hit Return. A folder is opened in which you can create your archive; note that the name you gave the archive appears at the top of the folder.

3. Drag the files/folders you want to compress into the archive folder window. Dragging in items automatically compresses (or Stuffs) them. For each file/folder in the archive, there are several columns of information: Name, Kind (file type), Date, Expanded (size in bytes when), Stuffed (size in bytes when), Saved (percentage smaller).

   Keep in mind that you can edit the various parts of the archive if you want. For each component, you can view information about it, delete it, etc., using menu items or buttons on the command panel. Rename files/folders in the archive just as you would any files/folders.

   You can also make the archive self-extracting by clicking the toggle box in the lower-left corner of the archive window. (The **Archive** menu also offers a **Make Self-Extracting** item.) This kind of archive unpacks itself automatically when someone tries to open it. You don't have to use an archiving program like StuffIt to do it.

4. If you want to mail or transfer the archive, you should also encode it for transfer using BinHex. The **Translate** menu offers a **BinHex4** submenu with two choices: **Encode** and **Decode**. Choose **Encode** to create a BinHexed version of the archive (*Archive.sit.hqx*).

BinHex files are in ASCII format. At the beginning of the file will be an informational line similar to this:

```
This file must be converted with BinHex 4.0.
```

This information will tell the person receiving the file how to unencode it—though if they have StuffIt, they should be all set. The BinHex delimiter character is a colon (:). If a colon does not appear at the end of the file, you'll know part of it was lost en route.

Unpacking an Archive (UnStuffing)

Many versions of StuffIt come with a small helper application called StuffIt Expander, which expands an archive you drag and drop into it. You can also open an archive using the primary StuffIt program:

1. Select **Open** from the **File** menu.

2. Select the archive filename in the resulting dialog. Then click Open or hit Return.

3. Select the items to UnStuff. Then select **UnStuff** from the **Archive** menu (or use the UnStuff button on the command bar or the Fan-U key shortcut). For each item to be UnStuffed, a dialog will ask you to confirm or change the item's name. Then you click UnStuff in the dialog to finish the operation.

   (Older versions of StuffIt may instead offer an Extract button to unpack the components of the archive.)

StuffIt Keyboard Shortcuts

The following table lists the keyboard shortcuts for some of the most common StuffIt operations. As is the case with a lot of Mac shortcuts, these involve the use of the Fan key.

Note that every one of these operations can also be performed using a button on the StuffIt command panel. Table 19–2 displays keyboard shortcuts for common StuffIt functions.

Table 19–2: Keyboard Shortcuts for Common StuffIt Functions

Function	Shortcut
Stuff	Fan-S
UnStuff	Fan-U
New Folder	Fan-F
Delete	Fan-D
Get Info	Fan-I
View	Fan-L
Launch	Fan-T
Move/Copy	Fan-M

PART VI

Helpers and Plug-ins

CHAPTER 20

Helper Applications

At one time, even the best browsers were extremely limited as to the the types of data they could display. Many graphic images, as well as video and audio files, were just too much for most browsers to handle. So, they needed a little help—in the form of external applications that could be called upon to display the files that were outside the browser's capabilities. Such programs are commonly referred to as *helper applications.*

Well, the smarter browsers get, the less help they need. The latest and greatest of the popular browsers (at least as of this writing)—the version of Netscape Navigator shipped in the Communicator 4.0 suite and Microsoft Internet Explorer 3.02—both handle files in a greater number of formats than their predecessors. But no browser as shipped can handle every kind of file you're liable to encounter. And if you're not using the latest version of your browsing program, it may need even more assistance.

When your browser comes across a file it doesn't know how to handle, you have a couple of options. You can download an appropriate helper application, which your browser can then call upon when it runs into this kind of file. Or, you can see whether you can enhance the browser itself by installing a *plug-in* (for Netscape) or *ActiveX control* (for MSIE).

Plug-ins and ActiveX controls are like helper applications that are embedded within your browser. While helper apps can be initiated from within the browser or run entirely on their own, plug-ins and ActiveX controls become in effect part of the browsing program itself.

The way the latest browsing programs are designed to work, if you encounter a file that the browser can't access and there's a plug-in or control that can help, you'll get a dialog asking if you want to go get it and install it. If you say yes, the program should step you through the installation. For the most popular plug-ins and controls, this should be pretty painless.

But if the only way you can deal with a file you encounter is an external helper application, you're largely on your own. You have to find it, install it, and tell your brower how to find it. Since there are no dialog boxes to tell you what's going on, you may not even have any idea what kind of application you need.

However, the scenario isn't as gloomy as all that either, because there are a number of common helper applications, some of which may already be installed on your computer. If you already have a helper app, it's simply a matter of letting your browser know—by editing its customization settings (generally called preferences or options).

The current chapter lists some of the most popular and useful helper applications, along with addresses from where you should be able to download them. Installation guidelines depend on the program and your environment, but each program should either be self-installing or come with detailed installation instructions.

As you look over the chapter, keep one important principle in mind: just because such applications exist doesn't mean you need them. As a matter of fact, chances are you don't need many helper applications. And if you have the latest version of your browser, you may not need any.

However, if you do need to install a helper—or if you have one your browser doesn't know about—you'll need to set up your browser to find it. We'll show you how for both Navigator and MSIE.

Of course, this discussion begs the question of what you should do if you can choose between installing an external helper app and an internal plug-in. Chapter 21, *Plug-ins and ActiveX Controls* , deals with these issues more fully, but the general principle is that you don't want to overburden your browser with internal enhancements because it will slow performance. If you tend to deal with a certain file type all the time—say you're a videophile—you might want to have the option of viewing files in the helper application (without having to run your browser). In addition, some helper apps let you edit the files in question. If you want to muck around with graphics, audio, video, etc., you'll definitely need some kind of external application. (The trickier issues become trickier in that some plug-ins—QuickTime for one—come with external apps as well. See Chapter 21 for more information.)

Common Helper Apps for Windows

There are a number of common helper applications for Windows environments. Luckily, two of the most important ones may not be an issue. The *telnet* remote login program (which also lets you access libraries worldwide) is probably already installed somewhere on your machine. All you have to do is make sure your browser knows where it is. If you have one of the latest and greatest browsers, there is a plug-in or ActiveX control you can easily install to view *.avi* format movie files. (If you did a full browser installation, you may even have it already.)

The current section covers these and some of the other popular helper applications for Windows, along with some pertinent details, including where to find them. See one of the following sections to learn how to configure your particular browser to use a helper application.

telnet

Chapter 8, *Accessing Libraries and Other Resources with Telnet*, describes some of the things you can do with *telnet*, including logging on to a remote system and accessing library catalogs. If you come across a Web page with a link to an address that begins with **telnet:**, your browser is going to need to launch a *telnet* application in order for you to visit that address.

Whether you've run into *telnet* before or not, there's a good chance some version of the program lives on your Windows system. Mine is hidden under *c:\windows*. Before you go out and download a *telnet* client, select Run from the Start menu, then enter "telnet" in the Run dialog, and hit Return. If there's a Telnet application in your path, it will run for you.

If Telnet isn't in your path, the Run dialog won't find it. The next thing to do is search for "telnet" using your Windows Explorer or File Manager. If you turn it up, skip to the appropriate configuration discussion for your particular browser, later in this chapter.

If you can't find *telnet* on your system, the following two versions are available for free via:

NCSA Telnet for Windows

```
ftp://gatekeeper.dec.com/pub/micro/msdos/win3/winsock/wintelb3.zip
```

Note that this program is an unsupported beta version.

Trumpet Telnet (VT100) terminal for Winsock

```
ftp://gatekeeper.dec.com/pub/micro/msdos/win3/winsock/trmptel.zip
```

AVI Video Player for Windows

Files with a *.avi* extension are Windows format video files. If you requested a complete install of MSIE 3.0, you should already have an AVI player plug-in. Thus, when you come across a video file in this format, the browser will simply open the AVI player and display the video file. Likewise, Navigator 4.0 is AVI-friendly. One of the default plug-ins can play AVI files within the browser window.

If you need or want an external AVI player, here's where to get it:

```
ftp://gatekeeper.dec.com/pub/micro/msdos/win3/desktop/avipro2.exe
```

More Video: MPEG Players

MPEG is another common video format, developed partly from the JPEG graphic image format (which most browsers handle just fine). Keep in mind that there are a number of plug-ins that handle MPEG and other video files. (See Chapter 21 for information on researching the right plug-ins for your needs.) However, if you want an external MPEG viewer, check out the offerings at:

```
ftp://gatekeeper.dec.com/pub/micro/msdos/win3/desktop/
```

and

```
ftp://ftp.winsite.com/
```

MPEGPLAY is a popular choice.

Audio: MPLAYER and WHAM 1.33 Audio Player

With sound files on many Web pages, audio may be one department where you should really go with a plug-in. RealAudio and its next generation RealPlayer are among the most popular and useful plug-ins. See Chapter 21 for more information.

If you want an external audio player, you might try *MPLAYER*. Versions should be available at both:

```
ftp://gatekeeper.dec.com/pub/micro/msdos/win3/desktop/
```

and

```
ftp://ftp.winsite.com/
```

Or the WHAM 1.33 Audio Player may suffice:

```
ftp://gatekeeper.dec.com/pub/micro/msdos/win3/sounds/wham133.zip
```

A JPEG Viewer

Again, JPEG has become a very browser-friendly format. However, if you want to have an external JPEG viewer, which also lets you alter the images, LVIEW is very popular. (So much so that it may already be hiding on your PC; search for it before doing anything.) If you need to get LVIEW, get the file:

```
ftp://gatekeeper.dec.com/pub/micro/msdos/win3/desktop/lview31.zip
```

Configuring Navigator 4.0 to Use Helper Apps

The specifics of setting up Navigator to use a helper application have changed between 3.0 and 4.0, but the principles remain the same—and it's still simple. Basically, you just have to let the browser know that for a particular type of file, it should launch an external application named such-and-such that resides in file such-and-such on your system.

Here's the procedure to configure Navigator 4.0 to use a helper application:

1. Select **Preferences** from the **Edit** menu. (Typing Alt+E, and then E again, accomplishes the same thing.)

2. Within the resulting Preferences dialog, open up the heading Navigator. (Click on the plus sign in front of the heading to do this.)

3. Click on the subheading Applications; this page of preferences allows you to specify helper applications.

4. In the Description column, click on the file or MIME type for which you want to specify a helper app. Then click the Edit button; enter the pathname to the helper app in the resulting dialog.

If the appropriate file/MIME type isn't included in the Description column, click the New Type button. Then fill in the resulting dialog with the text description, file extension(s) (if any), MIME type (if any), and the pathname to the helper application to use to deal with files of this type (e.g., *c:\windows\telnet.exe*).

5. Click OK.

When you next encounter a file that requires this particular helper application, Navigator should automatically open it. If this doesn't work, go back and check your settings under **Preferences**.

Configuring MSIE 3.0 to Use Helper Apps

It's easy to configure Microsoft Internet Explorer 3.0 to use helper applications. You set preferences like these using the Options dialog box.

1. Select **Options** from the **View** menu. (The keyboard shortcut Alt+V, and then O does the same thing.)

2. Within the Options dialog, the various preferences are organized on six overlapping tabbed windows, which look something like file folders. The tabs reveal the following categories:

- General

- Connection

- Navigation

- Programs

- Security

- Advanced

Click on the On the **Programs** tab; you'll find a section called **Viewers**, which lets you specify external viewers and players (i.e., helper apps).

3. Select the File Types button to open another dialog, which lists a number of file/MIME types with the default players/helper apps.

4. Select a file/MIME type.

5. Enter the pathname of an appropriate helper application (e.g., *c:\program files\mpeg\mpegplay.exe*).

6. Select OK.

When you next encounter a file that requires this particular helper application, MSIE should automatically open it. If this doesn't work, go back and check your settings under **Programs**.

CHAPTER 21

Plug-ins and ActiveX Controls

If you've been browsing around for a while, you may already have come across a situation in which your browser can't handle some type of information it encounters. Although Netscape Navigator and MSIE are state-of-the-art browsers, there are some things these programs can't do without a little enhancement. For instance, as it stands, there are certain audio and video file formats that a basic browser can't play for you.

As explained in Chapter 20, *Helper Applications*, when your browser comes up against a type of file it can't handle, you might install a separate program the browser can run to view/play the file. Or, you might be able to enhance the browser program itself by adding a so-called *plug-in*.

Suppose, for instance, you come across a link to a movie file in Apple QuickTime format. You really want to view the movie, but your browser can't understand data of that type. Well, the developers of QuickTime have also come up with a plug-in you can install to enable your browser (whether it's Navigator or MSIE) to show you the movie. This is a typical plug-in scenario. Apple QuickTime movies are common around the Net, and they're something most people will want to get a look at.

Many plug-ins are similar—they let you browse the various types of multimedia files you might encounter on the Web. For instance, another popular plug-in is Shockwave by Macromedia. Shockwave files include animation and sound. They're common at Web sites having to do with music, such as MTV's site (**http://www.mtv.com/**). The current chapter covers both of these popular plug-ins (QuickTime and Shockwave) in some detail.

However, there are also plug-ins that add more esoteric functionality to your browser: spreadsheet capabilities, calendar programs, file conversion, chat utilities, even graphics programs to illustrate chemical formulas. Later in this chapter is a partial list of some plug-ins that are currently mentioned at the Netscape site. Since this isn't a comprehensive list, the current chapter also mentions some other sites you can check to keep up with the latest available browser enhancements.

Keep in mind that while a number of plug-ins simply enhance your browser, many are development tools. Someone needs to create files like Apple QuickTime movies, right? Thus, when you install a plug-in, you may have to decide the level of installation you want. You may opt for a viewer/player only, where such a choice is possible. But in many cases, you'll need the more complete tools, even simply to view/play files. Since most plug-ins provide extensive installation help, at least for the more common plug-ins, you should have plenty of guidance in these matters.

While most plug-ins can be installed for either Navigator or MSIE, if you're an MSIE user, you may have another option. A number of so-called *ActiveX controls* provide an alternative to plug-ins by extending the capabilities of Microsoft Internet Explorer. The Shockwave plug-in mentioned previously, for instance, also exists as an ActiveX control.

The advantage of using an ActiveX control is that the installation tends to be seamless and automatic. When you come across a file MSIE can't handle, if MSIE knows about an ActiveX control that can do the job, you'll be prompted as to whether you want to download it. If you say yes, this process should happen quickly and without any further effort on your part. Although installing many plug-ins can also be very simple, installing a well-supported ActiveX control is about as easy as it gets.

While the current chapter is concerned only with those ActiveX controls that extend the functionality of your browser, you should be aware that ActiveX is also a development environment. In fact, many ActiveX controls are actually used for Web page authoring. These so-called *form controls* let you add various graphical elements to a Web page. If you consult one of the ActiveX resources mentioned later in this chapter, you can peruse these offerings as well.

Which Plug-ins or ActiveX Controls Do I Need?

Which browser enhancements you need largely depends on the tasks you like to accomplish with your system. However, there are a few plug-ins that are extremely useful just about across the board. The following plug-ins let you take advantage of some of the better and also more common multimedia offerings on the Web:

- Apple QuickTime

- Shockwave

- RealAudio (or the more recent RealPlayer)

Keep in mind that every browser enhancement you install has to be loaded each time you run the browser. You don't want to install superfluous plug-ins just to have ready access to them because it will slow your browser's performance. The three plug-ins discussed in the following sections should be worth having for a large percentage of users.

However, the way plug-in installations tend to work, it's a good strategy only to add one when you come up against a data wall—in other words, when you can't display, play or otherwise handle a file you come across during the course of normal browsing. Even though Shockwave files are all over the Net, I never run into them because they tend to be concentrated at sites related to music and pop culture, and those aren't high on my lists of interests. I made a point to visit sites that have Shockwave files so I'd know what I'm talking about. But the time to get a plug-in is basically when you need one.

Now, how do you know you need one? Well, if you click on a link for an audio file and you don't get any sound, you may need an audio plug-in like RealAudio. (Your PC might also need a sound card and speakers!)

When Netscape Navigator encounters an image, video, or other file it can't display/play, it will instead display an image that looks like a jigsaw puzzle piece—to indicate that something is missing. Clicking on this jigsaw piece should open up a dialog that lets you link to an appropriate plug-in. Here's the dialog I got when I tried to open a Shockwave file without having the Shockwave plug-in. (The MIME type of such files is "application/x-director.")

```
Plugin Not Loaded

This page contains info of type "application/x-director" that
can only be viewed with the appropriate plug-in.  What do
you want to do?

Get the Plugin            Cancel
```

If you get a dialog like this and select "Get the Plugin," Navigator will take you to the Netscape "Plugin Finder Page," which will have links to one or more plug-ins that can handle this type of file. In the previous case, the only plug-in (predictably) was Shockwave by Macromedia. You can download by clicking on the link, and you'll be led through the simple installation.

MSIE will also tell you when you need a plug-in and walk you through the process of obtaining and installing it. For well-supported plug-ins, you should get a dialog box like this one:

```
QuickTime Plug-In Error

The Plug-In could not load QuickTime for Windows.
Would you like to get QuickTime for Windows now?

Yes     No
```

Again, there's no mystery here. You need QuickTime, and MSIE will help you get it. Clicking Yes takes you to the QuickTime site, from which you can begin.

Plug-in installation is supposed to be simple. And installing popular plug-ins like these generally is. However, the plug-in market is huge, and there are plenty of exceptions. When in doubt, contact the developers of the particular plug-in.

Apple QuickTime

If you're going to be on the Web, why not enjoy some of the cooler offerings—like movies. Apple QuickTime is a popular movie format, offering genuine talking pictures. QuickTime movie files have a *.mov* filename extension. You can find QuickTime movies at movie-related sites, such as Paramount Pictures (http://www.paramount.com/) or Warner Brothers (http://www.warnerbros.com/), but they turn up all over the place. I ran into some at the Web site of the Boston Red Sox (more my kind of site). The Apple QuickTime site has an extensive samples page (http://quicktime.apple.com/sam/), with links to a number of movies on the Net.

You can install the QuickTime plug-in for either Netscape Navigator or MSIE. (As of this printing, there is no equivalent ActiveX control.) The easiest way to do this is to let your browser come up against a QuickTime file. It should then lead you through the installation process.

The preceding section includes an example of the kind of dialog box MSIE is supposed to provide when it encounters the need for a plug-in. The example dialog happens to be one I got when I tried to view a QuickTime movie without the appropriate plug-in, asking if I wanted to get QuickTime for Windows. Responding Yes takes you to the Apple QuickTime site, where you can download the necessary installation file.

If you're a Navigator user, you'll get a different dialog (also illustrated in the preceding section), but the point is the same. If you select "Get the Plugin," you'll be taken to get QuickTime and guided through the installation.

The installation procedure is virtually identical for Navigator and MSIE. However, there will come a point where you have to designate your preferred browser. Check the appropriate one.

Note that the Apple QuickTime site offers a few different packages (QuickTime 2.1.2, QuickTime Plug-in, QTVR Component). Select the QuickTime Easy Install Download, which includes all the parts—you'll need them to use the plug-in correctly.

Save the downloaded file onto your hard disk. Then go and open the file. You should get another dialog box that indicates the file is a "self-extracting" executable (i.e., a program file that will "unpack" its own parts). You then need to confirm the installation:

```
InstallShield Self-Extracting EXE

This will install QuickTime and the QuickTime Browser Plug-In
(32 Bit).  Do you wish to continue?
Yes        No
```

If you select Yes, the files that will install the application will be extracted. In order to install, you first need to quit out of other applications (including your browser). Then proceed with the installation and setup. The QuickTime Browser Plug-in Setup Wizard guides you through the simple procedure.

Along the way, you'll have to confirm the choice of directory for the plug-in, accept the license requirements for the product, and specify your default browser. If you have a previous version of QuickTime, it will be deleted.

Once the QuickTime plug-in is installed, you can watch QuickTime movies within your browser window. Many of these files are very large; they may take a while to download. You'll notice that a horizontal bar along the bottom of the QuickTime player fills up as a movie is loaded. Once the bar is filled, you can click on the adjacent play symbol, which looks like a right arrow key, to view the movie. Save a movie by using your browser's pop-up menu (displayed by clicking the right mouse button over the image).

Along with the plug-in you get two helper applications, MoviePlayer (*player.exe*) and PictureViewer (*viewer.exe*). You can use these programs, independent of your browser, to view QuickTime videos and images.

Shockwave by Macromedia

You want your MTV? Well, to appreciate MTV (and many other pop culture sites) on the Web, you'll need to enhance your browser with Shockwave by Macromedia. Shockwave files include animation and sound. The Shockwave application happens to come as both a plug-in and as an ActiveX control. It's easy to install either way, but adding the ActiveX control to MSIE redefines easy.

When you run into a Shockwave file using Netscape, you're liable to get one of those jigsaw puzzle images described in the section "What Plug-ins or ActiveX Controls Do I Need?" This puzzle piece indicates that the necessary plug-in is missing. Click on the puzzle piece to open a dialog that lets you "Get the Plugin" (also as illustrated in the earlier section). You'll then be taken to the Netscape Plug-In Finder Page, where you can link to Macromedia to get the Shockwave plug-in (**http://www.macromedia.com/shockwave/**).

Before the download, you'll have to give your name and email address. (No money is involved, however.) The site should be smart enough to gauge your operating system and browser. When I connected, it rightly surmised that I needed:

```
Shockwave Installer for Windows 95/NT

Plays Director, Flash, and Flash2 media
```

The second line refers to three of Macromedia's Shockwave family of applications (Shockwave Director, Flash, and Flash2). You'll be given a choice of "Download Now" buttons—corresponding to servers at different locations. You can choose to download from the U.S., Europe, or Japan.

Once the download is complete, quit out of your other applications, including your browser, and double-click on the Shockwave Installer to install the plug-in. This automated process is fairly easy.

If you're an MSIE user, you'll have it even easier. If you try to access a Shockwave file without the the necessary browser enhancement, you'll get a dialog like this:

```
Authenticode (tm) Security Technology

Do you wish to install and run [the Shockwave ActiveX control]?

Yes    No

Click each link below before replying on this certificate.

[Assorted links to the ActiveX developer's site]
```

You're asked to "click each link" to learn more about the ActiveX control before you agree to install it. If you then decide to install and run the ActiveX control, you don't have to quit the browser or any other application. When you click yes, the ActiveX control will be added to your browser, and you can continue working. The only possible disadvantage to this system is that you have to get separate ActiveX controls for Shockwave Director, Shockwave Flash, etc. (while a single plug-in covers them all). But, truthfully, the process is so seamless, only my notes make me realize I went through it more than once.

RealAudio by Progressive Networks

Progressive Networks' RealAudio has become a virtual standard for audio files on the Net. The files are everywhere. Radio and television broadcasts are commonly distributed by RealAudio. It isn't always the cleanest sound, but it's pretty neat to be able to sit at your computer and hear Paul McCartney sing live in London.

Because its presence on the Web is ubiquitous, RealAudio is probably the plug-in most people are likely to want (presuming their computer has the sound capabilities). In fact, RealAudio has become so close to a standard that Netscape and Microsoft are trying to eliminate the need to treat it as an add-on. Thus, if you do the complete install of MSIE 3.0, you'll already have RealAudio capabilities. Otherwise, you can easily get the RealAudio ActiveX control when you encounter the need.

If you need to get RealAudio and you're using one of the more recent releases of your browser, the browser should walk you through the installation (as illustrated for Shockwave and QuickTime). However, if you're using an older browser, you may need to install the stand-alone RealAudio player (which brings along the plug-in). You can find the player and the installation instructions at the RealAudio site (http://www.real.com/). The next generation of the RealAudio Player is called RealPlayer; as of this writing, the beta version is currently available.

Which Plug-Ins and ActiveX Controls Are Out There?

There are a few sites you can visit to peruse the available plug-ins and ActiveX controls. Netscape has its own directory of plug-ins that have been registered with them. As of this moment, there are 135 and counting. You can read about these plug-ins and access links to them, from the Netscape site.

When you connect to http://www.netscape.com/, on the righthand side of the frame notice the banner that reads "Get the Latest Netscape Software." Below the banner is a drop-down menu, labeled with the instruction "Pull down to select product." Clicking on the menu bar reveals a few dozen categories of Netscape software, including "Navigator Plug-ins." Once you select an item from this list, you can either "Try It," "Buy It," or obtain "Info" using one of three buttons that appear below the menu bar. Choose Info to browse the descriptions of the current plug-ins.

Naturally, Microsoft's Web site includes a list of ActiveX controls. Component Gallery (**http://www.microsoft.com/activex/controls**), there are 113 controls listed as of this writing. However, these particular ActiveX controls are mostly intended to be used by Web page developers. If you're interested, you can view them sorted by type of control or by company and also link to the resources.

Neither Netscape's nor Microsoft's list covers the whole market of available plug-ins and ActiveX controls. For more comprehensive lists of plug-ins and ActiveX controls, the place to go is the enormous BrowserWatch site, a product of *iWORLD*:

```
http://browserwatch.iworld.com/
```

Once you're at the BrowserWatch site, check out the **Plug-In Plaza** and **ActiveX Arena**, both of which include a huge number of listings and links.

Some of the Current Plug-ins

The Netscape Web site classifies the available plug-ins into five basic categories:

- 3D and Animation

- Business and Utilities

- Presentations

- Audio/Video

- Image Viewers

If a Web site can't keep pace with plug-in development, we certainly can't hope to do it here. However, we are including a short list of some of the more interesting and popular plug-ins, classified under the same categories Netscape uses. Note that while Netscape's site provides links to the actual plug-ins, we've opted for URLs to the companies involved—because the addresses are more stable.

3D and animation

Shockwave by Macromedia
> **http://www.macromedia.com/**
> An industry standard for delivering and experiencing quality interactive multimedia, graphics, and streaming audio on the World Wide Web.

Shockwave Flash by Macromedia
> **http://www.macromedia.com/**
> Provides vector-based animation, with interactive buttons, anti-aliased graphics, outline fonts, and zooming control.

Sizzler by Totally Hip Software
> **http://www.totallyhip.com/Products/Products.html**
> Allows simultaneous viewing and interaction with Web pages while streaming animation is delivered over the Web.

Business and utilities

Acrobat Reader by Adobe
http://www.adobe.com/
Lets you view, navigate, and print Portable Document Format (PDF) files right in your Navigator window.

Carbon Copy/Net by Microcom
http://www.microcom.com/
Lets you remotely control another PC over the Internet.

Day-Timer Organizer by Day-Timer Technologies
http://www.daytimer.com/
Enables you to view calendar and address information in a user-friendly interface.

Earthtime by Starfish Software
http://www.starfishsoftware.com/
Lets you tell time around the world without leaving your browser.

Formula One/NET by Visual Components
http://www.visualcomp.com/
An Excel-compatible spreadsheet with built-in Internet functionality.

Ichat Plug-In by Ichat
http://www.ichat.com/
Integrates chat capability directly into Netscape Navigator.

ISYS HindSite by ISYS/Odyssey Development
http://www.isysdev.com/hindsite.html
Allows users to perform full-text searches on the contents of previously accessed Web pages.

Keyview by FTP Software
http://www.ftp.com/
View, zip, convert, or secure any file, any time.

Look@Me by Farallon
http://www.farallon.com/
Gives you the ability to view another Look@Me user's screen anywhere in the world in real time.

Panorama Viewer by SoftQuad
http://www.softquad.com/
Allows users to view longer and more complex SGML documents on corporate intranets and the World Wide Web.

PointCast Grabber by SE&S
http://www.hohouse.com/pcn/
GrabPCN gathers and displays links to the PointCast Network files cached on your hard disk.

PointCast Network by PointCast Incorporated
  http://www.pointcast.com/
  A free service that broadcasts up-to-the-minute news, weather, financial news,
  sports, and other information to your computer screen.

Surfbot 3.0 by Surflogic
  http://www.surflogic.com/
  Lets you build agents that actively monitor, organize, retrieve, and filter information from your favorite Web sites.

Tcl/Tk Plug-In by Sun Microsystems
  http://www.sun.com/960710/cover/tcl.html
  Allows Navigator to display Tcl scripts and UI elements, and structured graphics written in Tk inside a Web page.

Techexplorer Hypermedia Browser by IBM
  http://www.internet.ibm.com/
  Processes TEX/LATEX—the flexible, concise, and pervasive markup language
  used for publishing in education, mathematics, and many of the sciences.

Presentations

Astound Web Player by Gold Disk Inc.
  http://www.golddisk.com/
  Plays dynamic multimedia documents created with Gold Disk's award-
  winning Astound or Studio M software.

PointPlus by Net-Scene
  http://www.net-scene.com/
  Allows you to view dynamic and colorful presentations embedded in HTML
  pages.

PowerPoint Animation Player & Publisher by Microsoft
  http://www.microsoft.com/
  Provides users with the fastest, easiest way to view and publish PowerPoint
  animations and presentations in your browser window.

Audio/video

Apple Quicktime Plug-In by Apple Computer, Inc.
  http://www.quickTime.apple.com/dev/devweb.html
  Lets you experience QuickTime animation, music, MIDI, audio, video, and VR
  panoramas and objects directly in a Web page.

CineWeb by Digigami
  http://www.digigami.com/CineWebPress.html
  Brings real-time, streaming audio-video to the Web using standard movie
  (AVI, MOV, and MPG) and audio (WAV, MID, and MP2) files.

ClearFusion by Iterated Systems
  http://www.iterated.com/
  Enables any Video for Windows AVI file to be viewed inline as it's received.

MacZilla by Knowledge Engineering
http://maczilla.com
Plays QuickTime; ambient MIDI background sound; WAV, AU, and AIFF audio; MPEG; and AVI.

Netscape Media Player by Netscape
http://home.netscape.com/comprod/mirror/media/download_mplayer.html
Performs high-quality streaming audio and synchronized multimedia. (Also distributed with the Netscape browser.)

OnLive! Talker by OnLive! Technologies
http://www.onlive.com/
Lets you use your browser to join voice conferences on some of your favorite Web pages.

PhoneFree by Big Bits Software
http://www.phonefree.com/
Allows Net surfers to engage in real-time, phone-quality conversations over the Internet without using a phone or long-distance phone charges.

RealAudio by Progressive Networks
http://www.realaudio.com/
RealAudio provides live and on-demand real-time audio.

Image viewers

CMX Viewer by Corel Corporation
http://www.corel.com/
Views smooth vector graphics.

CyberSleuth by Highwater FBI
http://www.highwaterfbi.com/
Lets you find out who owns the image you are viewing and puts you in touch with the owner if you want to use their images.

IPIX Viewer by Interactive Pictures Corporation
http://www.ipix.com/
View 360-degree images.

Pegasus Plug-In by Pegasus Imaging
http://www.jpg.com/product.html
Supports JPEG, progressive JPEG, and PIC (Pegasus's enhanced JPEG), offering the fastest decompression, best color mapping on 256 color displays, and fastest viewing speed for viewing images on the Internet with Navigator.

SmoothMove by Infinite Pictures
http://www.smoothmove.com/
Enables users to view and navigate high-quality computer graphics and photo-based panoramas in real time.

Surround Video by Black Diamond
http://www.bdiamond.com/
Adds seamless 360-degree panoramic images to applications and Web pages while maintaining real-time navigation and photo realism.

Helpers
and Plug-ins

PART VII

Web Authoring

CHAPTER 22

Authoring for the Web

The World Wide Web is an exciting new medium, bringing information, images, and (what do you know?) advertising to every desktop. But what makes it truly revolutionary is how easy it is to become a Web publisher as well as a user. All you need is some space on a Web server and a little bit of know-how, and you too can litter cyberspace with your wit and wisdom.

Web authoring is a big topic. But simple Web authoring isn't nearly as complicated as you'd think. In this chapter, you'll find out how to get a presence on the Web, and what to do with it once you're there.

Getting on a Web Server

There are basically two ways of getting on the Web: getting space on someone else's Web server, or running your own Web server. Think of it as renting versus buying.

If you have an Internet Service Provider, most likely you can publish your Web site through them. If all you want is to distribute some personal Web pages and show pictures of your newborn twins, then any ISP or Internet service (such as AOL or Prodigy) can give you some Web space and let you go to town. This is by far the easiest way to get your own Web site.

The only disadvantage to using your ISP to host your Web site is that you don't have control over some of the more advanced Web authoring techniques. For example, if you want to do CGI programming, you are at the mercy of your ISP's choice of software tools (if any). If you need more control over the Web server than an ISP is willing to give, or if you're just an ornery do-it-yourselfer, you can try to run your own Web server.

Renting Space from Your ISP

Practically every Internet Service Provider has a Web server and will either give you a certain amount of free Web space with your subscription or will allow you to purchase Web space fairly cheaply. If you don't mind paying for it, you might even be able to get your own domain name through them—for example, if your name were Joey Cannoli, you might try to register the domain name *cannoli.com*—only to discover a bakery had beaten you to it. (Note, however, that a domain name doesn't have to coincide with yours—ideally it should reflect the purpose of the site, and also be easy to remember.)

Your ISP will either let you edit your HTML files directly online or will give you detailed instructions on how to download files to their Web server via FTP. We'll give you an introduction to writing HTML later in this chapter, with a complete HTML reference in Chapter 23, *HTML Tags and Attributes*.

Running Your Own Web Server

If you choose to run your own Web server, it won't be as easy as renting space on someone else's server, but it might be more satisfying in the end. Like buying a home, it costs you time, money, and possibly peace of mind. In return you have a Web server of your own that you have complete control over.

Any host on the Internet can run a Web server. Most large Web servers run on UNIX machines, but Web servers for PC and Macintosh computers are easy to come by and easy to install.

Running a UNIX Web server

If you aren't scared by the idea of running a UNIX machine, then you'll have the opportunity of running the cheapest Web server configuration: Linux with the Apache server. Linux is a free version of UNIX that runs on Intel-based PCs, and Apache is a free Web server that's extremely stable and is by far the most popular Web server on the Internet.

You can get Linux from **ftp://sunsite.unc.edu/pub/Linux/**. To learn more about Linux, see the O'Reilly books *Linux in a Nutshell*, *Linux Multimedia Guide*, *Linux Network Administrator's Guide*, and *Running Linux*.

You can get Apache from **http://www.apache.org/**. To learn more about Apache, see the O'Reilly book *Apache: The Definitive Guide*.

Running a Windows Web server

On a Windows machine, you have several Web servers to choose from:

Internet Information Server
> The Internet Information Server (IIS) runs on Windows 95 and Windows NT. It is bundled with the NT server distribution and free (under the name "Personal Web Server") for Windows 95 and Windows NT Workstation. IIS comes with few other goodies and absolutely no documentation. For more information, go to **http://www.microsoft.com/**.

WebSite

WebSite is a complete commercial Web publishing package, with a Web server, extensive documentation, and several Web site management tools, including a site browser, HTML editor, and imagemap editor. There is also a "professional" version called WebSite Pro, which includes a secure server and database integration tools. For more information, go to http://website.ora.com/.

FastTrack

The FastTrack server is a commercial product from Netscape Communications. It supports server-side Java and JavaScript. For more information, go to http://www.netscape.com/.

Running a Macintosh Web server

For the Macintosh platform, StarNine Technologies provides the commercial Web-STAR server. For more information on WebSTAR, go to http://www.starnine.com/.

Creating and Editing HTML Documents

Whether you buy or rent—once you have space of your own, you'll want to furnish it. Your Web site will consist of files written with HTML, the Hypertext Markup Language. It might also contain graphics, animations, sounds, video, you name it—but most likely you'll start with some basic HTML.

HTML Editors

Later in this chapter, we'll walk you through a simple Web page and show you what's what. However, you can also get an HTML editor to make things easier for you.

Do you need an HTML editor? Maybe, but not for the reasons you think. HTML is not particularly difficult. So if the reason you want an HTML editor is because you don't think you can do it by hand, then you're wrong.

However, HTML is laborious. Inserting tags all the time can be tiresome. What an HTML editor does is to make it fast and simple to insert tags in your document. It also makes it easy to get a browser-view of the document as you edit.

Some of the best HTML editors are:

AOLPress

Although distributed by America Online, AOLPress is a freely available Web authoring program. For more information, go to http://www.primehost.com/press/.

FrontPage

A commercial, integrated Web-site development package from Microsoft. For more information, go to http://www.microsoft.com/.

Hot Dog

One of the most popular HTML editors, from Sausage Software (no joke). See **http://www.sausage.com/**.

HoTMetaL

Another very good, very popular commercial HTML editor from SoftQuad, Inc. For more information, go to **http://www.sq.com/**.

HTML Assistant

HTML Assistant, from Brooklyn North Software Works, claims to have been the first HTML editor on the market. For more information, go to **http://www.brooknorth.com/**.

Netscape Composer

Part of the base installation of Netscape Communicator.

Text Editors

If you don't use an HTML editor, you can use any text editor to edit HTML documents. Under Windows, you can use the ubiquitous Notepad editor. You can also use any word processor and just save as text-only. Under UNIX, you can use either the *vi* or *emacs* editor, whichever you prefer.

If you use a text editor, the only thing you need to remember is to save the file with the suffix *.html* (or *.htm* on Windows machines, a holdover from DOS filename restrictions). This suffix tells the server that the file is HTML, the server tells the Web browser, and the browser knows to format the file for HTML. If you use no suffix, or the default *.txt* suffix on Windows machines, the file will be interpreted as straight text and the browser will display typewriter text with all the HTML tags intact.

HTML Document Structure

An HTML document consists of text, which comprises the content of the document, and tags, which define the structure and appearance of the document. The basic structure of an HTML document is simple, with the entire document (header and body) bound by a pair of <html> and </html> tags:

```
<html>
<head>
<title>Barebones HTML Document</title>
</head>
<body>
This illustrates in a very <i>simple</i> way,
the basic structure of an HTML document.
</body>
</html>
```

Each document has a *head* and a *body*, delimited by the <head> and <body> tags. The head is where you give your HTML document a title and where you indicate other parameters the browser may use when displaying the document. The body is where you put the actual contents of the HTML document. This includes the text to be displayed and document control markers (tags) that advise the browser how to display the text. Tags are also used to incorporate special-effect files like graphics and sound and to indicate the hot spots (*hyperlinks* or *anchors*) that link your document to other documents.

HTML Tag Syntax

For the most part, HTML document tags are simple to understand and use since they are made up of common words, abbreviations, and notations. Every HTML tag consists of a tag *name*, sometimes followed by an optional list of tag *attributes*, all placed between opening and closing brackets (< and >). The simplest tags are nothing more than the tag name enclosed in brackets, such as <head> and <i>. More complicated tags have attributes, which may have specific values defined by the author to modify the behavior of a tag.

Tag attributes belong after the tag name, each separated by one or more tab, space, or return characters. The order of attributes in a single tag is not important. An attribute's value, if it has one, follows an equal sign after the attribute name. If an attribute's value is a single word or number, you may simply add it after the equal sign. All other values should be enclosed in single or double quotation marks, especially if they contain multiple words separated by spaces. The length of an attribute's value is limited to 1024 characters. Here are some examples of tags with attributes:

```
<a href="http://www.ora.com/catalog.html">
<ul compact>
<input name=filename size=24 maxlength=80>
<link title="Table of Contents">
```

Tag and attribute names are not case-sensitive, but attribute values can be. For example, it is especially important to use the proper capitalization when referencing the URLs of other documents with the href attribute.

Most HTML tags consist of start and end tags that enclose text and other elements of a document. An end tag is the same as a start tag except it has a forward slash (/) before the tag name. End tags never contain attributes. For example, to italicize text, you enclose it within the <i> tags:

```
<i>This text in italics.</i>
```

You should take care when nesting tagged elements in a document. You must end nested tags starting with the most recent one and work your way back out. In this example, a phrase in bold (<b>) appears in the text of a link (<a href=...>) contained in some body text:

```
<body>
This is some text in the body, with a
<a href="another_doc.html">link, a portion of which
is <b>set in bold</b></a>
</body>
```

There are a handful of HTML tags that do not have end tags because they are standalone elements. For example, the image tag (<img>) inserts a single graphic into a document and does not require an end tag. Other standalone tags include the linebreak (<br>), horizontal rule (<hr>), and tags that provide information about a document that doesn't affect its displayed content, such as the <meta> and <base> tags.

In some cases, end tags can be omitted in a document. Browsers often assume the end of one element when another begins. The most common example of this is with the paragraph tag (<p>). Since it is so often used in a document, a <p> tag usually only appears at the beginning of each paragraph. When one paragraph ends, another <p> tag signals the browser to end the paragraph and start another. Most authors do not use an end paragraph tag. There are other end tags that browsers function fine without, such as an ending </html> tag. However, it is best to include the end tags as much as possible to avoid confusion and mistakes in displaying your document.

Inside HTML

The simplest way to learn HTML is to siphon a page from someone else and play with it. If you see a page you like, you can just save it on your disk and then edit away. Every browser has a **Save As** command, generally on the primary menu. See the **File** menu for both Netscape Navigator and Microsoft Internet Explorer.

If you're using the version of Navigator that comes with the Netscape Communicator suite, you also have the option of opening up a document in the accompanying HTML editor, called Composer. See Chapter 2, *Netscape Navigator*, for more information.

If you just want to look at the code of a particular page to see what's used to create it, your browser should offer a "view the source code" function. In MSIE, select **Source** from the **View** menu. The Navigator **View** menu offers a **Document Source** item.

Is this stealing? Yes, but it's okay on a small scale. If you're going to borrow someone's HTML markup for your personal home page (with your own original content), no one's going to care—although if you see a copyright notice, you should be sure to respect it. On the other hand, if you take someone else's images, sounds, JavaScript programs, or video, you better ask permission and attribute credit where due.

So let's take a look at a sample HTML document. For this example, I'm using the personal Web page of a coworker, Kiersten Conner. Figure 22–1 shows the Web page.

In this page, we have the following features:

- Text

- Embedded images

- Non-standard fonts and colors

- Hypertext links

- Some simple JavaScript code

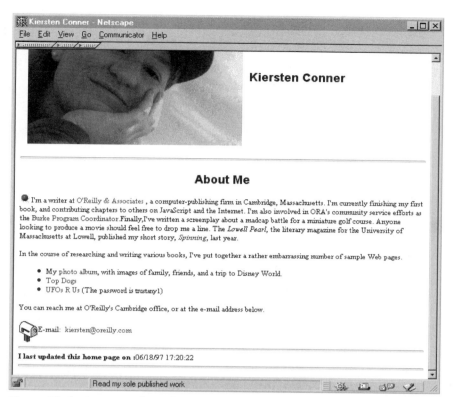

Figure 22–1: Anatomy of a Web page

Let's walk through the HTML that produced the page. (For more information on any of the tags discussed in this example, see the quick reference provided in Chapter 23.)

```
<!-- The HTML tag indicates the beginning of the document //-->

<HTML>

<HEAD>
    <TITLE>Kiersten Conner</TITLE>
</HEAD>
```

The first thing to notice is the lines beginning with <!--. These lines are HTML comments and are used extensively in this document. As any programmer will tell you, commenting is almost always a good idea. It's less important for a fairly simple personal Web page like this one (since there's only a single author and maintainer), but commenting becomes essential for a complicated page on a commercial Web site where others may some day need to decipher your work.

The <HTML> tag indicates the beginning of the document. It announces that the text from here to the close </HTML> tag is written in the HTML language. This may seem obvious to you, but browsers appreciate an explicit declaration.

Next is the *heading* of the document, enclosed by the <HEAD> and </HEAD> tags. The most important use for the heading is to declare the *title* of the page with the <TITLE> tag. This title is never actually shown in the document itself; instead, it is generally used by the browser to set the titlebar of the window, or to label bookmarks.

```
<!--In the BODY tag, set the text, visited link, and active link colors, and
    choose a background image //-->

<BODY TEXT="#400040" LINK="#0000FF" VLINK="#8000FF" ALINK="#FF0000"
    BACKGROUND="white.jpg">
```

The <BODY> tag generally follows </HEAD>, to declare the beginning of the *body* section of the document. In this case, we're using several attributes with <BODY> to set colors for the text, for links, and for the background of the page itself. (See Chapter 24, *Color Names and Values*, for more information on setting colors.)

```
<H2>
<IMG SRC="http://www.ora.com/people/staff/kiersten/newme.gif"
    ALT="I'm diagonal!" HEIGHT=200 WIDTH=320 ALIGN=MIDDLE HSPACE=10>
    <font face="helvetica">Kiersten Conner</font></H2>
```

Enough of the preparation. Now something you can actually see. Kiersten gives her name and shows her picture, using the <H2> tag for a second-level heading. The <IMG> tag is used to show Kiersten's picture, which had been saved as a GIF file. The SRC attribute points to the URL of the GIF file. The ALT attribute gives "alternate" text for people who can't see images or choose to configure their browser not to display images. The rest of the attributes to <IMG> describe the height, width, alignment, and spacing around the image itself. For Kiersten's actual name, she specifies the Helvetica font (using the <FONT> tag).

```
<P>

<!-- Insert a horizontal rule to separate the text //-->
<HR>

<!-- The CENTER tags center the second level heading, while the FACE attribute
    of the FONT tag displays the text in the type face Helvetica //-->
<CENTER>
<H2>
<FONT FACE="Helvetica">About Me</FONT></H2></CENTER>
```

Now a horizontal rule is displayed with the <HR> tag, and another second-level heading is shown with <H2>, but this time centered with the <CENTER> tag.

```
<P>
<!-- Use an image of a purple ball as a small bullet //-->
<IMG SRC="http://www.ora.com/people/staff/kiersten/purple.gif"
    HEIGHT=14 WIDTH=14>

<!-- Link to the O'Reilly web site. Use JavaScript to display a
description of the link in the status bar //-->
I'm a writer at
<A HREF="http://www.oreilly.com/" onMouseOver="window.status='The World Wide
Web site of my employer'; return true">O'Reilly &amp; Associates</A>, a
computer-publishing firm in Cambridge, Massachusetts. I'm currently
finishing my first book, and contributing chapters to others on JavaScript
and the Internet.
```

```
I'm also involved in ORA's community service efforts as the <A HREF=
"http://www.ora.com/oreilly/comservice/" onMouseOver="window.status=
Program Coordinator</A>.  Finally, I've written a screenplay about a
madcap battle for a miniature golf course.  Anyone looking to produce a
movie should feel free to drop me a line. The <I>Lowell Pearl</I>, the
literary magazine for the University of Massachusetts at Lowell, published
my short story, <I><A HREF="http://www.ora.com/people/staff/kiersten/
spinning.htm" onMouseOver="window.status='Read my sole published work';
return true">Spinning</A></I>, last year.
```

A paragraph introducing Kiersten is next. To create a link to her company's Web site, she uses the <A> tag with an HREF attribute. She also uses JavaScript to change the status line of the window when the user places their pointer over the link. (For more information on JavaScript, see Chapter 26, *GIFs, Applets, and Other Enhancements.*) Also note that she uses the <I> tag to place text in italics.

```
<P>
In the course of researching and writing various books, I've put together a
rather embarrassing number of sample Web pages. Observe at your own risk:

<UL>
<LI>My <A HREF="http://www.ora.com/people/staff/kiersten/photo.htm" onMouseOver=
"window.status='Exciting photo essays on my family and friends'; i
return true">photo album</A>, with images of family, friends, and a trip to
Disney World.
</LI>
<LI><A href="http://pckiersten.ora.com/topdog.htm">Top Dogs</a>
</LI>
<LI><A href="http://pckiersten.ora.com/ufosrus.htm">UFOs R Us</a> (The
password is <FONT SIZE=-1>trustany1</FONT>)
</LI>
</UL>
```

Here, Kiersten uses the <UL> and <LI> tags to create an unordered (i.e., bulleted, not numbered) list. She also puts text in a slightly smaller font size with the SIZE attribute of the FONT tag.

```
<P>
You can reach me at O'Reilly's Cambridge office, or at the e-mail address below.
<P>
<IMG SRC="http://www.ora.com/people/staff/kiersten/mailbox1.gif" ALT="[mailbox]"
HEIGHT=34 WIDTH=29 ALIGN=CENTER>E-mail: 
<A HREF="mailto: kiersten@oreilly.com">kiersten@oreilly.com</A>

<HR>

<!-- Using JavaScript, insert a date stamp that shows when this page was last
updated //-->
<B>I last updated this home page on :</B>06/18/97 17:20:22<HR>

</BODY>
</HTML>
```

For the convenience of anyone who wants to send Kiersten some feedback after reading her Web page, she uses the HREF attribute of the anchor tag to launch a mail window using a special link called *mailto*. Rather than directing the browser to another site, *mailto* opens up a mail composition window for the user, automatically addressed to Kiersten.

She adds another horizontal rule, and then she uses JavaScript to tell people when the page was last edited.

Finally, the </BODY> and </HTML> tags are used at the end of the page to signal the end of the body of the document and the end of the entire document, respectively.

CHAPTER 23

HTML Tags and Attributes

This section lists the known HTML tags and attributes currently available for use in Web documents. There are many different browsers out there, and they do not all support the same set of tags.

If keeping track of all the browsers and all their differences makes your head spin, no fear. Netscape Navigator and Microsoft's Internet Explorer are the two most popular browsers and are responsible for almost all of the non-standard extensions to HTML.

Tags and attributes specific to Netscape Navigator 3.0 and later revisions have *N3 and later* in their descriptions. Tags and attributes specific to Microsoft Internet Explorer 3.0 and later revisions are marked *IE3 and later*. Browser-specific tags for the earlier versions of the browsers (e.g., *IE2* or *N2*) are assumed to be supported in the later versions.

HTML Tag and Attribute Descriptions

`<a>` ... `</a>`

Create a hyperlink (`href` attribute) or fragment identifier (`name` attribute) within a document.

Attributes

`href=url`   Specify the URL of a hyperlink target (required if not a name anchor).

`methods=list`

Specify a comma-separated list of browser-dependent presentation methods.

`<a>`

$\rightarrow$

\<a\>
←
	name=*string*
	    Specify the name of a fragment identifier (required if not a hypertext reference anchor).
	
	rel=*relationship*
	    Indicate the relationship from this document to the target.
	
	rev=*relationship*
	    Indicate the reverse relationship of the target to this document.
	
	target=*name*
	    Define the name of the frame or window to receive the referenced document.
	
	title=*string*
	    Provide a title for the target document.
	
	urn=*urn* Specify the location-independent Uniform Resource Name for this hyperlink.
	
	Example
	
	To create an anchor named info at some point in a document called *doc.html*, use the \<a\> tag with the name attribute:
	
	`<a name="info">Information</a>`
	
	To provide a hyperlink to that point in *doc.html*, use the \<a\> tag with the href attribute appending the anchor name to the filename using a hash mark (#):
	
	`<a href="doc.html#info">Link to information</a>`

\<address\>	**\<address\> ... \</address\>** The enclosed text is an address.
\<applet\>	**\<applet\> ... \</applet\>** Define an executable applet within a text flow. ***Attributes*** align=*position* Align the \<applet\> region to either the top, middle, bottom (default), left, right, absmiddle, baseline, or absbottom of the text in the line. alt=*string* Specify alternative text to replace the \<applet\> region within browsers that support the

<applet> tag but cannot execute the application.

<applet>

code=*class* Specify the class name of the code to be executed (required).

codebase=*url*
URL from which the code is retrieved.

height=*n* Specify the height in pixels of the <applet> region.

hspace=*n* Specify additional space in pixels to the left and right of the <applet> region.

name=*string*
Specify the name of this particular instance of the <applet>.

vspace=*n* Specify additional space in pixels above and below the <applet> region.

width=*n* Specify the width in pixels of the <applet> region.

<area>

<area>

Define a mouse-sensitive area in a client-side image map.

Attributes

coords=*list*
Specify a comma-separated list of shape-dependent coordinates that define the edge of this area.

href=*url* Specify the URL of a hyperlink target associated with this area.

nohref Indicate that no document is associated with this area; clicking in the area has no effect.

shape=*shape*
Define the region's shape to be either circ, circle, poly, polygon, rect, or rectangle.

<b> ... </b>

<b>

Format the enclosed text using a **bold** typeface.

<base>

<base>

Specify the base URL for all relative URLs in this document.

Web Authoring

→

\<base\>
←
	Attributes
	
	href=*url* Specify the base URL.
	
	target=*name*
	     Define the default target window of all \<a\> links in the document. Mostly used for redirecting a link to other frames. There are four special values: _blank, _parent, _self, and _top:
	
	     _blank specifies that a linked document with target="_blank" will always be loaded into a newly opened, unnamed window.
	
	     _self is the default for all \<a\> tags that do not specify a target, causing the referenced document to be loaded in the same frame or window as the source document. The _self target is redundant and unnecessary unless used in combination with the target attribute of the \<base\> tag to override the default target value for all the links in the source document.
	
	     _parent causes the document to be loaded into the parent window or frameset containing the frame containing the hypertext reference. If the reference is in a window or top-level frame, it is equivalent to the target _self.
	
	     _top causes the document to be loaded into the window containing the hypertext link, replacing any frames currently displayed in the window.

\<basefont\>	**\<basefont\>** Specify the font size for subsequent text. ***Attributes*** size=*value* Set the basefont size of 1 to 7 (required; default is 3).
\<bgsound\>	**\<bgsound\>** *IE2 and later.* Define background audio for the document. ***Attributes*** loop=*value* Set the number of times to play the audio; *value* may be an integer or the value infinite.

src=*url* Provide the URL of the audio file to be played.	**\<bgsound\>**

\<big\> ... \</big\>

Format the enclosed text using a bigger typeface.

\<big\>

\<blockquote\> ... \</blockquote\>

The enclosed text is a block quotation.

\<blockquote\>

\<body\> ... \</body\>

Delimit the beginning and end of the document body.

\<body\>

Attributes

alink=*color*
> Set the color of active hypertext links in the document.

background=*url*
> Specify the URL of an image to be tiled in the document background.

bgcolor=*color*
> Set the background color of the document.

bgproperties=*value*
> *IE2 and later.* When set to fixed, prevent the background image from scrolling with the document content.

leftmargin=*value*
> *IE2 and later.* Set the size in pixels of the document's left margin.

link=*color* Set the color of unvisited hypertext links in the document.

text=*color* Set the color of regular text in the document.

topmargin=*value*
> *IE2 and later.* Set the size in pixels of the document's top margin.

vlink=*color*
> Set the color of visited links in the document.

Web Authoring

\<br\>

Break the current text flow, resuming at the beginning of the next line.

\<br\>

$\rightarrow$

**\ ** ←	***Attributes*** clear=*margin* Break the flow and move downward until the desired margin, either left, right, or all, is clear.

\<caption>	**\<caption> ... \</caption>**
	
	Define a caption for a table.
	
	Attributes
	
	align=*position*
	    For Netscape, set the vertical position of the caption to either top or bottom. Default is top, centered. For Internet Explorer, set the horizontal alignment of the caption to either left, center, or right, or even the vertical position to top or bottom. The default is top, centered. You cannot set both the horizontal and vertical position with this attribute alone.
	
	valign=*position*
	    IE2 and later. Set the vertical position of the caption to either top or bottom. Default is top. Use this with a horizontal specification to align to set both vertical and horizontal caption position in Internet Explorer.

\<center>	**\<center> ... \</center>** Center the enclosed text.
\<cite>	**\<cite> ... \</cite>** The enclosed text is a citation.
\<code>	**\<code> ... \</code>** The enclosed text is a code sample.
\<col>	**\<col>** *IE2 and later.* Set properties for a column (or columns) within a \<colgroup> of a table.

Attributes

<col>

align=*value*

>Specify alignment of text in the cells of a column. Value can be center, left, or right.

span=*n*

>Specify the number of columns to be affected by the <col> settings.

<colgroup>

<colgroup>

IE2 and later. Set properties for designated column or columns within a table. Also indicates where vertical rules will be drawn when rules=groups is set in the <table> tag.

Attributes

align=*value*

>Specify alignment of text in the cells of columns in the <colgroup>. Values can be center, left, or right.

span=*n*

>Specify the number of columns in the <colgroup>.

<comment> ... </comment>

<comment>

IE2 and later. Place a comment in the document. Comments will be visible in all other browsers. Comments can be placed within <!-- *comment text* --> for all browsers.

<dd> ... </dd>

<dd>

Define the definition portion of an element in a definition list.

<dfn> ... </dfn>

<dfn>

Format the enclosed text as a definition.

<dir> ... </dir>

<dir>

Create a directory list containing <li> tags.

Attributes

compact   Make the list more compact if possible.

<div> ... </div>

<div>

Create a division within a document.

$\rightarrow$

`<div>` ←	**Attributes** `align=`*type* Align the text within the division to `left`, `center`, or `right`.
`<dl>`	**`<dl>` ... `</dl>`** Create a definition list containing `<dt>` and `<dd>` tags. **Attributes** `compact` Make the list more compact if possible.
`<dt>`	**`<dt>` ... `</dt>`** Define the definition term portion of an element in a definition list.
`<em>`	**`<em>` ... `</em>`** Format the enclosed text with additional emphasis.
`<embed>`	**`<embed>` ... `</embed>`** Embed an object into a document. Additional parameters to those listed here may be included depending on the embedded object. **Attributes** `src=`*url* Specify the URL of the object to be embedded (required). `height=`*n* Specify the height of the area the embedded object will occupy. `name=`*name* Specify the name of the embedded object. `width=`*n* Specify the width of the area the embedded object will occupy.
`<font>`	**`<font>` ... `</font>`** Set the size, color, or typeface of the enclosed text. **Attributes** `color=`*color* Set the color of the enclosed text. `face=`*list* Set the typeface of the enclosed text to the first available font in the comma-separated list of font names.

size=*value* Set the size to an absolute value (1 to 7) or relative to the `<basefont>` size using +n or -n.

<code><font></code>

`<form>` ... `</form>`

<code><form></code>

Delimit a form.

Attributes

action=*url* Specify the URL of the application that will process the form. The default is the current URL.

enctype=*encoding*
> Specify how the form element values will be encoded.

method=*style*
> Specify the parameter-passing style, either get or post. The default is *get*.

target=*name*
> *IE3 and later.* Specify a target window for results of form submission to be loaded. The special attributes _blank, _top, _parent, and _self may be used. See `<base>` tag attributes.

`<frame>` ... `</frame>`

<code><frame></code>

Define a frame within a frameset.

Attributes

bordercolor=*color*
> *N3 and later.* Set color for frame border if border is turned on with frameborder=yes.

frameborder=[1|0]
> *IE3 and later.* Enable or disable the displaying of a 3-D border for a frame. Default is 1, which inserts the border. The value 0 turns the border off.

frameborder=[yes|no]
> *N3 and later.* Enable or disable the displaying of a 3-D border for a frame or a plain border. The default is yes (for 3-D borders).

marginheight=*n*
> Place *n* pixels of space above and below the frame contents.

→

\<frame\>	marginwidth=*n*
←	Place *n* pixels of space to the left and right of the frame contents.
	name=*string*
	Define the name of the frame.
	noresize Disable user resizing of the frame.
	scrolling=*type*
	Always add scrollbars (yes), never add scrollbars (no), or add scrollbars when needed (auto).
	src=*url* Define the URL of the source document for this frame.

\<frameset\>	**\<frameset\> ... \</frameset\>**
	Define a collection of frames or other framesets.
	Attributes
	border=*n* *N3 and later.* Set size in pixels of frame borders within a frameset. Default border width is 5 pixels.
	bordercolor=*color*
	N3 and later. Set color for frame borders in a frameset.
	cols=*list* Specify the number and width of frames within a frameset.
	frameborder=[yes|no]
	N3 and later. Enable or disable the displaying of 3-D borders or regular borders for frames. The default is yes (3-D borders).
	frameborder=[1|0]
	IE3 and later. Enable or disable the displaying of 3-D borders for frames within a frameset. The default is 1 (borders on).
	framespacing=*n*
	IE3 and later. Add additional space between adjacent frames in pixels.
	rows=*list* Specify the number and height of frames within a frameset.

\<h*n*\>	**\<h*n*\> ... \</h*n*\>**
	The enclosed text is a level *n* header; for level *n* from 1 to 6.

Attributes

align=*type*   Specify the heading alignment as either left (default), center, or right.

<h*n*>

<head> ... </head>

Delimit the beginning and end of the document head.

<head>

<hr>

Break the current text flow and insert a horizontal rule.

Attributes

align=*type*   Specify the rule alignment as either left, center (default), or right.

noshade   Do not use 3-D shading to render the rule.

size=*pixels*

    Set the thickness of the rule to an integer number of pixels.

width=*value*

    Set the width of the rule to either an integer number of pixels or a percentage of the page width.

<hr>

<html> ... </html>

Delimit the beginning and end of the entire HTML document.

Attributes

version=*string*

    Indicate the HTML version used to create this document.

<html>

<i> ... </i>

Format the enclosed text in an *italic* typeface.

<i>

<iframe> ... </iframe>

IE3 and later. Define a floating frame within a document with similar placement to <img>. This element requires a closing tag.

<iframe>

Web Authoring

$\rightarrow$

\<iframe\> ←	**Attributes** align=*type* Align the floating frame to either the top, middle, bottom (default), left, or right of the text in the line. frameborder=[1|0] 　　Enable or disable the displaying of a 3-D border for a frame. Default is 1, which inserts the border. The value 0 turns the border off. height=*n* Specify the height of the frame in pixels or as a percentage of the window size. hspace=*n* Specify the space in pixels to be added to the left and right of the image. marginheight=*n* 　　Place *n* pixels of space above and below the frame contents. marginwidth=*n* 　　Place *n* pixels of space to the left and right of the frame contents. name=*string* 　　Define the name of the frame. noresize Disable user resizing of the frame. scrolling=*type* 　　Always add scrollbars (yes), never add scrollbars (no), or add scrollbars when needed (auto). src=*url* Define the URL of the source document for this frame. vspace=*n* Specify the vertical space in pixels added at the top and bottom of the image. width=*n* Specify the width of the frame in pixels or as a percentage of the window size
\<img\>	**\<img\>** Insert an image into the current text flow. **Attributes** align=*type* Align the image to either the top, middle, bottom (default), left, or right of text in the line. *N2 and later*. Additionally, align to the texttop, absmiddle, absbottom, or baseline of the text. alt=*text* Provide alternative text for text-only browsers.

border=*n*	Set the pixel thickness of the border around images contained within hyperlinks.	**<img>**
controls	*IE2 and later.* Add playback controls for embedded video clips.	
dynsrc=*url*	*IE2 and later.* Specify the URL of a video clip to be displayed.	
height=*n*	Specify the height of the image in pixels.	
hspace=*n*	Specify the space in pixels to be added to the left and right of the image.	
ismap	Indicate that the image is mouse-selectable when used within an <a> tag.	
loop=*value*	*IE2 and later.* Set the number of times to play the video; *value* may be an integer or the value infinite.	
lowsrc=*url*	*N2 and later.* Specify a low-resolution image to be loaded by the browser first, followed by the image specified by the <src> attribute.	
src=*url*	Specify the source URL of the image to be displayed (required).	
start=*start*	*IE2 and later.* Specify when to play the video clip, either fileopen or mouseover.	
usemap=*url*	Specify the map of coordinates and links that define the hypertext links within this image.	
vspace=*n*	Specify the vertical space in pixels added at the top and bottom of the image.	
width=*n*	Specify the width of the image in pixels.	

<input type=checkbox>

<input>

Create a checkbox input element within a <form>.

Attributes

checked	Mark the element as initially selected.
name=*string*	Specify the name of the parameter to be passed to the form-processing application if the input element is selected (required).

→

<input> ←	value=*string* Specify the value of the parameter sent to the form-processing application if this form element is selected (required).

<input>	## <input type=file>
	
	Create a file-selection element within a <form>.
	
	Attributes
	
	maxlength=*n*
	    Specify the maximum number of characters to accept for this element.
	
	name=*string*
	    Specify the name of the parameter that is passed to the form-processing application for this input element (required).
	
	size=*n* Specify the number of characters to display for this element.

<input>	## <input type=hidden>
	
	Create a hidden element within a <form>.
	
	Attributes
	
	name=*string*
	    Specify the name of the parameter that is passed to the form-processing application for this input element (required).
	
	value=*string*
	    Specify the value of this element that is passed to the form-processing application.

<input>	## <input type=image> Create an image input element within a <form>. ***Attributes*** align=*type* Align the image to either the top, middle, or bottom of the form element's text. name=*string* Specify the name of the parameter to be passed to the form-processing application for this input element (required).

src=*url* Specify the source URL of the image (required).	`<input>`

`<input type=password>`

`<input>`

Create a content-protected text-input element within a `<form>`.

Attributes

maxlength=*n*
> Specify the maximum number of characters to accept for this element.

name=*string*
> Specify the name of the parameter to be passed to the form-processing application for this input element (required).

size=*n*   Specify the number of characters to display for this element.

value=*string*
> Specify the initial value for this element.

`<input type=radio>`

`<input>`

Create a radio-button input element within a `<form>`.

Attributes

checked   Mark the element as initially selected.

name=*string*
> Specify the name of the parameter that is passed to the form-processing application if this input element is selected (required).

value=*string*
> Specify the value of the parameter that is passed to the form-processing application if this element is selected (required).

`<input type=reset>`

`<input>`

Create a reset button within a `<form>`.

Attributes

value=*string*
> Specify an alternate label for the reset button.

`<input type=submit>`

`<input>`

Create a submit button within a `<form>`.

$\rightarrow$

<input>
←
	Attributes
	
	name=*string*
	    Specify the name of the parameter that is passed to the form-processing application for this input element (required).
	
	value=*string*
	    Specify an alternate label for the submit button, as well as the value passed to the form-processing application for this parameter if this button is clicked.

<input>	**<input type=text>**
	
	Create a text input element within a <form>. (This is the default input type.)
	
	Attributes
	
	maxlength=*n*
	    Specify the maximum number of characters to accept for this element.
	
	name=*string*
	    Specify the name of the parameter that is passed to the form-processing application for this input element (required).
	
	size=*n* Specify the number of characters to display for this element.
	
	value=*string*
	    Specify the initial value for this element.

<isindex>	**<isindex>** Create a "searchable" HTML document. ***Attributes*** action=*url* *IE2 and later.* Provide the URL of the program that will perform the searching action. prompt=*string* Provide an alternate prompt for the input field.
<kbd>	**<kbd> ... </kbd>** The enclosed text is keyboard-like input.

<li>

<li> ... </li>

Delimit a list item in an ordered (<ol>) or unordered (<ul>) list.

Attributes

type=*format*

> Set the type of this list element to the desired format. For <li> within <ol>: A (capital letters), a (lowercase letters), I (capital Roman numerals), i (lowercase Roman numerals), or 1 (Arabic numerals; default). For <li> within <ul>: circle, disc (default), or square.

value=*n* Set the number for this list item to *n*.

<link>

<link>

Define a link in the document <head> between this document and another document.

Attributes

href=*url* Specify the hypertext reference URL of the target document.

methods=*list*

> Specify a browser-dependent list of comma-separated display methods for this link.

rel=*relation*

> Indicate the relationship from this document to the target. For Internet Explorer 3.0, rel=style indicates the existence of an external style sheet.

rev=*relation*

> Indicate the reverse relationship from the target to this document.

src=*url* *IE3 and later.* Specify the URL for the external style sheet to be used in formatting the document.

title=*string*

> Provide a title for the target document.

type=text/css

> *IE3 and later.* Show type of outside link to be an external cascading style sheet.

urn=*urn* Provide the location-independent Uniform Resource Name for the target document.

Web Authoring

\<listing\>	**\<listing\> ... \</listing\>**
	Same as `<pre width=132>` ... `</pre>`; deprecated, do not use.
\<map\>	**\<map\> ... \</map\>**
	Define a map containing hotspots in a client-side image map.
	Attributes
	`name=string`
	Define the name of this map (required).
\<marquee\>	**\<marquee\> ... \</marquee\>**
	IE2 and later. Create a scrolling-text marquee.
	Attributes
	`align=position`
	Align the marquee to the `top`, `middle`, or `bottom` of the surrounding text.
	`behavior=style`
	Define marquee style to be `scroll`, `slide`, or `alternate`.
	`bgcolor=color`
	Set the background color of the marquee.
	`direction=dir`
	Define the direction, `left` or `right`, the text is to scroll.
	`height=value`
	Define the height in pixels of the marquee area.
	`hspace=value`
	Define the space in pixels to be inserted left and right of the marquee.
	`loop=value` Set the number of times to animate the marquee; value is an integer or `infinite`.
	`scrollamount=value`
	Set the number of pixels to move the text for each scroll movement.
	`scrolldelay=value`
	Specify the delay in milliseconds between successive movements of the marquee text.
	`vspace=value`
	Define the space in pixels to be inserted above and below the marquee.

width=*value* Define the width in pixels of the marquee area.	**\<marquee\>**

\<menu\> ... \</menu\> Define a menu list containing \<li\> tags. **Attributes** compact Make the list more compact.	**\<menu\>**

\<meta\>
 	
Provides additional information about a document.
 	
Attributes
 	
content=*string*
    Specify the value for the meta-information (required). For client pulls, content=" *n*;url=*url*" *tells the browser to load the specified url after n* seconds. If no URL is specified, the source document will be reloaded. Must be used with http-equiv="refresh" within \<meta\>.
 	
http-equiv=*string*
    Specify the HTTP equivalent name for the meta-information and cause the server to include the name and content in the HTTP header for this document when it is transmitted to the client. A value of refresh creates a "client-pull" within a document.
 	
name=*string*
    Specify the name of the meta-information.
	\<meta\>

\<multicol\> ... \</multicol\> *N3 and later.* Format enclosed HTML and text in multicolumn format. Text and elements will flow across specified number of columns to give them approximately equal length. **Attributes** cols=*n* Specify number of columns (required). gutter=*n* Specify amount of space in pixels between columns. Default is 10 pixels.	**\<multicol\>**

Web
Authoring

$\rightarrow$

<multicol>	width=*n* Specify width of columns in pixels.
←	
<nextid>	**<nextid>** Define the labeling start point for automatic document-generation tools. ***Attributes*** n=*n* Indicate the starting label number (required).
<nobr>	**<nobr> ... </nobr>** No breaks allowed in the enclosed text.
<noframes>	**<noframes> ... </noframes>** Define content to be presented by browsers that do not support frames.
<noscript>	**<noscript> ... </noscript>** *N3 and later.* Specify alternative content for browsers that do not support JavaScript. (See Chapter 26 for more information on JavaScript.)

<object>	**<object> ... </object>**
	
	IE3 and later. Insert an object into the document. This tag is used to specify applets, OLE controls, and other media objects.
	
	Attributes
	
	align=*value*
	    Specify how the object is aligned with other elements in the document. Values include: baseline, center, left, middle, right, textbottom, textmiddle, and texttop.
	
	border=*n* Set the width of the object's border if it is a hyperlink.
	
	classid=*url*
	    Identify the class identifier of the object. The URL syntax of the URL depends on the object type.
	
	codebase=*url*
	    Identify the URL of the object's codebase. The syntax of the URL depends on the object.
	
	codetype=*codetype*
	    Specify the media type of the code.

data=*url*	Specify the URL of the data used for the object. The syntax of the URL depends on the object.	**<object>**
declare	Declare an object without instantiating it.	
height=*n*	Specify the height of the object in pixels.	
hspace=*n*	Specify the amount of space in pixels between the sides of the object and the surrounding elements.	
name=*url*	Specify the name of the object.	
shapes	Indicate shaped hyperlinks in object.	
standby=*message*	Specify message to display during object loading.	
type=*type*	Specify the media type for data.	
usemap=*url*	Specify image map to use with object.	
vspace=*n*	Specify the amount of space in pixels above and below object.	
width=*n*	Specify object width.	

<ol> ... </ol>

<ol>

Define an ordered list containing numbered (ascending) <li> elements.

Attributes

compact	Present the list in a more compact manner.
start=*n*	Start numbering the list at *n*, instead of 1.
type=*format*	Set the numbering format for this list to either A (capital letters), a (lowercase letters), I (capital Roman numerals), i (lowercase Roman numerals), or 1 (Arabic numerals; default).

<option> ... </option>

<option>

Define an option within a <select> item in a <form>.

Attributes

selected	Make this item initially selected.
value=*string*	Return the specified value to the form-processing application instead of the <option> contents.

`<p>`	**`<p> ... </p>`** Start and end a paragraph. ***Attributes*** `align=`*`type`* Align the text within the paragraph to `left`, `center`, or `right`.

`<param>`	**`<param> ... </param>`**
	
	Supply a parameter to the `<applet>` or `<object>` surrounding this tag.
	
	Attributes
	
	`name=`*`string`*
	    Define the name of the parameter.
	
	`value=`*`string`*
	    Define the value of the parameter.
	
	`valuetype=`*`type`*
	    IE3 and later. Indicate the type of value. Can be one of three types: `data` indicates that the parameter's value is data (default); `ref` indicates that the parameter's value is a URL; `object` indicates that the value is a URL of another object in the document.
	
	`type=`*`type`* *IE3 and later.* Specify the media type.

`<plaintext>`	**`<plaintext>`** Render the remainder of the document as preformatted plain text.
`<pre>`	**`<pre> ... </pre>`** Render the enclosed text in its original, preformatted style, honoring line breaks and spacing verbatim. ***Attributes*** `width=`*`n`* Size the text, if possible, so that *n* characters fit across the display window.
`<s>`	**`<s> ... </s>`** The enclosed text is struck through with a horizontal line.

`<samp>` ... `</samp>`

The enclosed text is a sample.

`<samp>`

`<script>` ... `</script>`

Specify enclosed script in a supported scripting language to be used in the document.

Attributes

language=*lang*
> Identify language of the script, e.g., JavaScript or VBScript.

src=*url* *N3 and later.* Specify the URL of an outside file containing the script to be loaded and run with the document.

See Chapter 26 for more information on JavaScript.

`<script>`

`<select>` ... `</select>`

Define a multiple-choice menu or scrolling list within a `<form>`, containing one or more `<option>` tags.

Attributes

multiple
> Allow user to select more than one `<option>` within the `<select>`.

name=*string*
> Define the name for the selected `<option>` values that, if selected, are passed to the form-processing application (required).

size=*n*
> Display items using a pulldown menu for size=1 (without multiple specified) and a scrolling list of *n* items otherwise.

`<select>`

`<small>` ... `</small>`

Format the enclosed text using a smaller typeface.

`<small>`

`<spacer>`

N3 and later. Insert a whitespace element in a document.

Attributes

type=*type* Specify what type of spacer to use. vertical inserts space between two lines of text. horizontal inserts space between words or characters. block inserts a rectangular space like an `<img>`.

`<spacer>`

Web Authoring

$\rightarrow$

`<spacer>` ←	`size=n` Specify size in pixels for either width of horizontal spacer or height of `vertical` spacer. `width=n` Specify width in pixels of `block` spacer. `height=n` Specify height in pixels of `block` spacer. `align=value` Specify alignment of `block` spacer with surrounding text. Values are the same as for the `<img>` tag.

`<span>`	`<span> ... </span>`
	
	IE3 and later. Specify style-sheet formatting to text between tags.
	
	Attributes
	
	`style=elements`
	               Specify cascading style sheet elements for text in the span.

`<strike>`	`<strike> ... </strike>` The enclosed text is struck through with a horizontal line.
`<strong>`	`<strong> ... </strong>` Strongly emphasize the enclosed text.
`<style>`	`<style> ... </style>` *IE3 and later.* Surrounds list of style elements to be used in formatting of document. The `<style>` block comes before the `<body>` tag and outside all other elements except `<html>` ... `</html>`.
`<sub>`	`<sub> ... </sub>` Format the enclosed text as a subscript.
`<sup>`	`<sup> ... </sup>` Format the enclosed text as a superscript.
`<table>`	`<table> ... </table>` Define a table.

align=*position*
>Align the table either `left` or `right` with the surrounding text flow.

background=*url*
>*IE3 and later.* Specify an image to be tiled in the background of the table.

bgcolor=*color*
>*N3, IE2 and later.* Define the background color for the entire table.

border=*n*   Create a border *n* pixels wide.

bordercolor=*color*
>*IE2 and later.* Define the border color for the entire table.

bordercolordark=*color*
>*IE2 and later.* Define the dark border-highlighting color for the entire table.

bordercolorlight=*color*
>*IE2 and later.* Define the light border-highlighting color for the entire table.

cellpadding=*n*
>Place *n* pixels of padding around each cell's contents.

cellspacing=*n*
>Place *n* pixels of spacing between cells.

frame=[void|above|below|hsides|lhs|rhs|vsides| box|border]
>*IE3 and later.* Specify which sides of a table's outer border will be drawn. `void` removes outer borders. `box` and `border` display all. `hsides` draws horizontal sides; `vsides` draws vertical sides. `lhs` draws left side; `rhs` draws right side.

hspace=*n*   Specify the horizontal space in pixels added at the left and right of the table.

rules=[all|cols|groups|none|rows]
>*IE3 and later.* Turn off (none) or turn on rules between table cells by `cols`, `rows`, `groups`, or `all`.

vspace=*n*   Specify the vertical space in pixels added at the top and bottom of the table.

width=*n*   Set the width of the table to *n* pixels or a percentage of the window width.

Web Authoring

<tbody>	**<tbody>** *IE2 and later.* Specify the rows in a table to be grouped as the main table body. Requires no ending tag. This element is used to indicate where rules will be drawn when `rules=groups` is used in the `<table>` tag.
<td>	**<td> ... </td>** Define a table data cell. ***Attributes***

`align=`*type* Align the cell contents to the `left`, `center`, or `right`.

`background=`*url*
    IE3 and later. Specify an image to be tiled in the background of the cell.

`bgcolor=`*color*
    N3, IE2 and later. Define the background color for the cell.

`bordercolor=`*color*
    IE2 and later. Define the border color for the cell.

`bordercolordark=`*color*
    IE2 and later. Define the dark border highlighting color for the cell.

`bordercolorlight=`*color*
    IE2 and later. Define the light border highlighting color for the cell.

`colspan=`*n*   Have this cell straddle *n* adjacent columns.

`nowrap`   Do not automatically wrap and fill text in this cell.

`rowspan=`*n* Have this cell straddle *n* adjacent rows.

`valign=`*type*
    Vertically align this cell's contents to the `top`, `middle`, `bottom`, or `baseline` of the cell.

`width=`*n*   Set the width of this cell to *n* pixels or a percentage of the table width.

<textarea>	**<textarea> ... </textarea>** Define a multiline text input area within a `<form>`; contents of the `<textarea>` tag is the initial, default value.

\<textarea\>

cols=*n* Display *n* columns of text within the text area.

name=*string*
> Define the name for the text-area value that is passed to the form-processing application (required).

rows=*n* Display *n* rows of text within the text area.

wrap=*style* *N2 and later.* Set word wrapping within the text area to off, virtual (display wrap, but do not transmit to server), or physical (display and transmit wrap).

\<tfoot\> **\<tfoot\>**

IE2 and later. Specify the rows that will be grouped as the table footer. Requires no ending tag. Used to indicate where rules will be drawn when rules=groups is set in the \<table\> tag.

\<th\> ... \</th\> **\<th\>**

Define a table header cell.

Attributes

align=*type* Align the cell contents to the left, center, or right.

background=*url*
> *IE3 and later.* Specify an image to be tiled in the background of the cell.

bgcolor=*color*
> *N3, IE2 and later.* Define the background color for the cell.

bordercolor=*color*
> *IE2 and later.* Define the border color for the cell.

bordercolordark=*color*
> *IE2 and later.* Define the dark border-highlighting color for the cell.

bordercolorlight=*color*
> *IE2 and later.* Define the light border-highlighting color for the cell.

$\rightarrow$

<th>	colspan=*n*	Have this cell straddle *n* adjacent columns.
←	nowrap	Do not automatically wrap and fill text in this cell.
	rowspan=*n*	Have this cell straddle *n* adjacent rows.
	valign=*type*	
		Vertically align this cell's contents to the top, middle, bottom, or baseline of the cell.
	width=*n*	Set the width of this cell to *n* pixels or a percentage of the table width.

<thead>	**<thead>**
	IE2 and later. Specifies the rows that will be grouped as the table header. Requires no ending tag. This element is used to indicate where rules will be drawn when rules=groups is set in the <table> tag.

<title>	**<title> ... </title>**
	Define the HTML document's title.

<tr>	**<tr> ... </tr>**
	Define a row of cells within a table.
	Attributes
	align=*type* Align the cell contents in this row to the left, center, or right.
	background=*url*
	IE3 and later. Specify an image to be tiled in the background of the cell.
	bgcolor=*color*
	N3, IE2 and later. Define the background color for this row.
	border=*n* Create a border *n* pixels wide.
	bordercolor=*color*
	IE2 and later. Define the border color for this row.
	bordercolordark=*color*
	IE2 and later. Define the dark border-highlighting color for this row.
	bordercolorlight=*color*
	IE2 and later. Define the light border-highlighting color for this row.

valign=*type* Vertically align the cell contents in this row to the top, middle, bottom, or baseline of the cell.	`<tr>`

<tt> ... </tt>

Format the enclosed text in typewriter-style (monospaced) font.

`<tt>`

<ul> ... </ul>

Define an unordered list of bulleted `<li>` elements.

Attributes

compact   Display the list in a more compact manner.

type=*bullet*
     N2 and later. Set the bullet style for this list to either circle, disc (default), or square.

`<ul>`

<var> ... </var>

The enclosed text is a variable's name.

`<var>`

<wbr>

Indicate a potential word break point within a `<nobr>` section.

`<wbr>`

<xmp> ... </xmp>

Same as `<pre width=80>` ... `</pre>`; deprecated, do not use.

`<xmp>`

CHAPTER 24

Color Names and Values

Within Netscape Navigator and Internet Explorer, you can change the colors of various elements of your document. The following table lists some of the tags and attributes that give you color choice.

Element	Associated Tag and Attribute
Document background	`<body bgcolor=color>`
All document text	`<body text=color>`
Active hyperlinks	`<body alink=color>`
Visited hyperlinks	`<body vlink=color>`
Regular hyperlinks	`<body link=color>`
Small portion of text	`<font color=color>`
Table cells	`<table bgcolor=color>`
	`<tr bgcolor=color>`
	`<td bgcolor=color>`
	`<th bgcolor=color>`
Table borders (Internet Explorer only)	`<table bordercolor=color>`
	`<table bordercolorlight=color>`
	`<table bordercolordark=color>`
	`(same for <tr>, <td>, and <th>)`

Color Values

In all cases, you may specify the color value as a six-digit hexadecimal number that represents the red, green, and blue (RGB) components of the color. The first two digits correspond to the red component of the color, the next two to the green component, and the last two to the blue component. A value of 00 corresponds to the component being completely off; a value of FF (255) corresponds to the component being completely on. Thus, bright red is FF0000, bright green is 00FF00, and bright blue is 0000FF. Other primary colors are mixtures of two components, such as yellow (FFFF00), magenta (FF00FF), and cyan (00FFFF). White (FFFFFF) and black (000000) are also easy to figure out.

You use these values in a tag by replacing the color with the RGB triplet, preceded by a hash (#) symbol. Thus, to make all visited links display as magenta, use this body tag:

```
<body vlink="#FF00FF">
```

Color Names

Unfortunately, determining the hexadecimal value for more esoteric colors like "papaya whip" or "navajo white" is very difficult. You can go crazy trying to adjust the RGB triplet for a color to get the shade just right, especially when each adjustment requires loading a document into your browser to view the result.

The folks at Microsoft and Netscape thought so, too, and gave their browsers the ability to use color names directly in any of the color tags. Simply use the color name for the color-attribute value enclosed in quotes. Single-word color names don't require enclosing quotes, but it's good practice to include them anyway. For example, you can make all visited links in the display magenta with the following attribute and value for the body tag:

```
<body vlink="magenta">
```

The standard color names currently supported by Internet Explorer are:

aqua	gray	navy	silver
black	green	olive	teal
blue	lime	purple	yellow
fuchsia	maroon	red	white

Not to be outdone, Netscape 2.0 and higher supports named colors as well; they just don't document the fact. Even better, Netscape supports the several hundred color names originally defined for use in the X Window System. Note that color names may contain no spaces; also, both *gray* and *grey* are acceptable spellings of that color (and the alternative spellings are also valid for *slategray, slategrey,* etc.).

Colors marked with an asterisk (*) represent a family of colors numbered one through four. Thus, there are actually four variants of blue, named blue1, blue2, blue3, and blue4, along with plain old blue. Blue1 is the lightest of the four; blue4 is the darkest. The unnumbered color name is the same color as the first; thus, blue and blue1 are identical.

Finally, if all that isn't enough, there are one hundred variants of gray (and grey) numbered 1 through 100. Gray1 is the darkest, gray100 is the lightest, and gray is very close to gray75.

As an additional note in the "not to be outdone" category, Internet Explorer 3.0 also supports these color names, except for the *grey* variants and the numbered variants. The X11 color names in the following list are supported just as they appear (do not include the asterisks).

The X11 color names are:

aliceblue	darkturquoise	lightseagreen	palevioletred*
antiquewhite*	darkviolet	lightskyblue*	papayawhip
aquamarine*	deeppink*	lightslateblue	peachpuff*
azure*	deepskyblue*	lightslategray	peru
beige	dimgray	lightsteelblue*	pink*
bisque*	dodgerblue*	lightyellow*	plum*
black	firebrick*	limegreen	powderblue
blanchedalmond	floralwhite	linen	purple*
blue*	forestgreen	magenta*	red*
blueviolet	gainsboro	maroon*	rosybrown*
brown*	ghostwhite	mediumaquamarine	royalblue*
burlywood*	gold*	mediumblue	saddlebrown
cadetblue*	goldenrod*	mediumorchid*	salmon*
chartreuse*	gray	mediumpurple*	sandybrown
chocolate*	green*	mediumseagreen	seagreen*
coral*	greenyellow	mediumslateblue	seashell*
cornflowerblue	honeydew*	mediumspringgreen	sienna*
cornsilk*	hotpink*	mediumturquoise	skyblue*
cyan*	indianred*	mediumvioletred	slateblue*
darkblue	ivory*	midnightblue	slategray*
darkcyan	khaki*	mintcream	snow*
darkgoldenrod*	lavender	mistyrose*	springgreen*
darkgray	lavenderblush*	moccasin	steelblue*
darkgreen	lawngreen	navajowhite*	tan*
darkkhaki	lemonchiffon*	navy	thistle*
darkmagenta	lightblue*	navyblue	tomato*
darkolivegreen*	lightcoral	oldlace	turquoise*
darkorange*	lightcyan*	olivedrab*	violet
darkorchid*	lightgoldenrod*	orange*	violetred*
darkred	lightgoldenrodyellow	orangered*	wheat*
darksalmon	lightgray	orchid*	white
darkseagreen*	lightgreen	palegoldenrod	whitesmoke
darkslateblue	lightpink*	palegreen*	yellow*
darkslategray*	lightsalmon*	paleturquoise*	yellowgreen

CHAPTER 25

Character Entities

The following table collects the defined standard, proposed, and several nonstandard (but generally supported) character entities for HTML.

Entity names, if defined, appear for their respective characters and can be used in the HTML character-entity sequence &name; to define any character for display by the browser. Otherwise, or alternatively for named characters, use the character's three-digit numerical value in the sequence &#nnn; to define specifically an HTML character entity. Actual characters, however, may or may not be displayed by the browser depending on the computer platform and the display font selected by the user.

Not all 256 characters in the ISO character set appear in the table. Missing ones are not recognized by the browser as either named or numeric entities.

To be sure that your documents are fully compliant with the HTML 2.0 standard, use only those named character entities whose conformance column is blank. Characters whose conformance columns contain a "P" (Proposed) are generally supported by the current browsers, but they are not part of the HTML standard. Defy compliance by using the nonstandard (N) entities.

Numeric Entity	Named Entity	Symbol	Description	Conformance
&#009;			Horizontal tab	
&#010;			Line feed	
&#013;			Carriage return	
&#032;			Space	
&#033;		!	Exclamation point	
&#034;	&quot;	"	Quotation mark	
&#035;		#	Hash mark	

Numeric Entity	Named Entity	Symbol	Description	Conformance
&#036;		$	Dollar sign	
&#037;		%	Percent sign	
&#038;	&amp;	&	Ampersand	
&#039;		'	Apostrophe	
&#040;		(	Left parenthesis	
&#041;		)	Right parenthesis	
&#042;		*	Asterisk	
&#043;		+	Plus sign	
&#044;		,	Comma	
&#045;		-	Hyphen	
&#046;		.	Period	
&#047;		/	Slash	
0 #057;		0 - 9	Digits 0 – 9	
&#058;		:	Colon	
&#059;		;	Semicolon	
&#060;	&lt;	<	Less than	
&#061;		=	Equal sign	
&#062;	&gt;	>	Greater than	
&#063;		?	Question mark	
&#064;		@	Commercial "at" sign	
A #090;		A – Z	Letters A – Z	
&#091;		[	Left square bracket	
&#092;		\	Backslash	
&#093;		]	Right square bracket	
&#094;		^	Caret	
&#095;		_	Underscore	
&#096;		`	Grave accent	
a #122;		a – z	Letters a – z	
&#123;		{	Left curly brace	
|				Vertical bar	
&#125;		}	Right curly brace	
&#126;		~	Tilde	
&#130;		,		N
&#131;		ƒ	Florin	N
&#132;		"	Right double quote	N

Numeric Entity	Named Entity	Symbol	Description	Conformance
&#133;		...	Ellipsis	N
&#134;		†	Dagger	N
&#135;		‡	Double dagger	N
&#136;		^	Circumflex	N
&#137;		‰	Permil	N
&#138;		_		N
&#139;		<	Less than sign	N
&#140;		Œ	Capital OE ligature	N
&#145;		'	Left single quote	N
&#146;		'	Right single quote	N
&#147;		"	Left double quote	N
&#148;		"	Right double quote	N
&#149;		•	Bullet	N
&#150;		—	Em dash	N
&#151;		–	En dash	N
&#152;		~	Tilde	N
&#153;		™	Trademark	N
&#154;		_		N
&#155;		>	Greater than sign	N
&#156;		œ	Small oe ligature	N
&#159;		Ÿ	Capital Y, umlaut	N
			Nonbreaking space	P
&#161;	&iexcl;	¡	Inverted exclamation point	P
&#162;	&cent;	¢	Cent sign	P
&#163;	&pound;	£	Pound sign	P
&#164;	&curren;	¤	General currency sign	P
&#165;	&yen;	¥	Yen sign	P
&#166;	&brvbar;		Broken vertical bar	P
&#167;	&sect;	§	Section sign	P
&#168;	&uml;	¨	Umlaut	P
&#169;	&copy;	©	Copyright	P
&#170;	&ordf;	ª	Feminine ordinal	P
&#171;	&laquo;	'	Left angle quote	P
&#172;	&not;	¬	Not sign	P
&#173;	&shy;	–	Soft hyphen	P
&#174;	&reg;	®	Registered trademark	P
&#175;	&macr;	¯	Macron accent	P

Numeric Entity	Named Entity	Symbol	Description	Conformance
&#176;	&deg;	°	Degree sign	P
&#177;	&plusmn;	±	Plus or minus	P
&#178;	&sup2;	2	Superscript 2	P
&#179;	&sup3;	3	Superscript 3	P
&#180;	&acute;	´	Acute accent	P
&#181;	&micro;	µ	Micro sign (Greek mu)	P
&#182;	&para;	¶	Paragraph sign	P
&#183;	&middot;	·	Middle dot	P
&#184;	&cedil;	¸	Cedilla	P
&#185;	&sup1;	1	Superscript 1	P
&#186;	&ordm;	º	Masculine ordinal	P
&#187;	&raquo;	'	Right angle quote	P
&#188;	&frac14;	¼	Fraction one-fourth	P
&#189;	&frac12;	½	Fraction one-half	P
&#190;	&frac34;	¾	Fraction three-fourths	P
&#191;	&iquest;	¿	Inverted question mark	P
&#192;	&Agrave;	À	Capital A, grave accent	
&#193;	&Aacute;	Á	Capital A, acute accent	
&#194;	&Acirc;	Â	Capital A, circumflex accent	
&#195;	&Atilde;	Ã	Capital A, tilde	
&#196;	&Auml;	Ä	Capital A, umlaut	
&#197;	&Aring;	Å	Capital A, ring	
&#198;	&AElig;	Æ	Capital AE ligature	
&#199;	&Ccedil;	Ç	Capital C, cedilla	
&#200;	&Egrave;	È	Capital E, grave accent	
&#201;	&Eacute;	É	Capital E, acute accent	
&#202;	&Ecirc;	Ê	Capital E, circumflex accent	
&#203;	&Euml;	Ë	Capital E, umlaut	
&#204;	&Igrave;	Ì	Capital I, grave accent	
&#205;	&Iacute;	Í	Capital I, acute accent	
&#206;	&Icirc;	Î	Capital I, circumflex accent	
&#207;	&Iuml;	Ï	Capital I, umlaut	
&#208;	&ETH;	Ð	Capital eth, Icelandic	
&#209;	&Ntilde;	Ñ	Capital N, tilde	
&#210;	&Ograve;	Ò	Capital O, grave accent	
&#211;	&Oacute;	Ó	Capital O, acute accent	
&#212;	&Ocirc;	Ô	Capital O, circumflex accent	

Numeric Entity	Named Entity	Symbol	Description	Conformance
&#213;	&Otilde;	Õ	Capital O, tilde	
&#214;	&Ouml;	Ö	Capital O, umlaut	
&#215;	&times;	×	Multiply sign	P
&#216;	&Oslash;	Ø	Capital O, slash	
&#217;	&Ugrave;	Ù	Capital U, grave accent	
&#218;	&Uacute;	Ú	Capital U, acute accent	
&#219;	&Ucirc;	Û	Capital U, circumflex accent	
&#220;	&Uuml;	Ü	Capital U, umlaut	
&#221;	&Yacute;	Ý	Capital Y, acute accent	
&#222;	&THORN;	Þ	Capital thorn, Icelandic	
&#223;	&szlig;	ß	Small sz ligature, German	
&#224;	&agrave;	à	Small a, grave accent	
&#225;	&aacute;	á	Small a, acute accent	
&#226;	&acirc;	â	Small a, circumflex accent	
&#227;	&atilde;	ã	Small a, tilde	
&#228;	&auml;	ä	Small a, umlaut	
&#229;	&aring;	å	Small a, ring	
&#230;	&aelig;	æ	Small ae ligature	
&#231;	&ccedil;	ç	Small c, cedilla	
&#232;	&egrave;	è	Small e, grave accent	
&#233;	&eacute;	é	Small e, acute accent	
&#234;	&ecirc;	ê	Small e, circumflex accent	
&#235;	&euml;	ë	Small e, umlaut	
&#236;	&igrave;	ì	Small i, grave accent	
&#237;	&iacute;	í	Small i, acute accent	
&#238;	&icirc;	î	Small i, circumflex accent	
&#239;	&iuml;	ï	Small i, umlaut	
&#240;	&eth;	ð	Small eth, Icelandic	
&#241;	&ntilde;	ñ	Small n, tilde	
&#242;	&ograve;	ò	Small o, grave accent	
&#243;	&oacute;	ó	Small o, acute accent	
&#244;	&ocirc;	ô	Small o, circumflex accent	
&#245;	&otilde;	õ	Small o, tilde	
&#246;	&ouml;	ö	Small o, umlaut	
&#247;	&divide;	÷	Division sign	P
&#248;	&oslash;	ø	Small o, slash	
&#249;	&ugrave;	ù	Small u, grave accent	

Numeric Entity	Named Entity	Symbol	Description	Conformance
&#250;	&uacute;	ú	Small u, acute accent	
&#251;	&ucirc;	û	Small u, circumflex accent	
&#252;	&uuml;	ü	Small u, umlaut	
&#253;	&yacute;	ý	Small y, acute accent	
&#254;	&thorn;	þ	Small thorn, Icelandic	
&#255;	&yuml;	ÿ	Small y, umlaut	

CHAPTER 26

GIFs, Applets, and Other Enhancements

The original developers of the Web intended it to be used by academics, to enable them to share information, both effectively and economically, over a worldwide network. Then corporations heard about the Web. They saw that it could help them sell their wares. They called in their marketing firms and designers. And the Web hasn't been the same since.

In Chapter 22, *Authoring for the Web*, we showed you how to include an image in a fairly simple Web page that's mostly text. Well, once people saw the potential of the Web, text and images weren't enough. They needed the Web to dance and sing. Interactivity, animation, and dynamic content became the hallmarks of stand-out sites.

You may want to bring some of this jazz to your own Web pages. Perhaps you'd like your Web site to open with a splash page depicting a rocket roaring into the heavens. Where do you start? Should you write a Java applet from scratch? You'll need to learn an entire programming language, draw multiple images, and record the sound file. (And once you're done, only about fifty percent of the browsing public will be able to view it.)

GIF animation is easier, and you could embed a sound file to play as the page loads. What's more, images of rockets and sounds of blast-offs aren't esoteric; perhaps you could find these files on the Web. But how do you implement them?

Professional Web developers call on some fairly sophisticated tools in order to enhance documents with features like these. But you don't have to be a pro—or even a programmer—in order to enhance your Web pages.

The spirit of the Web remains freewheeling, and many people like to share their creations. Public domain sites on the Web contain literally thousands of animated GIFs, JavaScript programs, Java applets, CGI scripts, and audio files that are free to download and legal to use.

This chapter provides an overview of how to use these technologies and links to public domain resources to assist you.

Static GIF Images

You don't have any images at all on your Web page? For shame! You can draw an image from scratch, but this is easier said than done if you have no software and/or no talent. You can scan in a picture of your new puppy, but first you have to get a scanner and a puppy. Or, you can just copy an image from someone else's Web site and use it in your own.

It's easy to copy an image; Chapters 2 and 3 tell you how to copy an image you find on a Web page, using Netscape Navigator and Microsoft Internet Explorer, respectively. Keep in mind, however, that it's illegal to copy images (and other enhancements) other people have created and published on the Web. Practically speaking, no one's going to care if you take an image to use as your screen's wallpaper pattern. But republishing a pirated image on your own Web site is quite another matter.

Thus, you should only copy images for public use if you have express permission to do so. Luckily, there are many sites that give you such permission. The following sites are public domain repositories of GIF images that are free for use by anyone.

Dryden Research Aircraft Photo Gallery
> http://www.dfrf.nasa.gov/gallery/photo/index.html

The Clip Art Connection
> http://www.ist.net/clipart/index.html

Varian's AngelDreams—AngelClippings (FTP)
> http://users.aol.com/dreamweavn/angeldreams/clipart.html

JPL Image & Information Archives
> http://www.jpl.nasa.gov/pictures/browse

The VIRTUALibrary
> http://www.mindspring.com/~phaeton/Vsteve.html

Public Gif89A Animation
> http://www.oswego.edu/~acevedo/gif89a/public/

Graphics Are Cool
> http://www.niagara.com/~pmarquis/cool.html#Free

Welcome to Public Domain Images
> http://www.PDImages.com/

Welcome to ArtToday!
> http://www.arttoday.com/

Diamond Sports Icons
> http://www.diamondsports.com/icons/ww2-gifs.html

Cognitive Solutions Inc.—Free HTML and GIF Resources on the Web
> http://www.cognitives.com/links.html

Net-User
> http://www.net-user.com/graphics/

Free Graphics for Your Page
   http://www.geocities.com/SiliconValley/Park/9132/index.html

The Free Graphics Store Chronological Archives
   http://ausmall.com.au/freegraf/freegrfx.htm

Caboodles search engine
   http://www.caboodles.com/

Ender Design: Realm Graphics
   http://www.ender-design.com/rg/

A+ Art: Free clipart, icons, backgrounds, buttons, bars, animated GIFs, photos
   http://aplusart.simplenet.com/aplusart/clipart.htm

GIF Animation

GIF animation works much the way television and movies do: by moving a series of static images past your eyes so quickly that they appear to be a single, moving image. Although they don't have all the functionality of a full Java applet, animated GIF files don't take up as much memory as Java applets and they're easy to find on the Web.

To use an animated GIF, place the animated GIF on your page as you would any other image with the <IMG> tag. For example:

```
<CENTER><P><IMG SRC="mm.gif" HEIGHT=32 WIDTH=32><BR> </P></CENTER>
```

Public Domain Animated GIFs

There are a number of good sites on the Net for free animated GIFs, and a few are starting to support search engines. The quality and size of the images ranges wildly. Since they're all free, however, it's hard to complain. Many sites provide additional tips, advice, or tutorials on creating GIF animations.

The MicroMovie MiniMultiplex
   http://www.teleport.com/~cooler/MMMM/index.html

Animated GIFs
   http://www.compnetserv.com/robertf/ANGIF.HTML

Andy's Art Attack
   http://www.andyart.com/

Animated GIF Galleries
   http://ntweb1.imvi.com/global98/gal_anim_frm.htm

Animated GIFs
   http://http.tamu.edu:8000/~bkf3938/anim/anim.html

The Webmaster's animated GIFs index
   http://www.geocities.com/SiliconValley/7406/anigifs.htm

Dee Dee's Collection Of Animated GIFs
   http://www.NorCom.mb.ca/deedee/animat.htm

Club Unlimited Animated GIFs
http://www.wu-wien.ac.at/usr/h95a/h9552688/local.html

Amazing Instant Online Animated Banner Maker
http://www.andatech.com/vidcraft/banners.html

One final note: as with static GIFs, taking animated GIFs from other sources is just
as easy. It's also illegal.

JavaScript

JavaScript is a fairly simple object-oriented programming language, created to execute scripts within HTML on the client side. The example program in Chapter 22
showed how you can run a message through the browser's scrollbar. This is one
of the more trivial uses of JavaScript.

Now take a look at the example in Figure 26–1.

Figure 26–1: JavaScript example

This functioning calculator may be placed within any standard Web page. Here's
part of the JavaScript code that created it:

```
// CalcResult - the "=" button was pressed, display the result
//

function CalcResult(form) {
if (!errorstate) {
CalcDisplay(form.display);
oper = " ";
acc = 0;
startnum = true;
decpoint = false;

} else { // errorstate
alert('An error has occured. Please press the "AC" button');
}
}
```

This section of code defines the action for the browser to take when the user
presses the equals button: it should display the result of the calculation.

The best way for the amateur to include JavaScript programs in a Web site is by finding a public-domain JavaScript applet, saving it to the server, and sourcing it into the page.

Sourcing in Scripts

It's easy to source a script into your HTML code. Save the script to a file on your server with the extension *.js*. Then source in the file as you would with an image, within the <SCRIPT> tag:

```
<SCRIPT LANGUAGE="JAVASCRIPT" SRC="calculator.js">
```

Here's what the HTML code would look like. Notice the *onLoad* command in the BODY tag. *onLoad* is a JavaScript event handler; in this case, the "event" of the page loading is "handled" by the browser executing the function calcStart.

```
<HTML>
<HEAD>
<TITLE></TITLE>
<SCRIPT LANGUAGE = "JavaScript" SRC = "calculator.js">
</SCRIPT>
<BODY onLoad=calcStart()>
</BODY>
</HEAD>
```

Public Domain Sources for JavaScript

The following sites maintain libraries of JavaScript examples; if you use one of these scripts, be sure to attribute credit as requested.

All U Wanna Know About 'JavaScript'
   http://www.geocities.com/SiliconValley/Park/3091/main.htm

The JavaScript Index
   http://www.c2.org/~andreww/javascript/

Timothy's JavaScript Examples
   http://www.essex1.com/people/timothy/js-index.htm

JavaScript 411 Snippet Library
   http://www.freqgrafx.com/411/library.html

JavaScript Tip of the Week
   http://webreference.com/javascript/

The JavaScript Planet
   http://www.geocities.com/SiliconValley/7116/

Hunting the SNARK with JavaScript
   http://www.cs.cmu.edu/~jab/snark/

JavaScript: Simple Little Things to Add to Your Pages
   http://tanega.com/java/java.html

Benny's JavaScript World
   http://chelsea.ios.com/~benny3/javascript/

Java

Many people are confused about what Java is. You know your browser should support it, but what does Java actually do?

Java is a programming language designed to run on almost any platform, and a Java applet is a program that runs within the confines of a browser. All the hype about Java exists because it solves one of the great complications of computer software: platform dependence. Before Java, it was an unfortunate but accepted fact that applications written for a Windows machine won't run on a Macintosh, and vice versa. With Java, an application can be run on any machine with a Java interpreter—be it Windows, Macintosh, UNIX, or a microwave oven.

Java is entirely distinct from JavaScript and much more complicated. If you're interested in learning how to program in Java, see *Java in a Nutshell*, published by O'Reilly & Associates.

Implementing Java applets into your pages is slightly more complicated than implementing JavaScript applets. The sites provided below, however, make it easy, by including both the class files to download and the HTML to include in your page.

Let's say you wanted to include a guest book on your site (that's a program that lets visitors to your site record that they've been there). You could visit the Java Boutique, at **http://www.j-g.com/java/**, where you might find the applet for sending email pictured in Figure 26-2.

First, download the class files into the same directory in which your page resides by clicking on the file called *gb2.zip*. Next, paste the HTML code into your page within the <APPLET> tags (see Figure 26-3).

Notice the tags that begin with "param name." If you'd like to change some simple characteristics of the applet, change the parameters here. For example, to change the background color of the logo, replace the hexadecimal value in the following line:

```
<param name=BGCOLOR value="000000">
```

See Chapter 24, *Color Names and Values*, for more information on using colors in Web pages.

Here are some good sources for public-domain Java applets on the Web:

JARS.com
> **http://www.jars.com**

Gamelan
> **http://www.gamelan.com**

Apple Flavored Java
> **http://www.mbmdesigns.com/macjava/**

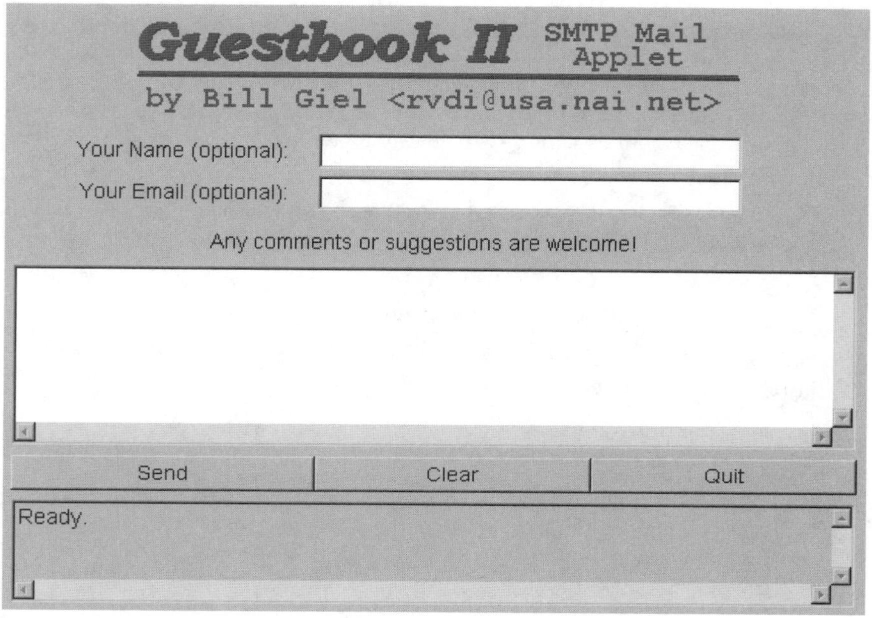

Figure 26-2: A Java applet

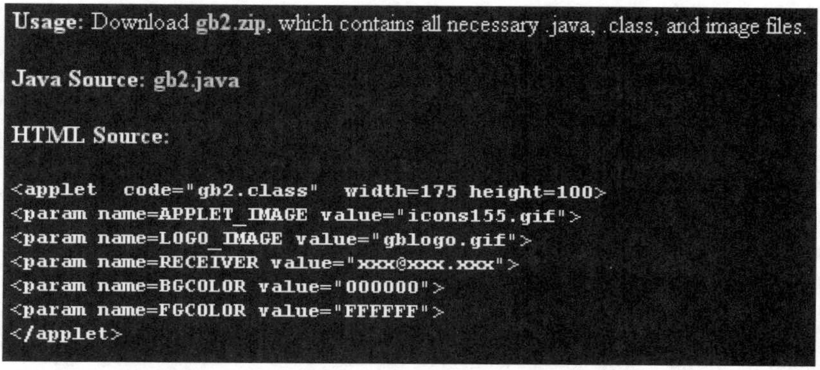

Usage: Download **gb2.zip**, which contains all necessary .java, .class, and image files.

Java Source: gb2.java

HTML Source:

```
<applet  code="gb2.class"  width=175 height=100>
<param name=APPLET_IMAGE value="icons155.gif">
<param name=LOGO_IMAGE value="gblogo.gif">
<param name=RECEIVER value="xxx@xxx.xxx">
<param name=BGCOLOR value="000000">
<param name=FGCOLOR value="FFFFFF">
</applet>
```

Figure 26-3: HTML code for the applet

CGI Scripts

CGI stands for Common Gateway Interface, and it's the oldest technology for interactivity on the Web. This server-side technology allowed for the first communication between browser and server. With CGI, users can submit information that is sent back to the server. The server then executes a program that analyzes the information and sends dynamic content back to the user.

There are several security hazards associated with CGI. So, unlike the other technologies listed in this chapter, you can't just plug a script into your Web page and expect it to work. However, many Internet service providers support CGI. If you find a script you would like to implement, contact your system administrator or service provider to find out whether you're allowed to use CGI, and if so, the details as to how. Many service providers have scripts (especially counters) already available for your use. (Of course, this is a mixed blessing: if your support is unreliable, it can make implementing CGI quite difficult. This is a factor to consider when choosing an ISP.)

The following Web sites provide CGI scripts and instruction for free; be sure to examine and debug scripts carefully.

Dave's List of CGIs
    http://www.nkn.net/nkn/resources/cgi.html

Selena Sol's CGI Script Archive
    http://www.eff.org/~erict/Scripts/

The Common Gateway Interface
    http://hoohoo.ncsa.uiuc.edu/cgi/

Introduction to CGI Programming
    http://ute.usi.utah.edu/bin/cgi-programming/counter.pl/cgi-programming/index.html

Grafman Productions—CGI & PERL
    http://www.graphcomp.com/grafman/perl/tips.html

The CGI Frequently Asked Questions List
    http://www.dwt.co.kr/~ymji/cgi-faq/faq.html

Audio Files

For better or worse, many Web sites now assault you with sound along with their sizzling graphics. Some provide a virtual jukebox, playing the greatest MIDI hits of all time. Others greet the user with a cheery hello while the page loads.

Sound files come in a number of different formats. While convergence seems to be occuring slowly, the different formats were created for different platforms: Sun Audio (*.au*) for UNIX, Audio Interchange File Format (*.aif*) for the Mac, Waveform Audio (*.wav*) for Windows, and Musical Instrument Digital Interface (*.midi*) for exchanging musical notation electronically.

If you'd like to supply a sound file for download or for the user's listening pleasure, save the file in the same directory as your Web page and include the file as a link:

```
<A HREF="blast.au">Lift off</A>
```

When the user clicks the link, the browser's media player plays the sound. See Figure 26–4.

Figure 26–4: Netscape Media Player

Embedding Background Sound Files

Instead of waiting for the user to click on a link, you can embed a background sound directly into the page so it plays automatically when the page loads. You'll need to include two tags (one for Netscape and one for Internet Explorer), and you'll want to place them near the end of the page's code so that the rest of the page is visible while the sound file loads. Background sound files should be small, especially in the *.wav* and *.au* formats; for longer sounds, consider using a MIDI file.

If we wanted to include the blast-off noise we discussed earlier using HTML, here's what the tags would look like:

```
<bgsound src="blast.au"> <-- Internet Explorer tag
<embed src="blast.au" autostart=true hidden=true></embed> <--
Netscape tag
```

You do, unfortunately, need both tags if you want the sound to play on both browsers. The "hidden" attribute tells Netscape not to display the media player, since "autostart" starts the sound when the page is loaded and plays it once through. If you'd like the media player to be displayed, simply omit "hidden=true."

Public Domain Sounds

As always, there are a number of sites on the Web with a plethora of sound files for download and use. If you're looking for a specific, more sophisticated sound effect, look at the sites providing Java and JavaScript files to find other sound functions.

Internet Underground Music Archive
   http://www.iuma.com/

SunSite USA
   http://sunsite.unc.edu/pub/multimedia/sun-sounds/

Australian National Botanical Gardens
   http://155.187.10.12:80/sounds/

Jammin Reggae Archives
   http://www.arrowweb.com/jammin/

Historical Speeches Archive
   http://www.webcorp.com/sounds/index.htm

Answering Machine Enhancements
   http://www.execpc.com/~mike1/ame/

Web Authoring

The Best MIDI
http://w3.one.net/~kklasmei/

MIDI: The Best of alt.binaries.sounds.midi
http://www.webthumper.com/midi/

PART VIII

Internet Relay Chat

CHAPTER 27

It's About Chat

Most of the ways people communicate over a network don't happen in the same timeframe they do in real life. When you send email or post news, you have to wait while it's distributed, wait while someone answers it, wait to read the answer, respond, etc. In nerd terms, events like these are described as happening *asynchronously*.

Chat is another story. Chat allows people to converse more in the way it happens in person or on the phone. You say something, people hear it and respond, you hear their responses on the spot and can reply, etc. (There are some momentary delays between someone saying something and everybody else hearing it, but you shouldn't be aware of it any more than you are for live television and radio broadcasts.) Only in the case of chat, this exchange happens in type on your computer's screen. In the nerd world, communications that happen pretty much in the order you'd expect are described as happening in *real-time*.

The most popular chat facility on the Net is called *Internet Relay Chat* or IRC. IRC allows groups of people to "get together" on various *channels*—which are basically virtual rooms in which you can have a conversation. What this means in practice is that you use a chat program to connect to a chat server, you poke around to see what kind of conversations are going on among the other people who are connected, and you might jump into one of their conversations or offer to start one on a different topic. Everybody "chats" by typing into their chat application. Everybody else in the particular room or channel sees the messages and can participate. A channel actually goes away when the last person exits it, though it can be restarted at any time. Some channels tend to stick around, while others are a one-shot deal.

Getting onto and using chat is not the no-brainer that browsing is. While there are friendly, Windows-based chat clients (such as *mIRC*), you need to know some commands in order to participate. And there are literally thousands of pages of "help" about chat out there on the Net! The *mIRC* list of frequently asked questions is 78 pages itself.

Do you need to read yourself into a stupor to participate in chat? No. You'll probably need to read some instructions in order to install a chat program. You'll need to learn a few commands. If you want to be a chat power user, that's another story. Depending on the chat program, you may be able to do some trickier things, like serve files to other people over a chat channel, share URLs, browse around together, play sound files to coincide with certain commands, etc. Whichever program you use, take a look at *some* of the help information (generally available at a Web site).

The current chapter provides an overview of some basic chat concepts, as well as some information about chat programs, with an emphasis on *mIRC*. (See Chapter 28, *IRC Command Reference*, for a quick reference to some of the more useful IRC commands in general, and *mIRC* commands in particular.)

An IRC Crash Course

OK, so you've read the course introduction, and you know the basic facts about chat. What else do you need to know?

Chat Info and Software

Don't let the thousands of pages of available chat help bury you. The following documents represent a substantial chunk of the more useful info:

* *IRC Primer* by Nicholas Pioch, available by FTP from **cs-ftp.bu.edu**.

* *IRC FAQ*. This list of frequently asked questions about chat is compiled and maintained by Helen Trillian Rose. You can get it via FTP at **cs-ftp.bu.edu** or in HTML format at **http://www.kei.com/**.

There's an entire branch of Usenet news devoted to chat; see the groups in the *alt.irc.** part of the hierarchy. You can also learn about chat by searching out resources with the WebCrawler search engine (described in Chapter 6, *Internet Directories and Search Engines*). WebCrawler's Internet directory points to a huge number of chat-related sites.

If chat seems like something you want to try, you'll need a chat program (or client, as they are commonly called). There are a number of chat clients available for Windows, among them *Global Chat*, *Pirch*, and *mIRC*. Most of these programs are shareware; it will cost you a nominal fee to register your copy.

We're going to take a closer look at *mIRC* because it's popular, fairly simple to use, and has a lot of neat features. *mIRC* is also very well supported, with tons of online help resources, from FAQs to tutorials. That's not to say that the other programs aren't popular or good; you'll just have to check them out for yourself. You can read about and download these programs at the following Web sites:

Global Chat: http://www.globalchat.com/

Pirch: http://www.bcpl.lib.md.us/~frappa/pirch.html

mIRC: http://www.mirc.co.uk/

The Web sites for these programs offer extensive help, in the form of FAQs, tutorials, and other information files, about the programs themselves and about chat in general. Browse these files and retrieve what looks useful. Be aware that some of the documents may be pretty big.

A number of anonymous FTP sites also archive chat programs. The site **ftp.winsite.com** is always a good choice. Look under the directory **/pub/pc/win3/winsock**. (For more information, see Chapter 17, *FTP and File Transfer*.)

We're not going to discuss many program specifics in this chapter. But where specifics help illustrate concepts, we're going to use *mIRC*, a Winsock client that was developed by Khaled Mardam-Bey. The section "mIRC Tips" highlights some of that program's more interesting features. (See Chapter 28 for a list of commands commonly used with *mIRC* and similar clients.)

About Chat Networks and Servers

In order to participate in chat, you first have to connect to a *chat server*, a system that makes chat channels available to users. A number of chat servers are connected to one another to form a *chat network*.

Many chat programs, *mIRC* included, come with a list of chat servers. Whatever chat program you use, the process of configuring it will involve telling the program which chat server to connect to.

Fortunately, for purposes of communication, but unfortunately in terms of explanation, the computer world is busting with chat networks. Different networks have different locations to which they distribute, different levels of system management, etc. A good network is one that reaches as far as you want it to and also has a server that is close to your location.

The following is a list of a few chat networks with some representative servers and their locations. This is by no means every network or every server on the selected networks. Note that while some chat server names include the chat network as part of the domain name, this is not always the case.

For more information about chat networks and servers, check out **http://www.irchelp.org/irchelp/networks/servers/**.

EFnet

The most popular chat network, Eris Free net has upwards of 20,000 users a day—so it can get logjammed. EFnet servers (which use port 6667) include:

irc.io.org (Internex in Canada)
irc-2.mit.edu (Massachusetts Institute of Technology, U.S.)
irc.opus.bridge.net (Miami, Florida, U.S.)
irc.mcs.net (Chicago, Illinois, U.S.)
irc.mo.net (Missouri, U.S.)

irc.cris.com (Cupertino, California, U.S.)
irc02.irc.aol.com (America Online, U.S.)

Undernet

Another popular, well-administered chat network. Again, the port to use is 6667. Also check out **http://servers.undernet.org/**.

amsterdam.nl.eu.undernet.org (Amsterdam, The Netherlands)
lulea.se.eu.undernet.org (Lulea, Sweden)
london.uk.eu.undernet.org (London, U.K.)
auckland.nz.undernet.org (Auckland, New Zealand)
pittsburgh.pa.us.undernet.org (Pittsburgh, Pennsylvania, U.S.)
dallas.tx.us.undernet.org (Dallas, Texas, U.S.)
lowell.ma.us.undernet.org (Lowell, Massachusetts, U.S.)

DALnet

A highly successful EFnet spinoff; these servers use port 7000.

raptor.DAL.net (Edmonton, Alberta, Canada)
xgw.DAL.net (Espoo, Finland)
liberator.DAL.net (Bristol, U.K.)
scorpion.dal.net (Phoenix, Arizona, U.S.)
voyager.DAL.net (San Diego, California, U.S.)
hebron.dal.net (Hebron, Indiana, U.S.)
stlouis.DAL.net (St. Louis, Missouri, U.S.)
uncc.DAL.net (Charlotte, North Carolina, U.S.)

There are plenty of other networks, with servers worldwide. NewNet is a young chat network with at least one server in South Africa (**irc.sprintlink.co.za**). There are a number of Brazil-based IRC networks, intended for a Portuguese-speaking audience. Icenet is a small Australian-based network, with some servers in the U.S. as well. For more information about these and other servers, see **http://www.irchelp.org/irchelp/networks/servers/**.

Channels and What Goes On There

Chat conversations are said to take place on channels. There may be hundreds, or even thousands, of channels open at a particular chat server at any given time. By convention, (public) channel names begin with a pound sign (#)—for example, *#pcusers*.

The name may or may not tell you what kinds of topics are being discussed on that channel. A channel called *#pcusers* would certainly be easy to tell, but there are also channels with names like *#happytime*.

All chat commands begin with a forward slash (/). You can list the channels open on a given server using the **/list** command, which returns each public channel name, the number of participants, and (an optional) description of the topic(s).

Before issuing the **/list** command, it's a good idea to set a parameter that prevents the list from scrolling by too quickly for you to read it. The command **set hold_mode on** lets you look at the channel names one window full at a time. Turn this mode off when you're done reading the listing with the **set hold_mode off** command.

The following are some typical public channels. Note, however, that some channels will only be available on certain chat networks.

- *#chat*—a long-established channel for general, mostly low-key socializing

- *#teenchat*—young people meet here

- *#cafe*—chat with an online coffee house feeling

- *#hottub*—pretty much what you'd expect—a social forum in which people may get, um, fairly loose

- *#Espanol*—Spanish spoken here

- *#freenet*—talk about Freenets

- *#irchelp*—if you can't find an answer in the FAQ, ask your question here

What is this "public" channel business? Well, some channels actually limit participation to a selected group. (More about this later in the chapter.) If you're included in one of these private chats, the channel name will begin with an ampersand (&).

The person who creates or moderates a channel is called the *channel operator*, or *op*, for short. Hypothetically, an op can exclude or bump someone from a channel. But, like getting thrown out of a bar, you'd have to make yourself pretty obnoxious for this to happen.

A caveat: A lot of chat is very sophomoric, to say the least. You're always going to have to pick and choose among channels—and you may even want to start your own.

Configuring Your Chat Program

Regardless of which chat program you run, before you can connect to a server and participate in chat, you'll need to give the program some basic information. Typically, you'll need to supply the following:

- Your name

- Your email address

- One or more "nicknames" you want to use to represent you in chat

- The IRC server you want to connect to

In the *mIRC* client, you use the menu sequence **File** → **Setup** (or Alt+E) to open the program's Setup dialog box. (In some implementations, this box will be opened for you automatically the first time you run the program.) Click on the IRC

Servers tab in the dialog to enter the necessary information. This tab includes a list of possible chat servers.

Your nickname is the name used to identify you in the chat. Nicknames must be unique for each channel. Thus, if you call yourself "Chatcat," and the channel you try to join already has a participant using that nickname, you'll need to choose another one. *mIRC* and some other clients will have you come up with an alternate name upfront. If you have an alternate, the program will automatically try it when your first nickname is rejected.

Once you enter your name, email address, and nickname(s), you can try to connect to a server by double-clicking on its name, or by selecting the name and then using the Connect button.

Some programs may also ask you for:

* Your computer's IP address

* The port number to use for the server

Every computer on the Net has a unique IP address, usually a set of four numbers connected by dots (e.g., 196.201.29.34), or a name that corresponds to the number. Some Internet Service Providers give subscribers a unique IP address (static) for their PC, while some assign a different IP address (dynamic) every time you connect. Certain chat programs will need to know your address or whether the address is assigned dynamically.

Most chat servers use port number 6667. If your chat program asks for a port and you're not sure what it is, choose 6667. However, keep in mind that some servers listen to other ports. For example, DALnet servers use port number 7000.

The Basics of Chatting

Once you choose and connect to a chat server, you can list the currently open channels (see the explanation of the **/list** command in the section "Channels and What Goes On There," earlier in this chapter). When you find a channel that interests you, you can try to join using the command:

```
/join #1_name
```

mIRC provides a graphic interface for many chat functions. You can choose channels in a List Channels dialog. You can also save the names of your favorite channels in a special Channel Folder and filter out channels you don't want to see.

As explained earlier, you need to precede all chat commands with a forward slash (/). Once you're on a channel, everything you type that *isn't* a command is broadcast to everyone on the channel. The text is preceded by your nickname, so that everyone knows who's saying what.

Here are some other useful commands:

/help [*command*]
　　Shows a general help message, or help for the specified *command*.

/whois *nickname*

> Gives you the lowdown on the person using the specified nickname (e.g., email address, what other channels they're on, etc.).

/away *message*

> Specifies a message to be sent to anyone who sends you a private message when you're away from your computer. When you want to get back into chat again, clear this message by entering **/away** with no arguments.

/me *what_I_am_doing*

> Tells everyone else something you're doing, or would like to do. For example,

```
/me kisses Chatdog on the cheek.
```

> which looks like this in the other people's chat clients:

```
*Chatcat* kisses Chatdog on the cheek.
```

/query *nickname*

> Starts a private conversation with *nickname*; this happens in a separate window.

/msg *nickname private_message*

> Sends a private message to the specified *nickname*. In most clients, private messages appear in a separate window. Only the sender and recipient get to see it. If you are sent a private message, a dialog will so inform you.

/notice *nickname private_message*

> Works like **/msg** but without the separate window.

/invite *nickname #channel*

> Invites someone to join a channel with you.

/ignore *nickname*

> Suppresses chat entered by someone who bugs you. What they write won't appear in your chat client.

/nick *name*

> Changes your nickname.

/part or **/leave**

> Exits the current channel.

/quit or **/bye**

> Exits IRC altogether.

For additional commands, see Chapter 28.

How to Be a Channel Operator 101

Anybody can start a channel simply by requesting to join one that is not currently active. This can be a channel name that has been used before or one you make

up on the spot. The following command would open up my own channel, with
the name *whatever*:

```
/join #whatever
```

If someone beat me to this idea, I would be added to the existing channel of that
name. Otherwise my command opens up a new channel called *#whatever*.

Whoever starts a channel becomes a channel operator, with the power to dump
people off of it as well as the ability to specify certain characteristics, or *modes*, of
the channel.

The former is accomplished with the the **kick** command,

```
/kick #mychannel nickname
```

which ejects the named person from the chat on the (public) channel called
#mychannel.

The **/mode** command lets the channel op control some important characteristics of
the channel. For example, the following command makes the channel private:

```
/mode #channel +p
```

You could open the same channel up to the public again using the command:

```
/mode #channel -p
```

Note that a channel is not limited to one operator; a current operator can grant the
same powers to another person using the command:

```
/mode #channel +o nickname
```

It's often a good idea to have at least a couple of channel operators. If your only
channel op quits out of a channel, you're left with no one who can do administration for the channel. Everyone would need to exit—dissolving the channel—and
then someone would rejoin first in order to become channel op. It's a lot easier for
a channel op to set up some other people in the same capacity.

Chapter 28 lists the various options of the **/mode** command.

CHAPTER 28

IRC Command Reference

Windows-based chat programs make it easier to connect to a chat network, request certain services, etc. Although some commands should be available via menus, you'll need to type commands on the keyboard in order to initiate many IRC functions. Staying on the keyboard will also let you keep chatting!

Each command must appear at the beginning of a line within the chat window while you're connected to a channel. Note that all commands must start with a forward slash (/).

The following list presents some of the IRC commands available via *mIRC*. Other chat programs should recognize a similar set of commands. Note that *nickname* refers to the name used by a chat participant; thus *nickname* basically equals *user*, but you must identify them by their "nick."

For more extensive information about any command, enter the following in your chat client:

    /help *command*

Now here's the command reference.

/	/
Reprints the previous command entered in the current window.	
/!	/!
Reprints the previous command entered in any window.	
/action *action_text*	/action
Sends the specified *action_text* to the active channel.	

Internet
Relay Chat

/add	**/add [*-a* | *-c* | *-e* | *-p* | *-u*]** *filename* Loads aliases (-a), commands (-c), events (-e), popups (-p), and users (-u) into *mIRC*.
/ame	**/ame** *message about what you're doing* Sends a message about what you're doing to all the channels to which you're connected. (See also **/me**.)
/amsg	**/amsg** *text* Sends the text to all the channels you're on at the time.
/auser	**/auser** *level nickname* | *address* Adds a user with the specified access level to the remote users list.
/auto	**/auto [** *on* | *off* | *nickname* | *address* **]** Toggles automatic operator status of a nickname or address or sets it on or off.
/away	**/away** *message* Specifies a response to be sent automatically to anyone who sends you a private message when you're away from your computer. For example: `/away Getting something to eat. Be right back.` To clear the message type **/away** with no arguments.
/ban	**/ban [** *#channel* **]** *nickname* **[** *type* **]** Bans the specified nickname from the specified channel, or the current channel, if none is given.
/beep	**/beep** *x delay* Specifies that a beep be sounded *x* times every *delay* minutes.
/channel	**/channel** When you're within a channel, this command pops up the channel central window.

/clear	/clear
Clears the text currently in the window.	

/clearall	/clearall
Clears text in all open chat windows.	

/closemsg *nickname*	/closemsg
Closes the query window you've opened to talk to the specified *nickname.*	

/commands [*on* | *off*]	/commands
Turns the commands section on or off; without an option, returns a status message.	

/creq [*ask* | *auto* | *ignore*]	/creq
Specifies your DCC "On Chat request" in DCC/Options.	

/ctcp *nickname* ping | finger | version | time | userinfo | clientinfo	/ctcp
Performs the specified CTCP request on *nickname.*	

/dcc *send nickname file1 file2 . . .*	/dcc
Sends the specified file(s) to *nickname.*	

/dcc *chat nickname*	/dcc
Opens a DCC window and sends a DCC request for a chat to *nickname.*	

/dde [*-r*] *service topic item* [*data*]	/dde
Allows DDE control between *mIRC* and other applications.	

/ddeserver [[*on* [*service*] *off*]]	/ddeserver
Toggles the DDE server mode.	

/describe *#channel action_text*	/describe
Sends *action_text* to the specified channel.	

/disable	**/disable** *#groupname* Deactivates a group of commands or events.
/disconnect	**/disconnect** Abruptly disconnects you from the IRC server.
/dlevel	**/dlevel** *level* Changes the default user level.
/dns	**/dns** *nickname* | *IP_address* | *IP_name* Specifies that your providers DNS be used to resolve an IP address.
/echo	**/echo** [*nickname* | *#channel* | *status*] *text* Displays the specified text to you only on the given place in color *n.*
/enable	**/enable** *#groupname* Activates a group of commands or events.
/events	**/events** [*on* | *off*] Shows the remote events status or toggles it to be listening or not.
/exit	**/exit** Forces *mIRC* to shut down its connection and exit.
/finger	**/finger** [*nickname*] Performs a *finger* command on user's address.
/flood	**/flood** [*lines seconds pause*] Controls flooding.
/flush	**/flush** [*levels*] Clears all nicknames that aren't currently on your channels from the remote users list.

/font /font

Opens a dialog in which you can specify fonts.

/fsend [*on* | *off*] /fsend

Shows *fsend*'s status; can also use it to toggle DCC fast send option.

/fserve *nickname max_gets home_dir* [*welcome_file*] /fserve

Opens a fileserver.

/groups [*-e* | *-d*] /groups

Without any options, shows all groups defined in the remote sections; -e shows enabled groups only; -d disabled groups.

/guser *level nickname* [*type*] /guser

Adds the user to the user list with the specified level and type of address.

/help [*command* | *keyword*] /help

Get help about IRC commands, or search help for particular command/keyword.

/ignore [*on* | *off*] | *nickname* | *address*] /ignore

Toggles ignoring of a nickname or address, or turns ignoring on or off.

/invite *nickname #channel* /invite

Invites a nickname to a channel.

/join *#channel* /join

Gets you onto the specified channel.

/kick [*#channel*] *nickname* /kick

Kicks *nickname* off of the specified channel.

/leave [*#channel*] /leave

Exits you from the specified channel.

Internet
Relay Chat

/list	**/list** [*#string*] [*-min #*] [*-max #*] Lists all currently available channels.
/load	**/load** [*-a* | *-c* | *-e* | *-p* | *-u*] *filename* Loads aliases (-a), commands (-c), events (-e), popups (-p), or users (-u) into *mIRC*.
/log	**/log** [*on* | *off*] Shows the logging status or toggles logging.
/me	**/me** *text* Sends a message about what you're doing to the current channel or query window. (See also **/ame**.)

/mode	**/mode** [*#channel* | *nickname*] [[+|-]*mode_characters* [*options*]]
	
	Sets channel or user modes if you are the channel operator. Each option starts with a plus (+) if you are turning the feature on, or a minus sign (−) if you are turning it off.
	
	For channel functions, the first argument is the channel name, followed by a plus or minus sign, then the "mode character" and any options it takes. Here are the various mode characters:
	
	b *nickname*
	    Ban the user *nickname* from the channel. For example, the following command bans "Chatrat" from the channel called *mychannel*:
	
	    `/mode mychannel +b Chatrat`
	
	i Make the channel by invitation only.
	
	l *number*
	    Limit the channel to *number* number of users.
	
	m Make channel moderated. Only channel operators, and others who have been granted "voice," may talk. See the "v" option.
	
	n Disallow private messages (**/msg**) from outside of the channel.
	
	o *nickname*
	    Set user *nickname* as a channel operator.
	
	p Set the channel as private.

s   Set the channel as secret.   **/mode**

t   Allow only a channel operator to set the topic.

v *nickname*
        Give *nickname* a "voice" in the channel. See the "m"
        option.

For user functions to /mode, the first argument is the user's nickname, followed by options:

i   Make your nickname invisible, i.e., your nickname will not
        appear in the member list.

o   For operators only, grant operator status to user.

s   Receive server messages.

w   Recieve wallops.

/msg *nickname message*   **/msg**

Sends a private message to specified *nickname* without opening
a query window.

/names [*#channel*]   **/names**

List the nicknames of all users on the current or specified channel.

/nick *nickname*   **/nick**

Change your nickname.

/notice *nickname message*   **/notice**

Send the notice message to *nickname*.

/notify [*on* | *off* | *nickname . . .*]   **/notify**

Creates a "notify" list of nicknames:

    /notify Chatcat Chatdog Ginny Ahab

You will then be notified when any of these people join or exit
IRC.

Without arguments, **/notify** tells you whether the people from
your notify list are on or off IRC.

Can instead be used to toggle notification on or off:

    /notify off

/omsg	**/omsg** [*#channel*] *message* Sends the specified message to all operators on a channel.
/onotice	**/onotice** [*#channel*] *message* Sends the specified notice message to all channel operators.
/part	**/part** [*#channel*] Exits you from the specified channel.
/partall	**/partall** Exits you from all channels.
/ping	**/ping** *server_address* Pings the specified server to see if it's active.
/play	**/play** [*-clmpqrt*] [*channel* | *nickname*] *filename* [*delay/ linenumber*] Let's you play text files over chat.
/pop	**/pop** *delay* [*#channel*] *nickname* Adds operator status (after a delay) to *nickname*.
/protect	**/protect** [*on* | *off* | *nickname* | *address*] Toggles protection of a *nickname* or *address*, or turns protection on or off.
/query	**/query** *nickname message* Opens a query window to *nickname*, displaying a private message.
/quit	**/quit** [*reason*] Close connection to server. If you include a message, it will be displayed to any channel you are on.
/raw	**/raw** *command* Sends a command directly to the server; use with caution.

/remote [*on* | *off*] Displays the remote command status, or toggles it on/off.	/remote
/rlevel *access_level* Removes all users with the specified access level from the remote users list.	/rlevel
/run *c:\path\program.exe* [*options*] Runs program.	/run
/ruser *nickname! address* [*type*] Removes *nickname* from the remote user's list.	/ruser
/save [*-a* | *-c* | *-e* | *-p* | *-u*] *filename* Saves remote sections into the specified file.	/save
/say *text* Displays the specified text to the active window.	/say
/server [*server_address* [*port*] [*password*]] Reconnects to the specified server or (without options) the previous server.	/server
/sound [*nickname* | *#channel*] *filename.wav action_text* Sends the specified action and sound file to the *nickname* or *channel.*	/sound
/speak *text* Uses the program Monologue to vocalize the written text.	/speak
/sreq [*ask* | *auto* | *ignore*] Specifies your DCC "On Chat request" in DCC/Options.	/sreq
/time Retrieves the current time and date from the server.	/time

Internet Relay Chat

/timer	**/timer** [*n repetitions interval command* [| *command2 . . .*]] Activates a timer to issue one or more commands *repetitions* times every *interval* seconds.
/timestamp	**/timestamp** [*on* | *off*] Sets timestamping on or off for all your chats.
/topic	**/topic** *#channel new_topic* Changes the stated topic for the specified channel.
/ulist	**/ulist** *level* Lists all users in the remote list with the specified access levels.
/url	**/url** [*-d*] Opens the URL in a browsing window.
/uwho	**/uwho** *nickname* Shows information about the specified *nickname*.
/wavplay	**/wavplay** *c:\path\sound.wav* Plays the specified *.wav* file on the local machine.
/who	**/who** *#channel* Displays the nicknames of everyone on the specified channel.
/who	**/who** **address.string** Displays the nicknames of everyone with the specified address.
/whois	**/whois** *nickname* Displays info about the specified user.
/whowas	**/whowas** *nickname* Displays info about the last person to use a given nickname.
/write	**/write** [*-cdil*] *filename* [*text*] Writes the specified text to a text file.

Glossary

Archie

A system for locating files that are publicly available by anonymous FTP.

bandwidth

The amount of data that can be transferred over a network connection. The phrase *wasting bandwidth* refers to transferring useless information over valuable network connections.

browser

A program that displays documents on the Internet. Browsers are primarily used to display HTML documents on the World Wide Web, but most programs can handle a variety of document formats. The most popular browsers on the market are Netscape Navigator (Chapter 2, *Netscape Navigator*) and Microsoft Internet Explorer (Chapter 3, *Microsoft Internet Explorer*).

BTW

Common abbreviation in mail and news, meaning "by the way."

buffers

Areas of memory that provide temporary storage for input devices.

bulletin board service (BBS)

In online terms, an area where messages can be posted, read, and responded to in a non-real-time discussion. Usenet newsgroups are basically bulletin boards. Traditionally, "BBS" has referred to a standalone computer or site where users can dial in and exchange messages and files, or access some other types of services (such as chat or mail). These "private" BBSs are self-contained services and are not part of the Internet, although many have gateway connections to the Net.

cache

Information saved in memory for later use. For example, Web browsers save recently viewed pages in a cache so the exact pages are not downloaded again, thereby saving Internet resources and time.

chat

A real-time conversation (in text, usually) among multiple users online. Discussions take place in virtual *rooms* or *channels*. Internet Relay Chat (IRC) is the Internet's chat facility. (For more information, see Chapter 27, *It's About Chat*, and Chapter 28, *IRC Command Reference*.)

client

A software application that works on your behalf to extract a service from a server somewhere on the network. For instance, a Web browser is a client that lets you view documents on remote servers.

DNS

The Domain Name System; a distributed database system for translating computer names (like **ruby.oreilly.com**) into numeric Internet addresses (like **194.56.78.2**), and vice versa. DNS allows you to use the Internet without remembering long lists of numbers.

Domain name

The name given to a network or site that is connected to the Internet—e.g., **oreilly.com** is the domain name of O'Reilly & Associates.

FAQ

Either a frequently asked question, or a list of frequently asked questions and their answers. Many Usenet (q.v.) newsgroups and some non-Usenet mailing lists maintain FAQ lists (FAQs) so that participants don't spend lots of time answering the same set of questions.

flame

A virulent and (often) largely personal attack against the author of a Usenet posting (or an email message). A free-for-all of this kind is called a *flame war*.

followup

A message posted in response to a Usenet posting.

freenet

An organization to provide free Internet access to people in a certain area, usually through public libraries.

FTP

(a) The File Transfer Protocol; a protocol that defines how to transfer files from one computer to another.

(b) An application program that moves files using the File Transfer Protocol. (See Chapter 17, *FTP and File Transfer*, and Chapter 18, *FTP Command Reference*.)

FYI (a) A series of informative papers about the Internet; they're similar to RFCs (q.v.), but don't define new standards.

(b) The more widely understood meaning: an acronym for the phrase "for your information." "FYI" is used commonly in email and Usenet (q.v.) news messages.

GIF

Common file format of graphic images displayed on the Internet. Also refers to the Graphic Interchange Format standard.

Gopher

A menu-based system for exploring Internet resources.

hostname

The name given to an individual computer attached to a network or the Internet; a host machine.

HTML

Hypertext markup language; the language in which World Wide Web documents are written.

hypermedia

A combination of hypertext (q.v.) and multimedia (q.v.).

hypertext

Documents that contain links to other documents; selecting a link automatically displays the second document.

IMHO

An acronym (used commonly in mail and news) for "in my humble opinion." In actual usage, the "humble" part often seems ironic. For those who don't aspire to humility, the acronym IMO is also available. :-) See also *smiley*.

IP The Internet Protocol; the most important of the protocols on which the Internet is based. It allows a packet to traverse multiple networks on the way to its final destination. See also *TCP*.

IP address

A 32-bit number defined by the Internet Protocol that uniquely identifies a resource on the Internet. It is usually shown in dotted-decimal or dotted-quad notation, which is four numbers separated by dots.

Internet Relay Chat (IRC)

See *chat*.

Internet Service Provider (ISP)

An organization that provides connections to a part of the Internet.

JPEG

A popular graphic file format on the Internet. Also the Joint Photographic Experts Group standard for encoding and compressing graphic images.

MIME

Multimedia Internet Mail Extensions. A protocol that defines a number of content types and subtypes, which allow programs like Web browsers, newsreaders, and email clients to recognize different kinds of files and deal with them appropriately. A MIME type specifies what media a file is, such as image, audio, or video, and a subtype identifies the precise file format.

mirror site

A computer that contains an exact replica of the directory structure of another computer to provide alternative access to information at a heavily accessed site. Mirror sites also provide geographically closer site access to save network resources.

MPEG

A popular video image format on the Internet. Also the Moving Pictures Experts Group standard for encoding and compressing moving video images.

multimedia

Documents that include different kinds of data; for example, plain text and images, or text, audio, and images, etc. See also *hypertext* and *hypermedia*.

netiquette

Network etiquette. A loose collection of undocumented rules that is supposed to govern acceptable social behavior on the Internet. Most of netiquette arises from simple politeness to other users. For example, don't post private email without the sender's permission. Also, read a Usenet newsgroup's list of frequently asked questions (FAQ) before participating in the discussion.

packet

A bundle of data. On the Internet, data is broken up into small chunks, called *packets*; each packet traverses the network independently. Packet sizes can vary from roughly 40 to 32,000 bytes, depending on network hardware and media, but packets are normally less than 1500 bytes long.

POP

The Post Office Protocol; a mail protocol that allows a remote mail client to read mail from a server.

port

(a) A number that identifies a particular Internet application. When your computer sends a packet to another computer, that packet contains information about what protocol it's using (e.g., TCP or UDP) and with what application it's trying to communicate. The port number identifies the application.

(b) One of a computer's physical input/output channels (i.e., a plug on the back).

Unfortunately, these two meanings are completely unrelated. The first is more common when you're talking about the Internet (as in "**telnet** to port 1000"); the second is more common when you're talking about hardware ("connect your modem to the serial port on the back of your computer").

posting

An individual article sent to a Usenet (q.v.) newsgroup; or the act of sending an article to a Usenet newsgroup.

PPP

Point-to-Point Protocol; protocol that allows a computer to use the TCP/IP (q.v.) protocols to connect to the Internet using a modem and a standard telephone line.

protocol

A protocol is just a definition of how computers will act when talking to each other. Protocol definitions range from how bits are placed on a wire to the format of an electronic mail message. Standard protocols allow computers from different manufacturers to communicate; the computers can use completely different software, provided that the programs running on both ends agree on what the data means.

RFC

Request for Comments; a set of papers in which the Internet's standards, proposed standards, and generally agreed-upon ideas are documented and published.

RTFM

An acronym (used commonly in mail and news) that stands for "read the f****** manual"—in other words, check your documentation before you bother me with that question.

server

A networked computer that provides some kind of service or information. Internet servers are classified by the type(s) of information they offer. A mail server provides electronic mail. A World Wide Web server provides *hypertext* (q.v.) documents, using the Hypertext Transfer Protocol (HTTP), and is thus called an HTTP server. A single computer can act as a number of different servers.

shell

On a UNIX system, software that accepts and processes command lines from your terminal. UNIX has multiple shells available (e.g., C shell, Bourne shell, Korn shell), each with slightly different command formats and facilities.

shortcut

A feature of Windows 95 that allows you to place an icon on the desktop or in a document and simply click on the icon to access a particular application.

signature

A file, typically up to five lines long, that people often insert at the end of email messages or Usenet news articles. A basic signature gives the user's name and email address. Many signatures also include a business or organization name, postal addresses, and telephone numbers, as well as personal touches like quotations, ASCII pictures, etc. Using a signature of more than five or six lines is considered to be poor netiquette (q.v.).

SLIP

Serial Line Internet Protocol; protocol that allows a computer to use the TCP/IP (q.v.) protocols to connect to the Internet using a modem and a standard telephone line.

smiley

A picture of a smiling face created using a few simple punctuation marks. Smileys are commonly used in electronic communication (e.g., email, Usenet news) to clarify meaning that might not be apparent in the words alone. The most common smiley is :-) to indicate approval, happiness, humor, etc.

However, there are many variations on the smiley, to allow you to express a wide range of moods. For example, :-(indicates sadness or disappointment. You might use :-o for surprise, or ;-) (notice the wink) to show that you're kidding.

SMTP

The Simple Mail Transfer Protocol; a protocol that is used to send mail over a TCP/IP network.

TCP

The Transmission Control Protocol; one of the protocols on which the Internet is based.

Telnet

(a) A "terminal emulation" protocol that allows you to log in to other computer systems on the Internet.

(b) An application program that allows you to log in to another computer system using the Telnet protocol. Telnet applications are commonly used to connect to online library catalogs. (See Chapter 8, *Accessing Libraries and Other Resources with Telnet*, for more information.)

timeout

A timeout is what happens when two computers are communicating and one computer—for any reason—fails to respond. The other computer will keep on trying for a certain amount of time, but will eventually give up.

Usenet

Usenet is an online discussion forum, somewhat analogous to a bulletin board service (q.v.). Usenet communications happen in the context of groups of users interested in the same subject. There are literally thousands of these "newsgroups" accessible via the Internet. Newsgroup communications are also carried over other networks and channels, including UUCP (UNIX to UNIX Copy). (For more information, see Chapter 12, *Getting Along in Usenet*.)

W3C

The World Wide Web Consortium. A consortium of many companies and organizations that "exists to develop common standards for the evolution of the World Wide Web." It is run by a joint effort between the Laboratory for Computer Science at the Massachusetts Institute of Technology and CERN, the European Particle Physics Laboratory, where the WWW was first developed.

White pages

Like the telephone books for which they are named, white pages refer to online listings of basic information about individuals, commonly their names, phone numbers, and email addresses. Online white page listings may also provide maps and directions. The Internet is loaded with white page services. (See Chapter 7, *Finding People and Places*, for more information.)

Winsock

Common term for "Windows Sockets," which is the set of specifications that programmers must use to write TCP/IP software for Windows.

World Wide Web (WWW)

A hypertext-based system for finding and accessing Internet resources.

Yellow pages

Like the telephone books for which they are named, yellow pages refer to online listings of basic information about organizations, commonly their names, phone numbers, and email addresses. Online yellow page listings may also provide maps and directions. The Internet is loaded with yellow page services. (See Chapter 7 for more information.)

Index

checkboxes in HTML forms, 349
CHECKED attribute, <INPUT> tag,
    349, 351
children, Web sites for, 85
chunksize command (ftpmail), 277
CineWeb plug-in, 322
<CITE> tag, 342
CLASSID attribute, <OBJECT> tag, 356
CLEAR attribute, <BR> tag, 342
/clear command (IRC), 397
/clearall command (IRC), 397
ClearFusion plug-in, 322
clickable image maps, 350
close command (FTP), 267, 283
/closemsg command (IRC), 397
CNET (Web site for), 74
CODE attribute, <APPLET> tag, 339
<CODE> tag, 342
CODEBASE attribute
    <APPLET> tag, 339
    <OBJECT> tag, 356
CODETYPE attribute, <OBJECT> tag,
    356
<COL> tag, 342
<COLGROUP> tag (HTML), 343
Collabra (see Netscape Collabra
    Discussions)
colleges, Web sites for, 86
color
    frames, 345
    hexadecimal values for, 366
    hyperlinks, 341
    names for, 367-368
    tables, 361, 363
    text, 341, 344, 366
COLOR attribute, <FONT> tag, 344
COLS attribute
    <FRAMESET> tag, 346
    <MULTICOL> tag, 355
    <TEXTAREA> tag, 363
COLSPAN attribute, table tag, 362, 364
columns, 342, 355
.com (URL suffix), 70
/commands command (IRC), 397
<COMMENT> tag, 343
comments in HTML, 333
commercial service providers (see
    ISPs)

Common Gateway Interface (CGI),
    381-382
comp. (computer-related) news-
    groups, 179
COMPACT attribute
    <DIR> tag, 343
    <DL> tag, 344
    <MENU> tag, 355
    <OL> tag, 357
    <UL> tag, 365
compact command (ftpmail), 277
companies (see businesses, searching
    for)
completion
    email addresses, 205
    URLs, 25
Component Bar (Navigator), 26
Component Gallery (Web site), 320
Composition window (Messen-
    ger/Collabra), 162, 190
compress command (ftpmail), 277
compress utility (UNIX), 302-303
compressing files, 159, 298-299
    compress utility (UNIX), 302-303
    filename extensions and, 300
    gzip utility (UNIX), 302-303
    StuffIt utility for (Macintosh),
      304-306
    WinZip utility for, 300-302
computers
    networked (see servers)
CONTENT attribute, <META> tag, 355
control markers, HTML (see tags,
    HTML)
CONTROLS attribute, <IMG> tag, 349
cookies, 13
    Microsoft Internet Explorer and,
      55-56
    Netscape Navigator and, 34-36
COORDS attribute, <AREA> tag, 339
cr command (FTP), 283
Crayola Art Site, 85
/creq command (IRC), 397
crossed-out text, 358, 360
/ctcp command (IRC), 397
CultureFinder (Web site), 89
customizing/configuring
    chat programs, 391-392
    Internet Explorer, 62-65

customizing/configuring (cont'd)
Internet Mail, 235-236
Internet News, 255-256
Links area (Internet Explorer), 51
MSIE (Microsoft Internet Explorer)
for helper applications, 313
Netscape 4.0
for helper applications, 312-313
Netscape Communicator, 43-47
personal toolbar (Navigator), 31-33
CyberSleuth plug-in, 323

D

DALnet chat network, 390
DATA attribute, <OBJECT> tag, 357
date and time
expiring browser history, 34, 54
sorting messages by (Messenger/Collabra), 201, 222
Day-Timer Organizer plug-in, 321
/dcc command (IRC), 397
<DD> tag (HTML), 343
/dde command (IRC), 397
/ddeserver command (IRC), 397
debug command (FTP), 283
DECLARE attribute, <OBJECT> tag, 357
decoding files, 159
decompressing files (see compressing files)
definition lists, 343
DejaNews search engine, 80, 96, 104, 184-187
delete command (FTP), 284
Deleted Items folder (Internet Mail), 221
/describe command (IRC), 397
<DFN> tag (HTML), 343
dictionaries online, 79
digest option (mailing lists), 172
dir command (FTP), 284
<DIR> tag (HTML), 343
DIRECTION attribute, <MARQUEE> tag, 354
directories
FTP management commands, 282, 286, 289, 294
listing contents of, 95-124, 284
FTP commands for, 287-289

directories of Web sites
Infoseek search engine, 96, 110-114, 126, 129
search engines versus, 94-95
WebCrawler site, 119-120, 130
Yahoo! (see Yahoo! directory)
/disable command (IRC), 398
disconnect command (FTP), 267, 285
/disconnect command (IRC), 398
discussion groups (see newsgroups)
<DIV> tag (HTML), 343
<DL> tag (HTML), 344
/dlevel command (IRC), 398
/dns command (IRC), 398
DNS (domain naming system), 70
Dock Component Bar (Communicator menu), 27
documentation, online, 78-80
documents (see files)
documents, HTML (see HTML)
domain naming system (DNS), 70
domains, 70
downloading files with FTP (see FTP)
Drafts folder (Messenger), 193
<DT> tag (HTML), 344
DYNSRC attribute, <IMG> tag, 349

E

Earthtime plug-in, 321
/echo command (IRC), 398
.gov (URL suffix), 70
education, Web sites for, 85-86
EFnet chat network, 389
Electronic Zoo (Web site), 86
<EM> tag (HTML), 344
email (electronic mail), 148-164
addresses, 149-151
address books, 152, 204-205, 222-224, 247-248
of mailing lists, 170
using multiple, 157
advice on, 153-154
attaching files to messages, 159-164
choosing service for, 158
filtering, 153
Communicator, 205-207
Internet Mail, 227-228
to prevent spam, 157
FTP via (ftpmail servers), 275-277

Message Center (Messenger), 189, 193-194
creating toolbar links to, 200
Message Composition window (Messenger), 162
Message List window (Messenger), 189, 192-193
messages, email (see email)
Messenger (see Netscape Messenger)
<META> tag (HTML), 355
METHOD attribute, <FORM> tag, 345
METHODS attribute
<A> tag, 337
<LINK> tag, 353
mget command (FTP), 267, 288-289
Microsoft
home page for, 49
Internet Explorer (see MSIE)
Internet Mail (see Internet Mail)
Internet News (see Internet News)
Search Wizard tool, 97
MIME (Multipurpose Internet Mail Extensions), 159
MIME types, 259-262
mIRC client, 387
command reference, 395-404
configuring, 391
mirror sites, 263
misc. (miscellaneous) newsgroups, 180
mkdir command (FTP), 289
MLB@BAT (Web site), 81
mls command (FTP), 289
mode command (FTP), 290
/mode command (IRC), 394, 400-401
moderated newsgroups, 177
moderators of mailing lists, 165
modes, channel (chat), 394
money, online resources for, 83
.mov filename extension, 316
movies, online resources for, 90
MPEG player for Windows, 311
MPLAYER Audio Player, 312
mput command (FTP), 267, 290
/msg command (IRC), 393, 401
MSIE (Microsoft Internet Explorer)
ActiveX controls, 315-323
color names, 367

configuring for helper applications, 313
cookies, 55-56
customizing, 62-65
Favorites list, 52-53
adding Navigator Bookmarks to, 54
interesting functions of, 48-57
Internet Mail, 146, 217-229
address book in, 222-224
attaching and receiving files, 160-162
customizing, 235-236
keyboard shortcuts, 224-226
quick reference, 229-235
windows for each message, 222
Internet News, 146, 217, 237-248
address book in, 247-248
customizing, 255-256
icons in, 238
keyboard shortcuts, 245-246
Internet News (Microsoft)
quick reference, 248-255
keyboard shortcuts, 57
performance, 51
quick reference, 57-62
specifying start page, 49
Toolbar and Status Bar, 50-51
<MULTICOL> tag (HTML), 355
multiline text input area, 352, 362
MULTIPLE attribute, <SELECT> tag, 359
Multipurpose Internet Mail Extensions (MIME), 159
museums, 83-84
music-related newsgroups, 180

N

NAME attribute
<A> tag, 338
<APPLET> tag, 339
<EMBED> tag, 344
<FRAME> tag, 346
<IFRAME> tag, 348
<INPUT> tag, 349-352
<MAP> tag, 354
<META> tag, 355

SCROLLDELAY attribute, <MARQUEE> tag, 354
SCROLLING attribute
   <FRAME> tag, 346
   <IFRAME> tag, 348
Sea World (Web site), 87
Search Wizard tool (Microsoft), 97
searching
   Archie utility for, 135
   for businesses, 127
   for email addresses, 127, 130-133
   FAQs (Frequently Asked Questions), 80
   Internet directories (see directories)
   library catalogs, 134-142
   for mailing lists, 168-169
   MasterSite (Web site) for, 97
   newsgroup postings, 80, 96, 104
      with AltaVista, 99
   for newsgroups, 178-181
      Internet News, 243
      Messenger/Collabra, 197
   for people/organizations, 29, 125-132
      finger utility for, 132-133
   search engines, 93-94
      AltaVista, 96, 98-104
      DejaNews, 80, 96, 104, 184-187
      directories versus, 94-95
      Excite, 96, 104-106, 129
      HotBot, 96, 106-110
      Infoseek, 96, 110-114, 126, 129
      list of, 95-124
      Lycos, 96, 114-118, 130
      NetGuide Live, 118
      WebCrawler, 119-120, 130
security, 13-15
   authentication (see authentication)
   cookies and, 14, 34-36, 55-56
   preventing spam, 156-159
   privacy issues (see privacy)
<SELECT> tag (HTML), 359
SELECTED attribute, <OPTION> tag, 357
selection lists, HTML, 359
_self target, 340
send command (FTP), 295
sendport command (FTP), 295
/server command (IRC), 403

servers, 4
   chat servers, 389
   names of, in URLs, 69
   Web, getting onto, 327-329
   Web, running your own, 328-329
SHAPE attribute, <AREA> tag, 339
SHAPES attribute, <OBJECT> tag, 357
Shockwave Flash plug-in, 320
Shockwave plug-in, 314, 318-319
shortcuts, keyboard
   Internet News, 245-246
   Messenger/Collabra, 198-200, 224-226
   MSIE (Microsoft Internet Explorer), 57
   Netscape Navigator, 23
   StuffIt utility, 306
showing/hiding
   MSIE status bar, 51
   MSIE toolbar, 50-51
   Netscape toolbars, 194
signature files, 149
   Internet Mail, 226-227
   Internet News, 246-247
SIZE attribute
   <BASEFONT> tag, 340
   <FONT> tag, 335, 345
   <HR> tag, 347
   <INPUT> tag, 350-352
   <SPACER> tag, 360
Sizzler plug-in, 320
slash (/)
   in HTML tags, 331
   in IRC commands, 390
<SMALL> tag (HTML), 359
smileys (emoticons), 153
The Smithsonian Institution (Web site), 83
SmoothMove plug-in, 323
soc. (society-related) newsgroups, 180
sorting messages
   Internet Mail, 222
   Internet News, 247
   Messenger/Collabra, 201-202
sound, 382-384
/sound command (IRC), 403
<SPACER> tag (HTML), 359
spam (junk email), 155-159

WS_FTP program, 264, 272-273
WWWebster Dictionary (Web site), 79

X

<XMP> tag (HTML), 365

Y

Yahoo! directory, 10, 73-74, 96,
      120-124, 130
   Yahoo! Travel (Web site), 88
   Yahooligans! (Web site), 85
Yellow Page searches, 29, 125-132
Yellow Pages Online, 132

Z

zip code directory, 132
Zip2 directory, 132
zoos online, 86

About the Authors

Valerie Quercia has co-written a number of books for O'Reilly & Associates, including the *X Window System User's Guide* (with Tim O'Reilly), *X User Tools* (with Linda Mui), and *WebMaster in a Nutshell* (with Stephen Spainhour). *Internet in a Nutshell* is her first solo book. Val is also the Managing Editor of The Left Field Press, a company that specializes in baseball publications.

Colophon

Our look is the result of reader comments, our own experimentation, and feedback from distribution channels. Distinctive covers complement our distinctive approach to technical topics, breathing personality and life into potentially dry subjects.

The image featured on the cover of *Internet in a Nutshell* is an alchemist. Alchemy, the precursor of modern chemistry, first appeared around 100 AD in Alexandria, Egypt—a product of the fusion of Greek and Oriental culture. The goal of this philosophic science was to achieve the transmutation of base metals into gold, regarded as the most perfect of metals.

Alchemy was based on three key precepts. The first was Aristotle's teachings that the basis for all material objects could be found in the four elements: fire, water, air, and earth. By altering the proportions in which the qualities were combined, elements could be changed into one another. The second precept arose from the philosophic thought of the time: metals, like all other substances, could be converted into one another. The third precept was taken from astrology: metals, like plants and animals, could be born, nourished, and caused to grow through imperfect stages into a final, perfect form.

Early alchemists were generally from artisan classes. As alchemy gained adherents, philosophers became more involved, and the cryptic language used by the early artisan-alchemists to protect trade secrets became virtually its own language, with symbols and fanciful terms. Over the centuries, the language of alchemy became ever more complex, reaching its height in Medieval Europe in the fourteenth and fifteenth centuries. Alchemy was superseded by the advent of modern chemistry at the end of the eighteenth century.

Edie Freedman designed the cover of this book, using a 19th-century engraving from the Dover Pictorial Archive. The cover layout was produced with Quark XPress 3.3 using the ITC Garamond font.

The inside layout was designed by Edie Freedman and Nancy Priest and implemented in gtroff by Lenny Muellner. The text and heading fonts are ITC Garamond Light and Garamond Book. Figures were created by Robert Romano in Macromedia Freehand 7.0 and Adobe Photoshop 4.0. This colophon was written by Michael Kalantarian.

Whenever possible, our books use RepKover™, a durable and flexible lay-flat binding. If the page count exceeds RepKover's limit, perfect binding is used.

Songline Guides

NetLearning: Why Teachers Use the Internet

By Ferdi Serim & Melissa Koch
1st Edition June 1996
304 pages, ISBN 1-56592-201-8

In this book educators and Internet users who've been exploring its potential for education share stories to help teachers use this medium to its fullest potential in their classrooms. The book offers advice on how to adapt, how to get what you want, and where to go for help. The goal: To invite educators online with the reassurance there will be people there to greet them. Includes CD-ROM with Internet software.

NetSuccess: How Real Estate Agents Use the Internet

By Scott Kersnar
1st Edition August 1996
214 pages, ISBN 1-56592-213-1

This book shows real estate agents how to harness Internet communications and marketing tools to enhance their careers and make the Internet work for them. Through agents' stories and "A day in the life"scenarios, readers learn what happens when technology is welcomed as a full working partner.

NetActivism: How Citizens Use the Internet

By Ed Schwartz
1st Edition September 1996
224 pages, ISBN 1-56592-160-7

Let a veteran political activist tell you how to use online networks to further your cause. Whether you are a community activist, a politician, a nonprofit staff person, or just someone who cares about your community, you will benefit from the insights this book offers on how to make the fastest-growing medium today work for you. Includes CD-ROM with Internet software and limited free online time.

Net Lessons: Web-based Projects for Your Classroom

By Laura Parker Roerden
1st Edition March 1997
300 pages (est.), ISBN 1-56592-291-3

When you use this book, you will inherit the advice, experience and project ideas of veteran Web users, teachers, and curriculum experts. This book includes:
• 100+ K-12 classroom lessons and ideas
• Standard lesson plan formats
• Assessment and goal-setting tools

NetResearch: Finding Information Online

By Daniel J. Barrett
1st Edition Winter 1997
240 pages (est.), ISBN 1-56592-245-X

Whatever your profession or avocation, NetResearch will show you how to locate the information in the constantly changing online world. Whether you're research statistics for a report, to find free software, or to locate an old college roommate, it pays to locate online information rapidly. But the Net is a very big, disorganized place, and it can be difficult to locate just the information you want, when you need it. In NetResearch, you'll learn effective search techniques that work with any Internet search programs. The author offers quizzes that allow you to practice your own research skills or that you can use as a teaching tool to help others. Covers the Internet, America Online, CompuServe, Microsoft Network, and Prodigy.

NetTravel: How Travelers Use the Internet

By Michael Shapiro
1st Edition Winter 1997
225 pages (est.), ISBN 1-56592-172-0

NetTravel is a virtual toolbox of advice for those travelers who want to tap into the rich vein of travel resources on the Internet. It is filled with personal accounts by travelers who've used the Net to plan their business trips, vacations, honeymoons, and explorations. Author and journalist Michael Shapiro gives readers all the tools they need to use the Net immediately to find and save money on airline tickets, accommodations, and car rentals. Includes CD-ROM with Internet software.

Net Law: How Lawyers Use the Internet

By Paul Jacobsen
1st Edition Winter 1997
254 pages (est.), ISBN 1-56592-258-1

From simple email to sophisticated online marketing, *Net Law* shows how the solo practitioner or the large law firm can turn the Net into an effective and efficient tool. Through stories from those who've set up pioneering legal Net sites, attorney Paul Jacobsen explains how lawyers can successfully integrate the Internet into their practices, sharing lessons "early adopters" have learned. Includes CD-ROM with Internet software and limited free online time.

O'REILLY™

TO ORDER: **800-998-9938** • **order@oreilly.com** • **http://www.oreilly.com/**
OUR PRODUCTS ARE AVAILABLE AT A BOOKSTORE OR SOFTWARE STORE NEAR YOU.
FOR INFORMATION: **800-998-9938** • **707-829-0515** • **info@oreilly.com**

How to stay in touch with O'Reilly

1. Visit Our Award-Winning Site
http://www.oreilly.com/

★"Top 100 Sites on the Web" —*PC Magazine*
★"Top 5% Web sites" —*Point Communications*
★"3-Star site" —*The McKinley Group*

Our web site contains a library of comprehensive product information (including book excerpts and tables of contents), downloadable software, background articles, interviews with technology leaders, links to relevant sites, book cover art, and more. File us in your Bookmarks or Hotlist!

2. Join Our Email Mailing Lists
New Product Releases
To receive automatic email with brief descriptions of all new O'Reilly products as they are released, send email to:
listproc@online.oreilly.com
Put the following information in the first line of your message (*not* in the Subject field):
subscribe oreilly-news "Your Name" of "Your Organization" (for example: subscribe oreilly-news Kris Webber of Fine Enterprises)

O'Reilly Events
If you'd also like us to send information about trade show events, special promotions, and other O'Reilly events, send email to:
listproc@online.oreilly.com
Put the following information in the first line of your message (*not* in the Subject field):
subscribe oreilly-events "Your Name" of "Your Organization"

3. Get Examples from Our Books via FTP
There are two ways to access an archive of example files from our books:

Regular FTP
- ftp to:
  ftp.oreilly.com
  (login: anonymous
  password: your email address)
- Point your web browser to:
  ftp://ftp.oreilly.com/

FTPMAIL
- Send an email message to:
  ftpmail@online.oreilly.com
  (Write "help" in the message body)

4. Visit Our Gopher Site
- Connect your gopher to:
  gopher.oreilly.com

- Point your web browser to:
  gopher://gopher.oreilly.com/

- Telnet to:
  gopher.oreilly.com
  login: gopher

5. Contact Us via Email
order@oreilly.com
To place a book or software order online. Good for North American and international customers.

subscriptions@oreilly.com
To place an order for any of our newsletters or periodicals.

books@oreilly.com
General questions about any of our books.

software@oreilly.com
For general questions and product information about our software. Check out O'Reilly Software Online at **http://software.oreilly.com/** for software and technical support information. Registered O'Reilly software users send your questions to:
website-support@oreilly.com

cs@oreilly.com
For answers to problems regarding your order or our products.

booktech@oreilly.com
For book content technical questions or corrections.

proposals@oreilly.com
To submit new book or software proposals to our editors and product managers.

international@oreilly.com
For information about our international distributors or translation queries. For a list of our distributors outside of North America check out:
http://www.oreilly.com/www/order/country.html

O'Reilly & Associates, Inc.
101 Morris Street, Sebastopol, CA 95472 USA
TEL   707-829-0515 or 800-998-9938
        (6am to 5pm PST)
FAX   707-829-0104

O'REILLY™

TO ORDER: **800-998-9938** • **order@oreilly.com** • **http://www.oreilly.com/**
OUR PRODUCTS ARE AVAILABLE AT A BOOKSTORE OR SOFTWARE STORE NEAR YOU.
FOR INFORMATION: **800-998-9938** • **707-829-0515** • **info@oreilly.com**

Titles from O'Reilly

Please note that upcoming titles are displayed in italic.

WEB PROGRAMMING

Apache: The Definitive Guide
Building Your Own Web Conferences
Building Your Own Website
Building Your Own Win-CGI Programs
CGI Programming for the World Wide Web
Designing for the Web
HTML: The Definitive Guide
JavaScript: The Definitive Guide, 2nd Ed.
Learning Perl
Programming Perl, 2nd Ed.
Mastering Regular Expressions
WebMaster in a Nutshell
Web Security & Commerce
Web Client Programming with Perl
World Wide Web Journal

USING THE INTERNET

Smileys
The Future Does Not Compute
The Whole Internet User's Guide & Catalog
The Whole Internet for Win 95
Using Email Effectively
Bandits on the Information Superhighway

JAVA SERIES

Exploring Java
Java AWT Reference
Java Fundamental Classes Reference
Java in a Nutshell
Java Language Reference
Java Network Programming
Java Threads
Java Virtual Machine

SOFTWARE

WebSite™ 1.1
WebSite Professional™
Building Your Own Web Conferences
WebBoard™
PolyForm™
Statisphere™

SONGLINE GUIDES

NetActivism   NetResearch
Net Law   NetSuccess
NetLearning   NetTravel
Net Lessons

SYSTEM ADMINISTRATION

Building Internet Firewalls
Computer Crime: A Crimefighter's Handbook
Computer Security Basics
DNS and BIND, 2nd Ed.
Essential System Administration, 2nd Ed.
Getting Connected: The Internet at 56K and Up
Internet Server Administration with Windows NT
Linux Network Administrator's Guide
Managing Internet Information Services
Managing NFS and NIS
Networking Personal Computers with TCP/IP
Practical UNIX & Internet Security. 2nd Ed.
PGP: Pretty Good Privacy
sendmail, 2nd Ed.
sendmail Desktop Reference
System Performance Tuning
TCP/IP Network Administration
termcap & terminfo
Using & Managing UUCP
Volume 8: X Window System Administrator's Guide
Web Security & Commerce

UNIX

Exploring Expect
Learning VBScript
Learning GNU Emacs, 2nd Ed.
Learning the bash Shell
Learning the Korn Shell
Learning the UNIX Operating System
Learning the vi Editor
Linux in a Nutshell
Making TeX Work
Linux Multimedia Guide
Running Linux, 2nd Ed.
SCO UNIX in a Nutshell
sed & awk, 2nd Edition
Tcl/Tk Tools
UNIX in a Nutshell: System V Edition
UNIX Power Tools
Using csh & tsch
When You Can't Find Your UNIX System Administrator
Writing GNU Emacs Extensions

WEB REVIEW STUDIO SERIES

Gif Animation Studio
Shockwave Studio

WINDOWS

Dictionary of PC Hardware and Data Communications Terms
Inside the Windows 95 Registry
Inside the Windows 95 File System
Windows Annoyances
Windows NT File System Internals
Windows NT in a Nutshell

PROGRAMMING

Advanced Oracle PL/SQL Programming
Applying RCS and SCCS
C++: The Core Language
Checking C Programs with lint
DCE Security Programming
Distributing Applications Across DCE & Windows NT
Encyclopedia of Graphics File Formats, 2nd Ed.
Guide to Writing DCE Applications
lex & yacc
Managing Projects with make
Mastering Oracle Power Objects
Oracle Design: The Definitive Guide
Oracle Performance Tuning, 2nd Ed.
Oracle PL/SQL Programming
Porting UNIX Software
POSIX Programmer's Guide
POSIX.4: Programming for the Real World
Power Programming with RPC
Practical C Programming
Practical C++ Programming
Programming Python
Programming with curses
Programming with GNU Software
Pthreads Programming
Software Portability with imake, 2nd Ed.
Understanding DCE
Understanding Japanese Information Processing
UNIX Systems Programming for SVR4

BERKELEY 4.4 SOFTWARE DISTRIBUTION

4.4BSD System Manager's Manual
4.4BSD User's Reference Manual
4.4BSD User's Supplementary Documents
4.4BSD Programmer's Reference Manual
4.4BSD Programmer's Supplementary Documents
X Programming
Vol. 0: X Protocol Reference Manual
Vol. 1: Xlib Programming Manual
Vol. 2: Xlib Reference Manual
Vol. 3M: X Window System User's Guide, Motif Edition
Vol. 4M: X Toolkit Intrinsics Programming Manual, Motif Edition
Vol. 5: X Toolkit Intrinsics Reference Manual
Vol. 6A: Motif Programming Manual
Vol. 6B: Motif Reference Manual
Vol. 6C: Motif Tools
Vol. 8 : X Window System Administrator's Guide
Programmer's Supplement for Release 6
X User Tools
The X Window System in a Nutshell

CAREER & BUSINESS

Building a Successful Software Business
The Computer User's Survival Guide
Love Your Job!
Electronic Publishing on CD-ROM

TRAVEL

Travelers' Tales: Brazil
Travelers' Tales: Food
Travelers' Tales: France
Travelers' Tales: Gutsy Women
Travelers' Tales: India
Travelers' Tales: Mexico
Travelers' Tales: Paris
Travelers' Tales: San Francisco
Travelers' Tales: Spain
Travelers' Tales: Thailand
Travelers' Tales: A Woman's World

International Distributors

UK, Europe, Middle East and Northern Africa (except France, Germany, Switzerland, & Austria)

INQUIRIES
International Thomson Publishing Europe
Berkshire House
168-173 High Holborn
London WC1V 7AA, UK
Tel: 44-171-497-1422
Fax: 44-171-497-1426
Email: itpint@itps.co.uk

ORDERS
International Thomson Publishing Services, Ltd.
Cheriton House, North Way
Andover, Hampshire SP10 5BE, United Kingdom
Tel: 44-264-342-832 (UK)
Tel: 44-264-342-806 (outside UK)
Fax: 44-264-364418 (UK)
Fax: 44-264-342761 (outside UK)
UK & Eire orders:
itpuk@itps.co.uk
International orders:
itpint@itps.co.uk

France

Editions Eyrolles
61 bd Saint-Germain
75240 Paris Cedex 05
France
Fax: 33-01-44-41-11-44

FRENCH LANGUAGE BOOKS
All countries except Canada
Tel: 33-01-44-41-46-16
Email: geodif@eyrolles.com

ENGLISH LANGUAGE BOOKS
Tel: 33-01-44-41-11-87
Email: distribution@eyrolles.com

Australia

WoodsLane Pty. Ltd.
7/5 Vuko Place, Warriewood NSW 2102
P.O. Box 935,
Mona Vale NSW 2103
Australia
Tel: 61-2-9970-5111
Fax: 61-2-9970-5002
Email: info@woodslane.com.au

Germany, Switzerland, and Austria

INQUIRIES
O'Reilly Verlag
Balthasarstr. 81
D-50670 Köln
Germany
Tel: 49-221-97-31-60-0
Fax: 49-221-97-31-60-8
Email: anfragen@oreilly.de

ORDERS
International Thomson Publishing
Königswinterer Straße 418
53227 Bonn, Germany
Tel: 49-228-97024 0
Fax: 49-228-441342
Email: order@oreilly.de

Asia (except Japan & India)

INQUIRIES
International Thomson Publishing Asia
60 Albert Street #15-01
Albert Complex
Singapore 189969
Tel: 65-336-6411
Fax: 65-336-7411

ORDERS
Telephone: 65-336-6411
Fax: 65-334-1617
thomson@signet.com.sg

New Zealand

WoodsLane New Zealand Ltd.
21 Cooks Street (P.O. Box 575)
Wanganui, New Zealand
Tel: 64-6-347-6543
Fax: 64-6-345-4840
Email: info@woodslane.com.au

Japan

O'Reilly Japan, Inc.
Kiyoshige Building 2F
12-Banchi, Sanei-cho
Shinjuku-ku
Tokyo 160 Japan
Tel: 81-3-3356-5227
Fax: 81-3-3356-5261
Email: kenji@oreilly.com

India

Computer Bookshop (India) PVT. LTD.
190 Dr. D.N. Road, Fort
Bombay 400 001 India
Tel: 91-22-207-0989
Fax: 91-22-262-3551
Email:
cbsbom@giasbm01.vsnl.net.in

The Americas

O'Reilly & Associates, Inc.
101 Morris Street
Sebastopol, CA 95472 U.S.A.
Tel: 707-829-0515
Tel: 800-998-9938 (U.S. & Canada)
Fax: 707-829-0104
Email: order@oreilly.com

Southern Africa

International Thomson Publishing Southern Africa
Building 18, Constantia Park
138 Sixteenth Road
P.O. Box 2459
Halfway House, 1685 South Africa
Tel: 27-11-805-4819
Fax: 27-11-805-3648